ALLIES FOR FREEDOM

BLACKS ON JOHN BROWN

BENJAMIN QUARLES

DA CAPO PRESS

Allies for Freedom
Copyright © 1974 by Oxford University Press

Blacks on John Brown
Copyright © 1972 by The Board of Trustees of the University of Illinois

Reprinted by arrangement with the Estate of Benjamin Quarles

A CIP record for this book is available from the Library of Congress.

First Da Capo Press Edition 2001
ISBN 0-306-80961-3

Published by Da Capo Press
A Member of the Perseus Books Group
http://www.dacapopress.com

1 2 3 4 5 6 7 8 9—05 04 03 02 01

Dedication for the Da Capo Edition

To grandsons James, Jonathan, and Kristopher

INTRODUCTION TO
THE DA CAPO EDITION

John Brown is one of the most vexing figures in American history. If a single soul can be said to have caused the Civil War, he has as a rival only Harriet Beecher Stowe who, writing *Uncle Tom's Cabin*, raised a more pacific weapon against slavery than Brown was to do. No one seems able to write or speak quietly about him. No one, that is, except Benjamin Quarles. With meticulous use of sources and unsurpassed knowledge of individuals in the black community of Brown's day, he tells the story with refreshing care. Concerning sources, for example, he notes the report in one older biography that one "Mary (Mammy) Pleasant gave Brown a draft for $30,000 at Chatham, Ontario," which the author, Franklin P. Sanborn, himself later said was a myth. With admirable astringency, Quarles adds, "Brown may have been bound by no canons but his own, but this liberty hardly extends to those who reminisce or write about him."

Benjamin Quarles was born in 1904 in an America far different for African-Americans than it was when he died ninety-two years later. He spent his whole long career teaching in predominately black colleges in the South. Professor of history at Morgan State University in Baltimore from 1953 until he retired, he did not follow the lead of other renowned black scholars to move when predominately white universities belatedly recruited black faculty members.

Quarles, a most generous scholar, was rewarded with sixteen honorary degrees. As a writer, he was always scrupulous in his use of sources in his many books, which include *Black Abolitionists* and *The Negro in the Civil War*. In his excellent biography of Frederick Douglass, there are psychological insights that others might have missed. Anyone teaching American history to students black, white, or both would be wise to choose this biography for the syllabus.

The most impressive chapter in *Allies for Freedom* and *Blacks on John Brown* explains both the failure of the raid in 1859 on Harpers Ferry and the failure of black people to rally to Brown's side. "No figure in American history," Quarles states, "could outdo Brown as a 'loner.' . . . He sought no one's advice; he asked no group to accept him as leader. In this respect, as in general, he treated blacks and whites alike, eliciting the counsel of neither and taking for granted the acceptance of both." Brown, carrying secrecy to "Byzantine proportions," provided would-be followers "with no sense of direction, of concrete purpose."

It was only after his bold attempt to raise a slave insurrection and his capture, imprisonment, and hanging that he became a hero to black America. With ringing rhetoric damning slavery, he went, with dignity, to his death. Countless black leaders who participated in the "canonization" of the "martyr" after Brown was hanged felt obliged to explain why they were not at his side when his tiny band of not very able fellow raiders took the arsenal and expected to arouse a general slave insurrection. Brown, awaiting his execution, did feel forsaken, as did his son John Jr. (who was not with him for the raid). Quarles concludes, laconically, that the "Browns, father and son, had some difficulty believing that some of the blacks who opposed the raid were motivated primarily by the conviction that such an undertaking was the height of folly."

Brown's armed attack on slavery may have been misguided in terms of immediate results, but it greatly increased the anxieties of the white South and the sympathy for his cause of many in the North. Not two years after his raid, the nation was engaged in the immense violence of the Civil War that became the attack on slavery that *did* work.

John Brown, far from being neglected as a figure important in our history, is remembered on all sides and is celebrated still in black America. *Allies for Freedom*, Quarles's biography of Brown (first published in 1974), appears here with its companion, *Blacks on John Brown* (1972). This valuable collection contains words written and said by a wide range of black spokesmen, both the great—Frederick Douglass, W. E. B. Du Bois, Langston Hughes—and the obscure, from 1858 to 1861, from 1870 to 1925, and from 1925 to 1972. As does Quarles in the later part of his biography, these pieces shed valuable light on how John Brown has been assessed over the years in the black community. Quarles leaves to others the study of the fervor in 1859, to the point of suspending judgment about the many devoted white antislavery people who delighted in having a martyr. On the other hand, proslavery advocates were equally sure the whole North would turn into a John Brown raid on the South. The road to war quickened.

The reason for Brown's attraction for black Americans, finally, is a simple one, though Quarles leaves recognition of the fact to the reader. Brown was, and to many black observers still is, the one white man who was unequivocally one of them. It is telling that in his introduction to *Blacks on John Brown* Quarles tells of the white writer Richard Henry Dana, Jr. wandering into North Elba, New York, the community in which Brown and black settlers lived, and being invited in for supper. Entering, Dana was introduced to a *Mr.* Jefferson and a *Mrs.* Wait, two black neighbors at the Brown table.

It is this civil side of Brown that so appeals to Quarles. He does not fail to notice the man's favoring violence when confronting the sin of slavery that must be vanquished at any cost. The incident at Pottawatomie Creek, in which a small band of unarmed white men, perhaps proslavery but not the owners of any slaves, were taken from their house by Brown's men and slaughtered—with broadswords—"forever tarnished" Brown's name. But even here Brown's action is seen in the context of the whole of the long struggle against slavery.

It is revealing of Benjamin Quarles that he gave meaning to his title, *Allies for Freedom*, only near the close of the book. He quotes the then-little-known poet Michael Harper, whose *History as Cap'n Brown*, from which the line comes, also closes *Blacks on John Brown*. Harper—and Quarles—has white John Brown say: "Come to the crusade . . . not Negroes, *brothers*." It is this alliance, rather than its failure at Pottawatomie and Harpers Ferry, for which Benjamin Quarles remembers John Brown.

William S. McFeely

ALLIES FOR
FREEDOM

Thomas Hovenden, *The Last Moments of John Brown.* Copyright Hovenden 1884. *The Metropolitan Museum of Art,* gift of Mr. and Mrs. Carl Stoeckel, 1897.

ALLIES FOR FREEDOM

Blacks and John Brown

BENJAMIN QUARLES

To my
two brothers
and
two sisters

PREFACE

Engaged in November of 1907 in working on a biography of John Brown of Harpers Ferry fame, newspaper editor Oswald Garrison Villard expressed his frustrations in a letter to Thomas W. Featherstonhaugh, himself a Brown scholar and collector.* "The further I get into this work" wrote Villard, "the more I am amazed and almost discouraged by the contradictions and mistakes in even the simplest matters." Villard soon overcame his misgivings and went on to produce a first-rate biography of Brown.

But the problem of untrustworthy sources still plagues the Brown researcher. Sometimes the contemporary records are at fault, such as their mention of one John Anderson, allegedly a free black from Boston who took part in the raid on Harpers Ferry or was en route there when it was launched. More often the researcher's problem lies with a narrator's long-belated and basically unprovable recollection of a statement allegedly made by Brown or of an incident allegedly relating to him. Such material, with proper cautions as to source and content, does have its uses. One would hesitate, however, to rely on such a highly questionable story as the one that Mary ("Mammy") Pleasant gave Brown a draft for

---

* In line with present-day usage I employ no apostrophe in Harpers Ferry except in direct quotation.

$30,000 at Chatham, Ontario, in the spring of 1858. "The legend you speak of is a myth," wrote Franklin B. Sanborn, a Brown confidant and biographer, to Villard on June 30, 1908, in response to an inquiry about Mrs. Pleasant. "The woman may have given Brown $10 or $100 but I doubt even that," he continued. "I looked this up years ago." Although appearing in print, such a story cannot be used by those who are governed by the rule of credible evidence. Brown may have been bound by no canons other than his own, but this liberty hardly extends to those who reminisce or write about him.

The problem of untrustworthy sources on this topic is almost as vexatious as the problem of no sources at all. The kinds of blacks who would be close to Brown would hardly care to keep any records of their legally questionable relationships with him. In the hue and cry following the raid at Harpers Ferry, black acquaintances of Brown were likely to do away with any written evidence that could be construed as revealing or incriminating. It is possible that at the time of the raid, Frederick Douglass, one of Brown's black confidants, decided to run the risk of retaining any Brown letters he may have been keeping, but if he did they were lost when his house in Rochester burned down in 1872.

But despite any gaps there might be in the formal record, there is no mistaking the attitude of blacks toward Brown. Admittedly it was not characterized by a sense of scientific objectivity, the reaction of black Americans being more likely to reflect their personal feelings. They tended to ignore or gloss over his shortcomings. They took him on his own terms—to them he was his own morality. Possibly as far as blacks were concerned Brown was a more towering figure than his actual career would seem to have warranted. But their evaluation of him had an enduring vitality—Brown's meaning to blacks did not die with his hanging. Brown was a symbol, typically bearing its own reality however well or ill supported by the initial hard facts.

If Brown meant much to blacks in their search for a relevant past, his relationships with them is revealing as to the America of a bygone day, particularly in its black-white interactions. And, equally important, the image of Brown projected by his black admirers has been, in no small measure, a factor in creating the figure that has lived in song and story and shows no signs of fading away. Thomas Wentworth Higginson, a Brown confidant, writing nearly fifty years later in a black monthly (*Alexander's Magazine,* August 1906), saw him in a dual relationship to blacks: "Brown's name is destined to be one of the permanent figures, as perplexing to many students as the Negro question itself, of which he is so central a figure."

Finally, this work differs from other Brown-centered histories in its broader focus and time span. Whereas most non-fiction treatments of Brown come to a close with his hanging, this work devotes considerable attention to the sequel to Harpers Ferry.

Baltimore, Md.   *B.Q.*
Spring 1974

ACKNOWLEDGMENTS

The bibliographical note to this volume indicates something of my indebtedness to a number of writers who have turned a searchlight on Brown, including his former friends and associates, critics and detractors, and scholarly biographers. Not attempting to duplicate their broad coverage of the man, I have naturally focused on their references to blacks, references often made in passing or otherwise unhighlighted. It is a commonplace that from the same source materials, one investigator, sensing a relationship hitherto not sufficiently elaborated, may find things on which another would not tarry. In addition to indicating my indebtedness, the bibliographical note to this volume will serve those whose curiosity about Brown might extend beyond the scope of this work. Their attention, as they will note, is particularly directed to two fine recent studies: Stephen B. Oates, *To Purge This Land with Blood,* and Richard O. Boyer, *The Legend of John Brown: A Biography and a History.*

I wish also to express my sincere thanks to the following, from whom I have sought and received information. These include James Egert Allen, Joyce Beachum, Howard H. Bell, August F. Benvenuti, W. E. Bigglestone, John W. Blassingame, Samuel E. Blount, Edwin C. Cotter, A. Mercer Daniel, M. A. Harris, Ruth W. Helmuth, Jean Blackwell Hutson, Theda Jackson, Martha E.

Johnson, Sidney Kaplan, Archie Motley, Vera S. Leclercq, Dorothy Inborden Miller, Pauli Murray, Mary Lawson Newby, Dorothy A. Plum, Nelson C. Reid, Richard Sherrill, and Daisy Stringer.

To the personnel at the following libraries and other repositories I am grateful: Boston Public Library, Carnegie Library, Windsor, Ontario, Chatham-Kent Museum, Chatham, Ontario, Cornell University Library, Columbia University Library, Fisk University Library, Henry E. Huntington Library and Art Gallery, San Marino, California, Kansas Historical Society, Library of Congress, Maryland Historical Society, Massachusetts Historical Society, Metropolitan Museum of Art, New-York Historical Society, New York Public Library, Ohio Historical Society, The Historical Society of Pennsylvania, the Library Company of Philadelphia, Virginia Historical Society, Virginia State Library, and the University of Windsor Library. Dorothy B. Porter called my attention to a number of references I otherwise would have missed. I am indebted to Vivian Marsalisi of Oxford University Press for her expert assistance in carefully reading the manuscript. To the Morgan College Library staff I owe an ever-increasing debt. My wife, Ruth Brett Quarles, has been most helpful.

CONTENTS

ALLIES FOR
FREEDOM

❧ 1 ❧

JOHN BROWN'S DAY

Thank God for John Brown.
Second Niagara Convention
"An Address to the Country," 1906

"John Brown could not have imagined as he looked through the barred windows of his dungeon that some day such a remarkable tribute would be paid to him on the very ground where he made his gallant stand. But the old Puritan is not one of the vanishing figures of history." [1] So wrote J. Max Barber, editor of the militant monthly, *Voice of the Negro,* while still in the exhilarating afterglow of his trip to Harpers Ferry, West Virginia.

Barber had been one of the nearly one hundred admirers who, on August 17, 1906, had assembled at the John Brown "fort" to commemorate the hundredth anniversary of Brown's birth and the fiftieth jubilee of his bloody skirmish at Osawatomie, Kansas, over the issue of slavery in the territories. These celebrants knew that in holding their observance in mid-August they were taking some slight liberties with the historical record, Brown having been born on May 9, 1800, and the Osawatomie engagement having taken place fifty years previously, true enough, but on August 30.

If the celebrants had taken liberty with the chronology, they remained faithful to the setting. Harpers Ferry, a government armory and arsenal, had been the scene of Brown's ill-starred attempt in 1859 to free the slaves. The fort, a fire-engine house which the sorely besieged Brown had converted into a defensive post, had been the site of his surrender. To black visitors Harpers Ferry evoked deep emotions.

The one hundred or so participants in this John Brown's Day

observance were the delegates to the convention of a one-year-old
black civil rights organization known as the Niagara Movement,
its first meeting having been held at Niagara Falls the preceding
summer. The planners of this second meeting had chosen Harpers
Ferry as the site in order that one full day might be spent paying
tribute to a figure who had become a legend among blacks even
before he went to the gallows.

John Brown's Day started early. At six in the morning his
admirers left the site of the convention, Storer College, a Baptist-
controlled school founded in 1867 for blacks, to make a pilgrimage
to the brick-walled fire-engine house, a mile away. As they neared
their destination they formed a procession, single file, led by Owen
M. Waller, a physician from Brooklyn. Defying stone and stubble,
Waller took off his shoes and socks and walked barefoot as if
treading on holy ground.[2]

Halting outside the engine house, the pilgrims listened to prayer,
followed by remarks from Richard T. Greener. A light rain was
falling, making the lack of any seating arrangements all the more
keenly felt. Greener was worth the discomfort. Harvard's first black
graduate and former dean of the Howard University Law School,
Greener was gifted in speech and handsomely magisterial in appearance. Forgoing a formal oration punctuated by the Latin
phrases he knew so well, Greener recited his personal recollections
of John Brown and the excitement in Boston and elsewhere immediately after the raid on Harpers Ferry. Closing with an incident more contemporary, Greener related that during his recent
tenure as American consul at Vladivostok he had heard the Russian
troops burst into the song, "John Brown's body lies a-mouldering
in the grave."[3]

Following the half-hour of Greener reminiscences, the group
marched around the fort single file. Almost as if to keep in step
they sang "The Battle Hymn of the Republic," supplementing it
with additional verses from the John Brown song. Once within
the fort, the pilgrims took turns climbing the wooden tower to
see the lovely Shenandoah Valley through the lessening mist.[4]

If the morning meeting was highly inspirational, the afternoon
proceedings were no less moving. True, the setting—Anthony

Hall of Storer College—was somewhat less symbolic. Overlooking the Shenandoah and Potomac rivers and the Blue Ridge Mountains, Anthony Hall afforded a scenic inspiration hard to match. But, like Storer itself, it postdated John Brown.

Anthony Hall had, however, echoed to John Brown's name before. Here, on Decoration Day in 1881, the peerless Frederick Douglass had delivered an oration on the hero of Harpers Ferry. On that memorable occasion the platform guests included Andrew Hunter, the attorney who had represented the Commonwealth of Virginia in its court case against John Brown. Moved by the Douglass speech, Hunter had fervently seized his hand, remarking that if Robert E. Lee had been living he would have done likewise.[5]

Douglass was lying in his grave when John Brown's Day came around. But standing in as his surrogate was an imposing roster of black leaders, most of them on the threshold of notable careers. Covering the meeting for the New York *Evening Post,* Mary White Ovington, a white social worker and later one of the founders of the N.A.A.C.P., was impressed by the participants. "Their power and intellectual ability is manifest on hearing or talking with them," she wrote.[6]

Not present at Harpers Ferry, however, were the most optimistic and the most pessimistic of the black leaders of the day, Booker T. Washington and Henry M. Turner. Not wholly the conservative and conciliatory figure he appeared to be, Washington waged an undercover war against segregation and disfranchisement. But as an avowed non-militant he would hardly have been at home at a John Brown's Day in a Southern town and under the auspices of the Niagara people. Doubtless, too, he shared the view of the pro-Washington *New York Age* that the real object of the Niagara Movement was to oppose Washington and "to tear down his work." In similar vein Charles Alexander, publisher of *Alexander's Magazine,* editorialized that the chief purpose of the Harpers Ferry gathering was "to minimize and destroy, if possible, the influence of Booker T. Washington."[7]

Bishop Turner, a back-to-Africa advocate, saw no need to be present, for he had simply given up on America. Earlier that year, in a speech at Macon, Georgia, he had said that the American flag was a dirty rag as far as the Negro was concerned, a remark that drew fire from President Theodore Roosevelt.[8]

But if these missing leaders were on anyone's mind as the afternoon exercises began, they must have faded as the first speaker was introduced. Her face, with its high cheek bones, had an Indian cast and her hair had "only a slight kink." She did not rise for she was bent and frail. Remaining in her chair, Henrietta Leary Evans talked of her brother, Lewis Sheridan Leary and her nephew, John A. Copeland, Jr., two of the five blacks with John Brown at Harpers Ferry. Her facial expression bright and alert but "in a voice made slender by age," Mrs. Evans said that the motivating force in the lives of Leary and Copeland had been their love of freedom. Each had fought valiantly with John Brown, she said, adding that Leary's courage had been attested to by the men who had fought against him. Mrs. Evans' brief remarks stirred an audience that did not need to be told that Leary had fallen on the field and that Copeland had been captured and hanged.[9]

As she took her seat, Henrietta Evans may have reflected on that bleak hour in the late morning of December 16, 1859, when her nephew mounted the scaffold. His family had assembled in the parlor of their home in Oberlin, Ohio, where they read aloud the New Testament passage beginning, "Let not your heart be troubled." And as the final minute came for the scheduled execution, the kneeling family commended Copeland's spirit to God. Then his bereaved mother had arisen and said, as reported by a visiting newsman, "if it could be the means of destroying slavery, I would willingly give up all my men-folks." [10]

Henrietta Evans was seated next to Lewis Douglass, who was introduced next. Son of Frederick Douglass, Lewis as a boy had seen Brown a number of times, particularly during a three-week period in early 1858, when Brown was a guest in the Douglass home in Rochester. To their delight, Brown had played with Lewis and the four other Douglass children, although they could not have guessed that the blocks he used and the games he played were a projection of his plans for Harpers Ferry. Lewis was introduced as one who had known John Brown. No spellbinder like his father, Lewis simply stood up and graciously bowed in acknowledgment of the generous applause.[11]

The packed audience, its interest stimulated by the sentimental, settled back for more thoughtful fare from the two orators of the day. Who present could not have known about the first of these, W. E. B. Du Bois? Physically he was slight and prematurely bald, but his steady eye, his unsmiling lips, neat beard, chiseled features, and careful dress gave him the look of a patrician. His aloof bearing, disconcertingly supercilious to some, bespoke a bookish temperament.

If Du Bois did not envelop the hall with passionate fervor or a folksy warmth, he commanded attention because of his intellectual power and his outspoken militancy. Of a scholarly bent, he had taken a doctorate in history at Harvard University in 1895 and had already published three books, one of them the arresting collection of essays and sketches, *The Souls of Black Folk*. He was founder of the Niagara Movement and was serving as its General Secretary.

For this John Brown's Day address Du Bois chose to give a history of slavery and Brown's relationship to it. He opened with an analytical study of slavery in modern times and the cause of its growth in the United States. Du Bois was on ground familiar to him, having written a pioneer study on the suppression of the African slave trade. As for Brown, said Du Bois, he lived in a world in which things were eternally right or eternally wrong, with slavery obviously in the latter class.[12] Du Bois then proceeded to describe the essential elements of Brown's thinking and planning in his crusade against slavery.

The speaker closed with the assertion that Brown's real contribution to his times was his effort to contain evil. "So much of life must go, not to forward right, but to beat back wrong." Yielding for once to oratorical convention and the whole spirit of the day, the highly individualistic Du Bois ended on a note of high commitment. Just as Brown sacrificed himself, he said, so must he and his listeners "sacrifice our work, our money, and our positions, in order to beat back the evil of the world." The applause was long-lasting.[13]

The second speaker, Reverdy C. Ransom, like Du Bois, was
sparely built, bronze-colored, and had a striking face. He wore a
moustache but no beard. His receding hair line and high cheek
bones gave him a professorial air. But his powerful speaking tones
left no doubt as to his calling—he was a clergyman, the pastor of
the Charles Street African Methodist Episcopal Church in Boston.
Outside of his own congregation, Ransom had attracted attention
for espousing a social gospel and for his ministerial leadership
in community welfare activities. He was more widely known,
however, for his fluency in public address. Appropriately enough,
the presiding officer W. J. Carter, introduced him as "the
thunderer." [14]

In essence Ransom's carefully prepared message, "The Spirit
of John Brown," was a summons to courage and self-sacrifice.
"Like the ghost of Hamlet's father, the spirit of John Brown
beckons us to arise and seek the recovery of our rights." The soul
of Brown "goes marching on" in those black men and women
who aggressively fought for equality despite the opposition of the
press and the public.

Ransom defended Brown against some of the time-worn charges
brought against him. If Brown were thought to be mentally unbalanced, "such insanity was required to arouse the nation against
the crime of slavery." If Brown's measures were extreme, it was
due to the desperate illness of the land. If Brown were a traitor to
the government, it was "in order that he might be true to the
slave."

As Ransom viewed it, Brown had not died in vain: "The rifle
shot at Harpers Ferry received answer from the cannon fired upon
Fort Sumter." Brown made the supreme sacrifice, added the
speaker, but before race hatred and class distinctions were abolished, many others would be called on to wear the martyr's crown.
Ransom had not once referred to himself, but as he spoke of the
danger of protest many in the audience remembered that he recently had been dragged, badly bruised, from a Pullman car labeled
for whites only.[15]

Ransom's address had been interrrupted several times by applause, sometimes lasting for minutes. His concluding sentence

brought the audience to its feet, clapping and cheering in tribute. "Women wept, men shouted and waved hats, and everybody was moved," wrote J. Max Barber. The evaluation of Mary White Ovington was equally enthusiastic: "Mr. Ransom delivered an oration which one wished that Phillips and Parker and Beecher might have heard." Nearly thirty years later J. B. Watson, a college president, called the speech Ransom's masterpiece, adding "Too bad the Bishopric had to lay hands on him." [16]

W. E. B. Du Bois, like Watson writing in a subsequent decade, asserted that Ransom's speech "led through its inspiration and eloquence to the eventual founding of the National Association for the Advancement of Colored People." [17] This was too generous an appraisal. Unquestionably, however, Ransom's speech was to remain as the most stirring single episode in the short life of the Niagara Movement.

With the Ransom exhortation, the observance of John Brown's Day officially ended. But the following morning some of the delegates made the eight-mile trip to Charlestown to view the courthouse where Brown had been tried, the jail that had housed him, and the spot where he had been hanged. Among the visitors were Mary Church Terrell and William Monroe Trotter. Oberlin graduate and a champion of woman suffrage, Mrs. Terrell was honorary president for life of the National Association of Colored Women, an organization she had founded.

Trotter, first black Phi Beta Kappa recipient at Harvard, was the strong-minded, independent editor of the Boston *Guardian*. Customarily going bare-headed, almost as if serving notice that he would wear no man's hat, Trotter had brought to the Harpers Ferry gathering a block of wood from the house in which John Brown had lived in Springfield, Massachusetts, the gift of the black pastor of the Springfield Baptist Church, William T. Amiger.[18]

With the final business session of the convention scheduled for that afternoon, the sightseers could not tarry long at Charlestown. Before leaving, however, they gathered souvenirs. Most of these were conventional items—a twig or a stone. But when William Monroe Trotter returned to Boston he brought with him a fox terrier which he named after Brown and which would become the official mascot of the John Brown Jubilee held in Boston on December 2, 1909.[19]

Within an hour or two after their return from Charlestown, Trotter and his fellow travelers made their way to Anthony Hall, there to join the other delegates. Here the convention gave its enthusiastic approval to a manifesto entitled, "An Address to the Country." Largely the work of Du Bois, this was a statement of black demands coupled with an invocation to the hero of Harpers Ferry. The "Address" disavowed a belief in violence but in the same breath affirmed its belief in John Brown and "the willingness to sacrifice money, reputation and life itself on the altar of right." The delegates pledged to reconsecrate themselves to the cause for which Brown died. With such ringing phrases the final business session of the second annual meeting of the Niagara Movement came to a close.

This organization would run its course in a few years, a combination of internal weakness and the powerful opposition of Booker T. Washington. But its influence would remain in many subtle ways, including its glorification of John Brown. It would be no accident that J. Max Barber, one of the Brown Day celebrants, would later become the co-founder and perennial president of the John Brown Memorial Association which in 1935 at Brown's burial site at North Elba presented a commemorative bronze statue to the state of New York.

For to Barber, as to the other blacks who had assembled on John Brown's Day in 1906, the man they idolized would never lose his luster. To them he would remain a figure who never faltered in freedom's cause, living proof that in the battle for human rights there were some defeats that were, in essence, delayed victories.

The man whom the blacks of the Niagara Movement regarded as a roadmark figure pointing from the past to the present was, in truth, not easy to assess objectively. Like other devoted people who were killed while working for a cause, the historical Brown soon tended to be replaced by the legendary Brown. The man, moreover, was somewhat of an enigma, raising questions in one's mind. Were the reformist activities of his later life an unconscious counter-poise to the rootless, rolling-stone quality of his earlier years, an effort to give meaning to a hitherto uneventful life?

In 1844, fifteen years before Harpers Ferry, he had, in a letter to his wife, expressed deep regret that he had thus far "done so very little to increase the amount of human happiness." Before becoming a full-time foe of slavery, Brown had, as he confessed to George L. Stearns in February 1858, "a steady desire to die." But, he added, he had "enjoyed life very much" on "becoming a 'reaper' in the great harvest." Writing to his children ten days before his scheduled hanging, he said that he had no complaint on leaving life, having enjoyed it so much.[20] Without doubt Brown's heightened anti-slavery activities gave him a sense of purpose he had not previously experienced, dispelling what might have become a chronic melancholia.

Had he set out to carve a career as a determined foe of slavery in order to compensate for a long history of business failures? Did his abolitionist zeal stem less from an acute sense of man's inhumanity to man than from a personality disturbance, a psychological disorder? Was he a social misfit rather than a flaming apostle of righteousness? Such questions admit no ready answers.

To blacks, however, Brown constituted no enigma. Focusing, as they did, on some of his traits to the exclusion of others, they viewed him as an admirable figure. Brown's endearment to blacks may be initially examined by taking note of a few of his personal characteristics that would come strikingly to the fore in his relationships with them, particularly to those in slavery. Brown, to begin with, was uncompromising in his basic beliefs, holding that moral truth was not amenable to bargaining, give-and-take procedures. Hence, to Brown, the familiar abolitionist phrase, "immediate, uncompensated emancipation," was a moral imperative rather than a trio of catchwords.

Brown's uncompromising attitude toward slavery was rooted, in part, in his Scriptural beliefs. "The religious element of his character was always the ruling motive of his life," Mary Brown informed a journalist, referring to her imprisoned husband a week before he was sent to the gallows. A product of the evangelical revivalism of his time, Brown viewed slavery as a sin—"the crime of crimes," and "the mother of all abominations." Writing in 1854 to the editor of a black weekly, Brown charged pro-slavery newspapers and editors with "insulting God." On the afternoon he was captured at Harpers Ferry a bystander asked him whether he considered his activities "a religious movement." Brown's reply sprang out of a deep conviction: "It is, in my opinion, the greatest service a man can render God." [21] Although not a member of a church congregation during his last twenty years, Brown, a believing Christian, had always considered himself an instrument of the Almighty.

Brown habitually carried and frequently read the Bible. He was not exaggerating when he said that he "possessed a most unusual memory of its entire contents." His vocabulary reflected its influence. His conversation, wrote Frank B. Stearns, was much like that of a Methodist divine, "without, however, the ministerial inflection." John Brown, Jr., remembered that his father "had twenty texts against the holding of human beings in bondage." Brown's oft-said prayers were abolitionist-flavored. One of his black followers, Osborne Perry Anderson, said that he never heard Brown pray without his making a strong appeal to God for the deliverance of those in chains.[22]

Prayer to Brown was a prelude to action, not a release from further involvement. He was an activist, a toiler in the Lord's vineyard, a rough hewer in shaping the Divinity's ends. Lyman E. Epps, Sr., a black neighbor of his at North Elba, New York, relates that Brown told him that he did not like to think of Heaven as a place of rest—it "must be a state of activity where all our powers are being continually developed for the better." [23] Although he was of the type that lived in expectation of a miracle, Brown felt that it was incumbent on him to help make it come to pass.

If one of the ways to serve Jehovah was to strike at slavery, Brown did not rule out the sword as a necessary instrument. In his later years he inclined more and more toward the use of direct, physical action, knowing that it might well entail violence and bloodshed. He had come to believe that the necessary change—the freeing of the slaves—could not be brought about in any other way, all other channels being closed or clogged beyond repair.

In the last decade of his life Brown was, in the words of a close associate, "an abolitionist of the Bunker Hill school." Certainly he did not belong to any of the abolitionist societies of his day. Of a direct actionist temperament, he regarded their dependence upon moral suasion as hopeless. Although he remained on friendly terms with conventional abolitionists, he did not always conceal a touch of contempt for them, holding that they effected "nothing with their milk-and-water principles." [24]

The platform eloquence of abolitionist orators drew his disdain. James Redpath relates that one day as he and Brown were walking in Boston he told Brown of a stirring speech he had recently heard by Wendell Phillips. When Redpath, in admiring tones, quoted one sentence that bore the mark of the Phillips eloquence but which expressed a viewpoint contrary to that held by Brown, the latter drily remarked, "Well, if it wasn't vulgar, I would say to that as the boys say—'Oh! shit.' " [25] To Brown a platform figure like Phillips had little to show for his efforts except torrents of words.

Bible-reading Brown knew of the New Testament's stern warning to those who took the sword. But he ignored that text, just as he brushed aside the pacifist viewpoint that reformers who opted for violence were, in effect, employing the same methods of the oppressors and hence were sanctioning and perpetuating the polarizing, counter-productive technique of force. To Brown violence was not necessarily a self-defeating primitive agency or the expression of a siege mentality. To him violence in a righteous cause was more of a rite of purification.

A final Brown characteristic that made for his canonization in black circles was his absence of color prejudice. Unlike the overwhelming majority of white abolitionists, Brown did not share the almost universal belief in black inferiority. While strongly opposing slavery, white reformers by and large had no feeling of fellowship with blacks, bond or free. Unlike most whites of their day the white abolitionists, with commendable courage, believed in legal equality for blacks. But in the matter of social equality white reformers reflected the general sentiment of the times, an attitude that can be summarized in the word "taboo."

Brown was of different mold, feeling no strain in the presence of blacks on a peer basis. Without color prejudice, he did not hold that whites were innately superior to blacks or vice versa. To him the color of a man's skin was no measure of his worth. If men were equal in God's sight, they were equal in Brown's sight too, his attitude and behavior toward blacks meeting the acid test in private conduct as in public advocacy.

By the time he had reached manhood Brown had divested himself of color prejudice if indeed he had ever harbored any. But to pinpoint the month or year that Brown reached his conclusions about racial equality is hardly possible. It is hardly easier to say just when he arrived at his decision to actively enter the ranks of those who were against slavery. There were, however, a few clues, even though they are something less than conclusive.

II

BROWN'S BLACK
ORIENTATION

John Brown, who is on his way to Kansas, is
well known as an active and self-sacrificing
abolitionist.
Frederick Douglass' Paper, July 6, 1855

In 1881 or 1882 the most versatile of the prominent blacks of his
day, George Washington Williams, then working on a lengthy
history of Negro Americans, sought information on John Brown
from Mrs. George L. Stearns, widow of a Brown benefactor. In
her long letter of reply, Mrs. Stearns related for the first time
the manner in which John Brown had come to write a brief account
of his boyhood. It was an autobiographical statement that had been
widely read and reprinted for its insights into the man and for
furnishing valuable information on him available nowhere else.
Mrs. Stearns told the story that Brown, while a visitor at the
Stearns home just outside of Boston in January 1857, had been
asked by thirteen-year-old Henry to tell him what sort of a boy
he had been. Brown had done so, and in writing, even though not
until six months later. This, concluded Mrs. Stearns in her letter
to Williams, was the story behind the story.[1]

Perhaps the most important disclosure in Brown's autobiographical letter was a recital of the incident that instilled in him a hatred
of slavery. When, wrote Brown, he was thirteen or fourteen, he
and a slave became friends. The black boy was about his own age
and, added Brown, was fully his equal, if not more. But whereas
the slave owner treated Brown in the kindest and most indulgent

manner, he was heartless and cruel in his treatment of the slave. This led young Brown to much sober reflection on the wretched, hopeless condition of parentless slave children, raising a question in his mind as to whether they had a father even in God.[2]

This story, told by a fifty-seven year old, could have been an example of almost total recall. Certainly the young Brown, having lost his mother at eight, had been an unusually thoughtful youngster, but this story could equally be an example of sentiment playing a trick on memory. It reads like a wishful reconstruction, however well intentioned and honestly held.

The first verifiable reference by Brown to blacks came late in 1834 in a long letter to his brother, Frederick. Writing from Randolph Township in northwestern Pennsylvania, where he served as postmaster, the thirty-four-year-old Brown said that he had been trying to devise ways to help those in bondage. To this end, he, his wife, and three sons had agreed to seek out a black boy and bring him up as one of the family, giving him a good education. They thought, continued Brown in his letter, that such a boy might be obtained without charge from a "Christian slave-holder." Failing that, they would try to get a free black. If unsuccessful in this, too, they would subject themselves to "considerable privation" in order to buy a young slave.

Brown's letter also spoke of a long-held interest he had in opening a school for blacks, expressing the opinion that in Randolph there would be no strong opposition to such a move. Urging his brother to join him in the undertaking, Brown pointed out that schools for blacks would do much to break the yoke they bore: "If the young blacks of our country could once become enlightened, it would most assuredly operate on slavery like firing powder confined in rock, and all slaveholders know it well." [3]

Nothing came of either of these proposals. Had Brown pursued the matter of a black school he would have found the opposition greater than he bargained for. But he left Randolph the following year, driven to northern Ohio by the financial troubles that were never to leave him.

In moving to northern Ohio, Brown was returning to the strongly abolitionist region of his boyhood years. The Western Reserve was congenitally hospitable to runaways, its ports receiving them and then spiriting them across Lake Erie to Ontario and freedom. Detesting slave-catchers, the villagers of Hudson were in the habit of signalling their arrival by loudly tolling the firebell.[4]

Brown shared these sentiments, inherited not only from the villagers of Hudson but from one of its key figures, his own father. Owen Brown had become an avowed abolitionist before John's birth. Later as a trustee of Western Reserve he resigned because his fellow trustees favored the colonization of blacks and opposed their admission to the college. Turning to the more liberal Oberlin College, Owen became a trustee for eleven years.

John, like his father, opposed the colonization of blacks. In this he ran counter to some of his fellow worshippers at the Hudson Congregational Church. Brown also came to loggerheads with the nearby Franklin Mills Congregational Church over blacks. At a revival meeting held in the summer of 1838 and open to all, a few blacks came and were given seats in the rear by the stove. Angered by such discrimination in the House of God, Brown struck back at the next meeting by inviting the black worshippers to sit in his family pew. Upon their acceptance, their vacated seats were taken by the Browns.[5]

This challenge to racial segregation came at a time when the murder of Elijah P. Lovejoy was still on the minds of many in Hudson. A clergyman-publisher with strong views against slavery, Lovejoy was shot and killed and his presses destroyed by a mob at Alton, Illinois, in November 1837. Shortly afterward at a Thursday evening prayer meeting at the Hudson Congregational Church, Brown, in attendance with his father, was deeply moved throughout the services. According to the recollections of two fellow attenders, Brown rose just before the meeting ended and pledged that he would devote his life to the overthrow of slavery.[6]

Having committed himself to abolitionism, Brown soon saw to it that his family followed suit. According to John, Jr., this signal event took place one evening while Brown, his wife, their three sons, and a "colored theological student" from Western Reserve were seated at the kitchen table. Gaining their attention, Brown announced that he had made up his mind to combat slavery "by force and arms." After reciting the evils of human bondage, Brown administered an oath to his solemn and quietly consenting listeners binding them to fight slavery tooth and nail to the best of their abilities.[7]

These early vows by Brown bore no immediate fruit. It was not until the late 1840's that his anti-slavery bent became unmistakably evident. By then he had moved to Springfield, Massachusetts, for business reasons, having become a wool merchant and exporter. Locating in Springfield in 1846, Brown found himself in an even stronger abolitionist environment than the one in Ohio he had left. The principal town in western Massachusetts, Springfield boasted an anti-slavery society of its own and not too far away was Boston, the citadel of the William Lloyd Garrison school of reformers. The transplanted Brown was not unfamiliar with Garrison's outspoken weekly, *The Liberator,* but its beam was brighter in Massachusetts than in Ohio. Not without a liberal organ of its own, Springfield boasted the *Daily Republican,* which did not take its cue from Garrison, but which consistently opposed slavery and championed civil rights.

Brown's two-year residence in Springfield would deepen his compassion for those in bondage. As he informed his wife in a letter dated January 8, 1847, his own mounting joy at the prospect of rejoining his family after a protracted absence made him even more sensitive to the lot of the "vast number" of slaves who experienced separation from their loved ones with almost no hope of ever seeing them again in this life.[8]

Springfield was a center of underground railroad operations, the valley of the Connecticut River having long been a preferred route for escaping slaves. In Springfield one branch of the underground railroad had a name of its own, the Subterranean Passage Way. If Brown stood aside from the organized underground railroad he found in Springfield, his individual efforts to assist runaways left no doubt as to his deep sympathies. Writing in 1858 to one of his backers, Brown said that since his boyhood days he had never let an opportunity pass to take part in "railroad business." [9]

In truth Brown's father had made it a point to assist runaways, hiding them in the barn, with John lending a hand. By the time he had reached manhoood John Brown "considered it as much his duty to help a slave escape as it was to help catch a horse thief," according to one of his employees. The first two blacks young John, Jr., ever saw were a runaway couple—the woman picked him up and kissed him. At Randolph township, Brown had a cleverly concealed, well-ventilated room in the haymow of the barn. Whenever his own slave-harboring facilities were overtaxed, he appealed to his neighbors to furnish shelter for the fugitives.[10] Hence when Brown came to Springfield he was acting in character in speeding slaves on to Canada.

In the spring of 1848 Brown rejoiced over the furore created by the attempt, however unsuccessful, of Captain Daniel Drayton of the schooner *Pearl* to smuggle seventy-seven slaves out of Washington to New York. "The slave case at Washington seems likely to set the Pot aboiling again in Congress," he conjectured wishfully in a letter to his eldest son.[11]

Brown's interest in runaway slaves led him to reflect upon the lot of those who succeeded in reaching Canada. Within a year after reaching Springfield he considered the possibility of starting "an African high school" in Ontario.[12] Nothing came of the idea. Brown's business in wool was destined to be unprofitable; he had no money for such a venture even if the candidate he had in mind for the mission, George Delamater, had been willing.

Although from boyhood Brown had formed short-time acquaintances with slaves in flight, he came to know blacks in a more personal way and in a more sustaining relationship only after he had come to Springfield. Unlike the Western Reserve where there were few resident blacks, Springfield boasted nearly 300 at the time of Brown's arrival. His first acquaintance among them was Thomas Thomas, whom Brown hired as a porter at the wool warehouse. "Have Thomas Thomas helping me," wrote Brown on May 15, 1847, in a private letter. After the Harpers Ferry raid Thomas said that he had learned something of Brown's plans to liberate the slaves on the first day he went to work for him in 1846.[13]

Of the blacks Brown came to know during his Springfield years, the most important was Frederick Douglass. Like Thomas, Douglass was a former fugitive from Maryland. But their similarities went little further, Douglass by 1847 having become a prominent reformist figure in America and the British Isles. Following his escape, Douglass had taken residence in Lynn, Massachusetts, and while there he joined the Massachusetts Anti-Slavery Society in 1841 as a lecturer. His imposing physique, handsome countenance, and thundering voice, combined with a clarity of thought and a steadily mounting command of the English language, had made him a prime drawing card in reformist circles.

In 1845, after the publication of the *Narrative of the Life of Frederick Douglass,* a moving and deservedly popular autobiography, Douglass spent twenty months touring the British Isles. Here his many admirers raised a purse to buy his freedom so that he would return to America with no price on his head. Back in his native land, Douglass established himself at Rochester in upstate New York and quickly proceeded to make one of his dreams come true—the publication of a weekly paper, *The North Star.*

Douglass symbolized the role of blacks in antebellum reform movements, particularly of the organized effort against slavery. Blacks had been instrumental in the formation of the new abolitionist societies that sprang up in the North in the 1830's, culminating in the emergence of the American Anti-Slavery Society in 1833. Black reformers—men, women, and children—were already on the scene in 1841 when Douglass came to the fore. But by 1846 he had become the most prominent of the black public figures, a position he would relinquish only upon his death nearly half a century later.

Inevitably a figure like Douglass would attract Brown's attention and interest. Douglass had committed his career to the crusade against slavery. Like Brown also, he had grown cool toward the church because of its timidity on the slavery question and its failure to witness against jim-crow practices even within its own congregational membership. Brown could have been in the audience when Douglass, appearing at the town hall in Springfield on February 1, 1848, denounced the Christian church as being pro-slavery and characterized America as "a slave hunting community." In any event it is not surprising that Brown invited the black orator to visit him on two occasions, late in 1847 and late in

1848, both invitations timed with Douglass' lecture tours in the vicinity.[14]

On the first occasion Douglass was an overnight guest. Commenting on his visit at the time, Douglass remarked that although Brown was white, he was in sympathy with blacks and as deeply interested in their cause as though he had been in chains. Brown, as Douglass reported in the *North Star,* also expressed pleasure at the growing number of militant blacks, a circumstance he felt would inevitably make for the downfall of slavery.[15]

In a much later account of this first visit, Douglass supplied additional details. Some of these were innocuous, such as the cordial welcome he received from every member of the family and the kind of supper fare. But some of the later details furnished by Douglass were of a type that could not have been divulged at the time. These included Brown's disclosure of a plan to establish squads of armed men at stations in the Alleghenies, to aid slaves to escape. Although the skeptical Douglass raised some questions which Brown hardly answered to his satisfaction, the black leader had been deeply impressed.[16] The two men would retain a cordial relationship until the eve of Harpers Ferry.

If Brown impressed Douglass, the sentiment was mutual. Brown knew full well, however, that Douglass was the exception rather than the rule. By 1848 Brown, for a white, had acquired an exceptional knowledge of the black rank and file. Deciding to spur them on, Brown in 1848 composed a satirical essay which he called "Sambo's Mistakes." Appearing in short-lived black weekly, *The Ram's Horn,* published in New York, the piece took on the quality of an in-house memorandum, an unburdening of confidences within the family circle.

The article attempted to get blacks to take a hard look at themselves, Brown posing as a Negro named Sambo who describes his varied and numerous mistakes. When he was a boy, writes Sambo, instead of reading good literature he spent his time on silly novels and other such miserable trash. Another of his early errors was the notion that smoking would make a man of him. Reaching the years of adulthood, he had joined secret societies and fraternal orders instead of seeking the company of educated men. Moreover at meetings of colored people, he had been so eager to display his "spouting talents" that he had lost all sight of the business at hand, and that in general discussions he would never yield any minor point of difference even at the expense of presenting a united front on important social issues.

Another of his small mistakes, continues Sambo, was his unwillingness to deny himself anything. "For instance I have bought expensive gay clothing, nice Canes, Watches, Safety Chains, Finger-rings, Breast Pins and many other things of a like nature." He had, writes Sambo, a weakness for expensive parties and fashionable amusements, indulging these habits whenever he had the means or could borrow them.

Another "trifling error" to which Sambo confessed was that of currying favor with whites "by tamely submitting to every species of indignity, and contempt and wrong," instead of nobly resisting brutal aggressions, instead of assuming his responsibilities as a citizen, a man, a husband, a brother, a neighbor, and a friend, as ordained by God. His reward for this submissiveness was little more than that received by Northerners who kowtowed to the Slaveocrats, counting themselves honored to be allowed "to lick up the spittle of a Southerner." [17]

If the impact of Brown's memorandum was slight, it provides further clues as to Brown's evolving pattern of protest. It was a call for resistance, for blacks to take their rightful place as men. It warned them not to honor their oppressors. "Sambo's Mistakes" urged the free blacks to slough off any such docile, fawning, cheek-turning traits that a present-day writer, Stanley Elkins, refers to as the "Sambo" personality of the slave.

However much Brown's abolitionist sentiments deepened during his sojourn in Springfield, his purse remained lean. The wool business went poorly, culminating in a disastrous business trip abroad in the fall of 1848. Facing bankruptcy and somewhat restless, Brown welcomed the opportunity to move to North Elba, a hamlet in northeastern New York. The wealthy philanthropist reformer,

Gerrit Smith, had purchased in 1846 a tract of 120,000 acres in the Adirondacks for the express purpose of granting the land to blacks. The Smith lands extended over eight counties, with the main settlement located at the township of North Elba with its 17,000 acres.

Brown may have first learned of the Smith grants from a notice in the *Springfield Republican* of April 20, 1848: "Great numbers of colored people are to leave New York City, this spring, to settle on farms in the Northern part of New York State, the land having been given them by Gerrit Smith." At any rate, Brown visited the region in November 1848, reporting to Frederick Douglass that he found the lands good. Some six weeks later, in a letter to his father, Brown said that, all things considered, he could think of no place that he would rather go than to North Elba, where he could live with "these poor despised Africans," helping and encouraging them.[18] The black grantees needed help, most of them having previously made their living in service occupations rather than in farming.

Brown had little trouble in negotiating a 244-acre tract with Gerrit Smith, at $1.00 an acre. The two were kindred spirits in their hatred of slavery, their concern about the welfare of free blacks, and their general moralistic outlook. Following Brown's visit to Smith's home in Peterboro, New York,, in April 1848, the two reformers formed a friendship that would be warm and enduring. In May of the following year Brown, his wife, and seven children arrived at North Elba. They had been driven from Westport through the Keene Valley by a hired black, named Thomas Jefferson, himself moving from Troy to North Elba with his family. The morning after their arrival, they were joined by a runaway slave, Cyrus, whom Brown employed as a farm hand and who lived with the family in a rented, rambling house with four rooms and an unfurnished attic.[19]

Brown's social relationships with his black neighbors were cordial to friendly. On his first trip to North Elba to scout out the land he was accompanied by Lyman E. Epps, Sr., owner of the farm that adjoined the one Brown later bought. During his periods at North Elba, Brown visited the Epps family, as his time permitted, and played with the children. On one occasion, he brought along a runaway slave. Brown's daughter, Ruth, remembered how grief-stricken he was at the death of a black neighbor who perished in the cold after losing his way in the woods.[20]

Brown's person-to-person behavior toward blacks was some-what puzzling to Richard Henry Dana, Jr., noted author of *Two Years Before the Mast,* who stumbled upon the Brown house after losing his way while camping in the Adirondacks with two com-panions. Brown invited the unexpected guests to stay for supper and they gratefully accepted. Seated at the long table were two blacks. Somewhat taken aback by this display of social equality, Dana was even more surprised when, in introducing the blacks Brown prefixed their last names with Mr. and Mrs. In his diary, Dana duly underscored these courtesy titles Brown gave to the black diners, *"Mr.* Jefferson," and *"Mrs.* Wait." [21]

With a large family of his own and an income that was both small and unsteady, Brown was hardly in a position to give money or supplies to his black neighbors. Once or twice, however, he sent them barrels of pork and flour, and in one instance he mailed a donation of $5.00.[22]

Although Brown himself could hardly have been called a good credit risk, he sought to help the black settlers in their business affairs. He surveyed their lands and collected payments due to their creditors, on one occasion sending Gerrit Smith $225 of such funds.[23] Stories of blacks being swindled out of their lands and being overcharged for supplies and for services, such as having their luggage or logs carted, decreased with the coming of Brown, the threat of a lawsuit by a white a far greater deterrent than a similar expression by a black.

If Brown helped blacks at North Elba, he was not too proud to seek their help in turn. In December 1850, in a letter to his children, he acknowledged that the "colored brethren" had been of marked assistance in clearing a piece of his land. Writing from Troy in the following October to his daughter, Ruth, and her husband, Henry Thompson, he told them to ask Lyman Epps to "take care" of some Brown-owned lumber. Writing in May 1853 to the same couple, who were about to build a house for him, Brown advised them to approach Epps to give a hand. "If he does I shall be glad," he added, "but I would not have him distress himself to do it." [24]

Brown's advice and counsel to his black neighbors extended beyond business affairs. He urged them to be honest, truthful, and industrious. Writing to black Willis A. Hodges, owner of 200 acres and a log house on the Smith lands, Brown expressed the hope that his "colored friends" would not be content to conduct themselves merely as well as whites "but to set them an example in all things." The colored families were doing well, he wrote his wife in late December 1852: "They have constant preaching on the Sabbath; and intelligence, morality, and religion appear to be all on the advance." [25]

Brown's propensity for giving advice to blacks found an outlet in the Fugitive Slave Law of 1850, a highly explosive enactment. It denied the alleged runaway a jury trial and the right to testify on his own behalf, thus assuming him guilty. The measure outraged the abolitionists, white and black, galvanizing them into action. To surmise, as Brown did, that the Fugitive Slave Law would create more abolitionists "than all the lectures we have had for years," one scarcely needed any unusual gift of prophecy.

Brown was in Springfield, closing out some business matters, when the law went into effect. Here he met with groups of blacks, publicly and behind closed doors, in an attempt to keep their spirits from falling. Some of them told him that they could not sleep, fearful that they or their wives or children would be seized. "I want all my family to imagine themselves in the same dreadful condition," wrote Brown to Mary.[26]

Bent on concrete action to thwart the hated law and at the same time embolden the blacks, Brown formed a new organization, the Springfield branch of the United States League of Gileadites. The name of the semi-secret organization came from the Bible. But the balm in Gilead which Brown had in mind was more of an excitant than a soother. As he pointed out, the title of the organization came from the Old Testament admonition: "Whoever is fearful or afraid, let him return and part early from Mount Gilead." Holding an organizational meeting on January 15, 1851, a group of forty-four "Gileadites," all of them black and many of them former slaves, listened while Brown delivered a prepared document under two headings, "Words of Advice" and "Agreement."

Following the quotation, "Union is Strength," Brown's words-of-advice section opened with the assertion that nothing charmed Americans more than personal bravery. No jury in the North, ran the statement, would convict a runaway slave for defending his rights at whatever cost. Brown called attention to the struggle of the Greeks against the Turks and the Poles against the Russians. Then after a brief castigation of blacks who indulged in idle show and luxury (reminiscent in tone and temper of "Sambo's Mistakes"), Brown mentioned a trio of whites who had made personal sacrifices for blacks—Charles T. Torrey, who was sentenced to hard labor for assisting runaways, Jonathan Walker, who was branded on his hand for a similar offense, and Elijah P. Lovejoy.

With exhortation accounted for, Brown proceeded to give specific directions as to behavior. He advised the Gileadites to assemble quickly if any of their members were arrested, thus outnumbering "your adversaries." Members should go armed but with weapons concealed. They were to be tight-lipped in the presence of others. When they were ready they must strike; otherwise their resolution would peter out. "Be firm, determined, and cool; but let it be understood that you are not to be driven to desperation without making it an awful dear job to others as well as to you." During a trial in a courtroom they might create a distraction by burning gunpowder in paper bags and, all else failing, they "might possibly give one or more of your enemies a hoist." As for dealing with a slave-catcher, a lasso might be used to good effect. Above all, unity was the watchword. Had the blacks in New York City had a well-defined plan of operations when runaway slaves James Hamlet and Henry Long were seized, the results would have been different. If Gileadites met with trouble while on rescue business they were to seek refuge in the house of influential white friends, thereby forcing them to take a stand one way or the other.

Brown's words-of-advice section was followed by a briefer "agreement" in which the signatories bespoke their trust in a just and merciful God, pledged their loyalty to the American flag, and promised to arm themselves at once. Their officers were to be chosen on the basis of their wisdom and stout-heartedness, as demonstrated "after some trial of courage." Brown's document came to a close with nine resolutions which simply reaffirmed the "agreement," often in the identical phraseology.

Apparently the document was accepted by the assembled blacks without change, some of them not only signing their names to it but adding their occupation, such as waiter, barber, laborer, woodworker, tinsmith, jobber, machinist, druggist, and sexton.[27] At least four of the Gileadites were women. Their names were listed but not their type of employment.

The Brown plan to which the Gileadites assented was basically revolutionary in import, envisioning a semi-militaristic organization whose aim of rescuing and protecting runaways was to be accomplished by any means necessary. Although the plan stressed resistance rather than attack, it had commando-raid and guerrilla-war elements.

The application of these techniques of warfare would have to await Harpers Ferry, however; they would not become operative in Springfield. The League of Gileadites apparently never functioned, in part because it was never put to the test; no slave-catchers showed up in the town. And the author of the plan, ever on the move, soon left Springfield for good.

Returning temporarily to North Elba, Brown resumed his advice-giving to his black neighbors, now including exhortations to resist the fugitive slave law. He ordered his family to be on the lookout for anyone who might come in quest of Cyrus, the runaway slave in their employ. Later that year, in a letter to Frederick Douglass, Brown entreated "his colored friends" not to faint or grow weary: "Let no man's heart fail him." Brown added a typically cryptic sentence, highly significant in retrospect, "The Lord our God shall raise for us a deliverer in the very best possible time; and who shall pretend to prove that he is *not even now born.*" In a postscript to this letter from his father, John, Jr., added that he was glad that there was one newspaper in existence whose mission was to teach the people the truth about the fugitive slave law "and that paper is your own." [28]

John, Sr.—it hardly need be added—never let up in his attack on the hated "blood-hound bill." In a long letter to Douglass in January 1854, he asserted that God commanded his followers to desist from delivering unto the master the servant who had escaped. On the contrary, one should open his gates to the escapee, inviting him in to dwell. A few months later when Brown, then at Vernon, New York, as a defendant in a law suit, heard of the seizure of runaway Anthony Burns, he announced that he was leaving for Boston on a rescue mission. His alarmed attorney finally talked him out of it.[29]

To its black settlers North Elba had its pluses and minuses, with the latter eventually winning out. Like blacks elsewhere who were beholden to Gerrit Smith, those at North Elba were appreciative of the man and his generosity. Similarly the North Elba blacks knew they had a staunch friend in John Brown. The remoteness of the region was reassuring to blacks who had escaped from slavery; no federal marshals were likely to be lurking around. North Elba, however, posed one all-important problem to its black settlers— that of making a living. They could find few markets for their farm produce and little work in the off season.

Hard pressed, some of them sold their lots to pay the taxes, prompting Lyman Epps to write a public letter beseeching his fellow black landowners to retain their holdings for their pine lumber, whose value was increasing as the supply diminished. But Timbucto, as the black settlers called it, remained little more than a sprinkling of crudely-built shanties, their flat roofs relieved by small, protruding stove-pipes. By 1855 not more than ten families remained.[30]

The smallness of the population at North Elba did not long act as a deterrent to Brown's black improvement program. Within a few years a measure far more explosive than the Fugitive Slave Law gave momentum to his efforts. This was the Kansas-Nebraska Act of 1854, a measure that widened Brown's contemplated field of action far beyond the confines of a semi-wilderness like North Elba, a hamlet like Hudson, or a township like Springfield. In addition, this act of Congress changed Brown's plan of action from resistance to slavery to a frontal attack upon it. And, finally, Kansas would provide for Brown a training-school for Harpers Ferry just as the bloody struggles in that territory would constitute a prelude to the Civil War.

The Kansas-Nebraska Act set aside the Missouri Compromise of 1820, which had prohibited slavery in those territories. Enactment of this measure had an electric effect, immediately touching off a desperate race between free-state advocates and pro-slavery advocates, each bent on organizing the territory. Sectional control of Kansas became the paramount issue, with Northerners being determined to prevent the addition of more slave states and Southerners bent on thwarting such a containment. Pro-slavery sympathizers flooded into the territory. Northerners countered with organizations such as the New England Emigrant Aid Company, its purpose to organize emigration to Kansas thereby securing it to freedom by outnumbering their opponents at the polls.

Opening Kansas to slavery drew bitter condemnation from black leaders. "The Nebraska business is the great smasher in Syracuse as elsewhere," wrote Jermain Wesley Loguen, a runaway slave turned clergyman and underground railroad operator. To Loguen the bill was so monstrous as to arouse widespread feeling against it, thus inadvertently helping the anti-slavery cause. Calling it a hell-bent scheme for extending human bondage, *Frederick Douglass' Paper* urged that companies of emigrants from the free states be organized and "sent out to possess the goodly land." [31]

Blacks in Philadelphia held an "Anti-Colonization and Anti-Nebraska meeting," declaring that the Kansas-Nebraska bill contemplated the extension of slavery and hence peculiarly affected them by virtue of their close identification with the slave. Stamping it as a foe to freedom, "a document meriting the execration of every friend of man," they pointed out that whether the bill violated this or that compromise was irrelevant.[32]

Kansas beckoned inexorably to Brown, although he held back for over a year. Writing from Akron, Ohio, in September 1854 to his daughter, Ruth, he confessed that he was uncertain as to which

would benefit the colored people more—his returning to North Elba
or setting out for Kansas. He asked her to sound out Lyman Epps
and "all the colored people" for their advice. Brown addressed a
similar inquiry to Gerrit Smith, Frederick Douglass, and J. McCune
Smith, a physician-reformer of New York City. As the donor of
the lands at North Elba, Gerrit Smith understandably advised
Brown to return. No reply came from the two black abolitionist
leaders.[33]

While the elder Brown pondered his proper course, his five sons
joined the migration to Kansas, three arriving in the fall of 1854
and two the following spring. Their motivation was mixed. Two of
them, as their sister, Annie, later put it, "went to Kansas to settle
and make homes for themselves," and would fight in self-defense
but otherwise with reluctance.[34] But to Salmon, Oliver, and John
Brown, Jr., the lure of free land was combined with the desire to
strike a blow against slavery.

In a long letter to Frederick Douglass, written in mid-August
1855 from Lawrence, John Brown, Jr., discussed the key question
confronting the emigrants from the Northern states: "Shall Kansas
be a free *White* state only, or a state in which *all* shall have their
rights protected irrespective of color?" Unfortunately, continued
young Brown, most of his co-settlers seemed to be in favor of
making Kansas a state for whites only, while imposing the "most
outrageous restrictions upon the colored man." In passages expressing deep concern, young Brown said that he hoped and prayed
that the free-staters would not consent to a scheme which robbed
black fellow citizens of their rights.[35]

Anti-Negro sentiment, however, turned out to be far stronger
than John, Jr., had anticipated. Despite his efforts a convention
of free-staters at Big Springs, held less than three weeks after he
had written to Douglass, denounced abolitionists of the Garrison
stripe and recommended stringent Negro-exclusion laws. As
John, Jr., would discover from a territory-wide vote held three
months later, in which a stipulation barring free Negroes was
carried by a large majority, Northerners who settled in Kansas,
like those of other Midwestern states and localities, wanted no
blacks, bond or free.

In an editorial, "Our Plans for Making Kansas a Free State," Frederick Douglass in September 1854 had urged blacks to go to the territory and become permanent settlers. But neither he nor the Browns had sufficiently weighed the antipathy in Kansas to people of color. Northerners who went to Kansas had an aversion to both African slavery and Afro-Americans. Indeed excluding slavery from the territory was also a way of excluding blacks. A handful of whites like the Browns might be emancipationist and equalitarian in racial matters but most of the Northerners who emigrated to Kansas were anti-slavery and anti-Negro. To them equal rights for blacks was a notion not worth serious consideration.[36]

Black leaders would soon come to the conclusion that the Kansas struggle was, in the main, little more than a contest between free white labor and black slave labor. But they did not write the territory off, holding that to save it for partial freedom was an important first step.[37]

This half-a-loaf attitude made sense to John Brown. By the late spring of 1855 he had made up his mind to go to Kansas. Letters from his sons had described its lovely and fertile prairies, but Brown's motivation was his growing urge to strike a direct blow at slavery. According to Charles Robinson, a prominent Free State leader in the territory and later the first governor of the state, Brown told him "that he did not come to Kansas for the purpose of settling at all." Kansas to Brown "was an opportunity to get at slavery in the country and abolish it; and he came there for that purpose, and not simply to operate in Kansas, and for Kansas alone." [38]

Leaving his wife, daughters, and a grown son at North Elba, Brown first traveled downstate to Syracuse, bent on raising funds at the organizational meeting of the Radical Abolitionist party. Offshot of the dying Liberty party, but with the similar aim of striking at slavery through the ballot box, the Radical Abolitionist party numbered two Negroes—Frederick Douglass and J. McCune Smith—among its five founders. At the meeting the delegates chose Smith for the chairmanship, a move dictated less by his color than by his abilities.

John Brown was in attendance during the entire three days of the convention, meeting a warm reception on the whole. Invited to speak at the closing session, he appealed for men and means to make Kansas a free state, presenting two letters from John, Jr. The reading of these drew tears "from numerous eyes in the great collection of people present," wrote Brown to Mary. Hyperbole aside, Brown's remarks seem to have been well received. Douglass, in an editorial reference to the meeting, spoke of Brown as an active and self-sacrificing abolitionist who had presented his case most feelingly.[39] Perhaps as pleasing to Brown as praise was the purse of about $60 that he received from the delegates.

Brown used part of this windfall to go to Springfield to purchase firearms and flasks. Taking advantage of this opportunity, he called on Thomas Thomas and tried to induce the former slave to accompany him westward. Except for their once having attended the theater, along with John Jr., to see *Uncle Tom's Cabin,* the two had seen little of each other in five years. Brown's invitation to go with him to Kansas brought a negative response, Thomas saying that he had made other plans.[40] When Brown finally entered the territory on October 4, 1854, he was accompanied only by his son, Oliver, and his son-in-law, Henry Thompson.

Reflecting the temperament of the true believer, Brown's early assessment of the free state prospects in Kansas were optimistic. His first letters to Mary were strongly up-beat in tone. On October 14, he reported that the outlook was brightening every day, and a week later he voiced the opinion that Missouri's sister slave states had now begun to share her unhappiness about the dimming prospect of winning Kansas. Writing from Brownsville on November 2, he expressed his growing confidence that slavery in the territory would soon be a thing of the past, "and to God be the praise." [41]

In a letter to Douglass' weekly in mid-December (undoubtedly the lengthiest he ever wrote) Brown spoke of the brave, non-drinking volunteers who were "holding on" in Kansas, adding that the territory would soon be free if "friends in the States" retained the high ground on which they stood. This long letter to Douglass contained Brown's version of a skirmish that came to be known as the Wakarusa War. Brown's role in this action illustrates that his efforts in Kansas were not confined to writing hopeful letters. Within a week after his arrival in the territory, he and his sons, hearing that there might be trouble on Election Day at the voting precinct nearby, had appeared on the scene "most thoroughly armed," as Brown put it.[42]

Two months later Brown and four of his sons made an overnight march from Osawatomie to Lawrence. Bands of pro-slavery Missourians had gathered on the banks of the Wakarusa River near Lawrence, their mission to sack the town. Brown arrived at Lawrence on December 7, 1855, bearing the title "Captain of the Liberty Guards" and heading a company of twenty men. But before the newly commissioned officer could put himself or his recruits to the test, the Missourians withdrew. The governor of the territory, having hastened to the town, negotiated an agreement with the free state spokesmen to which the pro-slavery leaders reluctantly acquiesced, thus bringing to an end the unfought Wakarusa War. Brown's company was discharged within a few days afterward, but the title of captain would cling to him, not without reason perhaps. It "fitted him readily," wrote Villard; "where he was, he led." [43]

Becoming an active leader of the free state volunteers, Brown demonstrated a courage sometimes bordering on recklessness. Badly outnumbered at Black Jack on June 2, 1856, the Brown forces refused to wilt under fire, winning the battle after an instillation of new courage from their leader. Twenty-five Missourians were taken prisoner, Brown exchanging their two leaders for his previously captured sons, John, Jr., and Jason.

If Brown's willingness to mix with his enemies was never questioned, the same could not be said of his judgment as a leader of armed men. Brown's name would be forever tarnished by an incident at Pottawatomie Creek on May 24, 1856. In an action planned by Brown and carried out under his direction, five pro-slavery men were cruelly put to death. According to his son Jason, Brown himself "never raised a hand in the slaying of the men," although he put a bullet through the head of one of them a half hour after he had expired.[44] The victims had been seized in their cabins late at night and ordered outside to be put to death, Brown's party of eight washing their broadswords in the creek.

Six weeks before the Pottawatomie slaying Brown had expressed the opinion that the pro-slavery people would, by their constant aggression, bring about their own undoing: "Their foot shall slide in due time," he wrote to his family.[45] But, as Pottawatomie showed, Brown was not prepared to wait indefinitely before giving "due time" a personal assist.

Brown's act, however unpardonable when taken by itself, came to be viewed by his defenders as hardly more than the spirit of the times on the Kansas border. Alleging that there were mitigating reasons for Pottawatomie, they pointed out that the code of violence and a willingness to wink at the law were not uncommon on the frontier. True, to the men in the territory, Kansas was in an undeclared state of war, with ruffianism on both sides. Unquestionably the free state men were convinced that the pro-slavery forces were intractable and violence-oriented. "Our enemies are determined to drive us into forcible resistance," wrote John, Jr., to Douglass six weeks before Pottawatomie. "Hourly are we moving in the midst of inflammable material which it needs but a spark to ignite." This letter had scarcely reached its destination before a series of sparks had been touched off, with Pottawatomie the kindle. In the words of Charles Robinson, "Brown was ready to kill any pro-slavery man he could find simply because he was pro-slavery." [46]

Brown had a stern sense of duty, and a favorite text of his was an admonishment that without the shedding of blood there could be no remission of sin. But he was not proud of the Pottawatomie killings, preferring to avoid the topic. Writing to his family shortly after the incident, he inserted a sentence that sounded like an apology, a purging of something from his mind: "We feel assured that He who sees not as men see, does not lay the guilt of innocent blood to our charge." [47]

The Pottawatomie murders would constitute a stain on Brown's career, particularly when his own grim role in the incident became fully substantiated some years afterward. But to his black supporters, no blame attached to his conduct in Kansas. With a perception born of an oppressed minority, blacks were keen in their critical analysis of their detractors. But to their friends, few at most and generally at bay for their lack of color bias, blacks tended to operate on an uncritical, or sub-critical, level. One hardly need subject his few friends to a searching inquiry when he had a legion of belittlers to attend to.

It was not that blacks condoned the Pottawatomie killings. It was simply that they viewed the incident from a wider perspective of aberrant behavior in their country, from a greater familiarity with the climate of violence, both legitimate, and extra-legal, in the land of their birth. The whole pattern of black-white relations in antebellum America was to blacks a form of violence, often concealed under familiar, institutional forms, but pervasive and ever on the march. To blacks, five men slain at Pottawatomie was sobering indeed. But so to blacks was it sobering to think of nearly 5 million of their kind subject by their color to a killing of their dreams, a snuffing out of their manhood and womanhood, day-in and day-out.

The battle that gave Brown his nickname, "Old Osawatomie Brown," also confirmed his commitment to a war to the death against slavery and on its own ground. Brown encountered the pro-slavery forces on August 30, 1856, at Osawatomie, on the Marias des Cygnes River, after being summoned by a messenger who told him his son, Frederick, had been killed and that the small settlement was being attacked. Brown's band of some thirty-five fought stubbornly against decidedly superior numbers. Eventually they had to fall back, however, driven across the river in a disorderly retreat. The victors put the settlement to the torch, a sight that enraged Brown, still nursing a back bruise from a spent bullet. "I will give them something else to do than to extend slavery," he vowed in Jason's hearing. "I will carry the war into Africa." [48]

For a few days after Osawatomie it was widely reported that

Brown had been killed in the action. When the story proved to be false, Brown's well-wishers were overjoyed. A relieved Frederick Douglass spoke of the exultation among the pro-slavery forces as they savored the news that the stalwart form before which they had so often fled had been "stiffened in death." But bravery such as Brown's deserved a better fate "than to perish in an obscure fight with the ruffian hordes of Missouri." Douglass expressed the hope that Brown would outlive the dangers that beset him and would succeed in planting in Kansas a free and prosperous community.[49]

Brown would never lose his anti-slavery zeal but he would not retain his interest in Kansas as the scene of his operations. Five weeks after the Osawatomie incident Brown left the territory, to return only temporarily and as a diversionary operation to conceal his real intentions.

Yet his participation for a year in the civil strife in Kansas had been a shaping force in his life. No longer would he be bothered by any role confusion. "Previous to this he had devoted himself entirely to business," wrote his half-brother, Jeremiah R. Brown, "but since the Kansas troubles he has abandoned all business and become wholly absorbed in the subject of slavery." In a letter to Joshua R. Giddings in June 1848, Brown stated that he wished to manage his business in such a way as to benefit the abolitionist cause. But after his Kansas experience Brown no longer attempted to combine his business with his calling, the latter having become his one increasing purpose. One who neglected the obligation of striking at slavery, he wrote in April 1857, would be held accountable by God.[50]

Brown now stood ready to give his all to a cause in which he felt every man, woman, and child had a deep and awesome interest. To this end his own militant abolitionism would henceforth seek new forms of expression, forms which might well take their cue from "bleeding Kansas."

III

REHEARSAL
PATTERN

I wish you Godspeed in your Glorious work.
James N. Gloucester to Brown,
February 19, 1858

During the twelve months after he left the Kansas territory, Brown, in chronic need, spent most of his time raising money. Traveling even more than was his wont, he sought financial backers like George L. Stearns who, sharing his convictions, might be induced to share their means. To this end he spoke at meetings, generally in New England, having prepared for delivery a short talk, "An Idea of Things in Kansas." He also approached the press. In a letter to the *New-York Tribune,* which appeared conspicuously on the editorial page, he asked all lovers of liberty to support his work by sending "contributions of pecuniary aid," and he asked all friendly newspapers to reprint this fund-soliciting letter, giving it "some half dozen insertions." [1]

To donors, proved or prospective, Brown did not reveal the full scope of his plans. At one time he might say he wanted funds for the defense of Kansas; at another time he might say that he was raising money for "the cause." But whatever "the cause" might be, by November 1857 Brown had decided that its locus was no longer Kansas but Virginia.

It was at Tabor, Iowa, that Brown first announced to his nine followers that Virginia was his destination. Of the four newest recruits, three were unhappy about this change of plans. The other recent volunteer, Richard Richardson, was apparently less reluctant, expressing no dissent. Richardson was a former slave from Lexington, Missouri, and his enlistment gladdened Brown, fulfilling his effort to bring at least one black into the fold.

Early in December 1857 the Brown band moved eastward across Iowa, stopping at Springdale when their money ran dangerously low. Bent primarily on tapping familiar sources, Brown left Springdale in mid-January, to be gone three months. His men broke up the long winter days at Springdale by drilling in the morning, followed by military studies. In the afternoons they did odd jobs, including corn husking, except on Tuesdays and Thursdays. These afternoons were devoted to holding a mock legislature. Following parliamentary procedure, the men debated the constitutionality of the Fugitive Slave Law and passed resolutions, one of which affirmed that John Brown was more entitled to the nation's sympathy and honor than George Washington.[2] Former slave Richardson spent many of his spare moments learning how to read. His teacher was Richard Realf, an English-born man of letters turned revolutionary for a time.

In their mock legislature Brown's followers drew up a set of laws for their so-called "State of Topeka." In this document Brown, of course, had no hand. No matter; at that very time he was formulating a more elaborate frame of government of his own— the Provisional Constitution, copies of which he would carry to Harpers Ferry. This document was being written at the home of Frederick Douglass.

Thirteen days after leaving his men, Brown presented himself at the Douglass residence in suburban Rochester. He asked for a room, insisting on paying for it and saying that he would be staying for only a short time. He felt confident that Douglass would acquiesce. Since leaving the Kansas regions, Brown had kept in touch with the black leader. En route westward in October 1856 Brown's son, Watson, had stopped in Rochester to see Douglass. Two months later Brown himself showed up, responding to a Douglass invitation "to take a mouthful" with him. In March 1857 when Douglass delivered an address to an anti-slavery gathering at Worcester,

Massachusetts, with the mayor presiding, Brown had been a platform guest. Douglass "was powerful indeed," he wrote.[3]

During his stay with the Douglass family, beginning on January 27 and lasting for three weeks, Brown proved to be an undemanding lodger. He spared the feelings of Douglass by not paying him directly, giving the money to his wife or to his eldest daughter, Rosetta. He did impose on Douglass to the extent of taking some of his busy hours, making a listener of one who was generally a speaker. "He has promised me $50," wrote Brown to John, Jr., "and what I value vastly more he seems to appreciate my theories & my labours." [4]

At the Douglass home Brown spent most of his time drafting a constitution and writing letters. Brown's brainchild, a "Provisional Constitution and Ordinances for the People of the United States," was a document comprised of a preamble and forty-eight articles. In typical fashion Brown kept its contents to himself, preferring not to unveil it prior to a ratification convention he was planning to hold three months later at Chatham, Ontario.

Many of Brown's letters written from the Douglass residence went to black opinion-makers, seeking to line up as many of them as possible for a meeting in Philadelphia in March. To this end Brown wrote to John Jones and Henry O. Wagoner in Chicago, Jermain Loguen in Syracuse, Henry Highland Garnet in New York, Martin R. Delany in Chatham, George T. Downing in Providence, and clergyman James N. Gloucester in Brooklyn. To conceal his identity Brown advised his correspondents to address him as N. (or Nelson) Hawkins, in care of Frederick Douglass, or else to send their letters in a sealed envelope inside another envelope addressed to Douglass. To avoid check-cashing problems Brown advised James N. Gloucester to make out to Douglass any remittances he was sending. To post his letters and pick up his incoming mail Brown engaged Charles Remond Douglass, thirteen-year-old son of his host.[5]

Brown left Rochester on February 17, 1858, expecting to meet many of his black correspondents within three weeks. He spent one of these intervening weeks at the Brooklyn home of the Gloucesters at their invitation. Both originally from Richmond, the Gloucesters were moderately wealthy. Elizabeth ran a furniture shop and dabbled in real estate. James had written Brown on February 19 commending him for his efforts to deliver the slave and vowing not to falter in his support of the work. In his letter the black clergyman cautioned Brown about the faith he had expressed in the rank and file: "The *masses* suffer for the want of intelligence and it is difficult to reach them in a matter like you propose." He did not despair, however, added Gloucester, and he hoped that his observation would not dampen Brown's ardor.[6]

As Gloucester soon learned when his guest arrived, Brown's optimism was not easily dimmed. True to form, he wrote to Mary that he was finding among the colored people more earnest feeling than ever before. Providence, he added, seemed to be intoning the words, "Try on." [7]

Brown's conference with black leaders, delayed until March 16 to suit a change in plans by Douglass, was held at the well-appointed home of Stephen Smith on Lombard Street, Brown's headquarters during his seven-day stay in Philadelphia. Smith was a well-to-do lumber dealer and a well-known underground railroad operator. Gloucester was not at the meeting; he had sent a letter expressing his regrets and pledging "$25 more" to the cause. Absent, too, was Jermain Loguen, who had been unwell but had planned to be present.[8] Brown and Loguen had originally planned to travel together from upstate New York.

The attendance at the meeting in Philadelphia on March 16, 1858, was below Brown's expectations. But the calibre of those who were there must have diminished his disappointment. The four blacks listed as present were among the most prominent in the abolitionist crusade—Douglass; the even more militant Henry Highland Garnet; the courageous and resourceful William Still, second only to Harriet Tubman in underground railroad operations; and Still's fellow Philadelphian and Brown's host, Stephen Smith.

To what extent Brown divulged his plans to the assembled group, which included his eldest son, is not known. One of the topics which certainly received attention was the forthcoming Chatham convention.[9] It is more than likely, too, that Brown made his customary appeal for men and money and equally probable that he left the meeting confident that its participants would bestir themselves to that end.

Two weeks after this meeting Brown went to North Elba for ten days—just before his planned impending foray into Virginia. This visit to his homesite in the Adirondacks was designed as a leave-taking with his wife and younger children. Possibly it was meant to be a renewal of inner strength, a lifting up of his eyes to the hills.

While at North Elba he did not completely set aside matters of business. He sent at least one letter—a request to Gloucester to collect whatever monies he could and to send them to Douglass in the form of a draft. Three days after leaving North Elba, Brown paid a short visit to Rochester where he and John, Jr., spent a night at the Douglass home. In this instance Brown had prepared his host for his coming, having on March 18 written to Douglass and to Loguen that he "expected to be on the way by the 28th or 30th." [10]

Joined by Jermain W. Loguen at Rochester, Brown crossed the border during the first week of April 1858, bound for St. Catherines, a settlement whose population of 6000 included some 1000 blacks. Writing of St. Catherines in 1856, part-time journalist Benjamin Drew noted that "nearly all" of the town's adult blacks had been slaves, a circumstance that made it an appropriate site for Brown's purpose in coming there—a scheduled meeting with legendary underground railroad operator, Harriet Tubman. "Among slaves she is better known than the Bible, for she circulates more freely," remarked Loguen.[11]

Herself an escaped slave with a price on her head, the resourceful and daring Harriet had an especial attraction for Brown. She could be invaluable enlisting needed volunteers for his army of liberation. And her familiarity with the Appalachian Mountains' routes, over which she had traveled so often on business, would make her indispensable as a master road guide and conductor of the many Virginia slaves whom he envisioned setting free.

Apparently his meeting with Harriet fulfilled all of Brown's hopes, fully justifying the payment of her traveling expense of

$15.00 from his thin purse. In elation he informed John, Jr., in a letter of April 8, that "Harriet Tubman hooked on his whole team at once." Brown had bestowed masculinity on his newly met collaborator, as his next sentence bore out: "He (Harriet) is the most of a man, naturally, that I ever met." Brown added that he was succeeding beyond his expectations and that there was abundant material of the right quality "in this quarter." As an indication of his high regard for Harriet, Brown gave her $25 on April 14, his last day at St. Catherines.[12]

It was on this note of high hope that Brown remained on Canadian soil for ten more days. During this period the most important person he interviewed, other than Mrs. Tubman, was Martin R. Delany, then residing in Chatham, having moved there from Pittsburgh in February 1856. But unlike many blacks who had come to Canada, Delany was free-born, although of a slave father. He had edited a reformist weekly in Pittsburgh, had toured as an abolitionist lecturer, and had studied medicine at Harvard. In whatever he did, Delany reflected a deep pride in his race and ancestry, holding that black Africa would one day regain its ancient glory. To his delight, Brown succeeded in winning Delany's promise to be an active participant in the proposed convention and to sound out others who might be interested in attending.[13]

With the Chatham convention scheduled for early May, Brown returned to the states for a quick trip to Chicago and Springdale. At the former he visited John Jones, a prosperous black tailor, to pick up his mail, having for two weeks informed his correspondents to address him as Nelson Hawkins or Jason Brown, in care of John Jones, Esq., Box No. 764, Chicago. Brown then turned his steps toward Springdale, Iowa, where he found that his "flock of sheep" now counted a few more but with Richard Richardson still the only black.

Two days after the arrival of their leader, Brown's small band left Springdale, bound for Chatham. As the passengers changed cars at Rock Island, an attempt was made to seize Richardson as a fugitive slave, but the conductor hurried him into the car and started the train. Stopping en route at Chicago for half a day, the group went to the Massasoit Hotel for breakfast, only to be told by the proprietor that Richardson would not be served. Muttering angrily, Brown marched out of the diningroom, his men a step behind. Nearby they found another hotel, the Adams House, "where we could take a colored man with us and sit down to breakfast," as Richard Realf put it. On the following day Brown and his party, now numbering a total of twelve, took their morning meal in a less charged atmosphere, a hotel patronized primarily by blacks, the Villa Mansion, located in Chatham, forty miles above Detroit and under the British flag.[14]

Chatham was an appropriate setting for a convention composed largely of blacks, the majority of the Negroes in Canada residing within a radius of fifty miles. For twenty years a major terminus of the underground railroad, Chatham's population of 4466 in 1863 was nearly one-third black. Unlike many other towns just across the border, Chatham's non-white population was concentrated in one section, heightening one's impression of blackness. "In my walk from the railroad station to the hotel," wrote William Wells Brown in September 1861, "I was at once impressed that I was in Chatham, for every other person whom I met was colored." An active self-improvement organization, the Chatham True Band, numbering some 400 members, men and women, gave the town's black residents a sense of unity and common purpose.[15]

Brown's men took rooms in Villa Mansion Hotel, where their leader joined them after spending a few days with J. Madison Bell. A twenty-eight-year-old plasterer who wrote poetry, Bell had left Cincinnati in 1854 for Canada. Although he had heard of Brown's exploits in Kansas, Bell had never seen him prior to the time of the convention. Brown simply presented himself at the Bell home with a letter of introduction from William Howard Day, then at Toronto, introducing the bearer as "John" and asking Bell to do whatever he could under the circumstances. To all persons to whom he sent letters while at Chatham—backers such as Thomas Wentworth Higginson and George L. Stearns and family members—

Brown asked that they direct all communications to James M. Bell, as usual using outer and inner envelopes. Bell could later say with truth that through his hands went every letter that Brown received during his stay at Chatham.[16]

In seeking conventioneers Brown sent out a printed, two-sentence letter earnestly requesting the recipient to attend a quiet gathering of the true friends of freedom. Undoubtedly this invitation was sent to whites in sparing numbers and on a highly selective basis. One of the half-dozen or so went to Alexander Milton Ross, a Canadian physician. Ross had doubled as an underground railroad conductor, personally assisted thirty-one runaways over a five-year span, and furnished guns to a few of them.[17] But with the exception of Brown, the twelve whites who would attend the convention were the recruits who had drilled at Springdale.

Among the known black invitees who did not attend were Douglass, Loguen, and Charles Lenox Remond. Brown wrote to Douglass on March 6 asking him to issue a call for the convention. One of Brown's white followers, John E. Cook, said that Douglass had been sent one of the printed letters of invitation.[18] If so, the invitation brought no response.

Loguen did reply to his invitation. Writing to Brown on May 6, he expressed his regret at his inability to attend and said that he would "like very much to see you and your brave men before you go to the *Mountains*."

Charles Lenox Remond, a long-time abolitionist lecturer from Salem, Massachusetts, was a friend and follower of William Lloyd Garrison, although of an independent mind and a lashing tongue. No reply came to a Chatham-stamped letter to Remond, dated April 29, 1858, signed by Brown, Bell, and Martin R. Delany, and stipulating that his travel expenses would be paid.[19] Brown had also been unsuccessful in trying to get in touch with the elusive, on-the-move Harriet Tubman.

Possibly there were one or two black leaders who did not attend because Brown had turned to Delany for help in enlisting supporters. Because of his strong emigrationist views, signalized by his leaving the United States to live in Canada, Delany had become somewhat of a pariah to many prominent American blacks. These critics were well aware, too, that the forceful Delany was likely to assume that in the Chatham convention he would be to the colored delegates what John Brown would be to the white ones. Not that Delany, proud and highly individualistic, would ever have thought of himself as a black John Brown (or, for that matter, of Brown as a white Martin R. Delany).

After nearly ten days of somewhat unproductive letter-writing, Brown was ready to hold the convention. On May 8 he assembled the delegates at a black schoolhouse, a one-story building which gave the appearance of a double log cabin. Brown's own semi-military band, including Richardson, comprised 13 of the 46 delegates. Of the blacks present the Chatham contingent was the largest in number and in repute. In addition to Bell and Martin R. Delany the other Chathamites included Israel Shadd, mulatto publisher of the *Provincial Freeman;* James Monroe Jones, Oberlin graduate and a gunsmith and engraver; Alfred Whipper, a school teacher; Isaac Holden, a surveyor and civil engineer with whom Brown may have stayed overnight; and James W. Purnell, a twenty-five-year-old merchant who later that year would serve as secretary and commercial reporter of the Emigration Convention, a Delany operation. Before moving to near-by Buxton, Thomas W. Stringer, one of the delegates, had lived at Chatham, helping to establish its Methodist Episcopal Church, as he would assist in the setting up of thirty-five similar churches in Mississippi after the Civil War.

Of the ten blacks who crossed the border to attend the convention, coming primarily from Detroit, Cleveland, and Sandusky, the best known was the prosperous tailor William Lambert, Trenton-born son of a self-purchased slave and for many years the head of the Colored Vigilance Committee of Detroit, an agency to assist runaways.

Detroit would also have the distinction of furnishing the convention's presiding officer, William Charles Munroe, rector of St. Matthew's Protestant Episcopal Mission, the first black church of that denomination west of the Alleghenies. In 1854 and again in 1856 Munroe had presided at the National Emigration Convention, each affair held in Cleveland and each largely the work of Delany. As a delegate to the Colored Convention held in Buffalo in

1843 Munroe had voted for the adoption of Henry Highland Gar-net's fiery address to the slaves.

Munroe, like Lambert, had been active in both the Michigan Anti-Slavery Society and in local Liberty party politics. Staunch supporters of the movement to win the ballot for blacks, both had played prominent roles in the state conventions held periodically by reform-minded blacks in Michigan. Episcopalian churchmen (Lambert held the lay office of warden at St. Mathew's where Munroe was rector), both were of a reflective turn of mind, men not given to rashness in rhetoric or behavior. Their decision to meet with John Brown at Chatham was a reflection of their feeling that the conventional methods of striking at slavery were simply not working well, the times calling for new approaches.

The selection of Munroe as the presiding officer at the Chatham convention was a sound one, both from his previous experience in that capacity and from his even temperament. He needed his savoir faire. Hardly had he taken the chair than he had to call for a change in venue, a move to a new meeting place. Typically operating in a hush-hush, somewhat conspiratorial atmosphere, the planners of the convention had given the townspeople the impression that the meeting was for the purpose of setting up a Masonic lodge. Badly backfiring, this planted rumor brought to the school-house a host of curiosity seekers, some bent on learning the secrets of Masonry and others who, knowing that there were no racially mixed Masonic lodges, wondered as to what was really afoot. Beating a retreat from the school, the delegates marched two blocks to a frame building which housed the hand apparatus of Volunteer Fire Company, No. 3, an all-black unit. This somewhat makeshift fire-engine house had been donated to the town by Isaac Holden.

The convention resumed its deliberations with a request from Delany that Brown describe the objective he had in mind and the methods by which he hoped to accomplish them. This was the moment that Brown had long awaited. He had, he said, on taking the floor, been governed for years by the idea of freeing the slaves, to that end making on-site studies of military fortifications in Europe and reading books on insurrectionary warfare, including the uprisings in Haiti and the role of its patriot-liberator Toussaint L'Ouverture therein. Slaves in the South would rise up, he said, upon the first concrete evidence of a plan for their liberation, repairing to the mountain strongholds he and his men would have prepared for them.[20]

The delegates voiced two misgivings. A few pointed out that Brown's plan could succeed only at a time when the United States was at war with a major power. Brown gave this short shrift, holding that he would not take advantage of his country in her extremity. James Monroe Jones expressed his doubts as to whether the slaves could be counted on to rally round the invading forces, American slaves being less impetuous and warlike than their counterparts in the West Indies. Brown quickly begged to differ, adding that he hoped "Friend Jones" would keep that viewpoint to himself inasmuch as there would be plenty of others to advance it, a remark that drew some tension-releasing laughter.[21]

Following the acceptance of his orally presented project and its manner of operation, Brown then produced his "Provisional Constitution and Ordinances for the People of the United States," which he had written while a paying guest at the Douglass home earlier that year. As the secretary prepared to read the document aloud, Thomas M. Kinnard, a Toronto clergyman, proposed that the delegates bind themselves to maintain secrecy. Watering down Kinnard's proposal, although in general concurrence with its spirit, Delany presented a mildly worded resolution stating that anyone who divulged the business of the organization would be denied its protection. This "parole of honor" was administered by presiding officer Munroe.[22]

Brown's "Constitution" was then taken up, to be read by the secretary of the convention, John Henry Kagi, just turned twenty-three but Brown's closest associate and strong right arm. The presentation of the Constitution was indeed a high moment for Brown—as he said at the time of his trial, it was a document "of my own contriving and getting up." But his peak occasion was marred by one circumstance—Kagi had to read from a handwritten copy whereas Brown had originally planned to have printed copies ready for distribution at the convention. To this end Brown on April 8 had turned his manuscript over to a black printer, William Howard Day, paying him a $15.00 deposit four days later. Day had learned the printer's trade before entering Oberlin, from which he was graduated in 1847. After serving as a type-setter and local editor of the *Cleveland Daily True Democrat,* he had in 1853 edited the short-lived *Aliened American,* the city's first black weekly. Residing in St. Catherines since 1857, abolitionist Day had arranged the meeting between Brown and Harriet Tubman. Writing from St. Catherines five days before the convention, Day regretfully informed Brown that he would not be able to deliver the "pamphlet." Not only was he having trouble with "the mechanical part" but he could work on such a confidential document only behind closed doors—"the privacy of things of course embarrasses me to a certain extent." In the absence of the vainly hoped for printed copies, Day mailed the original manuscript, which barely reached Brown by convention time.[23]

The document that Kagi read to the delegates opened with the assertion that slavery was a barbarous state of affairs which pitted one citizen against another and that to combat this evil the people establish "for the time being" a provisional constitution. This two-paragraph preamble was Brown at his best; it was a forceful and moving statement, its style, unlike that of Brown's other writings, measured and not staccato-like. Kagi then read the constitution's forty-eight combination articles and ordinances, many of them relating to the various branches of the proposed government, particularly to the powers of each. Some of the provisions reflected Brown's stern notions of morality—those, for example, touching upon profanity, unhallowed sexual intercourse, rape of a female prisoner, and a strict observance of the Sabbath.

The delegates challenged only one article—number 46 which stated that the constitution-makers wished to reform the government rather than to overthrow it and that their flag "shall be the same that our fathers fought under in the Revolution." Some of the black delegates, particularly those who had settled in Canada, were not enthusiastic about fighting under the Stars and Stripes: "Too many of them thought that they carried this emblem on their backs," reported James Monroe Jones.[24] But in the final vote the loyalty to country and flag proviso was adopted almost unanimously, after remarks in favor of its retention were made by Brown and his son, Owen; Kagi; Richard Realf; and three blacks—

Delany, Kinnard, and Munroe. One delegate, coppersmith J. G. Reynolds, an underground railroad worker from Sandusky, went on record as opposing article 46. Some minutes later, however, Reynolds joined the other delegates in a unanimous vote accepting the constitution as a whole. Brown felt an inner glow.

After a break of one hour and a half the delegates reassembled for the sole purpose of affixing their signatures to the Constitution, after which Delany and Kinnard made "congratulatory remarks." The evening session, beginning at six o'clock, was twice as long, and its results were no less predictable. The group now became a new organization, the Constitution having stipulated that the president of the original convention should, once the Constitution was ratified, summon another convention charged with the election of officers. To this new convention, as in the old, Munroe was elected president and Kagi secretary. By acclamation John Brown was elected commander-in-chief and Kagi as secretary of war.

On Monday the delegates gathered at 9 a.m., their meeting place the black First Baptist Church where Brown had attended services the previous morning, Sunday, May 9, his fifty-eighth birthday. Less than a block from the fire engine hall, this new convention site would hitherto be known among blacks as John Brown's Meeting House. Here the election of officers was resumed. Thomas M. Kinnard was nominated for president, declining after a lengthy speech. The absent Jermain W. Loguen's name was offered, only to have it withdrawn on someone's announcement that Loguen would not serve if elected. After Brown's motion that the election of the president be postponed, the convention proceeded to select two of the members of its projected Congress, the honors falling to Osborne P. Anderson, a printer's devil at the *Provincial Freeman,* and Alfred M. Ellsworth.

Three exeutive positions were filled—secretary of state, treasurer, and secretary of the treasury. None of these offices went to a Negro, although the signature of black William C. Munroe, president of the convention, was affixed to each commission certificate, Brown having brought along a supply of printed commission forms, leaving blank spaces for appropriate insertion.[25] Final adjournment of the convention came after the passing of Brown's motion that a committee be appointed to fill all remaining vacancies, its fifteen-man membership to be made up of him and his twelve recruits plus Congressmen Anderson and Ellsworth.

As the presiding officer brought the final session of the convention to its close, the black delegates felt a sense of satisfaction. True enough, only three of them had been named to the committee to complete the roster of officers. But they had fully participated in the convention's deliberations. Aside from Brown himself, no delegate had offered more motions, put more names in nomination, or had more to say than Martin R. Delany, his prominent role made all the more evident by what William Wells Brown referred to a year later as his stentorian voice and "a violence of gestures." As Richard Realf later testified, Delany "was one of the prominent disputants, or debaters." [26]

In large measure the satisfied feeling of the departing black delegates came from their highly favorable reactions to Brown himself. According to Anderson they had listened to him with profound attention. Perhaps some of them had been disappointed upon first setting eyes upon him. Like his handwriting, Brown was on the pinched and pointed side—he was under six feet and weighed not more than 150 pounds. His eyes were flinty and restless; his voice had a nasal twang. Nonetheless, to Osborne P. Anderson and perhaps to other black delegates, Brown had "a thoughtful and reverent brow and physiognomy" reminiscent of a Puritan at his best.[27] His milk-white beard, long and flowing, heightened this impression of a church dignitary.

Obviously the black delegates had no inclination to subject Brown's constitution and ordinances to careful analysis. The sound charges by later critics that this document was confused and contradictory would not have been relevant to them. To the black delegates the test of the Constitution's workability was a pointless topic of discussion at that early stage. Their trust was not in Brown's paperwork; it was in the man. They saw in him a firebrand, "the man to do the deed if it must be done," as he was characterized by the schoolmaster-philosopher Bronson Alcott five months before Harpers Ferry.[28]

The satisfied feeling of the black conventioneers was more than matched by Brown's own high spirits. The local newspaper, the *Chatham Tri-Weekly Planet,* which billed itself as the "Official Paper of the County," had not given the convention a single line of coverage and so there was little publicity beyond word-of-mouth speculation. The speeches of the black delegates, particularly those of Delany, had given Brown the impression that the Negroes of Canada would assist him en masse upon call. "Had a good Abolition convention," he wrote on May 12, in a letter to his family.[29]

Perhaps not all of the participants fully shared Brown's enthusiasm for his constitution and ordinances. To him, however, this document was basic to his entire plan, providing as it did for a "legal" interim government during a period of great national crisis which he and his associates were about to usher in. Hence it followed that a generous supply of copies of this document should be on hand when the action began. Brown would indeed have a "large number" of them at Harpers Ferry, as his captor, Robert E. Lee, would report.[30]

To put the document in print, Brown resumed his negotiations with William Howard Day, writing him about "the work" on the day after the convention adjourned. Two days later Brown sent the document entrusted in the care of Kagi, who would assist in the printing job and take possession of the completed copies. Nearly four weeks after the convention Brown paid Day a total of $10 in two payments, signalling the completion or near completion of the work.[31] As produced in print the document was a fifteen-page booklet, its hand-stitched binding suggesting a shop with limited equipment. The pamphlet carried no date and, doubtless for discretion's sake, the name of no publisher. But Brown was glad to have it in print; the readers he had in mind were not likely to notice any crudeness of pressroom mechanics.

Brown's sense of elation over the Chatham convention was lessened within two weeks after the delegates had departed. It had been his intention to stage his raid within a few weeks after the adoption of his constitution and his election as commander-in-chief.

In a letter to Frederick Douglass on April 14 he had written that
he would need all the help he could get by May 1.[32]

Brown's plans for an armed thrust into Virginia had to be postponed due to a lack of money and to the unreliability of drillmaster Hugh Forbes. Brown's fundraising problems reached their
peak in the spring of 1858, the country itself in recovery from the
depression of the preceding year. Right after the convention,
Brown was immobilized because of "the scantiness of his funds," he
wrote on May 25, fifteen days after the convention's adjournment.[33]

Brown's chronic insolvency was a factor in the second reason
for the postponement of the foray into Virginia—the disaffection
of Hugh Forbes. When Brown began to recruit his band, early in
1857, his first task was to hire a drillmaster. For $100 a month,
Forbes, an English soldier of fortune who had seen military experience in Italy under Garibaldi, contracted to train Brown's men
and to seek the recruitment of additional army officers. But within
a half-year Forbes had become disgruntled. His pay was slow in
coming, as he complained to F. B. Sanborn,[34] and in military matters he did not care to subordinate his judgment to that of Brown.

Forbes' search for personal funds led him in November 1857 to
the residence of Frederick Douglass in Rochester. Douglass was
not favorably impressed by the unexpected visitor, but for Brown's
sake he took him to a hotel, paying his bill in advance and giving
him "a little money." In a lapse of his generally sound judgment,
Douglass also furnished Forbes with letters of introduction to
abolitionist friends of his. Forbes immediately wrote to them, soliciting loans or donations. When this brought disappointing re-
turns, Forbes followed with letters threatening the slow givers with
exposure of their complicity in Brown's plot.[35]

The alarmed Douglass relayed the intelligence to Brown. But
other Brown supporters had already learned of Forbes' disaffection, including his willingness to talk with political figures in
Washington. Early in May 1858, Forbes leaked out something of
Brown's plans to three senators. In alarm, one of them, Henry
Wilson of Massachusetts, got in touch with Samuel Gridley Howe,
one of Brown's backers, who convened a secret meeting of the

small coterie that had furnished him with funds. These supporters decided that Brown should, for the time being, return to Kansas, thus ostensibly discrediting Forbes' allegations.

When he learned of Forbes' tell-tale behavior, Brown surmised that the Englishman may have gotten some of his information from J. McCune Smith of New York City. A black physician and reformer, able and dedicated in both capacities, Smith did not support the proposed thrust into Virginia. According to Richard J. Hinton, a Brown supporter, Smith was opposed to any black freedom movement that was not all-black, favoring a "separate and violent resistance," and wanting "no help from white men." Hinton doubtless did not know of Smith's cooperation with whites in the work of the Radical Abolition party in 1855 and 1856. But whatever the relationship between Smith and the disaffected Forbes, most other black leaders, feeling that the Englishman had talked out of school, would have agreed with Osborne P. Anderson's characterization of him as a Judas.[36]

A security breach might not be confined to the disaffected, as Richard Realf soon learned. Three weeks after the Chatham convention, delegate J. G. Reynolds had disclosed some of its business to a black military society in Sandusky. "I suppose these are good men enough," wrote Realf, "but to make a sort of wholesale development of matters at hazard is too steep a risk." Realf may have gotten his information about Reynolds from another white delegate, George B. Gill, who had made a trip to Sandusky for the express purpose of learning more about the secret military society. Reynolds had been his host, showing him the group's combination assembly hall and arsenal, displaying "a fine collection of guns." [37]

Forced to delay his Virginia expedition, Brown made ready to return to Kansas temporarily, arriving at Lawrence late in June 1858 under the name of Shubel Morgan. Accompanying him were seven of his twelve followers, the others having been left to their own devices while awaiting the summons to rejoin the band. Among the latter was black Richard Richardson, who went to Cleveland with Richard Realf a few weeks after the convention but returned to Canada shortly thereafter.

Brown remained in Kansas for six months, ill with ague much of the time. But if his operations during his second and final stint in Kansas had attracted few headlines, his departure was newsworthy enough—the seizure of eleven slaves whom he escorted to the Canadian border. During his half-year of relative quiet in Kansas, Brown's thoughts had remained on Virginia. In a family letter, written from Osawatomie on December 2, 1858, he let it be known that he was "still preparing for my other journey." [38] The dramatic manner in which Brown departed from Kansas three weeks later was, in its way, a foreshadowing of his forthcoming foray into Virginia—a dress rehearsal for Harpers Ferry.

This incident was the only one in which Brown conducted an underground railroad operation. But it would have been hard to match, an eighty-two-day wintertime trek of over 1000 miles while harassed for a time by troops. The episode began on a Sunday in late December when a slave, Jim Daniels, informed one of Brown's scouts that he, the other three members of his family, and a fifth slave, had been advertised for sale by their master, a resident of Vernon County, across the border in Missouri and ten miles from the Brown campsite. Daniels had been given the day off to sell his homemade brooms but instead had come to Kansas to enlist Brown and his men to guard him and his family as they made their escape.[39]

Learning of his request, Brown at once decided to go to the rescue. Dividing his forces Brown led one of the groups, his first stop the home of Harvey C. Hicklan, with whom Daniels and his family had been entrusted. Here at gun-point, the Brown-led unit, numbering approximately fifteen, seized the five blacks. Within the hour the band was on its way to the residence of another slaveowner, John B. Larue, just a mile away. Here they took another five blacks. They also gathered two whites, Larue and a guest of his, thus preventing them from raising a hue-and-cry for rescue. The duo would be released within the week.

In the meantime the second of the two columns, numbering fewer than the Brown-led group but also armed and mounted, had gone to the house of David Cruise and taken one slave, Jane—the other, George, being absent. Cruise was killed, one of the raiders firing on him after he had made a sudden move which the raider construed to be a gun-draw. As if sobered by this unexpected and dangerous turn of affairs, the unit made no other visits. With the coming of daybreak the two groups of liberators were united. It had been a bitterly cold night but "to our contrabands the conditions produced a genial warmth not indorsed by the thermometer," wrote George B. Gill.[40] After laying low during the day, the group moved back into Kansas.

In addition to slaves the raiders had also seized horses, oxen, foodstuffs, bedding, and clothing. Inevitably and despite Brown, a few of the men in his band were loot-minded. Brown, too, believed in taking the belongings of slaveholders. But his justification was not the spoils-of-war theory; rather it was a conviction that the masters should bear the costs of transporting their former slaves to freedom. And in a larger sense Brown held that whatever his party took belonged in reality to the slaves, their labor having produced it.

The value of the liberated slaves was not inconsiderable, if somewhat less than the figure of $16,000 which Brown gave. Three of the eleven slaves were men and five were women; of the three children two were boys. Four families, or parts of families, were represented. The Daniels contingent consisted of the husband, his pregnant wife, a boy, and a girl. A second family had five in number—a widow, her two grown daughters, one grown son, and a boy. A third family was represented by one young man, and a fourth family likewise had one representative, Jane Cruise.[41]

Moving northwestward Brown and his party bypassed Mound City to stop overnight at the home of Augustus Wattles, a long-time abolitionist lecturer. His daughter would remember "the chattering and laughing of the darkies" as they awaited supper.[42] Wattles was not unfamiliar with blacks at close range, having boarded with a black family while in Cincinnati where he taught black children.

Before the week was at end the eleven liberated slaves had been deposited in an abandoned cabin in an out-of-the-way spot along

Pottawatomie Creek, away from the prying eyes of the curious or the armed search parties of aroused Missourians. Brown kept watch for nearly a month, holding his men in readiness to receive any party or parties that might be in pursuit. He did not need to be told that the news of his invasion had spread over Missouri "like the wind, carrying with it everywhere the most intense excitement," as the Kansas reporter for the *Tribune* put it.[43]

But as it turned out the most exciting event of the Pottawatomie sojourn was the birth of Mrs. Daniels' son. The proud parents christened him John Brown Daniels, the first of Brown's black namesakes. Fortunately for the party the mother and baby had the services of a physician, James G. Blunt, who practiced in the neighborhood and was sympathetic to Brown.

In mid-January 1859, while his black flock was still enfolded along the Pottawatomie, Brown attempted to justify his raid, writing a letter, "Old Brown's Parallels," to the friendly *New-York Tribune*. He first described a bloody incident in Kansas less than a year earlier in which eleven "quiet citizens" had been assailed by an armed pro-slavery group which put five of them to death and left five others wounded. Brown then compared this affair with his own recent action in Missouri in which eleven persons were restored to their natural and inalienable rights, with only one resultant fatality. Both state and federal governments had remained silent on the brutal treatment of the "quiet citizens," said Brown. But the almost bloodless liberation of eleven persons in Missouri had brought an instant reaction in official quarters—all "Hell is stirred from beneath." Brown asked his readers to consider the two cases and the double-standard response of "the Administration party." [44]

By January 20, Brown was ready to resume the trek northward through the Kansas territory. On the first leg of the journey the total party consisted of fourteen—Brown, George B. Gill, and the twelve blacks, the latter huddled in an ox-drawn wagon. After two weeks of slow travel the party reached Lawrence, where it rested overnight.

A week later came their last day in Kansas, and it was appropriately marked by a battle between Brown and the federal forces sent by the commandant of Fort Leavenworth. The Brown party, aided by some fifteen volunteers from Topeka, defeated a force nearly four times its number and took prisoners. One of the captives reported that all of them were treated well by their captors but that "it did go a little against the grain to eat with and be guarded by 'damned niggers.' " After a few days the prisoners were released without their horses. "It was obviously not for the safety of our colored emigrants to have these men return very speedily," as one member of the party explained.[45]

As far as the "colored emigrants" were concerned, Brown's chief problem, at least in the early stages of the trip, was a certain exuberance on their part. Black Samuel Harper would remember that on first being freed "we used to cut up all kinds of foolishness." But Brown, continued Harper, would look as solemn as a graveyard. On occasion, however, he would "let out de tiniest bit of a smile an' say: 'You'd better quit yo' foolin' an' take up your book.' " [46]

With Kansas and their most dangerous encounter behind them, the Brown entourage traveled in Nebraska for four days, crossing the all-but-frozen Missouri River on February 4 to enter Iowa. Their journey east across this state was made at the rate of twenty-five miles a day. The blacks were armed with rifles provided by the foresighted Brown and had practiced daily in order to become familiar with their use.

At Tabor, their first stop in Iowa, the party met with a rebuff. Although the majority of the townspeople were abolitionist in their sympathies, they did not like some of the things they had heard of Brown's raid, notably the killing of David Cruise and the seizure of non-slave property. Remembering a previous visit to the town, Brown had expected a warm welcome. But a local church at which he had requested to speak proceeded to adopt a resolution expressing sympathy for the fugitive slaves but condemning those who took life or seized property while assisting them. As if to demonstrate their goodwill toward runaways, the townspeople permitted the twelve blacks in Brown's party to use the schoolhouse for a lodging place.

Ten days after leaving Tabor the party reached Grinnell where their reception could hardly have been more enthusiastic. The overjoyed Brown prepared a written statement describing their cordial treatment, sending it to newspapers in an attempt to counteract the reports of the group's cool reception at Tabor. As Brown pointed out, the Grinnell people bore the entire cost of the party's two-day stay in their town, provided "sundry articles of clothing" for the blacks, prepared food for the travelers to carry on their journey, and held two well-attended public meetings, at which speakers Brown and Kagi were loudly cheered.[47]

Sharing the platform with the two travelers was the key figure in their warm reception, Josiah Bushnell Grinnell, a founder of the town and of the college that bears his name and subsequently active in state and national politics. He found lodgings for the travelers, dividing them between his own parlor, which he later named the "liberty room," and the local hotel. Grinnell's barn provided stalls for the party's horses.[48] Not surprisingly some of the neighbors of J. B. Grinnell, as he customarily signed himself, began to refer to him as John Brown Grinnell.

Three days after leaving Grinnell the journeyers reached the Quaker settlement of Springdale, where they remained for two weeks. A band of Brown's was no novelty to Springdale residents who received this second contingent with typical cordiality. Some of the travelers were accommodated at the one-story, tree-surrounded house of abolitionist William Maxton, and others found lodging at other private homes. During their stay at Springdale a small group of men in Iowa City, ten miles away, toyed with the idea of assaulting the Brown party but had second thoughts about it.

Moving to West Liberty, a railroad town seven miles away, on March 9, the party found that its journey was to become faster and less hazardous. As his final benefaction J. B. Grinnell had hired a boxcar for $50 to take the party to Chicago. Grinnell had not, of course, specified the kind of freight for which it was intended. Following a night's lodging at a grist mill the party, three whites, Kagi having put in his appearance, and twelve blacks, moved on foot to the railroad station nearby. The loading permit in his pocket, Brown led the way into the closed boxcar, then located on a side-track. Two hours later the Chicago-bound train rolled into West Liberty. When it pulled out two hours later it carried an unbilled cargo—a procedure quite unusual but no more unusual than the cargo itself. Possibly, however, it was just as well that nobody was curious enough to make an investigation. He would have been given a "through ticket to hell," said Kagi, who stood sentinel at the door.[49]

When the train reached the city early the next morning Brown sought out Allan Pinkerton, head of the famed detective agency that bore his name. After breakfast Pinkerton took Brown to the home of John Jones, the city's most prominent black and no stranger to Brown.[50] Pinkerton then departed, bent on raising train fare to Detroit for the group. Brown and his white companions remained at the Jones residence during the forenoon. To keep the slaves out of sight they were taken to the mill of Henry O. Wagoner, a black reformer, who put up a "closed for repairs" sign on the mill.

Pinkerton had little trouble in his quest for donations, enlisting the full support of C. G. Hammond, superintendent of the Michigan Central and a friend of black people. With their car generously provisioned, including a barrel of fresh water, and clean straw spread upon the floor, the band left Chicago that afternoon, Kagi in charge. Brown himself, his mind on other things now that journey's end was near, had taken an earlier train to Detroit, not wanting to miss talking with Frederick Douglass, scheduled to be there for two speeches. Brown had already sent a letter to Douglass, apparently designed to arrange a meeting.[51]

When the Brown-rescued slaves arrived at Detroit on March 12, 1859, the weather was at its worst. But the cold and sleet had little effect on their soaring spirits—they had reached their last stopping point on American soil. Now they would have no doubts that the new life for which they yearned was a certainty. That afternoon, they were taken to the wharf to embark for Windsor, Ontario, then as now a main point of entrance into Canada. Their joy was complete when Brown met them shortly before they boarded the ferry. To each he spoke a cheerful word.

To these former slaves it must have been a moving occasion, even if they left no record of their emotions as they said goodbye to their benefactor. Of his feelings as he watched the boat move into the choppy, ice-flexed waters, we know a bit more. A little later he was asked by his daughter, Ruth, as to his sentiments at the parting scene. Ruth was quite prepared for his reply—a quotation from Scripture, "Lord, now lettest they servant depart in peace, for my eyes have seen thy salvation." [52]

It was to hasten the day of salvation that Brown met late that evening with Frederick Douglass and a group of black Detroiters, following Douglass' appearance at City Hall. The Douglass address would be covered by the two local dailies, the *Advertiser and Tribune* and the *Free Press,* although the latter would express wonder as to "why Fred should have come into so inhospitable a region." [53] One of the reasons for the coming of Douglass was, of necessity, hardly the kind that could be divulged to the press—to attend the behind-closed-doors meeting held later that evening at the home of William Webb, variously listed as a grocer and as the manager of a plug tobacco factory. The other Detroiters present included two with whom Brown had become acquainted at Chatham—William Lambert and William C. Munroe.

The most prominent of the other four black Detroiters in attendance was George DeBapiste, successively a barber, a baker, and a steamship steward, and successful in each. The successor to Lambert as head of the city's Colored Vigilance Committee, DeBaptiste was second to few as an underground railroad operator. "Had within the last 10 or 15 days 53 first class passengers; expect 10 more tonight," wrote DeBaptiste to Frederick Douglass on November 5, 1854. A long-time admirer of Toussaint L'Ouverture, DeBaptiste would in 1867 pay $50 for a portrait of him.[54]

At the meeting DeBaptiste seems to have been the most vocal and forceminded of the blacks, advocating a bolder course than even Brown envisioned. Brown apparently proposed a program of single raids on plantations, thereby setting in motion a chain reaction of slave defections. Douglass seems to have been cool toward this proposal. This may have brought on some hot words from Brown, in which he raised a question as to Douglass' courage. The black leader would much later deny, however, that any heated interchange had ever taken place between him and Brown at Detroit.[55]

Although DeBaptiste shared Douglass' coolness toward the Brown proposal, no one could raise the question of cowardice as to his reason for objecting. To him the Brown proposal did not go far enough. In its place DeBaptiste suggested a gunpowder plot in which fifteen large churches in the South would be blown up on a predetermined Sunday, thus arresting national attention and firing the imagination of the more militant-minded. Brown, a bit taken aback, demurred on the grounds of humanity, avowing that he did not wish to shed blood unless it was absolutely necessary. DeBaptiste held to his position, however, pointing out that the bloody Nat Turner insurrection had caused the Virginia legislature to consider seriously the abolition of slavery in the commonwealth. Whatever the dissenting voices as to Brown's proposal, the Detroit meeting appears to have come to a close amicably in its personal relationships, if not of one accord as to program and ways and means.[56]

Three days after the Detroit meeting Brown arrived in Cleveland, now accompanied only by Kagi. Seeking to help defray the cost of the Missouri slave rescue, Brown held a public meeting, charging 25¢ admission. To a disappointingly small audience he asserted that he considered it his duty to free any slave whenever the opportunity came, thus weakening the whole system of human bondage. He also treated his listeners to a rare bit of wry humor, stating that inasmuch as President Buchanan had offered $250 for his capture, he wanted it known "that he would give two dollars and fifty cents for the safe delivery of the body of James Buchanan in any jail of the Free States." [57]

Brown could thus confidently challenge federal authority in Cleveland because the city was in a highly emotional state over the so-called Oberlin-Wellington rescue. Thirty-seven rescuers of runaway slave John Price were lodged in a Cleveland jail awaiting trial. Sensing the angry mood of many citizens, the federal marshal's office in the city quietly ignored the numerous posters calling for Brown's arrest.

By early April 1859 Brown was ready to leave for the East, on a money-raising trip for what he was sure would be the last time. He had reason to be pleased with his progress during the past twelve months. He had conferred with black leaders in Philadelphia and Detroit, had held a convention in Chatham, had led an armed band into a slave state and by force had freed eleven slaves, and had boldly walked the streets of Cleveland with a price on his head. Curtain time could not be far off.

IV

THE RECRUITMENT
OF BLACKS

Have you all the hands you wish?
Lewis Hayden to Brown, September 26, 1859

As Brown traveled east in the early spring of 1859 the main thing on his mind was money for Harpers Ferry. Manpower, in his analysis, would be less of a problem, particularly the enlisting of black recruits. According to an insider, Richard Realf, Brown "expected that all the free negroes in the Northern States would immediately flock to his standard." [1]

What was it that made Brown so sanguine about recruiting blacks—on what were his high expectations based? Brown believed that blacks were basically militant and hence ready to take direct action as soon as a purposeful leader stepped forward. His belief about a black resistance ripe for the harvesting came from two main sources—the abolitionist literature that he read and the kind of black men and women he had come to know personally.

Brown subscribed to and read the abolitionist weeklies, and of these he relied chiefly on the one edited by Frederick Douglass, first entitled *The North Star* and later *Frederick Douglass' Paper*. He informed his family on January 23, 1852, that if they had trouble paying for Douglass' paper to let him know since as he had taken "some liberty in ordering it continued." From December 22, 1851, to April 22, 1858, Brown on seven occasions sent to Douglass amounts varying from 75¢ to $5.00 in payment for the weekly. "I found here last night one of Frederick Douglass' papers; for which I am grateful," wrote Brown to his family on January 9, 1856, while at Osawatomie.[2]

A reader of a black journal like the one edited by Douglass might well have gotten the impression, spurred by wishful thinking, that many slaves were potential Nat Turners. An editorial in the *Ram's Horn,* a black weekly which was read by John Brown, bore the title, "Slaves of the South, Now is the Time!" The slaves were advised that the time had come to strike for their liberty, dying rather than submitting.[3] The pacifist-oriented white abolitionist newspapers, such as *The Liberator,* which Brown also read regularly, avoided such fiery exhortations to the slave population, but they too, like their black counterparts, gave prominence to slave uprisings, past and present, real and merely rumored. Small wonder then that a reader like Brown might conclude that by and large the mood of the slaves was combustible.

Brown well knew of Negro behavior patterns that he regarded as drawbacks to the race, having called attention to them in "Sambo's Mistakes." But although he might inveigh against a want of spirit in blacks he did not believe that they were wanting in physical courage or fighting potential. On this point Brown was questioned in February 1857 by a reporter for the *New-York Tribune* who told him that blacks were a peaceful lot, seemingly incapable of resentment or reprisal. Brown's reply came quickly: "You have not studied them right and you have not studied them long enough." [4]

Brown could lay claim to having done some study on black resistance to oppression, having read about brave black leaders, slave and free. Brown knew that not all slaves were militant, if only from his reading of *Uncle Tom's Cabin,* a copy of which he bought for his daughters Sarah and Annie in January 1853.[5] But Brown's reading about slaves included those of a different stripe from Mrs. Stowe's central character. Brown preferred to dwell upon slave uprisings and their leaders. He could tell in full the stories of Toussaint L'Overture, Denmark Vesey, and Nat Turner, holding the last named as high in his admiration as George Washington. From his reading of ancient history Brown knew the story of Spartacus, a slave who had headed a servile war and routed several Roman armies before his ultimate defeat. To Brown these stories were proof that slaves, black and white, past and present, fought and would fight for their freedom if given half a chance. Brown's black heroes also included those who had obtained their freedom by means other than servile war. Ranking high among these was Joseph Cinque, who in the summer of 1839 led a successful mutiny of fifty-four slaves aboard the schooner *Amistad*.

Blacks who ran the gauntlet of the underground railroad drew Brown's attention and approval. He shared the belief expressed in May 1858 by his friend and supporter, Thomas Wentworth Higginson, that as a result of his years of acquaintance with the underground railroad "we white Anglo-Saxons on this continent must yield the palm of native heroism to the Negro." In this speech to the New York Anti-Slavery Society, Higginson had gone on to say that "the aroused strength of the African" would surface when he sensed that the time was propitious—when the necessary "preliminary agitations had created the sympathy he needed for his support." [6]

Brown personally knew many of the stout-hearted slaves who had made the dash for freedom, particularly those who had become leaders in the North. It was this one-to-one relationship with so many blacks of daring and courage that contributed markedly to Brown's image of the black people as protestors and activists. He believed that they had their full complement of potential Harpers Ferry raiders and supporters of the raid.

Brown's personal acquaintance with former slaves who had become active in the abolitionist crusade included such figures as Harriet Tubman, William Wells Brown, and Lewis Hayden. The three former slaves whom he knew best and longest were Jermain Loguen, Henry Highland Garnet, and Frederick Douglass. Each of this trio had voiced strong and incendiary anti-slavery sentiments, confirming Brown's opinion that he had not misread the militant mood of the black community as a whole.

Loguen's bold and fiery language drew Brown's plaudits. At a meeting in Syracuse in October 1850 called to defy the Fugitive

Slave Law, Loguen announced that he didn't respect it, he didn't fear it, and he wouldn't obey it. In August 1853 he wrote to *Frederick Douglass' Paper* concerning his indictment by the federal government for taking part in the rescue of slave William Henry ("Jerry") at Syracuse. Loguen expressed his pride at having taken part in the rescue, adding that he welcomed an appearance "in a Republican Court of Justice for loving liberty for a Brother." He had an old mother, sisters, and brothers still in slavery, he added, and he would, as God was his judge, rather hear of them swimming in blood in quest of their liberty than having them remain slaves for the rest of their days.[7]

No sooner had Brown read this letter than he wrote to *Frederick Douglass' Paper* expressing his highest commendation of it: "It has a certain music to it that so fills my ear, that I cannot well suppress the pleasure it affords." He had, said Brown to "Friend Douglass," been waiting and watching with longing eyes to see colored men leap to their full length above the surface of the water. When he next saw Loguen he would give him a handshake that would make his hand snap.[8]

Henry Highland Garnet, a Presbyterian clergyman, was another firebrand after Brown's own heart. At a national Negro convention held in Buffalo in 1843 the twenty-seven-year-old militant took his fellow delegates by surprise when he addressed himself not to them but to the slaves. His sentiments were incendiary, his language unequivocal. Invoking such names as "the patriotic Nathaniel Turner" and "the immortal Joseph Cinque," he admonished the slaves to arise and strike for their lives and liberties. There was, he said, little "hope of redemption without the shedding of blood"; it was better for them to die seeking freedom than to continue their existence as slaves. Let your motto be resistance, he exhorted, closing with a reminder that they numbered 4 million.[9]

Garnet's address was voted down by the convention but its main ideas soon became more palatable among most of the other black leaders. In 1848 Garnet published the *Address to the Slaves of the United States of America (Rejected by the National Convention of 1843)*, which he combined with an earlier revolutionary document by David Walker, a black in Boston. The Walker pamphlet, which had been barred in several Southern states, shared much the same viewpoint as that of Garnet, and bore an even longer title, *Walker's Appeal, in Four Articles, Together with a Preamble, to the Coloured Citizens of the World, but in Particular, and Very Expressly to those of the United States of America. Written in Boston, in the State of Massachusetts, September 28, 1829.*

There can be little doubt that Brown was familiar with this pamphlet, combining as it did the two most militant utterances by black Americans up to that time. J. McCune Smith said that Brown had the pamphlet republished at his own expense.[10] This is unlikely considering the absence of copies of such a publication and Brown's constant need of money. But the story had a credence of sorts based on Brown's pronounced predisposition for the sentiments the pamphlets aired.

Among those opposing Garnet's address at the Buffalo convention in 1843 was Frederick Douglass, then an exponent of the moral suasionist, nonviolent technique espoused by William Lloyd Garrison. But by the time Brown and Douglass became acquainted the latter had abandoned the pacifist approach to slavery. Speaking in Boston's Faneuil Hall in June 1849, Douglass said that he would welcome the intelligence, should it come, that the slaves had rebelled and "were engaged in spreading death and devastation." [11]

In the 1850's the Douglass tone became as sharp and forthright as Brown could have wished. Douglass, for example, condemned the Fugitive Slave Law with bitter language, asserting that the only way to make it a dead letter was to make a half-dozen or more dead kidnapers. In May 1857 at an abolitionist gathering in New York, Douglass challenged the idea that blacks "were a nation of Uncle Toms, good at psalm-singing, but not caring enough for liberty to fight for it." The contrary was true, he asserted, as demonstrated by every slave insurrection in the South.[12]

While still residing in Springfield, Brown had told Douglass that he was pleased to note an increase in the number of outspoken blacks. Those he had in mind were not only former slaves but free-born blacks such as David Ruggles and Charles Lenox Remond. Brown may never have met Ruggles, the latter having reached the

peak of his abolitionist activity in the late 1830's as secretary and
agent of the New York Committee of Vigilance. Ruggles had urged
a bold course of action. In August 1841 at a New York meeting of
the American Reform Board of Disfranchised Commissioners, an
organization he had created, Ruggles asserted that "in our cause"
action was everything, mere words were nothing. "Rise, brethren,
rise! Strike for freedom or die slaves!" By 1846 Ruggles had become a hydropathic practitioner, founding his own establishment,
The Northampton Water Cure. One of his patients was Mary
Brown. "Mother has gone to Northampton, Mass., to take water
cure under Dr. Ruggles," wrote John, Jr., on September 18, 1849,
to his father in London.[13]

Charles Lenox Remond, although counting himself a follower
of William Lloyd Garrison, spoke in a vein more like that of Brown.
At a meeting in Abington, Massachusetts, in June 1847, Remond
said that if the slaves were to rise en masse and throw off their
fetters, he would rejoice. Returning to this theme at a meeting in
New Bedford in August 1858, he recommended that an address
be sent to the slaves in the South urging them "to rise in their
might and majesty for their own freedom." [14] Remond's increased
bitterness stemmed from the Dred Scott decision which he and the
abolitionists in general regarded as a glaring example of racial
prejudice having donned judicial robes.

As a man with some military experience in Kansas and the potential leader of a proposed armed foray into Virginia, Brown undoubtedly knew of the efforts of black men to join the militias in
their states or, failing that, to form military companies of their
own. State laws, North as well as South, barred blacks from the
militia, reflecting national policy, an act of Congress in 1792 having
restricted military service to able-bodied white males.

The protest of blacks against laws restricting the militia to
whites became stronger than ever during the years that Brown
was shaping his revolutionary plans. A Negro national convention

held in Rochester in July 1853, the largest of its kind during the antebellum period, called for the repeal of "all laws and usages which preclude the enrollment of colored men in the militia," holding that such a restriction was unconstitutional.[15]

Denied admission to the state militias, blacks formed their own companies. Sixty-five blacks in Massachusetts drew up a petition which, after strongly condemning their exclusion from the state militia, requested a charter authorizing them to form an independent military company. On February 4, 1853, William J. Watkins delivered this petition to the Legislative Committee on the Militia, accompanying it with an address, "Our Rights as Men." Watkins made much of the fact that the signers of the petition were descendants of men who had fought and bled for America. "Our fathers were not able-bodied white male citizens but they were able enough to face British cannon, in 1776 and 1812." [16]

This petition would be rejected, as similar ones to the same body would later be treated in a like manner. But the blacks in Boston proceeded, even though without official authorization, to form a military company, furnishing their own stand of arms when the state refused a loan of equipment. As if to call attention to the exclusionary policies of the state, the black militia company invited into its ranks any citizen of good moral character.[17]

The company took the name "Massasoit Guards" after an Indian chief who in 1621 had signed a treaty of friendship with the Plymouth colonists. Although proud of this name, the company would have preferred "Attucks" but this designation had already been appropriated by at least two colored military units elsewhere, notably the "Attucks Guards" in New York and the "Attucks Blues" in Cincinnati. New York had two other black companies, one of them named after the Carthaginian general, Hannibal.

Among the other black military companies of the 1850's two were named after acquaintances of John Brown. Binghamton, New York, had its "Loguen Guards," and in the summer of 1859 the blacks of Harrisburg, Pennsylvania, organized the "Henry Highland Garnet Guards." The local paper in Harrisburg, the *Patriot and Union,* disapproved of the company, calling it the "rank and file, but mostly *rank,*" and also castigated the name of the person it bore, characterizing Garnet as foul-mouthed, depraved, vicious, and having done more "to excite the colored people of the North" than anyone else.[18]

Greatly contributing to Brown's belief that Northern blacks were in a mood for a direct, physical confrontation with slavery was their role in effecting the rescue of fugitive slaves. To wrest a runaway from his master, his master's agent, or a federal marshal was a risky business even though the rescuers could rely on widespread sympathy and support. Prior to 1850 the rescue of slaves had been an enterprise almost exclusively in the hands of blacks. With the passage of the Fugitive Slave Law of 1850 many whites took an increased interest in the effort.

One of these was John Brown. As has been noted, he had urged runaways to stand their ground despite the law and had formed an organization to help them do so. Brown had taken due note of the sense of threat and alarm that the Fugitive Slave Law had brought to the black community, particularly to its runaways. But it is certain that he could not have missed the defiant language that was the response of a great many blacks.

At a meeting of colored Bostonians, held in March in historic Faneuil Hall, a meeting typical of many others that year, a resolution was unanimously adopted proclaiming the right of revolution, a right that they would "sacredly maintain" at whatever cost. Later that year a meeting of blacks held at Zion Chapel in New York adopted a series of resolutions, one of them declaring that the provision of the Fugitive Slave Law left them no alternative other than to adopt the motto of Virginia, "Resistance to tyrants is obedience to God."

The reader of the resolutions, George T. Downing, who had recently purchased two pistols, declared that if "any fiend in human shape" crossed his threshold he would send him to hell before he had accomplished his mission. Charles W. Gardner, a Presbyterian clergyman from Philadelphia, advised "his brethren and sisters" to take the life of anyone who attempted to deprive them of their liberty. John S. Jacobs, a fugitive from South Carolina, had these words of advice: "My colored brethren, if you have not swords, I say to you, sell your garments and buy one." [19]

Two months later a group of runaways, meeting in Cazenovia, New York, drew up an "Address to the American Slaves," informing them that if the American patriots in the Revolutionary War had an excuse for shedding one drop of blood it must be granted that the American slaves had every justification for making blood flow "even unto the horsebridles." The Colored National Convention of 1855, which was held in Philadelphia, strongly condemned the Fugitive Slave Law on the grounds that "every man and woman are by right the owners of themselves." [20]

Brave words by blacks against the Fugitive Slave Law were supplemented by action on the field. The dramatic rescues of the 1850's invariably numbered blacks in the role of deliverers, a fact that could not have been lost on John Brown. In the Jerry Rescue of Syracuse in the fall of 1850 five blacks were included among the eighteen rescuers indicted by the federal authorities, including the clergymen-leaders Jermain W. Loguen and Samuel Ringgold Ward. Only one of the eighteen was found guilty, black Enoch Reed. In another celebrated rescue action taking place within a month's time, the "Christiana Riot" in southern Pennsylvania, thirty-five of the thirty-eight rescuers arrested on the charge of treason were black, including the leader of the party, William Parker, himself a fugitive slave.

In the highly publicized Passmore Williamson case in 1855 the six rescuers of Jane Johnson and her two sons were black Philadelphians, led by William Still. The case, however, took its name from a white Quaker who was jailed for contempt of court, having refused to give information about the rescue. Brown must have been greatly pleased when he learned of these slave rescues, just as he was saddened by the dramatic failure to prevent Anthony Burns from being seized in Boston in 1854 and carried away.

The slave rescue that came within Brown's personal purview and undoubtedly left its mark on him was the Oberlin-Wellington rescue. Of the thirty-seven indicted in this action, twelve were black, and, of the two brought to trial as leaders, Simeon Bushnell and Charles H. Langston, the latter was black. His address before a crowded courtroom, just prior to his sentencing, was an impassioned plea for liberty. In language that moved everyone, including the judge, Langston said that his father, a Revolutionary War veteran, had instructed him that in America all men had the right to life and liberty.

Brown spent ten days in Cleveland during the court trial of the rescuers. At his own trial after Harpers Ferry, Brown testified that inasmuch as he had been sick while in Cleveland he had not conversed with any of the defendants but that he had spoken publicly on the rescue. Unquestionably he was aware of the case and the furore it created. Following his departure from the city, his lieutenant, John H. Kagi, gave much of his time to assisting the rescuers.[21]

Brown may well have read into the Oberlin-Wellington rescue the things he wanted to believe about the militancy of blacks, perhaps causing him, in the words of Mary Land, "to universalize the characteristics of the Negroes he knew on the Reserve." Certainly the blacks in northern Ohio were not deferential or meek, particularly those in Oberlin. In 1859 black Oberlinites numbered only 340, of whom 28 were fugitives, but they bore themselves as though they were not "afraid of the white man," wrote William J. Watkins. "There is a sort of you-touch-me-if-you-dare about them."[22] Brown's knowledge of Oberlin extended to the college that bore its name, his father having served as a trustee and Brown himself having surveyed land under its employ.

Brown's twin belief that black militancy was widespread and that any number of action-oriented blacks would join him in his planned foray into Virginia was put to test at Harpers Ferry. At this raid, however, the entire assaulting party, including Brown himself, numbered only twenty-two, of whom five were black. This low black enrollment was a major miscalculation on Brown's part. Why had he failed in his efforts to enlist more blacks? We may first note some typical individual blacks who might have joined Brown but did not, and then note some of the circumstances militating against the recruitment of a sizable colored component.

In making an assessment of the black potential for such a raid as Brown had in mind, two groups need be defined—those blacks whom Brown could hardly have expected to join him, viewed objectively, and those whom he could, with some justification, however slight, have expected to swell his ranks.

Brown obviously could hardly have expected recruits from among black militants he had never met—H. Ford Douglas of Chicago and George T. Downing of Newport, Rhode Island, for example. An entry in Brown's diary for October 8, 1859, a week before Harpers Ferry, listed E. D. Bassett, 718 Lombard Street, Philadelphia, under the heading, "Names of Men to Call on for Assistance," but it is doubtful that Brown ever met the man himself, the Principal of the Institute for Colored Youth.[23] A good portion of the black militant leaders in antebellum America were clergymen—among them Garnet, Loguen, Gloucester, Daniel A. Payne, Leonard A. Grimes, and J. W. C. Pennington, figures not likely to join a raiding party themselves, however much they might countenance it for others.

Some black abolitionists were temperamentally unsuited for a raiding action. A person of a speculative and reflective turn of mind, like the well-to-do William Whipper, was likely to feel that his best contribution did not embrace the barracks. The somewhat patrician-mannered Robert Purvis, at home with the wealthy and well educated, was hardly the type for guerrilla warfare, although unsurpassed for militancy in language and general stance.

Some black abolitionists would not have joined Brown because of their preference for their own technique of liberation. Brown knew William Still, to whom Kagi wrote four days before Harpers Ferry,[24] but Still's forte was underground railroad operations and doubtless he felt that his best base was Philadelphia rather than the prairies of Kansas or the mountain passes of western Virginia.

The blacks whom Brown might more logically have expected to join him in his proposed foray included those who attended the Chatham convention and a handful of others. Only one of the thirty-four blacks at the convention, Osborne P. Anderson, would be with the Brown party at Harpers Ferry. One of the reasons for this low level of response among the conventioneers was the delay of eighteen months between the convention and the raid. During this long interim the zeal of most of the black participants had abated and some of them from Chatham had left that region for good. Three months after the convention Delany, in a letter to Kagi, said that he had been anxiously awaiting news of "uncle's movements." Delany assured Kagi of his own continued support and that of the other Chathamites, but it was evident that he and they felt frustrated by the delay.[25]

Delany himself was to be numbered among those who left Chatham months before Harpers Ferry. He first learned of the raid while he was in Abbeokuta, West Africa, having left New York on the black-owned bark, *Mendi,* on May 24, 1859, bent on making an expedition to explore the Niger Valley. One of Delany's traveling companions aboard the *Mendi* was the Reverend William C. Munroe, presiding officer at the Chatham Convention, but now bound for Liberia, under Episcopalian auspices, with his wife and two children.

When Delany wrote to Kagi in August 1858, he reported that William H. Day, among others, was then in Chatham. But, like Delany, Day was abroad when Brown made his move at Harpers Ferry. On June 24, 1859, Day had sailed for Dublin to attend an international religious conference as a delegate from the Canadian Presbyterian Church. Bound in a different direction prior to Harpers Ferry, some of the Chatham residents who attended the convention had left for the American Pacific Coast region, among them James Monroe Jones, and two had gone to British Columbia, one of whom was Isaac Holden.[26]

J. Madison Bell, who would move to San Francisco three months after the raid, kept in touch with the Brown people longer than any other resident of Chatham except Osborne P. Anderson. In mid-September 1859 Bell wrote to John Brown, Jr., that he had dispatched Anderson on the preceding day. Bell also reported that Richard Richardson was "anxious to be at work as a missionary to bring sinners to repentance," and would start his journey in a few days, possibly bringing "another laborer" with him. Bell added that he would like to hear of Brown's congregation numbering "more than 15 and 2 to commence a good revival." [27] When the "revival" was held it did not include Richardson, however, who would remain in Canada.

Possibly there were some blacks in Canada who had grown cool about joining Brown because his methods had been deplored by William King, founder of Buxton and a white pastor who had proved himself to be a trusted and energetic friend.[28] But the greatest cause of the disaffection among Canadian blacks was the long delay in implementing the recommendations of the Chatham Convention, especially when they had been led to expect a promptness of action.

Trying to rekindle their enthusiasm, John Brown, Jr., in company with Jermain Loguen, busied himself during the summer of 1859 in forming branches of the "League of Liberty," an agency to recruit black followers and supporters. Although the duo managed to set up cells in Buxton, London, Hamilton, St. Catherines, Windsor, and Chatham, the response was considerably less enthusiastic than they had hoped. In an overly optimistic vein, young Brown reported that he had met with a hearty response at Chatham and that one of the members of the convention, Robinson Alexander, was arranging his affairs so as to join the group and had promised that in the meantime he would give money to help recruit two or three others. But Robinson would not show up in Harpers Ferry, a circumstance predicted by Bell in mid-September 1859, nor would the anonymous "hand" for whom young Brown sent a draft to Bell on October 1.[29]

While generally looking on the bright side, young Brown did not hesitate to express pessimism as to the enlistment possibilities of such prominent figures as his sometime traveling companion, Jermain Loguen, and Charles H. Langston. Two months before the raid, John, Jr., informed Kagi that Loguen was too fat and, more important, that his heart was only passively in "our cause." In a letter to Kagi ten days before Harpers Ferry, young Brown reported that Langston "was discouraged about the mining business," believing that the hands were too few. "Physical weakness is his fault," concluded the writer.[30]

In his comment on Langston, young Brown made the natural assumption that anyone who showed skepticism about his father's project was more concerned about his own skin than about anything else, including the practicality of the proposed raid. The Browns, father and son, had some difficulty in believing that some blacks who opposed the raid were motivated primarily by the conviction that such an undertaking was the height of folly. One of the blacks holding this point of view and daring to express it to Brown himself was William E. Ambush of Cleveland who, in the early stages of the Civil War, would write to Governor David Tod of Ohio offering to raise two regiments of Negro soldiers.[31]

Henry Highland Garnet was another black militant who, although urging the slaves to rebel in 1843, cautioned Brown against making a direct strike at slavery, if we can accept the word of John S. Rock, in a speech delivered on December 2, 1859, the day of Brown's hanging. According to Rock, in 1857 Garnet told Brown that the time was not ripe, blacks in the South not being sufficiently aware of their rights and of the widespread sympathy for them in the North. Blacks in the North were equally unprepared for such a venture "in consequence of the prejudice that shuts them out from both the means and the intelligence necessary." Moreover, added Garnet as a clinching point, the breach between the North and the South had not widened enough for the success of such a move as Brown contemplated.[32]

The belief that a raid on Harpers Ferry was foredoomed to failure was shared by Frederick Douglass, leading him to reject Brown's invitation to join the party. Brown viewed Douglass as a role model, one whose very name would attract others, giving the venture an air of credibility. Hence he made an especial effort to win Douglass over, asking him to meet him at Chambersburg, Pennsylvania, and sending him $22 by John, Jr., to help defray his expenses from Rochester. Brown had come to Chambersburg in June 1859 ostensibly to engage in mineral development but using the town, forty-five miles due north of Harpers Ferry, as a place to store arms and ammunition.

Douglass arrived in Chambersburg accompanied by Shields Green, a runaway slave who had taken residence in Rochester.

Brown had asked Douglass to bring Green, having previously met him while a paying guest of the Douglass family in February 1858. Douglass also brought a letter from Mrs. E. A. Gloucester to Brown, with $10 enclosed. Dated August 19, 1859, the letter extended her best wishes for Brown's welfare and for the good of his cause.[33]

Douglass and Green were escorted to Brown's hideaway, an old stone quarry, by Henry Watson, whose barbershop was the center of underground railroad operations in the town. Brown knew of Watson's activities and counted on his support along with that of "his reliable friends." Watson did not tarry for the meeting, whose fourth member was the ever-present Kagi.

To his trio of listeners Brown described his plans—in essence, the seizure of the government arsenal at Harpers Ferry. This venture caught Douglass off guard, since it represented what he considered to be a major departure from the plan of running off slaves and defending them from would-be pursuers. An earnest discussion ensued, lasting much of the day, with Green having little to say. He was, as Douglass put it, a man of few words.

That evening, Saturday, August 20, Douglass had to give a speech at the town hall in order to divert suspicion from his true mission to Chambersburg. The ruse proved successful: "All supposed that he came solely for delivering a lecture and pocketing the profits," wrote a correspondent to the *Baltimore American* a week after the raid.[34]

On the next morning, Sunday, Brown and Douglass resumed their earnest discussion. The latter, our only source for this meeting summed it up thus:

> Brown for Harpers Ferry and I against it—he for striking a blow that should instantly arouse the country, and I for the policy of gradually and unaccountably drawing off the slaves to the mountains, as at first suggested and proposed by him.

Douglass says that he made it clear to Brown that this new plan was impractical and that he could not support it. As the discussion drew to its end, Brown made one last appeal. Putting his arm around Douglass, he vowed that he would defend him with his own life and that he wanted him for a special purpose: "When I strike, the bees will begin to swarm, and I shall want you to help hive them." Douglass was moved by Brown's "more than friendly manner," in making this plea, but he remained unconvinced.

The meeting was by no means unfruitful for Brown, however. As Douglass prepared to leave he turned to Shields Green and asked him what he decided to do. Douglass was suprised when Green coolly replied, "I b'leve I'll go wid de ole man." [35] The pleased Brown would hardly have minded being called old, regarding the word in its Old Testament sense as denoting respect and wisdom.

Douglass would always categorically maintain that he had advised Brown against the foray and had turned down the invitation to join the raiding party, yet some lingering doubts would remain as to what was said and agreed upon at the meeting in the old stone-quarry. "I wonder to what extent Frederick Douglass's recollections were correct as to the degree of his definite advice to Brown against the raid," wrote Alfred Webb in 1907. Webb was the son of the Dublin abolitionists, Richard and Hannah Webb, who knew Douglass from his visits to the British Isles. "Douglass is to be one of us," wrote Jeremiah G. Anderson on June 17, 1859.[36] Anderson, who would fall at Harpers Ferry, had recently called on Douglass at his Rochester residence. It hardly need be pointed out, however, that Anderson's visit took place prior to the Douglass-Brown meeting at Chambersburg.

Annie Brown Adams would later relate that when her father and Kagi returned from that meeting with Douglass they said that he had promised that he would follow Brown "even unto death." John E. Cook, one of the men taken at Harpers Ferry, charged Douglass with having failed to keep his promise to furnish the party with additional men and weapons on the eve of the foray. Mrs. Thomas Russell, who visited Brown in jail after the raid, gathered that "he had no fondness for Fred Douglass." [37]

But it is hard to believe that Brown, however given to wishful thinking, could have expected Douglass to join him at Harpers Ferry. Alex R. Boteler, an eyewitness to the raid and a congressman from the district, related that he had seen a list of the persons Brown expected to rally around him, with the list divided in two columns, "reliable," and "not reliable." The name of Frederick Douglass headed the latter column. John Brown, Jr., wrote in 1885 that neither his father or Kagi ever wrote him a word as to the visit of Douglass to Chambersburg. Nor, continued John, Jr., had his brother, Owen, an escapee from the Ferry, ever heard their father or Kagi refer to the meeting at the stone-quarry. John, Jr., surmised that Douglass could have regarded Shields Green as sort of a substitute for him. But Brown's son admitted that he had no positive knowledge as to the extent of Douglass' commitment. "It may be," concluded John, Jr., "that the mist will never be cleared away respecting this actor in the drama." [38]

One of Douglass' sons charged that the story that his father was scheduled to take part in the raid was a concoction by Southerners to discredit the Negro, picturing him as undependable and unmanly. It was, wrote Charles R. Douglass, a charge that Brown himself never made.[39]

Whatever Brown's hopes for Douglass, they were higher for Harriet Tubman, but in this quarter, too, he was destined for disappointment. By June 1859 he had set his heart on having Harriet go to Canada to recruit followers. Harriet herself had suggested the Fourth of July as a particularly appropriate day "to raise the mill." But it was not long before Brown began to receive reports that Harriet was under the weather. She was "probably in New Bedford sick," wrote F. B. Sanborn to Brown on August 29.[40]

John, Jr., and Sanborn went to considerable effort to enlist her services, hoping that her health would mend. Writing on September 14, 1859, to Thomas Wentworth Higginson, another Brown supporter, Sanborn reported that Harriet was "to be sent forward soon." But ten days later Sanborn had to admit ruefully that he had not yet heard from her.[41]

Growing impatient over the delay in the enlistment of Mrs. Tubman, Brown sought the aid of the energetic Lewis Hayden of Boston, like Harriet a runaway slave. Hayden wrote to Harriet, urging her to come to Boston. He also wrote to Gerrit Smith, asking for and receiving a sum of money to give to Harriet for the support of her parents while she was engaged in the raid.[42]

Despite all efforts, Harriet took no part in the operation. Later, in the Civil War, she served as a nurse and scout in the Sea Islands of South Carolina, and she lived until 1914. But during the weeks preceding Harpers Ferry she apparently remained in poor health and hence hors de combat. As the date for the impending foray drew closer and closer Brown must have grown increasingly unhappy about the absence of "General" Tubman.

James H. Harris, a member of the Chatham convention, was exasperated at the response from the fellow blacks he sought to enlist in and around Cleveland for service with John Brown. From some he got promises "and that's all," he explained in a letter to Kagi on August 22, 1859. From others he got only excuses. In a bitter outburst, Harris summed up his sense of frustration: "I am disgusted with myself and the whole Negro set, *God dam em!*" [43]

Harris' angry words doubtless relieved his feelings for the moment but it hardly explained the lukewarm responses of most blacks toward joining John Brown. Certainly it was not a want of physical courage or the lack of fighting qualities, as the impending Civil War would amply demonstrate.

Brown's failure to win blacks to his banner in invading Virginia sprang in some measure from his extreme reticence to divulge his plans and perhaps, and to a lesser degree, to his apparent change of dates for the attack. Brown also made the mistake of misjudging black rhetoric as declaimed by black spokesmen, orators, and firebrands. That some blacks may have hesitated to join a movement led by any white seems to have influenced not more than a few. It is to be noted, however, that black abolitionists and their white counterparts were often in sharp disagreement as to priorities and role, with black reformers becoming more self-consciously black during the 1840's and 1850's. And even among Brown's black followers there might have remained some distrust of whites. In the secret order formed in Detroit to assist Brown and headed by William Lambert, white enlistees were put to stricter tests than black ones and were not made privy to the order's most confidential data.[44]

It may be noted, too, that Brown "never thought to ask the Negroes if they would accept him as a leader, and if so, what kind of policy they wanted him to pursue," in the words of historian David M. Potter.[45] But this circumstance was not a racial or Negro-oriented policy of Brown's; rather it was typical of the man. No figure in American history could outdo Brown as a "loner." In Kansas he did not work with other Free State leaders or take part in the conventions they held. He sought no one's advice; he asked no group to accept him as leader. In this respect, as in general, he treated blacks and whites alike, eliciting the counsel of neither and taking for granted the acceptance of both.

This is not to say, however, that Brown's great reticence in revealing his plans, even to his immediate followers, may not have caused some blacks to withhold their support. Their basic civil rights flouted to a far greater degree than those of any white-skinned minority, blacks knew that in their struggle for full freedom in the land of their birth, the exercise of confidentiality had its uses. Black Americans were well aware that freedom for them was considered by many whites as subversive, as somehow not in the national interest. Hence blacks knew that in their struggle there was a time to speak out and a time to remain tight-lipped, a beleaguered minority hardly needing to be told that there are some things that might better be said or done in private.

To many blacks, however, Brown carried secrecy to such Byzantine proportions as to provide them with no sense of direction, of concrete purpose. Brown was "incapable of uttering a falsehood," said his friend, Richard J. Hinton, on the day of his hanging. But if Brown never lied about his plans it was due in part to his having uttered so little about them. He had an abiding passion for secrecy, believing it essential to his success and doubtless sensing that the role of the revolutionary was necessarily solitary. Augustus Wattles testified that he had never seen anyone as disposed to secrecy as Brown.[46]

In organizing the League of Gileadites in 1851 Brown advised his colored followers to divulge their plans to nobody. In a letter to his son, written from the Douglass residence in February 1858, Brown warned him not to so much as "lisp" his plan or theories, other than by "mere hints," even to committed friends. Two months before the raid Brown, in a letter to Kagi, pointed out that anyone who expected his friends to keep for him that which he could not keep to himself was a "stupid Fool." [47]

John Brown "never went around Robin Hood's barn, but always straight to the point," wrote J. Ewing Glasgow, a young American black studying at the University of Edinburgh at the time of the raid. If Glasgow could ever have heard Brown speak of his plans, he would have known better. Whenever necessity forced him to discuss his plans, Brown presented them in an indefinite fashion, blurring things over. As Richard Realf pointed out, Brown never stated more than was absolutely necessary, leaving his followers with only the minimum of information required to hold them. Mrs. Sturtevant, a Clevelander who sent him money, told a newspaper reporter that many of those who aided Brown financially "never understood his plans." Wealthier backers could echo the same sentiment. To reveal one's plans is the worst possible policy, Brown told George H. Stearns during their first discussion of affairs in Kansas.[48]

Brown acted on the sound premise that if some of his followers and supporters had known the full dimensions of his plans they might have shied away. To have let them in on his proposed operations might have entailed losing them. But too much concealment also had its drawbacks, making the thoughtful wary and hesitant. Admittedly the line between telling too much and telling too little was thin. Brown never bothered to seek it, however, and to this extent his excessive secrecy might have been counter-productive.

The band that invaded Harpers Ferry on October 16, 1859, might have been a bit larger if Brown had not struck prematurely. Apparently Brown made the raid a week or so earlier than he had originally intended. F. B. Sanborn, a confidant, said that Brown had originally planned to strike "about" October 25. According to this same source, Brown's raid caught Harriet Tubman unaware, coming while she was engaged in recruiting followers for him. If so, Harriet's absence stemmed more from poor advance information than from poor health. Richard J. Hinton relates that when the raid took place he was at a black-operated underground railroad post in Chambersburg, awaiting word to join the band.[49]

John Brown, Jr., might have been present had Harpers Ferry operations begun later. It was only on September 27, 1859, less than a month before the march, that young Brown received word that his father "intended to open the mines before spring," a step contrary to his original plans. Beyond this vague information John, Jr., remained in the dark as to the new time, and he was never to have any advance word as to place.[50] After Harpers Ferry there were rumors that a number of blacks in New York had been expecting that the raid would take place on October 24. These were matched by stories from Ontario that at the time of the raid three black companies, one each from Buxton, Chatham, and Ingersoll, were on their way to Detroit, their ultimate destination John Brown's headquarters.

Osborne Perry Anderson, a participant, said that suspicious neighbors at the Kennedy Farm rendezvous of the group caused Brown to move before "other parties" had reached him. In addition to the fear of exposure, Brown believed that the slaves in and around Harpers Ferry were in a bitter mood as a result of a slave hanging himself when his wife was sold.[51] Brown may have wished to capitalize on such slave discontent before it died down.

Brown's over-sanguine expectations of black support stemmed in some measure from the revolutionary rhetoric of violence so characteristic of black expression in the press and on the platform during the decade before Harpers Ferry. In this respect, however, and this was something that Brown failed to consider sufficiently, black rhetoric mirrored the national pattern for this period. In the 1850's the anti-slavery movement as a whole became more receptive to the verbal expression of violence, resulting in part from the Fugitive Slave Law and the bloody clashes in Kansas.[52]

Himself a man of action on the physical level, John Brown failed to realize that much of the violence that black and white reformers and their opponents were conjuring up was in reality the threat of violence rather than a commitment to its use. The use of threat had always been a weapon in the rhetorical arsenal of reformers as it was, too, of those against whom it was directed. Invoking violence was a means to achieve one's end.[53]

But, and here is where John Brown may have erred, not everyone who preached violence was prepared to practice it. To many of its users the rhetoric of violence was primarily a form of tension release, having little more than a narcotic effect. They had found the fulfillment they sought by using brave words.

It is to be noted too that a man who read selectively, like John Brown, may not have sufficiently weighed the extent of non-militancy among blacks. In the 1850's Brown could not have failed to note with satisfaction that the stories of men like Denmark Vesey and Nat Turner were increasingly being carried in the public press. "The increase of interest in the subject of slave insurrections is one of the most important signs of the time," wrote T. W. Higginson to Lysander Spooner in November 1858. But Brown might have missed the observation of a black like Edward V. Clark, who at a Fugitive Slave Law protest meeting in October 1850 at Zion's Church in New York pointed out that "the principle of dying before your time is much better in theory than in practice." Clark added, perhaps with tongue in cheek, that "all the lives we lose in opposing this bill would be a dead loss to us."[54]

Those marching with John Brown to strike at slavery on that fateful October morning would be small in number, sixteen whites and five blacks, and this leanness in count could hardly have been offset by any superior qualities they might have had. Obviously, however, they were men of spirit and courage. Obviously, too, they shared their leader's convictions, each of them being "anti-slavery by association and training," wrote Richard J. Hinton from first-hand knowledge.[55] They did not match their leader in life span, Brown, the father of three of them, being twice the age of the eldest, except for Dangerfield Newby.

Information on the antecedents of the five blacks who took part in the raid is far from complete. "I trust that a systematic effort will yet be made to collect all the facts and reminiscences of the Colored Martyrs of Harper's Ferry," wrote William C. Nell in July 1861, "for of all classes in the United States, Colored Americans are least likely to have justice awarded them." [56] Nell himself was not prepared to make this "systematic effort," and none of his contemporaries heeded his word.

Of the five blacks who took part in the raid, two had met Brown early in 1858, Shields Green and Osborne P. Anderson. The former had escaped from Charleston, South Carolina, on a sailing vessel, spurred by the death of his wife. He had had to leave his young son behind. Going to Rochester in 1856 and changing his name from Esau Brown to Shields Green, he then went to Canada for a year or two, where he found employment as a waiter and house servant. Upon his return to Rochester he changed occupations, his card announcing that he was "prepared to do clothes-cleaning in a manner to suit the most fastidious and on cheaper terms than anyone else." [57]

Lucy N. Colman, a Rochester abolitionist, relates that Green told her that an overseer's lash had cut deeply into his soul and that he was willing to lose his life with John Brown if it would help free his race.[58] Doubtless these were Green's sentiments, although, as one unable to read or write, he could hardly have expressed them in the literary form ascribed to him by interviewer Colman.

Dark-skinned and well built, Green was about twenty-five years old when he joined John Brown. At that time he was sometimes called "Emperor," a nickname that could have come from the self-confident manner with which he bore himself or from the rumor that he was the son of an African prince who had been sold into slavery. Green was the first black to be recruited for Harpers Ferry operations, joining the band at the close of the Chambersburg meeting between Douglass and Brown in August 1859.

Brown's first meeting with Osborne Perry Anderson took place at the Chatham convention in May 1858. Indeed when Anderson joined the Brown band he was dubbed "Chatham" Anderson by his fellows. He was born at Chester County, Pennsylvania. There he had attended the public schools, going hungry on occasion in order to buy books. A printer by trade he had gone to Canada in 1850, eventually finding employment at the offices of the *Provincial Freeman* in Chatham. His full face, prominent nose, chin-whiskers, "Afro" hair style and serious mien reminded one of a younger Frederick Douglass. A mixed blood like the famed orator-abolitionist, Anderson was somewhat lighter in complexion, his color yellowish-brown. A bachelor, he left Chatham for good on September 13, 1859, reaching the Brown forces at Chambersburg twelve days later.

Anderson was the third black arrival at the Brown headquarters, having been preceded by Green on August 21 and by Dangerfield Newby two or three days later. Born in Fauquier County, Virginia, perhaps in 1825, Newby was a former slave, like Green, but he was no runaway. His owner-father, a Scotsman, had freed him and his two brothers after taking them to Ohio. A blacksmith by trade, Dangerfield returned to Virginia, hoping to raise enough money to purchase his slave wife, Harriett, a seamstress, and their six children.[59]

Newby's decision to join John Brown may have been due in some measure to the heart-rending letters he received from Harriett, a mixture of love and despair. Writing on April 11, 1859, Harriett poured out her feelings: "Oh, Dear Dangerfield, *com* this fall without fail, *monny* or no *monney*. I want to see you so much. This is the one bright hope I have before me." Eleven days later, after hearing from her husband, Harriett wrote: "*Com* as soon as you can, for nothing would give more pleasure than to see you." [60]

Two months before the raid Harriett wrote to Newby, urging him to buy her as soon as possible "for if you do not get me some body else will." In this letter, as in the preceding two, Harriett

spoke of their children. And again she laid bare her love for him:
"*Their* has *ben* one bright hope to cheer me in all my troubles,
that is to be with you, for if I thought I should never see you this
earth would have no charms for me." [61] Shortly after this letter
was sent, Newby joined Brown. Possibly he also asked his two
brothers, Gabriel and James, to do likewise.

A light mulatto with high cheek bones and an oval face, concealed below the mouth by a profusion of whiskers, Newby was
a quiet member of the party. He had much on his mind. He was
"a smart and good man for an ignorant one," wrote Annie Brown,
who kept house for the raiders.[62] Writing in November 1859,
Annie used the past tense. Newby would fall at Harpers Ferry.

The last of the black arrivals at the Brown headquarters were
Lewis Sheridan Leary and John Anthony Copeland, Jr., both reporting Wednesday, October 12, four days before the outbreak.
Leary had seen Brown for the first time at the latter's public lecture
in Cleveland in March 1859 before a sparse audience. At that time
Leary had been a resident of Oberlin for three years, having come
there from Fayetteville, North Carolina, his birthplace. His father,
Matthew, was the son of an Irishman, Jeremiah Leary, who fought
in the Revolutionary War. Defying convention Jeremiah had
married Sally Revels, of mixed Croatan Indian and Negro blood.
Matthew Leary's own wife was French-born Julie Memriel,
daughter of a Guadaloupian. Lewis was their oldest child, followed
by Henrietta and John.[63]

Lewis attended school at Fayetteville and later became a saddler
and harness maker, going to Oberlin to work at his trade. Here
he joined a debating society and developed a sense of racial concern, urging blacks to learn trades and save their money in lieu
of going to parties and dances. "Men must suffer for a good cause,"
he said, eleven months before Harpers Ferry.[64]

A year before he met Brown young Leary married Mary Simpson Patterson, like him born in 1835 in Fayetteville. She had come
to Oberlin to attend the preparatory department of the college
enrolling for the school term 1857–58.[65] She withdrew after one
year, the birth of a daughter the probable cause.

Leary was instrumental in recruiting his nephew, John Anthony

Copeland, Jr. "I have a hardy man, who is willing and in every way competent to dig coal, but like myself, has no tools," wrote Leary to Kagi on September 8, 1859. "His address is John Copeland, Jr., Oberlin, Ohio." [66]

Born in Raleigh, North Carolina, in 1834, Copeland had been brought to Oberlin eight years later by his parents, Delilah Evans, a domestic, and half-white John Anthony Copeland, a carpenter and joiner. One of seven children, John, Jr., had to go to work as his father's helper but he received sufficient schooling to enable him to enter the preparatory department of Oberlin College, where he spent the academic year 1854–55. He joined the town's anti-slavery society and at its meetings he listened with an unusual tenseness whenever a fugitive slave spoke, "signifying often by the deep scowl of his countenance, the moist condition of his eyes and the quivering of his lips, how deeply he was moved by the recital of wrong and outrage," writes John Mercer Langston, a contemporary Oberlinite. Not surprisingly, Copeland was one of those indicted and jailed for his role in the Oberlin-Wellington rescue case. [67] Indeed it was Copeland who had escorted former slave John Price during the final stages of his flight into Canada.

For travel expenses to reach the Brown party Copeland received $15, the money put up by Ralph and Samuel Plumb, white residents of Oberlin, although handed to him by Leary. The latter also furnished him with the names of the Isaac Sturtevants in Cleveland. En route to his destination, Copeland reached the home of the Sturtevants on Monday, October 10, staying overnight. His next Monday night would be more eventful—the place, Harpers Ferry.

During the four months before they launched their raid, John Brown's men divided their time between Chambersburg, Pennsylvania, and the Kennedy Farm, an isolated spot in western Maryland, five miles from Harpers Ferry. Brown and Kagi had chosen Chambersburg as the site for the initial storage of arms, including a supply of 954 pikes. Made of steel, and with a ten-inch, double-edge blade, these were considered especially suited for hand-to-hand combat and hence just the type of weapon for rebellion-minded slaves who might know little about the handling of firearms.

The first three blacks to join the band—Green, Newby, and Anderson—spent some eight to ten days each at Chambersburg. To avoid suspicion they did not share the lodging house rented by the white Brownites. They were able to find some place to stay without trouble, however, owing to the efforts of the black barber, Henry Watson.

Beginning in early August 1859 Brown began to transfer his men and munitions to Kennedy Farm, which he had rented in July. Shields Green was the first of the blacks to make the transfer of sites, arriving in company with Owen Brown after nearly being seized by a white trio who thought that Green might have been a slave in the process of making his escape. Anderson arrived at Kennedy Farm on September 25, in company with Brown himself, the duo having driven all night. By then, if not shortly thereafter, Newby had also come to this launching site Brown had chosen.

The Kennedy Farm served jointly as a center for mobilizing the men and as a depot for the arms and material they would need. The building in which the men were housed and in which the pikes were stored was a two-story log-house, with a sizable basement. A small cabin, fifty rods away, was used as a storage place for the pistols and rifles. At the Kennedy Farm whites and Negroes had to stick close to the house during the day, keeping out of sight as much as possible. "We have to be very careful here how we act in every-thing," wrote white Dauphin Thompson on September 4. "We have one colored man in our company who has been seen by a neighbor woman, but she thinks he is a fugitive, and that we are trying to help him to his freedom." After this episode the occu-pants were even more restricted in their movements: "The colored men were never allowed to be seen by daylight outside of the din-ing room," wrote Annie Brown. "After Mrs. Huffmaster saw Shields Green in that room, they stayed upstairs closely." On the occasion that Green had been seen by Mrs. Huffmaster he had ventured down from the loft where the men were lodged and hid-den so that he might ask Martha, daughter-in-law of Brown, to mend his coat in exchange for some ironing he would do for her.[68]

To keep Green out of sight was somewhat of a problem, despite warning him of a second unexpected visitor like Mrs. Huffmaster. Confinement came somewhat easier to Osborne P. Anderson, his previous employment in a printing office having accustomed him to long hours indoors. Anderson managed to get some daytime exercise by suspending a sack of bran from the rafters and using it as a punching bag. He spent his less strenuous moments in studying military tactics from an army manual and in conversing on reform movements. In such discussions Dangerfield Newby took little part. Brooding and self-contained, he seemed impatient for operations to begin, indifferent apparently as to whether he was upstairs or down, inside or out.[69]

The Oberlin men, Leary and Copeland, hardly had the problem of adjusting to the prison-like atmosphere of the farm, spending only four days there before Brown's decision to move toward Harpers Ferry. Until that morning of October 16, Leary, Copeland, and Green were among the six or seven who had not been informed of Brown's timetable or plan of operations, according to John E. Cook. Whether these newly informed members, or any others in the band, were ready or not, Brown had reached a decision that was not reversible and one from which there was no option of non-concurrence. If the attack on Harpers Ferry turned out to be a rash and fatal move, as some of the men at Kennedy Farm doubtless believed it would,[70] they knew that no argument could prevail against Brown's conviction that the Almighty was guiding their footsteps and would not forsake His own.

On that Sabbath morning Brown, after assembling the men in the Kennedy livingroom, opened with a worship service at which he read a Bible passage and one of the blacks led in prayer. Then the group went into a council meeting with Osborne P. Anderson presiding. Brown, as commander-in-chief, made battle assignments, including the appointment of a rear guard of three which would remain at the farm house for the time being. Brown also gave out army commissions, none of which went to a Negro. Anderson would later explain that he had been offered a captaincy and the other blacks had likewise been offered commissions but that they all declined because of "a want of acquaintance with military tactics." [71]

The men spent the afternoon quietly. Each one was left to his own thoughts, composing himself for the stern effort at hand. That evening at eight o'clock Brown ordered them to get their arms, hardly needing to add, "We will proceed to the Ferry." [72]

V

HARPERS FERRY:
SCENE AND SEQUEL

*I thank you, that you have been brave enough
to reach out your hands to the crushed and
blighted of my race.*
Frances Ellen Watkins to Brown, Nov. 25, 1859

By moving into Harpers Ferry with his small band, Brown sought
to strike at slavery on its own grounds, not where it was trying
to get a toehold, as in Kansas. By carrying the war into the earliest
bastion of slavery in the original thirteen colonies, proud Virginia
itself, Brown felt that the whole system of American bondage
would feel the tremors. Harpers Ferry, moreover, was less than
sixty miles from Washington, and an outbreak so near the seat of
the national government was bound to arrest attention if not to
create apprehension.

Brown's specific intentions once he reached Harpers Ferry are
considerably less clear. It appears that he did not have in mind
running the slaves to the north, as he had done in the Missouri
rescue. Rather, he intended to liberate them and then to provide
them with the weapons to maintain their freedom where they were.
Thus the former slave would be in a position to confront his former
master instead of fleeing from him.

The spot Brown chose for this opening confrontation was dramatic enough. Long a tourist attraction for its beautiful and imposing scenery, Harpers Ferry stood at the confluence of the
Potomac and Shenandoah, the two rivers tumbling through a cleft

in the Blue Ridge Mountains. The majesty and beauty of Harpers Ferry had no influence, however, on Brown's decision to strike at that spot. He had a more mundane reason. Harpers Ferry was an arms-producing center at which the United States maintained an armory and an arsenal. It was, moreover, under civilian supervision with no corps of soldiers stationed on the grounds. Harpers Ferry beckoned insistently to one as arms-conscious as Brown.

The eighteen men who marched with Brown from Kennedy Farm included the five blacks. None of them would play a distinctively individual role at Harpers Ferry. Like their white comrades, they were components in a collective cast, playing supportive roles to John Brown. Bearing this in mind we may still attempt to focus our attention on these five and on such other blacks as were caught up in the drama. Indeed one of the latter, Hayward, or Heyward, Shepherd, a free Negro, would be the first to die in the affray.

When the Brown invaders marched into Harpers Ferry, rifles under their long gray shawls, they met with no resistance. No civilian or military guards were stationed at the three key building complexes seized by Brown's men—the armory which doubled as a fire-engine house, the arsenal, across the street, and Hall's Rifle Works, half a mile away. These arms-making and arms-storing facilities were wrested from their single guards without bloodshed.

Determined to delay news of his coup, Brown decided to lay hold of the depot and stop the train scheduled to pass through Harpers Ferry en route from Wheeling to Baltimore. Seizing the night watchman stationed on the bridge, Brown's men halted the train. Hearing the noise, the porter and baggage-master, Hayward Shepherd, came out to the bridge, looking for the night watchman and trying to find out what was going on.

Muscular, black-skinned, and soft-spoken, Shepherd "was a very noice nagur, and was, too, very well off, being worth upwards of $15,000," according to Patrick Higgins, one of the two night watchmen on the bridge.[1] An employee at the station for some twelve years, Shepherd got along well with whites, particularly with his supervisor, Fontaine Beckham, mayor of the town and the local general agent of the Baltimore and Ohio Railroad. In Beckham's absence at the station, the trusted Shepherd was in charge, not only doing janitorial and porter work but also selling tickets.

When Shepherd moved toward the toll-gate on the bridge that fateful morning he probably thought that the confusion was being created by marauders or revelers. If so, he was quickly disabused. Confronted by two armed men and commanded to halt, Shepherd turned around to retrace his steps. Before he could reach the office he was shot, one of the balls taking "effect in his back, going through his body and coming out at the nipple of his left breast," reported the train conductor, Andrew J. Phelps. "The Doctor says he cannot survive," he added.[2]

Shepherd's loud cry of distress had brought John D. Starry, a thirty-five-year-old local physician, to the railroad office. There he found Shepherd lying on a plank resting between two chairs. But there was nothing anyone could do except to answer his plea for water. As soon as he swallowed it one could hear its gurgle in his stomach. He would linger until mid-afternoon.[3]

Who killed Shepherd, whether one of Brown's sons or another of his followers, Stewart Taylor, cannot be determined. It was, of course, supremely ironic that the first discharge fired by Brown's men should have felled a member of the racial group Brown had come to liberate. But the shooting took place in the darkness, the man who pulled the trigger having no idea of the color of the person who was refusing to obey the order to halt. In his final instructions to his men, Brown had enjoined them to avoid taking lives except where absolutely necessary in self-defense.

An hour or two before the Shepherd incident Brown sent a raiding party of six to seize prominent slave-owners and their able-bodied male slaves. This raiding contingent included three of the blacks—Osborne P. Anderson, Shields Green, and Lewis S. Leary. Taking the road toward Charlestown in a four-horse farm wagon driven by Green, the six men made their way to the home of Lewis W. Washington, five miles from Harpers Ferry. Colonel Washington was not only a slave-owner but also the possessor of two

Osborne P. Anderson.
Library of Congress.

Dangerfield Newby.
Library of Congress.

Lewis S. Leary.
Library of Congress.

The military taking the prisoners, Shields Green and John A. Copeland, Jr., to the place of execution.
Frank Leslie's Illustrated Weekly.

Shields Green.
Library of Congress.

John A. Copeland, Jr.
Library of Congress.

Charles White, *John Brown.*
Courtesy Charles White and the Heritage Gallery,
Los Angeles.

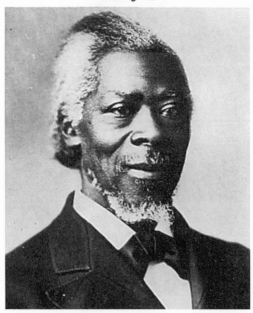

William Lambert.
Courtesy Burton Historical Collection, Detroit
Public Library.

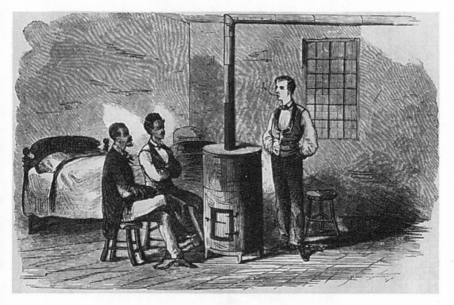

The prisoners, Shields Green, John A. Copeland, Jr., and Albert Hazlett, at the Charlestown Jail.
Frank Leslie's Illustrated Weekly.

Jacob Lawrence. To the people he found worthy of his trust, he communicated his plans.
The Detroit Institute of Arts, gift of Mr. and Mrs. Milton Lowenthal.

Jacob Lawrence. John Brown formed an organization among the colored people of the Adirondack woods to resist the capture of any fugitive slave.
The Detroit Institute of Arts, gift of Mr. and Mrs. Milton Lowenthal.

Jacob Lawrence. John Brown took to guerrilla warfare.
The Detroit Institute of Arts, gift of Mr. and Mrs. Milton Lowenthal.

Jacob Lawrence. John Brown was found "Guilty of treason and murder in the first degree," and was hanged in Charles Town, Virginia, on December 2, 1859.
The Detroit Institute of Arts, gift of Mr. and Mrs. Milton Lowenthal.

Horace Pippin, *John Brown Going to His Hanging.*
The Pennsylvania Academy of the Fine Arts.

relics given to his great-grand uncle, George Washington—a pistol he received from Lafayette and a sword given him by Frederick the Great.

When the party reached Colonel Washington's house, shortly after midnight, four of them entered, leaving Leary and Green to guard the approaches. The colonel was roused from his bed and, in his night-shirt and slippers, was ordered to hand over the sword of Frederick the Great to Anderson, a bit of symbolism Brown had planned. Then, given time to dress, Washington was ordered to get into his own carriage. Three slaves—two of them his, and one of them the husband of one of his slaves—were placed in the wagon. "My other servants," explained Washington later, "were almost all away, that being Sunday night." [4]

On the return trip to Harpers Ferry the raiders stopped at the home of John H. Allstadt, midway between Washington's house and Harpers Ferry. Allstadt and his grown son were ordered to dress and as they were marched out to the carriage they found all seven of their male slaves clothed and waiting. All nine were put in the wagon, along with one additional black, a slave who had been hired by Colonel Washington and who had caught up with the raiding party upon hearing that "something was wrong," as Washington put it.[5]

When the wagons returned to Harpers Ferry the two whites were taken to the armory yard where they were received by Brown. He told Washington that when morning came and the light was better he would have to write to some of his friends directing each of them to send an able-bodied black.[6] It was clear that Brown's purpose in taking white hostages was to swap them for strong black males—his party had taken no women. Upon their return to Harpers Ferry, the six raiders were given other assignments.

Newby would be the first of the invaders to fall. Early that morning the bell-ringer at the armory, James Darrell, had struck at him with a lantern when Newby ordered him to halt. Assuming that he had been confronted by a local black in an exuberant or drunken mood, Darrell realized his error only after being conducted to Brown.[7]

Newby, along with two white recruits, was then sent to defend the wagon bridge over the Shenandoah. The trio would not be there long. Two of the town's residents, Thomas Boerly and George W. Turner, were shot, reportedly by Newby, for walking within the sixty-yard ring of his picket line. Both were armed when killed, one of them, Turner, as he leveled his rifle.

Newby did not survive them. When a detachment of the Jefferson Guards seized the bridge, its three defenders were forced to fall back. Before reaching the armory, Newby was cut down by a six-inch spike which, in lieu of a ball, had been inserted in the gun. Coming from an elevated position the spike struck the lower part of his neck and plunged into his body, killing him instantly.[8]

Newby lay in the streets for several hours, a hog rooting at his body after some of the citizens had cut his ears off into little bits for souvenirs, kicked his lifeless body or beat it with sticks.[9] His death was an ominous sign, as was the manner in which his corpse was abused.

Militia forces had been gathering with far greater speed than Brown could have foreseen, imperilling his small band which had received no re-enforcements. Brown hastened to send Leary on his second assignment—to join Kagi and Copeland at the rifle works which the two latter had captured before midnight from the lone watchman. With Leary's coming the two-man garrison was hardly much better off. Taking note of the swelling crowd, Kagi sent a message to Brown telling him that his ammunition was low and urging him to retreat to the hills without delay. Misreading the situation, Brown sent back word to hold firm.

In mid-afternoon Kagi's fears proved sound—the rifle works were surrounded and attacked. With their position breached and with armed men firing from the cliffs overlooking the rifle works, the defenders were in an untenable position. To cross the Shenandoah, their only means of escape, the trio entered the rapids and fired one round each at their pursuers. In turn they met a hail of fire from the banks. Two-thirds of the way across the river Kagi was shot through the head, his body quickly sinking in the swirling waters. Leary fared little better. As he swam the rapids he was hit by a succession of rifle slugs, causing him to float, mortally wounded.[10]

Copeland succeeded in reaching the middle of the stream where he found a rock formation partially concealed by bushes. His pursuers thought that he had sunk to his grave but he was spied by a group that had come to pull in the wounded Leary. Bent on capturing Copeland single-handedly, one of the members of the assaulting party, James H. Holt, dashed into the rapids. When he came upon Copeland, both fired but their weapons were wet and refused to discharge. Copeland then threw down his gun, further resistance being hopeless with the bank of the rapids bristling with armed men poised for his next move.

Copeland's surrender might have been followed immediately by his hanging, some of his captors having already knotted their handkerchiefs. But some others, including the influential Dr. Starry, advised against such summary action, "not being such cowards as to want to kill a man when disarmed and a prisoner," as Copeland himself explained it.[11] Instead the young mulatto was put in a wagon and taken to the jail in Charlestown.

In the meantime the badly wounded Leary was pulled out of the water and carried to a cooper shop. Interviewed by newspaper reporters he entreated them to write to his wife. He lingered until the next morning, dying ten hours after he had been struck.

Only two of the original five blacks now remained with Brown. One of these, Anderson, had been assigned to hold the arsenal, along with another Brown follower, Albert Hazlett. But on that Monday afternoon, as the local military forces steadily increased their strength, Anderson and Hazlett thought in terms of escape while it was still possible. In the late afternoon when Shields Green arrived with a message from the armory headquarters, the duo sought to persuade him to join them in their planned escape. Green declined, much in the manner in which he had done at the old stone quarry meeting of Brown and Douglass.

Anderson and Hazlett went through with their plans, sensing that all other avenues of escape had been cut off. With the attention of the besieging party on the engine house rather than on the arsenal, Hazlett and Anderson climbed down the back of the building and made their way along the Shenandoah. Finding an old boat they paddled to Maryland and made their way to the Kennedy

Farm, now abandoned. From there they moved into Pennsylvania, traveling by night. Ten miles from Chambersburg, they separated, fortunately for Anderson. Before the week was over Hazlett was arrested in Carlisle and was soon extradicted to Virginia. Anderson, after a stopover in Philadelphia, returned to Canada.

During Brown's final twenty-four hours at the engine house, Shields Green was the only black member of the Provisional Army present. However, for a day and a half Brown had a handful of local blacks, the Washington-Allstadt slaves, under his control. These he put to various uses.

Five of them, three of whom belonged to Allstadt, were assigned to three of his men whom they would assist in transporting rifles from the Kennedy Farm to a schoolhouse one mile from Harpers Ferry. Here, according to plans, these weapons were to be guarded until Brown came to get them, ostensibly for the blacks he was expecting to join him. At five on that Monday morning the party left for Maryland, traveling in the four-horse wagon driven by one of the slaves.

En route to the Kennedy Farm the party stopped at the home of Terence and Joseph Bryne where the leader of the expedition, John E. Cook, ordered the brothers to give him their slaves. But the Brynes had only two male bondmen, both of whom were away for the weekend. The brothers were made prisoners and were held by two of Brown's men. The other member of the white trio, along with the five blacks, proceeded to the Kennedy Farm. Here they procured a quantity of the arms from the rearguard threesome stationed there.

The blacks and their white leader then returned to the Brynes house and the reunited party, along with the two prisoners, made their way to a schoolhouse about three miles from the Ferry. Classes were in session. Cook demanded that the teacher, Lind F. Currie, turn the building over to him for use as an arms depot. Currie had no choice and dismissed the alarmed children.

The three white members of the Brown band then split up. One of them escorted the Bryne brothers to Harpers Ferry. Cook himself, with one of the blacks, remained at the schoolhouse as guards. The third of the Brown band, C. P. Tidd, took the four other blacks back to the Kennedy Farm to procure another wagon load of arms. Some four hours later they returned, their mission fulfilled.

Upon the return of Tidd and his task force in the late afternoon, Cook decided to find out what had transpired at Harpers Ferry. He took with him one of the blacks, who had armed himself with a double-barreled shotgun. The two men had gone but a short distance before a black woman they met informed them that hard fighting had been going on in the town. Learning that Brown was hemmed in, Cook sent his black companion back to the schoolhouse to inform Tidd.

Cook, after reconnoitering, saw himself that Brown's position was hopeless, troop re-enforcements having been coming into Harpers Ferry all day from surrounding counties. His range of choices very narrow, Cook made his way back to the schoolhouse, only to find it deserted. Tidd, with one of the blacks, had gone to the Kennedy Farm, seeking the assistance of the three men. Tidd, upon leaving, had stationed the other blacks "in good position in the timber back of the schoolhouse." They had, however, disappeared before Cook's return.[12]

Not tarrying at the abandoned building, Cook made his way to the Kennedy Farm, where he joined his three white companions and the single black. The five men gathered some blankets and prepared, as a precautionary measure, to spend the night some yards from the farmhouse itself. About three o'clock in the morning one of the Brown men, happening to awaken, discovered that their black companion had left. Alarmed, the four members of the Provisional Army hastily left the region, now convinced that flight was their only recourse.

Their instincts were sound; the black who had disappeared would soon divulge their whereabouts. This informer, along with the other Washington-Allstadt slaves, would return to their masters on the following night, some hours after Brown's surrender.

What of the slaves who remained in the besieged engine house? Originally there had been a total of twelve slaves—the seven belonging to Allstadt, the four from Washington's house, and the one belonging to Daniel Moore, a neighbor of Allstadt. Of this total, five had been assigned to the Kennedy Farm operation. This left seven at the engine house, four of whom belonged to Allstadt. A walled partition separated these blacks from Brown's men and their ten white prisoner-hostages, but movement from one compartment to the other was as simple as it was apparently continuous.

The role of the blacks in the engine house, including that of Shields Green, is not easy to assess accurately. The bulk of the evidence comes from sources hostile to Brown—the official reports from military and state government sources and the testimony of the ten prisoner-hostages. The blacks in the engine house gave Brown only "involuntary assistance," according to the official report of Robert E. Lee. One of the prisoners, John E. P. Daingerfield, said that the blacks carried "awkwardly and unwillingly" the spears placed in their hands. John H. Allstadt bore similar witness, testifying that the seven blacks in the engine house "did not appear hostile to anyone." A local newspaper, the *Shepherdstown Register,* reported that one of Washington's slaves not only refused to accept a pike but when told that he was free and should fight with his liberators, replied that he "was free enough before you took me. I am not going to fight until I see Massa Lewis fighting, and then I fights for him." [13]

Two of the slaves, both of whom were destined to be fatalities, appear to have taken a more prominent role than the others. Twenty-year-old Phil, whom Allstadt rated as his most "valuable fellow," was given a set of mason's tools and proceeded to drill port holes in the windowless walls. When the engine house was captured, Phil was committed to the Charlestown jail, apparently on the charge of sympathizing with the invaders. A week later, however, and before his case could be investigated by the magistrate, he died of pneumonia.

Jim, a slave coachman whom Colonel Washington had hired from Dr. W. M. Fuller of Winchester, willingly accepted a pistol and a supply of ball cartridges from Brown's men. He had "joined the rebels with a good will," reported the Virginia Committee of Claims in turning down Dr. Fuller's petition for recompense.

When the engine house fell, Jim fled. He succeeded in reaching the Shenandoah only to be drowned, giving his pursuers the grim satisfaction of fishing up his body.

As for Shields Green, he was, like the rest of Brown's men, armed with a rifle, a revolver, and a sheathed butcher knife. The guns he used "rapidly and diligently" during the Monday morning of the occupation. Colonel Washington found Green's behavior "impudent" in the forenoon but far less cocky as the day wore on and Brown's situation worsened. Undoubtedly the passing hours of the late afternoon and early evening brought to the beleaguered raiders the realization that the engine house, like the town itself, had become a trap. From a military standpoint Harpers Ferry was practically untenable, as its Civil War defenders would also learn.

Shortly before midnight the outlook of the hard-pressed band became even more ominous with the arrival of federal troops under Robert E. Lee. On learning that a number of white citizens were being held as hostages, Lee decided that for their protection he would wait for daylight to strike. "During all this time no one of Brown's men showed the slightest fear, but calmly awaited the attack," wrote one of the prisoners, John E. P. Daingerfield.[14]

Calm waiting would avail the raiders little, however, the end coming with almost merciful speed. Early the next morning a detachment of marines battered down the engine house doors and within five minutes Brown was forced to surrender. The triumphant troops bore an order from Colonel Lee not to injure any of the slaves in the engine house unless they offered resistance.

Shields Green apparently tried to take advantage of this concern for the property of the masters. Before coming from behind one of the engines, where he had been stationed by Edwin Coppoc, he laid down his weapon, pulled off his cartridge box, and assumed the air of one of the Washington-Allstadt slaves. It was a futile ruse, Colonel Washington quickly informing the troops that Green was a member of Brown's party.

An hour or two later Lee wired the Secretary of War: "Please direct me what to do with Brown and the other white prisoners."[15] The Provisional Army had run its course in less than two days.

Ten of its twenty-two men were killed and seven were captured, with Brown among the latter. Four non-Brown whites lost their lives, a marine and three Harpers Ferry residents, one of them Fontaine Beckham. To this number must be added Beckham's black assistant, Hayward Shepherd, and the slaves Phil and Jim.

When Brown took possession of Harpers Ferry he expected that he would be quickly joined by white farmers and farmhands, mountain people, and blacks, free and slave. He told one of his prisoners that he expected to have 1500 men by Monday noon, a point of time only some fourteen hours after he had entered the town. He was disappointed "in his expectations of aid from the black as well as the white population," reported Colonel Lee.[16]

The slave-owners and the Southern press would not fail to call attention to this apparent lack of response by blacks. Harpers Ferry would be remembered for "the entire disinclination of the slaves to insurrection, or to receive aid for that purpose," asserted two members of the Mason Committee, Senators Jacob Collamer and J. R. Doolittle. Governor Henry A. Wise of Virginia gave assurance that there "was no danger from our slaves or colored people." A Baltimore daily asserted that the failure of the slaves to join the Harpers Ferry proceedings, except under duress, "will not be without its usefulness." [17]

White Southerners insisted that Brown was ignorant of the bonds of affection between the slaves and their masters. Speaking on the Senate floor, J. M. Mason of Virginia said that Brown's failure was due to the loyalty of the slaves, "to the affection, the kindness, the love which they bear to their masters and to their master's homes." The *Richmond Whig* asserted that the chief unhappiness of the slave was his apprehension that he would be abducted from his humane master and comfortable home and be taken to the free North or to Canada. The able Virginia lawyer, William Green, in an exchange of correspondence with John A. Andrew of Massachusetts, said that Brown had made a "fatal misapprehension as to the contended happiness, cheerful submission, and attached fidelity of our slaves." [18]

Governor Wise received a letter demanding that he take away Colonel Washington's commission for permitting himself to be taken prisoner when all he had to do was to give one yell to his Negroes and they would have made short the work of the raiders. Joseph Barry would relate the story that while cornered by four of Brown's men on a side street in Harpers Ferry, he had been rescued by Hannah, slave of Margaret Carroll, who had protectively extended her arms in front of him and begged that his life be spared.[19]

Virginians were told of blacks, slave and free, who offered their services in keeping the peace and preserving the status quo. On the day that Brown was captured, a group of blacks in Georgetown informed the mayor that they were at his service for suppressing the outbreak at Harpers Ferry and maintaining law and order. Lomax B. Smith, who in 1824 had the honor of shaving Lafayette, tendered his services and those of his friends to the mayor of Richmond. They were, according to Smith, ready to go to Charlestown either as fighting men or in the capacity of body servants. The Richmond correspondent of the New York *Herald* reported that a group of prominent members of the state legislature were thinking of raising a regiment of free blacks of good character to repel any future invasion by the types like Brown.[20]

It appears, too, that some slaves did not want to be left out in defending the way of life they knew. Bawley, a slave in Culpepper, was advertised as having received his master's permission to go to Charlestown to take a shot at an abolitionist. The *Richmond Enquirer* reported that a number of slaves in Staunton had wanted to contribute to the fund for the Harpers Ferry volunteers, following the lead of two free blacks who subscribed $5 each. The *Richmond Whig* voiced the wish that Governor Wise had constituted the guard at Charlestown entirely of slaves "with the exception of one white man to 10 Negroes." [21]

To dramatize their affection for blacks who had spurned the invaders, the whites of Harpers Ferry region buried Hayward Shepherd with military honors at Winchester. There was a procession through the streets, led by the mayor and the leading citizens, followed by a band, three companies of militia, and "several hundred" citizens. An elderly black clergyman read the burial service. It would not be the last time Shepherd would be honored by the local whites.[22]

The loyalty of blacks was not the only reason advanced by white Southerners for Brown's failure to win their support. The region's writers and cartoonists made much of black fear and fright, a staple of antebellum folklore in the region. The only emotion evidenced by blacks, wrote Senator Mason on October 21, 1859, was alarm and fear. Slave state whites reassured one another with stories of blacks who took to their heels at the approach of Brown's men, hiding wherever they could—in barns and stables and under hay ricks. Neither threats nor promises could induce "this good-humored, good-for-nothing, half-monkey race" to join John Brown, wrote David H. Strother, a Virginian.[23]

Loyalty or fear were not the only reasons why many of the slaves who were aware of Brown's raid did not join it. A slave's experiences left him with a sense of suspiciousness, of self-protectiveness. The slaves in the Harpers Ferry region had no foreknowledge of the Brown raid—they had known nothing of his plans or of the man himself. They had no way of knowing whether he could be trusted. Slaves had heard stories of dishonest liberators who made a business of reselling them to their masters or to the lower South. Hence some of them may have held back, as the *New York Times* put it, "not because they loved Virginia more but because they loved Louisiana less." [24]

Some slaves may have been reluctant to join any foray in which a white was the leader. J. Sella Martin, himself a former fugitive, said that slaves would not bring themselves to trust whites unless the latter furnished a demonstration involving bloodshed. "They have," explained Martin, "learned this much from the treachery of white men at the North, and the cruelty of the white men at the South, that they cannot trust the white man, even when he comes to deliver them." [25]

Slaves in and around Harpers Ferry, however unschooled, had some sense of relative numbers. They knew that the mountainous region in which they lived was hardly teeming with blacks. The band that invaded Harpers Ferry was hardly reassuring as to head count —a most unimpressive figure of nineteen, the other three having remained at the Kennedy Farm.

Quickly suppressed, the Harpers Ferry expedition was over before many slaves could possibly have joined it. Very likely the raid would have drawn more blacks if it had lasted a bit longer. William A. Boyle, a Chambersburg physician, informed Governor Wise that "a portion of our Negroes" knew of the foray and would have joined it had it not come to so abrupt an end. The Harpers Ferry slaves, wrote Frederick Douglass, were sensible enough not to shout before they got the prize.[26]

One of the raiders who escaped, C. P. Tidd, reported that the Allstadt-Washington blacks who had made the trips to the Kennedy Farm were overjoyed at the prospect of being free but had gone back to their masters after they learned that Brown had surrendered. Two of these slaves told him that they had planned to escape during the coming summer, a not uncommon goal for bondmen in the region: "Slaves on Virginia's northern borders found it easier to run away than to conquer their freedom," wrote the *National Era*. In his annual message to the state legislature in December 1859 Governor Wise struck the same note: "It is no solace to me that our border slaves are so liberated by this exterior system, by this still, silent stealing system, that they have no need to take up arms for their own liberation."[27]

The efforts by white Southerners to disparage the valor of a Shields Green and to honor a black like Hayward Shepherd were grounded in part in deep-seated psychological necessities. Despite their avowals of confidence in the loyalty or in the timidity of the slaves, Harpers Ferry had a profoundly emotional impact on Virginia and her sister slave states. Brown had struck at more than a little town of a few thousand inhabitants. He had struck at the greatest anxiety of the white South—the fear of a servile insurrection.

George Sennott, a lawyer for Brown, reported that he found Charlestown to be in a state of excitement and suspicion resembling insanity. This apprehension was not confined to the Harpers Ferry theater—the John Brown foray deeply affected white Southerners everywhere, cutting across political and social lines. "John Brown did not only capture and hold Harpers Ferry for twenty hours," wrote Osborne P. Anderson, "but he held the whole South." [28]

Many in the North believed that the South over-reacted to Harpers Ferry. Northern newspapers carried the story of a Harpers Ferry farmer, James Moore, who mistook the cry of the whippoorwhills for the screams of his neighbors being murdered by abolitionists and blacks and rode into town calling upon the people to arm themselves. J. Sella Martin charged that at Harpers Ferry if a rat struck his tail against the lathes the whites in the house would organize a search party, "taking good care always to make a Negro go before." One New York daily was critical of white Southerners for their propensity to see danger in the merest trifles, finding abolitionists behind every bush and treason in every peddler's pack. Another daily in the same city editorialized that if an outbreak of such small proportions as that of John Brown had taken place in the North it would have been put down by the village police whereas in a slave community it required "the interposition of Governors, Presidents, marines, militias and mobs." [29]

The white South, however, did not measure Brown's raid by the size of the invading party—they measured it in terms of its possible chain reaction on the institution of slavery. Harpers Ferry revived memories of previous slave uprisings. The white South, wrote Charles H. Langston to a Cleveland daily, saw in every colored man the dusky ghost of "General Nat Turner." [30]

Harpers Ferry strengthened the Southern belief that the abolitionists, despite their protests to the contrary, were bent on fomenting slave rebellions. Brown's band, moreover, had included five blacks, making the experience all the more traumatic for the white South. A black weekly asserted that Virginia would never have trembled at 17 or 1700 white men in arms, even if they had all been John Browns. It was the 5 black men, armed to the teeth, and the 500,000 black men in their midst, "armed with a quarrel," who caused the Virginians to shudder in fear.[31]

Seeking to forestall another Harpers Ferry, various Virginia counties organized and strengthened their mounted patrols, authorizing them to arrest any outsider who could not furnish a local person who would vouch for him. Hand weapons experienced a sales boom. Within a four-week period Baltimore arms dealers sold over 10,000 pistols to Virginia buyers. "Colt ought to do something handsome for Brown's family," observed the *Springfield Republican*. The governor of Maryland, Thomas H. Hicks, ordered special "police or scouting" detachments for the counties that bordered Virginia—those of Allegany, Frederick, and Washington.[32]

The whites at Harpers Ferry had reason to be nervous about the loyalty and conduct of the local blacks. On the night Colonel Washington was taken a free black who had been visiting among the slaves had not raised the alarm at Charlestown, leaving its inhabitants to find out about the raid from other sources and several hours later. Train engineer William Wooley reported that before the early morning train which had been halted at Harpers Ferry was permitted to resume its journey some 300 slaves had gathered around the cars, shouting that they wanted their freedom, having been slaves long enough.[33]

A great change came over the Harpers Ferry slaves immediately after the raid, wrote local resident Jennie Chambers. They were not as reliable as before, often congregating without their masters' knowledge. Another resident of the neighborhood, Presbyterian minister Charles White, wrote on November 10, 1859, that "several masters have been beaten or attacked by their servants." A Northern journalist reported that Harpers Ferry blacks "burned with anxiety to learn every particular" of the raid, although they feared to show it. But whatever one found out, the others soon knew— "they have a pretty effective and secret Free Masonry among them." [34]

Harpers Ferry whites sought to pretend that the local blacks were indifferent to the raid rather than "burning with anxiety" about it. But in the weeks after the raid there could be no pre-

tending about the unprecedented number of fires in the county.
Night after night, reported a Richmond daily, "the heavens are
illuminated by the lurid glare of burning property." The torch was
put to stock yards, barns, stables, haystacks, and agricultural implements, causing a general suspension of work on some farms.
Wheat was thrashed earlier than usual, its owners not daring to
let it stand in stack until the other fall work had been done, as was
customary before the raid. In a letter to his wife, dated November
12, Brown expressed his disquietude about "the fires which are
almost of *daily and nightly* occurrence in this *immediate* neighborhood," fearing that "we shall be charged with them." [35]

The alleged arsonists could not be identified but most people
believed that they were Negroes, as Colonel J. Lucius Davis, commanding the troops at Harpers Ferry, wired Governor Wise on November 19. This belief that blacks were behind the burnings was
strengthened by the fact that included among those suffering loss
of property were three of the jurors who had tried and convicted
Brown, among them the foreman of the jury, Walter Shirley.

Driving from Harpers Ferry to Charlestown on the eve of
Brown's execution, newspaper correspondent Murat Halstead
called to the attention of his traveling companion, the superintendent of the rifle works, the marks of recent fires along the route.
"The niggers have burned the stacks of one of the jurors who found
John Brown guilty," explained the superintendent. Wheatland, the
home of George W. Turner, a Harpers Ferry victim who had not
been liked by the blacks, was set to fire. His brother, William F.
Turner, had several of his horses and sheep die suddenly, as if by
poison. "Reports of alarm still come in," wrote Robert E. Lee on
December 6 from Harpers Ferry where he had been sent "to look
after the friends of Mr. John Brown." [36]

The misgivings of the whites at Harpers Ferry and elsewhere in
the South were not allayed by the trial and imprisonment of Brown
and his men. During this period between their capture and their
hanging, their words, written and spoken, and their bearing evoked

a widespread sympathy and admiration in the North, thereby vexing white Southerners and deepening their fears.

Brown and his men were tried at Charlestown, the county seat of justice. On October 24, a week after the raid, the five of them were brought into the courtroom, with Copeland and Shields handcuffed together. The prisoners listened to the grand jury indictment—treachery, "conspiring with Negroes to produce insurrection," and murder in the first degree. Each of these offenses carried the death penalty.

The judicial process would permit no delay. Brown, the first of the group to be tried, was found guilty nine days after his indictment. Given permission by the court to say why he should not be sentenced, Brown gave a short speech, moving in its sentiment and language. Had he interfered on behalf of the rich and powerful, he said, he would have been praised rather than punished.

Taking note of the Bible used in the court proceedings, Brown stated that his reading of the Holy Scriptures had told him to remember those who are in bonds as being bound with them. Despite his years he was still too young to "understand that God is any respecter of persons." He had, he continued, believed that in working for God's despised poor, he had not been wrong, but right. If the court deemed it necessary that his life should be forfeited and his blood mingled with that of millions "in this slave country whose rights are disregarded by wicked, cruel, and unjust enactments," so be it. This last speech of Brown's was "unequalled in the history of American oratory for simplicity and power," wrote Thomas Wentworth Higginson nearly fifty years later in a black monthly.[37]

With Brown's case disposed of, the Virginia court tried the other four who were indicted with him, Green and Copeland coming before the jury during the latter part of the same week. Green was brought to trial on November 3 and found guilty on November 4, the jury deliberating for one hour.

Green's quick conviction was due to no fault of his attorney, George Sennott of Boston. In defending his client the young Sennott picked flaws in the indictment, stating that the statute under which it was issued was loosely drawn and that no proof could be produced that Green had conspired with slaves to foment insurrection. Sennott's technicalities were overruled by the court and his keenly drawn arguments, although eliciting compliments from the opposing counsel, Andrew Hunter, influenced the jury not at all.

The twelve men brought in a verdict of guilty on all three counts, but consented that the charge of treason be dropped inasmuch as a black man, not being a citizen according to the Dred Scott decision, could hardly be termed a traitor. This ruling that Negroes had no treasonable capabilities drew the ire of the young black abolitionist, William J. Watkins: "It was the climax of tyranny to rob us of the paltry privilege of being traitors to this devil-inspired and God-forsaken government." [38]

Copeland's trial was of a pattern with that of Green, and like Green he was found guilty of murder and of inciting slaves to rebel. As in the case of Green, Sennott's defense of his client was spirited. He challenged the court's description of Copeland as a free man of color, pointing out that in Southern states a black was presumed to be a slave unless otherwise proved. Sennott also argued that to put a pike in a slave's hands was not tantamount to inciting him to revolt.

Two days before his trial, Copeland had been interviewed by two United States marshals, one of them, Matthew Johnson, from his own home district in Ohio. In answering one of the seventeen questions they put to him concerning the raid, Copeland said that Brown intended nothing more than to run off the slaves. Based on this "Confession," as Copeland's statement came to be called, Sennott argued that his client might be charged with stealing slaves but not with inciting them to rebel.[39]

The verdict in the trial of the Brown supporters was highly predictable. On November 11 Judge Richard Parker sentenced each to be hanged by the neck until dead on December 16, the two blacks in the forenoon and the two whites, John E. Cook and Edwin Coppoc, in the afternoon. Asked if they had anything to say as to why sentence should not be passed, Green said he had nothing to say and Copeland said nothing at all. All four received their sentence with "great firmness," although some of the spectators, almost in spite of themselves, were sniffling. Judge Parker himself showed signs of being deeply moved.

Sentenced on November 2 to die on December 2, Brown made the most of his last month, greatly influencing public opinion in the North. His quiet self-possession in jail won admiration. In his final bold effort to free the slaves he seemed to have liberated himself from private ghosts. It was as though an outer turbulence had been transformed into an inner tranquility, as though he felt he had found rest beyond the river even while still on this side of the Jordan.

Brown's peace of mind owed something to the kind treatment he received from John Avis, the county jailer. Repeatedly referring to the considerate attitude of Avis, Brown informed his family that he was in the custody of a jailer "like the one who took charge of Paul and Silas," and that kind hearts and kind faces "are more or less about me." In a codicil to his will, Brown left Avis a Sharpe's rifle. Two days after Brown's death, Avis sent $2.00 to his widow. Born in the vicinity, Avis had been a childhood playmate of Martin R. Delany. It was Delany's belief that Avis treated Brown with such marked consideration because he knew of Brown's acquaintance with him. It may be, however, that Avis, like many others, had come to admire Brown for his courage and dedication.[40]

Like others who came within earshot, the jail attendants soon came to know Brown's views. To one of the guards he told the story of Toussaint L'Ouverture, ranking him with Socrates, Luther, and John Hampden. For a dozen years, Brown said, he had read everything he could find on Toussaint.[41]

Newspaper reporters kept the jailed Brown and his views before the public. Having used his rifles, said Wendell Phillips, Brown began to use the press: "Having taken possession of Harper's Ferry, he began to edit the *New York Tribune* and the *New York Herald* for the next three weeks." To journalists Brown was "good copy," and invariably quotable even though his views were

well known. In his interviews with reporters he frequently referred
to the plight of the blacks, on one occasion, for example, stating
that he respected the rights of the poorest and weakest of the
colored people just as much as he did those of the wealthy and
powerful. In answer to one correspondent's question about intermarriage, he replied that although he was opposed to it, he would
prefer that a son or daughter of his marry an industrious and
honest Negro than an indolent and dishonest white man.[42]

Brown cordially received visitors except for clergymen who
supported or condoned slavery. He refused to accept the ministra-
tions of such pastors, informing them that they stood more in need
of prayer than he. Brown let them know that to him a clergyman
who was not against slavery was an abomination to God. "I of
course respect you as a gentleman," he told the Reverend James H.
March, "but as a *heathen* gentleman." [43] In Brown's theology no
slave-owner could be a Christian.

One of Brown's more highly acceptable visitors was Rebecca
Spring of Perth Amboy, New Jersey, a foe of slavery. As a result
of her visit to Brown's cell, Mrs. Spring received a letter from
Jonathan C. Gibbs of Philadelphia, a black graduate of Dartmouth
College and later destined to hold a high public office in Florida.
Gibbs invoked heaven's blessing upon her for sitting with Brown
and quietly knitting. Brown, he added, gave to this wicked world
the highest illustration of the power of divine principle working
on the hearts of men.

When black Samuel Jackson of Ohio learned that Lydia Maria
Child had requested permission to visit Brown and nurse his
wounds, he asked the well-known abolitionist and author to send
him a picture of her in the act of pouring oil on Brown's wounds.[44]

It was Brown's letters from his prison cell that were to give him
much of his historic fame. His punctuation remained his own and
so did his spelling. But his Harpers Ferry experience seemed to
have given him a new eloquence, a touch of the poet infusing the
roar of the prophet. "Where," asked Thoreau, "is our professor of
belles-lettres, or of logic and rhetoric, that can write so well?"
Brown's more than one hundred jail-written letters quickly found
their way in print, their recipients sensing their importance.

Brown's last writings bore his anti-slavery and equalitarian principles. In his long letters to his family he restated convictions with which they were familiar. In his first letter to them dated October 31, 1859, he urged them never to forget the poor "even though they may be as black as Ebedmelech, the Ethiopian eunuch, who cared for Jeremiah in the pit of the dungeon; or as black as the one to who Philip preached Christ." His last letter to his family urged them to abhor with undying hatred that sum of all villainies—slavery.[45]

Brown's letters from Harpers Ferry consistently expressed a broad humanity. He informed one correspondent that he had tried to better the condition of those "who are always on the under-hill side." To another he sent word that he went to his death cheerfully on behalf of those millions who had no rights that this "great and glorious Christian nation" was bound to respect. He besought Alexander Ross not to give up his labors for the poor that cried and for those who were in bonds. His letter to the Reverend H. L. Vaill had a note of benediction: "May the God of the *poor & oppressed* be the God & Savior of you all." [46]

Brown's views were reflected and confirmed in many of the letters he received. "Please remember me to all those noble prisoners, colored as well as white," wrote his daughter Ruth from North Elba. In mid-November he received a letter from a group of blacks in Chicago expressing deep sympathy, offering prayers, and pledging material aid to his family. A week later came a letter from a group of colored women in Brooklyn commending him as one whom America would one day regard as its greatest patriot. When they viewed things from a religious viewpoint, continued the women, the earth was not worthy of him, that his spirit yearned for a higher and holier existence.[47]

Writing from Kendalville, Indiana, on November 25, Frances Ellen Watkins, a slender and graceful public speaker and poet, with a soft and musical voice, expressed her thanks to Brown. She did so, she said, in the name of the young girl sold from "the warm clasp of a mother's arms to the clutches of a libertine," and in the name of the slave mother, "her heart rocked to and fro by the agony of mournful separations." Closing her long letter in a vein reminiscent of Brown's benedictory tones, Miss Watkins asked him to convey her sympathy to his fellow prisoners, telling them to be of good courage and to seek a refuge in the Eternal God.[48]

Writing to Brown was but one of the ways in which Northern Negroes expressed their feelings about him. Like most of his admirers they judged his Harpers Ferry venture by the motives which prompted it. As one black spokesman put it, "Men will soon begin to look away from the plot to the purpose." [49] Bible reading blacks felt that although Brown had not set at liberty those who were oppressed, he had proclaimed the acceptable year of the Lord.

As the most prominent black of his day and a close acquaintance of the captured leader, Frederick Douglass would of necessity have something to say. On Tuesday, October 18, while the headlines were carrying the news about the raid, Douglass was in Philadelphia, filling a speaking engagement. Near the close of his lecture on "Self-Made Men," he digressed to speak of Harpers Ferry, calling it the legitimate fruits of slavery.[50]

The applause was deafening but hardly reassuring. Douglass felt that he might be in danger of being seized as a Brown accomplice or an accessory before the fact. Hastening to his home in Rochester he proceeded to destroy any papers or letters that could be used to implicate him. He than fled to Canada, a preliminary step to embarking for the British Isles.

A black weekly deplored the flight of Douglass as not worthy of the man or the occasion, stating that it was not the response a man of heroic mold should have taken in so sublime a drama. J. Sella Martin criticized Douglass for "writing letters from the broad latitude of Canada West." Douglass had long been planning to make a trip abroad, however, and it was well for his safety that he sped up his timetable by a fort-night or so. He would have been seized before he got out of Philadelphia had not telegraph operator John W. Hurn, an admirer of his, delayed the delivery of a dispatch to the city sheriff instructing him to arrest Douglass.[51]

Governor Wise wanted Douglass badly. On November 6, 1859, he urged special prosecutor Andrew Hunter to get an indictment against Douglass, pointing out that if the latter had incited, aided, or abetted the Harpers Ferry foray he violated the laws of Virginia and could be demanded of England or any of the states of the Union. A week later Wise again urged Hunter to "have a bill found against" Douglass. In an attempt to speed matters along, Wise employed a detective, Bryon W. Barnard, whose specific duty was "to find out the *whereabouts* of the Negro Frederick Douglass and keep an eye on his movements and associates." Hired at $100 a month, and given the name, "C. Camp," Barnard was to "ascertain when and where a requisition of arrest could reach Frederick Douglass" and the best means of getting him to Virginia.[52]

On December 21 Wise addressed 200 Southern medical students at the executive mansion. In the address Wise expressed his vexation at his failure to get Douglass. If, he said, he had had one good, well-armed steamer in Hampton Roads, he would have placed it on the Newfoundland banks with orders to remove Douglass from any British packet he might have boarded. Wise said that he would have instructed the captain of the Virginia vessel not to hang Douglass before "I had the privilege of seeing him well hung." Wise had received a letter from a Mississippian suggesting a lesser penalty: "If you manage to get holt of that Boy, and send him to me I will make my Negro Jim take him out and whip him until he says thank you Sir, or Please Master." [53]

To justify his flight and to explain his connection with the Harpers Ferry affair, Douglass wrote a long letter to a Rochester daily, under the date of October 31, a letter which was very widely reprinted. In it he gave unstinted praise to Brown, reflecting the views of the overwhelming majority of blacks. Brown, wrote Douglass, was a "noble hero" who had shaken the foundation of the American Union and whose ghost would haunt the bed chambers of Virginia slave-owners, filling them with dread.[54]

Douglass' flight had caused him to cancel a speaking engagement in Boston, the so-called Fifth Fraternity Lecture. As a substitute, the managers selected Henry David Thoreau, who had once spent a night in jail for refusing to pay poll taxes as a protest against slavery. Delivering a ninety-minute plea for Captain Brown, a classic of its kind, Thoreau opened his address by saying that the reason why Douglass was not there was the reason why he was.[55]

To ascertain the reaction of New York blacks to Harpers Ferry was the assignment of a reporter from one of the city's dailies. The first thing he found out was that the blacks preferred to "keep shady" on the topic, being reluctant to express any opinion whatever. As he pointed out, blacks were always suspicious of white reporters, even on relatively trivial matters. When the subject was insurrection, they were even harder to draw out, their utterances taking on the form of riddles "dark as the Delphian oracle." The reporter was, therefore, frank in admitting that his impressions were formed from "dark hints and innuendoes" rather than from direct assertions.

Within these limitations he learned that one group of blacks believed that the slave states were destined for trouble, with the flames lighted at Harpers Ferry spreading to the banks of the Mississippi, carrying desolation to some and emancipation to others. Another and much similar group of blacks believed that Harpers Ferry signalled the coming of the irrepressible conflict and that its arrival might as well come then as later. Another group condemned, or, as the reporter sagely added, professed to condemn, the Harpers Ferry foray, holding that it was suicidal and would exasperate the whites, thereby rivetting slavery more securely.[56]

Some New York blacks apparently preferred to express no interest in Harpers Ferry, thereby drawing the ire of a black correspondent of the *Weekly Anglo-African*. "Are our young men gagged by the Metropolitan Hotel?" he asked. "Does Col. Fifth-Avenue or Com. Washington-Square or Murray-Hill tell his colored waiter or coachman that if he dare say Captain Brown is a hero, he shall not pass around the silver tray in his family, or sit in the box of his handsome coach, or wipe the kitchen of his palace?" [57]

The sermons and speeches delivered in New York by blacks

left no doubt as to their sentiments toward Brown and Harpers Ferry. On the Sunday following the raid, Henry Highland Garnet told his congregation that it was the duty of every freedom-loving person to affirm the rightness of the raid and that anyone who could not do so had better keep still. Ten days later in the lecture hall of the church, a plain brick structure supported by four pillars, Garnet asserted that the only right slavery had was to die. In a speech that the New York *Herald* described as "not distinguished by a tone of moderation," Garnet said that Colonel Washington had not slept soundly since Harpers Ferry, even though the sword of his great ancestor hung above his bed, and that the time was nearing when slaveholders would not dare to go to bed at all. Brown had made one mistake, continued Garnet. He had thrown away $20,000 when $20 would have done the job. "All that was needed was a box of matches in the pocket of every slave, and then slavery would be set right." [58]

At Shiloh the following night J. Sella Martin, dressed in black and wearing a Byron collar, held forth in a similar vein at a public lecture at which "a black man sold tickets outside and black man took them inside. A black man played the organ and a black boy managed the organ-bellows." Martin's topic was a eulogy to Nat Turner, in which he gave great praise to Brown. Invoking a third figure who sought to stir the slaves in Virginia, Martin declaimed that if he had the language of Gabriel he would say, "Brethren, let us rise and liberate John Brown." From the audience of 800 came "tremendous cheers." [59]

Later that week at a meeting held in the city and designed "for all who loved liberty rather than slavery," James Green, a former fugitive, urged his listeners to get a gun and to use it when necessary. Another speaker, J. J. Simons, said that blacks should follow Brown's example and that this was not to be done by prayer, the best prayer for the slaveholder being powder and shot. [60]

Similar sentiments about Harpers Ferry and its leader were echoed by black speakers elsewhere. Speaking to an all-white audience at Brockett's Bridge, New York, William J. Watkins extolled Brown, calling him a hero as brave and holy "as ever the sun flashed on." Watkins added that the slaves were destined to be free even though they might have to wade through seas of blood. A gathering of blacks at the Zion Church in Providence, Rhode Island, although calling attention to their abhorrence of bloodshed and civil war, expressed their full sympathy with their friend, Captain Brown, proclaiming him a hero, a philanthropist, and an unflinching champion of liberty.[61]

In Pittsburgh at a meeting of blacks headed by such local leaders as John Peck, Lewis Woodson, Jr., and Benjamin T. Tanner, a resolution was adopted declaring that "We see in the Harpers Ferry affair what Daniel Webster saw when speaking of Crispus Attucks, the black revolutionary martyr who fell in Boston—viz: 'the severance of two antagonistic principles.' " [62]

Blacks in Cincinnati, meeting on November 14 to petition the state legislature to pass a stronger law against kidnaping, adopted a resolution declaring that the death of Brown and his associates would mark an era in the abolitionist crusade.

In Cleveland a well-attended meeting of Negroes passed a resolution declaring that it was a duty of the "freemen" of the North to go to Charlestown and liberate John Brown. The *Cleveland Plain Dealer* voiced a sharp disapproval: "It never rains but it pours, the treason is falling in torrents, and from black clouds." More fallout from dark clouds came from a convention of Ohio blacks who approved a resolution, worded by John Mercer Langston, hailing Brown and his men as the "Heralds and Prophets of that new lesson, the lesson of Insurrection." [63]

The fugitives in Windsor, Ontario, whom Brown had rescued earlier that year, were deeply affected by his capture, weeping when a newspaper reporter read to them his speech at the time of his sentencing by the court. Two of the seven said that they would willingly die in his stead. Another one of them remarked that if the Bible were true, John Brown, as one who lived by it, would surely be rewarded by "old Master" on High.[64]

On one thing about Brown all blacks seem to have been in agreement—their single-minded negative reaction to the charge that he was mentally unbalanced. In an effort to save Brown's neck, and without his knowledge, his counsel collected nineteen affidavits attesting to his insanity. Overruling his attorney, Brown repudiated this plea and the court upheld him. The insanity of Brown was rejected by both sides. To white Southerners such a ruling would have left them without a culprit and without a cause for their alarm. To abolitionists such a ruling would have deprived them of a hero-figure and potential martyr.

Blacks particularly would have none of the insanity theory. An editorial in *Douglass' Monthly* asked whether heroism and insanity were synonomous in the American dictionary. Anyone who would declare Brown insane would have sent Gideon to a madhouse, put Leonidas in a straitjacket, treated the defenders of Thermopylae as demented, and shut up Caius Marcus in bedlam. J. Sella Martin asserted that if Brown were mad, his madness not only had "a great deal of 'method' in it, but a great deal of philosophy and religion." [65]

Blacks held that society, rather than John Brown, was deranged. They were innately suspicious of such a charge against any friend of theirs. They were accustomed to hearing that reformers, particularly those who championed blacks, were wrong in the head. They knew that any white who advocated equal rights for blacks was likely to be regarded by any other whites as being not sound of mind. Blacks did not want their heroes put down.

Convinced of the sanity of their advocate and friend, his black admirers awaited with mounting emotion Brown's day of execution, and that of four of his Harpers Ferry associates scheduled for two weeks later.

❧ VI ❧

HANGING DAYS
IN VIRGINIA

The John Brown of the second Revolution
is but the Crispus Attucks of the first.
John S. Rock, Boston, March 5, 1860

John Brown's last day was peaceful enough on the surface. The sky
was sunny; nature was at its serenest for that time of year. All was
quiet in Charlestown, most of its citizens remaining at home to
protect their property in case of trouble. They had no cause for fear.
The military authorities had taken every precaution to thwart any
rescue attempt, as commanding officer William B. Taliaferro had
assured Governor Wise on the preceding day.[1]

As Brown left his cell for the last time he was permitted to say
a word to the other captives as he passed down the corridor. Going
first to the cell jointly occupied by Copeland and Green, he exhorted
them to conduct themselves as "becomes a man." He then handed
each a twenty-five-cent piece, telling them it was a keepsake from
him.[2]

As Brown descended the steps of the jail he did not kiss a black
baby, contrary to a widely circulated story that he did. From the
time he left his cell until he mounted the scaffold, Brown was
flanked by jailor Avis on one side and by sheriff James W. Campbell on the other. As soon as the trio stepped outside the jail they
were surrounded by soldiers, thus preventing direct contact with the
public. No black baby was in sight, General Taliaferro having

ordered, on November 28, that women and children be excluded from the grounds. Four days earlier Governor Wise had directed Taliaferro to see to it that women and children remained at home.[3]

Apparently the only black on the field was William Brent, the governor's body servant, and he never got nearer than within fifty feet of the scaffold. A good hour before Brown left the jail the streets had been cleared except for those persons charged with official duties to perform. A few blacks on the surrounding hills or at the windows of distant dwellings might have caught a glimpse of the proceedings.[4]

The story that the about-to-be-hanged Brown kissed a black baby was the invention of a newspaper reporter, Henry S. Olcott, whose story appeared in the *New-York Tribune*. As Brown stepped out of the door, wrote Olcott, he saw a black woman with a child in her arms. "The twain were of the despised race for whom emancipation and elevation to the dignity of children of God, he was about to lay down his life." Breaking his stride, Brown "stooped over and, with the tenderness of one whose love is as broad as the brotherhood of man, kissed it affectionately." [5]

If the colored baby were Olcott's brainchild, its acceptance as fact owed a little to John Brown himself. Three days before his execution he had expressed the wish that at the time of his "judicial murder" his religious attendants be confined to "poor *little, dirty, ragged bare headed, & bare-footed Slave boys; & Girls;* led by some old *grey headed Slave Mother.*" [6] It was therefore in character for Brown to have kissed a black baby had there been an opportunity.The fact that the story was symbolically true, if historically inaccurate, was enough for Brown's followers. Kissing the black baby quickly became an imperishable part of the Brown legend, spurred on by John Greenleaf Whittier and a trio of painters who were inspired by his lines.

"Brown of Osawatomie" was Whittier's most influential poem as it was the most widely read single writing on Brown. Two weeks before Brown's day of execution Lydia Maria Child, an abolitionist associate of Whittier, asked him for something ("a dirge, or martyr's hymn, or whatever") for the John Brown meeting to be held in Boston on December 2. Whittier did not make that deadline,

but a few weeks later he published a poem on the baby-kissing
scene, its two opening stanzas running thus:

> John Brown of Osawatomie
>   Spake of his dying day;
> "I will not have to shrive my soul
>   A priest in Slavery's pay.
> But, let some poor slave-mother
>   Whom I have striven to free,
> With her children, from the gallows-stair
>   Put up a prayer for me!"
>
> John Brown of Osawatomie,
>   They led him out to die;
> And lo!—a poor slave-mother
>   With her little child pressed nigh.
> Then the bold blue eyes grew tender,
>   And the old harsh face grew mild,
> As he stooped between the jeering ranks
>   And kissed the negro's child! [7]

Following Whittier's example the prolific Mrs. Child turned out
a poem for the occasion. Hers ran seven stanzas, of which the following is typical:

> As that dark brow to his upturned,
> The tender heart within him yearned;
> And, fondly stooping o'er her face,
> He kissed her for her injured race.[8]

Whittier's poem, writes Cecil D. Eby, made Brown's kiss the
most famous in American history and perhaps the most famous in
all history, excluding that of Judas. By the magic of Whittier's
pen, "the fable that might have died as journalism was thereby
perpetuated as literature." [9]

Although an instantaneous success, Whittier's poem would not
stand alone in its popular appeal. The Brown–black-baby theme
attracted painters, beginning with Louis Ransom in 1860, his

"John Brown on His Way to Execution" being widely exhibited in city halls. Not one to miss out on a public attraction, P. T. Barnum exhibited the painting in his museum in New York for two months in 1863, withdrawing it in July in order to save the building from destruction during the anti-Negro riot that broke out during that month. In 1863 and 1870 Currier and Ives lithographed the Ransom painting, selling thousands of copies, especially to blacks. In 1867 Thomas S. Noble produced a similar mass-appeal painting, "John Brown's Blessing," exhibiting it in Boston in December of that year and in New York the following month.[10]

Although focusing on Brown and the baby, neither Ransom nor Noble had actually shown them in the act of kissing. Thomas Hovenden concentrated on this feature in his striking, "The Last Moments of John Brown," produced in 1884. Hovenden had spent more than a year on the commissioned work, including a visit to Harpers Ferry. Hence, however dubious the incident itself, the oil painting was careful as to authentic detail down to the last button on a militia man's uniform. Lithographed many times before coming into the possession of New York's Metropolitan Museum of Art in 1897, Hovenden's creation immediately struck the public fancy while simultaneously impressing the professional critics.

To stand before it, wrote the *Philadelphia Inquirer,* was like being a witness to a "thrilling tragedy." The *Chicago Daily Inter-Ocean* called it the best American historical painting yet produced, an opinion with which the *New York Times* fully concurred. Appraising it in equally unrestrained terms, the *Magazine of Art* proceeded to assert that the incident upon which the painting was based was "well established fact." But, added the magazine's critic, true lovers of art need not be disturbed even if some doubt as to the incident still lingered. They need only be reminded of one thing— "the fact that so popular a legend has been created and has gained such a foothold within our own generation, would only go to show the mythopoetic process which, according to Mr. J. Addington Symonds, is necessary to the creation of works of art, is still at work." [11] But whatever the necessary ambiguities between art and nature and regardless of the skepticism of the sticklers for fact,

Hovenden's picture fixed itself into the hearts and minds of tens of thousands, taking on a life of its own.

The baby-kissing story was kept alive by black speakers, their sentiments much the same as those voiced by Robert Purvis at the annual meeting of the American Anti-Slavery Society in New York in May 1860: "Who can look at the noble hero and see him stoop on the way to the scaffold to kiss the Negro child, and not be struck with admiration at his fidelity and sublime consistency?" The story would be kept alive by the periodic emergence of persons purporting to have been eye-witnesses to the kissing. Inevitably, too, someone would surface who would claim to have been the baby Brown had kissed.[12]

If Brown had no contact with a black young one as he stepped from the jail, he did leave a prophecy. He handed to jail guard Hiram O'Bannon a statement he had written earlier that morning, his final words of revelation to his countrymen:

> I John Brown am now quite certain that the crimes of this *guilty land: will* never be purged *away;* but with blood. I had *as I now think: vainly* flattered myself that without *very much* bloodshed; it might be done.[13]

Brown went to the gallows in complete possession of himself. He knew how to die, although an unsympathetic Baltimore newspaper observed that the way a man died was "no proof of the justice of his cause or the purity of his intentions." [14] When the trap door was sprung, Brown fell five inches and soon his lifeless body was dangling against the noon-day sky. After thirty minutes the attending physicians mounted the thirteen steps to the scaffold platform and pronounced him dead.

"We are very apt to sympathize with almost anybody who is going to be hung," observed George Sennott, one of the Brown defense attorneys.[15] But the hanging of John Brown brought him more than sympathy—it brought him canonization. The hour of his hanging was the hour of his glorification—"Martyr Day," as blacks called it. On that Friday, deeply moving exercises were held in cities and towns throughout the North.

These meetings were marked by the conspicuous presence of blacks. Indeed in many instances the meetings were initiated and conducted by them. "Negroes were the chief actors in creating excitement in many of the towns and cities," wrote a New York newspaper.[16] Moving from east to west, we might well take note of a cross-section of these commemorative meetings on December 2, both for their impact in fixing Brown's fame and for the prominent role which blacks played in them.

In Boston on December 2 it would hardly be accurate to say, as did one reporter, that the Negroes seemed determined "to pass the time as gloomily as possible." But their mood was somber and funereal. To them it was a day of fasting and of prayer. Many of them wore crepe on their arms, a practice largely confined to blacks. Some of the crepe arm-bands were decorated with rosettes or pictures of John Brown. By prior agreement all black stores and business places were closed and draped. "Dark barbers darkly doomed their razors to one day of rest; at dinner waiters were abstracted; to get one's boots blacked was difficult; to have a carpet shaken impossible," observed the New York *Herald,* accurately enough, but unable to resist a touch of raillery in dealing with people of color.[17]

That night the abolitionists held a standing-room-only meeting at Tremont Temple, with 3000 gathered outside. "Tremont Temple was crowded with people of all colors, mostly black, however," wrote one reporter. Of the speakers, among them William Lloyd Garrison and James Freeman Clarke, none was more eloquent than J. Sella Martin, then pastor of the Joy Street Baptist Church. Telling the audience that he fully endorsed Brown's course, Martin said that the only difference between Brown and patriots of the Revolutionary War was that his program was designed to help black men. Martin upbraided the slaveholders, defended the blacks from the charge of having failed to rally behind Brown, and closed with high praise for the man himself. "Though his body fall, the spirit of slavery and despotism falls with it, while John Brown goes up to heaven." [18]

The journalist who reported that all the colored people of Boston and vicinity were present at Tremont Temple did not give note to the predominantly black meeting held at the Twelfth Baptist Church that night. This meeting, the culmination of three meetings held there that day, was itself part of a continuous prayer meeting which had begun the night before and would not end until the following day. In the forenoon the speakers included the church's able pastor, Leonard A. Grimes, a former runaway, and Charles Lenox Remond. Those giving addresses during the two-hour afternoon session included William C. Nell. Many remained after the meeting, singing anti-slavery songs, "so worked upon were their feelings." The songs they sang were not specified in the record but they might appropriately have sung the Negro spiritual, "My Lord, What a Mourning." Like its predecessors the evening session "was one of no little impressiveness." [19]

Among the many attending all three sessions was Lydia Maria Child, the white abolitionist and woman of letters. Mrs. Child found nothing, she said, to offend her sensibilities. True, some of the prayers were uncouth, she said, white men having deprived the petitioners of their "chance for mental culture." But many of the prayers were eloquent, she made haste to add. Moreover, she found no one there who questioned Brown's sanity or his right to be reverenced. Of one thing everyone appeared to be certain—Brown was a friend of the blacks, and he had proved it with his life. [20]

Blacks in other Massachusetts towns took note of the occasion. Those in Worcester, having pledged themselves to abstain from work from 11 a.m. to 3 p.m. on that day and to wear crepe for a week, held a meeting convened by the Anti-Slavery and Temperance Society of the Colored Citizens of Worcester. The gathering expressed its sympathies for Brown's family and also for the families of his black followers who were killed or captured. New Bedford blacks would hold a mass meeting two days later. In Lowell, a black mounted a bell on a cart and marched through the streets, the bell tolling. [21]

Blacks in New Haven, Connecticut, voted to set aside December 2 as a day of condolences "from this time forth." At Hartford on that morning, two men, one black and one white, went to the cupola of the State House and robed the statue of justice in black cambric. The highlight of a three-hour, packed-house meeting at Pratt Hall in Providence, Rhode Island, under white auspices, was an address by William Wells Brown, "The Heroes of Insurrection." Reportedly well received, Brown's presentation included "personal reminiscences of John Brown." [22]

The Martyr Day meetings in New England were peaceful. In Philadelphia the story was different. At a mid-morning meeting in National Hall, called by the abolitionists and attracting upward of 4000, an address by Robert Purvis brought the meeting to an abrupt close by orders of the police. A group of medical students from the South, along with other anti-Brownites, managed to keep their seats and, to a lesser degree, their tempers, while the other speakers held forth, including Lucretia Mott, Theodore Tilton, and Mary Grew.

The uneasy calm was shattered by Purvis. The dark deed of slaying John Brown, he said, would work out to the salvation of the slave, making it all the more difficult to keep down the irrepressible conflict between right and wrong, between honor and dishonor. Amid the growing swell of groans, hisses, and stamping of feet, intermingled with loud applause, Purvis expressed his unbounded admiration for Brown, calling him the great apostle of liberty and the Jesus of the nineteenth century. Catching the mounting excitement of the crowd, Purvis remarked that "the coward fiends of Virginia have sowed the winds, to gather, in the coming wrath of God, the whirlwind." [23]

He got no further, the rest of his address lost in the wild confusion that erupted. Fearing violence, the large contingent of policemen, taken from regular duty and stationed throughout the hall, proceeded to adjourn the meeting, letting the women out by the back doors. A Philadelphia paper expressed no surprise that blacks should revere John Brown but was shocked and bewildered "that placid and pleasant looking white women and white men should display any other emotion than loathing and terror at a conspiracy for butchery and devastation" such as Brown had engineered.[24]

The audience at National Hall included a "thick sprinkling" of blacks. Even more would have been present except for a similar Brown prayer meeting being held that morning at the Shiloh Baptist Church. Called mainly by black clergymen, this meeting had originally been scheduled for historic Bethel Church, which seated 2500 and was the largest black church in the city. Rowdies had threatened to burn down the building, worth $60,000, if such a meeting were held. The Bethel Trustees had then reversed their decision, opening them to bitter criticism. "Is it possible," wrote a black Philadelphian, "that a Negro church in the City of Brotherly Love is afraid of the consequences of offering prayers for a man who has sacrificed his life for the deliverance of their race?" [25]

At the filled church, with a thin sprinkling of whites, four clergymen, led by Jonathan C. Gibbs, were the chief speakers. Each struck a joint note of reverence for Brown and forceful action against slavery. Jabez Campbell, for example, invoked a covey of angelic hosts to guard Brown's immortal spirit: "Let cherubic legions attend him—let seraphims of glory be about him." Almost in the same breath, Campbell then expressed the hope that Brown's hanging be the opening wedge for the overthrow of slavery, an overthrow that he hoped would come peacefully but "let it come anyhow." After three hours the meeting came to a close, much to the relief of the strong detachment of police stationed outside the church.[26]

Neither of these two meetings in Philadelphia was attended by William Still. On that solemn day Mary Brown was a guest in his home and her hosts did not care to leave her. At the breakfast table she was composed, but as the hour of her husband's execution approached she grew paler and soon the tears came down. Folding her hands across her breast she looked straight ahead for nearly an hour, as if in reverie. Mary would not forget Still and his wife, sending them a lock of her husband's hair and, on a later occasion, conveying her sincere thanks through J. Miller McKim, a mutual friend.[27]

New York City blacks assembled in Shiloh Church, with eight

clergymen sharing the pulpit, including Charles B. Ray and Amos G. Beman. The prayers and speeches were punctuated by sobs. Henry Highland Garnet referred to Brown as the purest and best man of that age or any other. A visiting clergyman from Demerara, Robert C. Henderson, recounted the martyrdom of a missionary there, John Schmidt, who had preached insurrectionary sermons in 1823. Sampson White asserted that whatever need be done for liberty would be approved by God, even to the shedding of blood. A white abolitionist, William Goodell, questioned this sanction of violence, only to find himself the target of several of the black speakers. Backing down a bit before such a united assault, Goodell explained that he did not mean to rule out the right to use arms but that in his opinion the ballot box was better.[28]

One black woman who purposely absented herself from the memorial exercises at Shiloh was discovered by a New York daily which roundly disapproved of Brown. Interviewed on the streets while she was selling her "bunches of savory herbs," she condemned such activities as "burning up, tearing down and dragging out." Why, she asked, didn't Brown wait and pray until God chose to act peacefully? "Freedom was not likely to present itself to the black with both hands red," she added.[29] She spoke as one of the sparse handful of blacks who might have attended one of the numerous anti-Brown meetings held throughout the North.

At Albany the blacks met in the afternoon at the Hamilton Street Baptist Church, their hearts overflowing in gratitude to the city officials for having fired 100 guns in commemoration of Brown's death. At the white Wesleyan Church that night the featured speaker was William J. Watkins, his theme, "Blackmen, be of good courage, for the day of liberty draws near." Pausing in his hour-and-a-half address, Watkins challenged anyone in the audience to rise, face him, and say that John Brown was not right. No one arose among a listening group that included the militant black clergyman, T. Doughty Miller and the long-time black underground railroad operator, Stephen Myers.[30]

Among the other Northern cities and towns in which blacks held commemorative services, none exceeded the one in Detroit in its program variety. The meeting there, held at the densely packed

Second Baptist Church, was called to order by William Lambert, who had met Brown at the Chatham convention. The first half of the meeting had a distinctly religious flavor, with three clergymen holding forth on the Christian virtues of John Brown. Between their addresses a group called the Brown Liberty Songsters held the stage, one of their selections being an original composition, an "Ode to Old Capt. Brown."

Following the religious exercises the meeting assumed a more militant tone, with George Hannibal Parker, the president of the "Old Capt. John Brown Liberty League," in the chair. The main business was the adoption of a declaration of sentiments and resolves. Read by Lambert, this statement asserted that Brown had "put the liberty ball in motion," which would continue to roll until the slavery had been crushed. Brown was hailed as "our temporal redeemer whose name shall never die." While lavish in its praise of Brown, the declaration called on blacks to bestir themselves as a group, stating that an oppressed people's liberties were gained only in proportion to their own efforts.

From the floor came one additional resolution, a proposal that the city's black churches be dressed in mourning for thirty days. During that period each church would schedule a funeral sermon for Brown. The meeting adjourned with the singing of "On, on to battle—we fear no foe." [31]

Such public celebrations of Martyr Day were hardly to be expected by blacks in the South. Those at Harpers Ferry and Charlestown were reported spending the day gathering corn, felling timber, and making fences. A Scottsville, Virginia, paper carried the story that the local blacks spent the evening by staging a mock hanging of Brown, complete with a wagon and a scaffold. The black spectators, ran the the report, greatly enjoyed the proceedings, thereby convincing the reporter that they would if necessary arm themselves with Brown's pikes to defend their masters. [32]

If blacks in the South found it expedient to conduct themselves discreetly on hanging day, their brothers in Canada were not to be outdone in their commemorative observances. At Chatham "every moment seemed to be devoted to the sad event." Here five prayer meetings were held, beginning at four o'clock in the morning and divided between two black churches. At an evening mass meeting held at Princess Street Methodist Church, eulogies were delivered by two members of the Chatham convention, J. Madison Bell and James H. Harris. Toronto blacks had marked the day as one of prayer. At a memorial service at St. Lawrence Hall, the chief speaker was Thomas M. Kinnard, a former Chatham delegate. Kinnard said that Brown had told him that he intended to liberate the slaves or die in the attempt.[33]

Montreal blacks had previously set the day aside for prayer and fasting. In the morning they held a public meeting of worship, followed by a meeting devoted to expressing their sentiments about slavery. At Victoria, the capital of Vancouver Island, the blacks gathered to express their sympathy for Brown's widow and children.[34]

The removal of Brown's body to North Elba and its burial there gave a few of his admirers an opportunity for a final accolade. Eight members of the Medical College of Virginia had asked for Brown's body for dissection purposes, and a professor of anatomy, A. E. Peticolas, had expressed a desire for Brown and his men in order "to add their heads to the collection in our museum" if the cost did not exceed five dollars each. But Governor Wise delivered Brown's body to his widow's agents, as he had promised.[35] The corpse went first to Baltimore by the Saturday morning train and was then taken to Philadelphia, arriving at 12:40 p.m.

A large crowd had assembled at the station, including the mayor and the chief of police. The gathering, however, was predominantly black, including many colored women, "whose tongues ran rather free," and a committee of fifty men dressed in black who had come to escort the body through the city on its way to New York. Remembering the excitement at National Hall on the preceding day and dreading an outbreak, Mayor Alexander Henry hit upon a ruse to divert the crowd from the blocked depot. An empty, oblong tool-box on the train was draped in deerskin and solemnly conveyed to a furniture wagon by six policemen.

As the mayor had intended, this box was mistaken for the coffin. As the wagon that bore it pulled out of the station and moved rapidly through the streets, it was followed by a stream of blacks, many of them in a highly emotional state. Most of them were on foot but some rode in the several carriages that formed a part of the procession. The blacks had been led to believe that the wagon was on its way to the anti-slavery office, where the body would lie in state for a few hours. But when the wagon by-passed the office and pulled up at the Camden depot, its black followers realized that they had been deceived. In the meantime the real coffin had been quietly and safely driven to the Walnut Street wharf to catch the New York ferry.[36]

For the remainder of its five-day journey Brown's body had a relatively peaceful passage as it moved toward North Elba. Bells were tolled at most of the towns through which it passed, the people gathering to greet Mrs. Brown and express their sympathies. At Troy the Brown admirers included "not a few of the colored class," who pressed forward to shake his widow's hand and murmur condolences. The funeral party reached North Elba on Wednesday, December 7, after an all-day trip.[37]

At the funeral exercises, held at the unpainted farmhouse on the following day at 1 p.m., blacks made up "quite one half of the company." The eulogy was given by the matchless Wendell Phillips and the prayers were offered by Joshua Young of Burlington, Vermont, who in June 1854, had delivered a bitter attack on the Fugitive Slave Law in a sermon on the rendition of Anthony Burns. But the blacks were not left out in the funeral proceedings. "The singing was done by colored people chiefly," wrote Ruth Brown Thompson. As she listened to their voices "it seemed as though my dear father was with us in spirit and joined in the chorus of his favorite hymn, Blow ye the trumpet blow, to the tune of Lenox." [38]

The singing was led by an Epps family quartette, Lyman, Sr., his son, and two daughters, Amelia and Evelyn. Lyman Epps, Jr., would never forget the opening of the coffin, just before the final lowering. Brown, he said, looked as natural as if he were about to speak even though his throat bore a deep red ring where the rope had left its imprint.[39]

Brown's body was laid beside a massive boulder, an impressive physical monument somehow suggestive of the man. But his grave was something more than a site in the stillness of the majestic Adirondacks. It was, in the sentiment expressed by Frances Ellen Watkins on the day after his interment, "a new altar where man may record more earnest vows against slavery." [40]

From his post at Harpers Ferry on December 1, Robert E. Lee expressed the opinion that "tomorrow will probably see the last of John Brown. There will be less interest for the others." If Lee's first observation might be open to question, his second was not— Brown's captured followers received far less attention than he. Lydia Maria Child expressed regrets that Brown's jailmates did not have as many manifestations of sympathy to sustain them "as their grand old leader had," a circumstance she found all the more poignant since they were young and did not want to die. Frances Ellen Watkins held that because "Brown towered up so bravely," the public tended to overlook the other doomed men.[41]

Brown's fellow prisoners received fewer visitors—indeed Cook, Coppoc, Copeland, and Green requested that as few persons as possible be allowed to see them. Although overshadowed by Brown, however, the other prisoners were not forgotten by the foes of slavery.

During the first five weeks Sheilds Green occupied the same cell as Edwin Coppoc, sharing a common bed. But before Brown's execution there was a re-shuffling of cell-mates, with Green and Copeland being put in the same room. Reports on the behavior of the blacks varied. Writing in late November one reporter found them to be in good spirits and as having made professions of religious conversion.[42]

Another newspaperman reported the two black prisoners as keeping close to the stove and reading the Bible, the correspondent offering no explanation of Green's newly found acquaintance with the printed word. The two blacks had nothing to say, wrote one journalist, and were awaiting their fate "with a sullenness of determination characteristic of their race." A despatch from Harpers Ferry to a Baltimore daily on December 9 carried a terse sentence: "The

Negroes attract very little attention and no sympathy." The
staunch abolitionist J. Miller McKim construed it as a good sign
that so little was being heard of Copeland and Green. He reasoned
that if anything could have been said to their disadvantage, it would
have been said.[43]

Neither of them normally talkative, Green and Copeland had
little to say to reporters. David H. Strother managed to get a few
words from Green but he learned little beyond the well-known facts
that he had been a clothes-cleaner, that he could neither read nor
write and that he had been designated as a member-elect of the
temporary legislature Brown had planned to establish. Pondering
this information, Strother drily reported that he could have no
regret that Brown failed inasmuch as "the Congress of the proposed
Provisional Government would hardly be an improvement on the
present body." With his fixed ideas on Negro inferiority, Strother
likewise had an unflattering opinion of Copeland, even though he
was literate. Characterizing him as a "likely mulatto," who "would
make a very genteel dining-room servant," Strother wrote that
Copeland was cowed and penitent as he sat in jail, bewailing that
he had been deceived as to Brown's real plans.[44]

On the other hand, two of the prominent figures in the trials,
both white Virginians like Strother, held a high opinion of Copeland. Richard Parker, the presiding judge, said that Copeland "was
the prisoner who impressed me best." According to Parker, "there
was dignity to him that I could not help liking. He was always
manly." Andrew Hunter, the special prosecutor in the trials, held
a similar point of view. Copeland, he said, "behaved himself with as
much firmness as any of them and with far more dignity. If it had
been possible to recommend a pardon for any of them it would have
been this man Copeland, as I regretted as much, if not more, at
seeing him executed than any other of the party." [45]

Like his leader, Copeland wrote of his good treatment by the
jail personnel. In a letter to his brother Henry he referred to John
Avis as a kindhearted gentleman who had protected the prisoners
from insult and abuse. John Sheats, one of the assistants of Avis,
had also been considerate, added Copeland, doing all he could to
make them comfortable. Copeland closed by asking his brother to

do a favor for Avis or Sheats if it were ever in his power to do so, "for my sake." [46]

Copeland did not send a letter to his parents until nearly six weeks after he had been captured. He had, however, previously sent them word by Matthew Johnson that although troubled in spirit, he had made up his mind to meet his fate. In a letter of November 26 to his family, Copeland explained that his silence did not reflect a want of love for them but because he "wished to wait and find out what my doom would be." Perhaps remembering an earlier dictated letter from his unschooled father saying that his mother's sorrow knew no bounds, Copeland told his parents not to grieve for him but instead to remember that he would be dying in a holy cause, trying to liberate a few of his poor and oppressed people.[47]

During his final days Copeland sent a long letter each to two Oberlin residents, Addison W. Halbert and Elias Green. He told Halbert he was doing well in mind and body but he confided to Green, his best friend, that whenever he thought of the sorrow his death would bring to his mother and father he could not keep from shedding tears. To both correspondents he justified his participation in the Harpers Ferry raid. Like Brown he was confident that history would vindicate him. He assured Green that although the foray had not succeeded in freeing the slaves, it was "the prelude to that great event." [48]

On the Sunday before his execution, Copeland sent a letter to the Oberlin Anti-Slavery Society assuring his former associates that his heart was with them even though he would never attend one of their meetings again. Somberly he added that even as he wrote he could see from his cell the pile of pine boards assembled to construct the gallows upon which he would soon stand.[49]

On the morning of his hanging, Copeland sent a farewell letter jointly addressed to his parents, his three brothers, and two sisters. "The last Monday, Tuesday, Wednesday and Thursday that I shall ever see on this earth have now passed by," he noted. He spoke reassuringly of being reconciled to his fate, and he absolved everyone other than himself from any blame for his having joined John Brown. Though separated from his beloved ones on earth he would

meet with them in heaven, where they would not be parted by the
cruel monster, Slavery. A fine example of Christian resignation,
Copeland's letter prompted a Cleveland newspaper to observe that
heroism and a sense of man's humanity to man were not deficient
in the colored race. *The Provincial Freeman,* a black weekly published at Chatham, published this letter, jointly with Copeland's
letter to his brother, Henry, as a broadside.[50]

Copeland still had one last line to pen. The son of jailer Avis
asked him for his autograph. Copeland took a sheet of paper, placed
it on the book which he used in lieu of a desk, and proceeded to
write, "Jno. A. Copeland was born at Raleigh, North Carolina,
August 15th 1834." These were not deathless words, such as those
Brown handed to the jailer on his last morning, but they indicated
that Copeland did not expect his name to die and that he wished
to set the record straight as to a few vital statistics.[51]

The day of the hanging was clear and sunny, although the ground
was white and a cold wind was stirring. Two clergymen made
joint calls on the four condemned men, going from one cell to the
other. As in the case of Brown, armed guards were everywhere.
One of the military units, the sixty-man Fincastle Rifles, had a
black fifer, Daniel Hall, perhaps the only one of his color close to
the proceedings.[52] The atmosphere was less tense than at the Brown
hanging even though Cook and Coppoc had tried to escape the
night before, having sawed their shackles off with two knives, one
of which they got from Shields Green.

Scheduled to be hung before the two whites, Copeland and Green
left their cell at a quarter of eleven, their arms pinioned. Helped
into the open furniture wagon drawn by two horses, they took their
seats on their coffins. Flanked on each side by a company of rifle-
men, the vehicle moved from the jail. Within a quarter of an hour
the condemned men reached the field, and three minutes later they
were at the foot of the gallows. In the company of three clergymen
they stood for a few moments, Copeland quiet and Green's lips
moving as if in earnest prayer.

Exchanging farewells with the clergymen, both mounted the scaffold, their steps firm. The caps were fitted on their heads and the ropes affixed around their necks. Green was made ready first and just before his hands were joined he extended one of them toward Copeland, as if in a final goodbye. The two were then led forward to the trap, and the noose was adjusted to the hooks on the beam. At 11:11 Sheriff Campbell cut the ropes, thus springing the trap.[53]

Green died easily and within five minutes, his body having only a slight motion. It was in painful contrast that death came to Copeland. His body writhed in contortions. With his pinioned arm he tried to grasp the rope around his neck, drawing up his arms and legs and swinging to and fro. The index finger of his right hand was over his thumb and the index finger of his left hand was under his thumb, the other fingers curling inward. The rope slipped a bit, Copeland dying of strangulation.

After dangling for 31 minutes Copeland and Green were examined by three physicians, one of them Dr. John D. Starry, and pronounced dead. Profiting by the agonizing experience of Copeland, the officers in charge would give Cook and Coppoc a considerable longer fall than they had given the two blacks, resulting in a quicker death.[54]

That night the bodies of Cook and Coppoc were carried by Adams Express from Harpers Ferry to relatives in Williamsburg, New York, and Springfield, Ohio. The bodies of the two blacks never left the locality. Taken down by four guards shortly before noon, the remains of Copeland and Green were placed in plain poplar coffins, transported to a nearby field, and buried. The interment lasted for less than an hour, a group of students from the Winchester Medical College digging up the bodies to use them in dissection.

The disposal of the remains of Copeland and Green had been a matter of no small concern to abolitionists and to blacks. On December 14 seven white reformers in Orange, New Jersey, headed by Lucy Stone and her husband, Henry B. Blackwell, wrote to Governor Wise asking for the bodies. They said that they wrote on behalf of themselves and the other abolitionists of the town, men and women who felt honored to identify themselves in life and death with the prescribed race to which Copeland and Green belonged. They requested Wise to name an official to whom they should apply. The governor did not receive the letter until December 21, five days after the hanging, and evidently never sent a reply.[55]

On the day before the executions George L. Stearns, one of Brown's financial backers, sent a request, via telegraph, to J. Miller McKim asking him to obtain the bodies if nobody else claimed them. Stearns urged McKim to do all that he could in the matter lest the world say that "we honoured the White but forgot the Colored Brother." Mrs. Rebecca B. Spring of Perth Amboy also made an unavailing effort to get the bodies.[56]

Blacks in New Bedford, Massachusetts, appointed a committee on December 4 to correspond with jailer John Avis as to the impending disposal of the bodies. A group of New York City blacks expressed a similar concern, pointing out that however obscure and unknown Copeland and Green might have been, they were nonetheless of African blood, and they would be dying for the freedom of their race. The New York group said that it was desisting from any efforts of its own to procure the bodies, however, because they had learned of a similar effort being put forth by the blacks in Philadelphia.[57]

But the people of color in Philadelphia were having internal problems both over the request for the bodies of Copeland and Green and the holding of a memorial service for them on December 16. In line with black groups in some other cities, the members of the Banneker Institute, a self-improvement group founded in 1854 by younger men, had planned to commemorate the hangings on the day of their occurrence. To this end they had hired the Masonic Hall and engaged Jonathan C. Gibbs to deliver the eulogy, sending notices to four black churches. On the evening specified a large number of sympathizers came to the hall only to find it closed.

The agent of the Masonic Hall and two members of its board informed the Banneker Institute spokesman, David D. Turner, that they were fearful that the building would be burned down, white public sentiment being so strongly against Brown and his followers.

The officials said, however, that if Turner would assure them that no publicity would be given to the meeting they would grant permission. With a reporter from the *Weekly Anglo-African* already present, Turner was in no position to furnish such a guarantee. The board members thereupon refunded Turner his small deposit, the hall remaining closed. The crowd dispersed, doubly angry because it was then too late to find a substitute meeting place, unlike the instance, three weeks earlier, when Bethel Church had rescinded its permission for a John Brown service. The Banneker Institute subsequently condemned the two Masonic Hall board members and its agent, charging that they had showed a contemptible servility to the slave power.[58]

Philadelphia blacks also differed on the wording of a petition to Governor Wise. At the John Brown meeting held at Shiloh Church on December 2, a committee of three was appointed to write to Wise requesting the bodies of the two blacks who were to be hanged. On the following day the committee sent Wise a long letter, flattering him for his undying love for the Negro and pleading for his intervention on behalf of "those poor, miserably misguided men," Copeland and Green, who had "recklessly torn themselves from home and friends." The committeemen, Alfred M. Green, and two members of the clergy, Jabez P. Campbell and Jeremiah Asher, had couched their letter not in terms of their true feelings but in the hopes that soft language would be more likely to obtain the bodies or even win for the black prisoners a commutation of sentence.

Two weeks later when the committee letter became public, two meetings were held in condemnation of it. At a gathering in Wesley Church a number of speakers bitterly criticized the committee's reference to Copeland and Green as having been "misguided." At a later meeting at the Philadelphia Institute a series of resolutions was passed stating that the letter of the committee to Wise did not express the true feelings of the black community, and that said letter exhibited "a total want of dignity, frankness, and independence, that would crush its authors." Governor Wise took far less interest in the letter than did the Philadelphia petitioners, apparently not deigning to answer it even though it included a short postscript, addressed to "Most Honored Sir," asking that he direct his answer to Jabez P. Campbell, Box 430, Philadelphia Post Office, and concluding with "Profoundest Respect." [59]

Copeland's father, aided by the townspeople of Oberlin, tried hard to obtain his son's body. Two weeks before young Copeland's scheduled execution, his father sent a letter to Governor Wise asking his permission to send a "messenger," perhaps the congressman from his district, to take charge of the body. Copeland deemed it expedient to add that he never had the slightest foreknowledge of his son's intention to go to Harpers Ferry. [60]

Eight days after sending his letter Copeland wired the governor: "Will my son's body be delivered?" Yes, said Wise, in an answering wire, but only on the condition that the body would be given to a white person: "You cannot come to this state yourself." In a wire sent two days later, on December 14, Copeland requested that his son's body be delivered to K. H. Stevens "on order from Washington City." [61]

Stevens did not come to Charlestown. Instead he sent a letter to Sheriff Campbell requesting him to express Copeland's body to A. N. Beecher, mayor of Oberlin. Campbell referred the letter to General Taliaferro who ignored it on the grounds that he had received no instructions from Wise on the matter. [62]

The governor seemingly was prepared to deliver the body to an agent but not to ship it out. On December 17 Beecher wired him requesting that if Copeland's body had not been delivered to anyone, to send it to him via express and collect. Wise sent no reply, scribbling on the wire itself that he had previously notified Copeland's father that his son's body would have been handed over to a white person. [63]

On the eve of the execution the distraught parents of Copeland, having heard rumors that their son's body was to be taken to the medical college at Winchester, called at the home of James Monroe, member of the Ohio Senate and a professor at Oberlin, seeking his assistance. Against his better judgment but moved by Mrs. Copeland's entreaties, Monroe consented to make the trip to Winchester to try to recover Copeland's remains. Armed with Wise's wire to Copeland and carrying a letter of introduction to Judge Parker, Monroe left Oberlin on December 19 and arrived in Winchester two days later. Registering at the Taylor House he signed his name, "James Monroe, Russia," using the name of the township in which Oberlin was located. To have registered as a resident of Oberlin, with its reputation as an abolitionist hotbed, would have been inexpedient in view of the prevailing tension in the locality.

After private talks with Judge Parker and the president of the Winchester Medical College, followed by a meeting with the faculty, Monroe was sure that he would soon have Copeland's body. But he and the faculty reckoned without the students. As Monroe was awaiting a call from the undertaker who had been preparing the body for its journey, he opened the door to find instead a delegation of grim-faced young men.

They told him that the body of Copeland belonged not to the faculty but to the students—that they were the ones who had dug him up and that they alone had title to him. The meeting ended courteously enough, with the surprised Monroe saying that he would get in touch with the faculty. He quickly found that the faculty did not propose to have a show-down in the matter. A faculty representative advised him to abandon his mission, otherwise "the whole country about us would soon be in a state of excitement." [64]

Monroe may not have sensed it, but he faced some competition from within the faculty itself. On December 12 Medical Director Edmund Mason, in a letter to Wise, said that although he had a "dislike to trouble you about small matters," he sought his permission to obtain the bodies of the two blacks. His object, he explained, was to place their skeletons in the college museum, the need being pressing inasmuch as none of the eleven patients then in the hospital was sick enough to be in danger of dying. "By granting this request you will confer a great favor," Mason concluded. Two days later Wise replied to the effect that if the bodies of the blacks were "not demanded by their proper relatives," Mason had his consent "to receive them for the purpose named," assuming that he also obtained permission of the sheriff of Jefferson County.[65]

The opposition of the students and the college's need for skeletons meant that Monroe would leave empty-handed. During his short stay he had been permitted to view the unclad body of Shields

Green as it lay in a garret, frozen and bloody, its unseeing eyes staring upward. But at best this macabre sight was but the grimmest of recompenses for the journey. The Winchester Medical College would be burned to the ground by the Union armies less than three years later. With the disappearance of its buildings went, presumably, the remains of Copeland and Green.[66]

Monroe reached Oberlin on Christmas Eve, low in spirits and much reduced in purse, having paid considerable sums to the undertaker to prepare Copeland's body for a trip it would never take. Monroe's dejection, however, was short-lived. The day after his return from Winchester he attended a funeral service for Copeland and Green, an audience of over 3000 having gathered on short notice. The eulogy was delivered by Henry E. Peck who earlier that year had spent eighty-five days in the county jail for his role in the rescue of runaway slave John Price. In his address Peck said that at Harpers Ferry the Supreme Being had furnished for the Colored race a "not less firm, heroic and Christlike champion than had the white race in the person of the immortal John Brown." [67]

As he expected, Monroe was called to the platform to describe his trip to Winchester. As he proceeded to relate his story, the audience listened silently but sympathetically, as if they approved his course and absolved him of any blame for the mission's failure. But to Monroe the response that gratified him above all others was that of Copeland's parents. He had dreaded to face them, but he found that they were grateful to God and grateful to their neighbors. They were far more self-possessed than they had been at the memorial exercises held for Copeland and Green ten days earlier at the College chapel.[68]

The last two of Brown's captured followers, Aaron D. Stevens and Albert Hazlett, were put to death on March 16, 1860. Stevens had sufficiently recovered from his horrible wounds to face the gallows, and Hazlett had been tried and sentenced early in 1860, after having been captured in Pennsylvania and extradicted to Virginia. While in jail Stevens had received a letter from Frances Ellen Watkins, dated December 28, 1859, in which she enclosed a copy of her poem, "Bury Me in a Free Land." In his letter of acknowledgment, Stevens said that the poem went to the innermost parts of his soul.[69]

The poem was not new to Stevens. Oliver Brown, slain at Harpers Ferry, had carried a copy of it to Chambersburg shortly before the raid. According to Annie Brown, "all or nearly all" of the men stationed there said that they did not want to be buried in the land of the slave. "I have often thought and spoke of these verses," wrote Annie on May 29, 1860.[70]

Stevens was another who would not forget them. One week before his death he copied the poem in longhand for Mrs. Rebecca Spring; she found it in a trunk which he sent her enclosing those of his effects that had meant the most to him.[71]

Blacks did not sever their ties with Brown and his fallen comrades following the funeral exercises for them. The reverse was the case. Blacks would find a number of ways to demonstrate anew their lasting affection for the figures of Harpers Ferry and their deepened commitment to the ideals for which those slave-rescue-bent invaders had given their lives.

VII

THE NOOSE'S
BLACK SHADOW

Thus Liberty goes marching on
Step for step, with "hero John!"
In whom oppression basely slew
The bravest son e'er freedom knew.
J. Madison Bell, 1862

To blacks, as to other admirers of the Harpers Ferry raiders, there was no better way to honor the memory of those men than to raise money for their families. The men who accompanied Brown to Virginia were hardly affluent types. One of them, Dangerfield Newby, left a widow who was a slave. Four others, including Leary and Brown himself, had very little to bequeath to their impoverished widows. Five additional ones, including Copeland, left parents who were needy.

The financial plight of Mrs. Brown, as might be expected, drew especial attention. On November 11, 1859, her husband had advised her not to come to visit him in jail because the journey would take what little money she had. "For let me tell you," he admonished, "that the sympathy that is now aroused in your behalf may not always follow you. There is little more of the romantic about helping poor widows and their children than there is about trying to relieve 'poor niggers.'" On the following day in a letter to Lydia Maria Child, who had volunteered to nurse him, Brown replied that she might instead "give 50¢ to his wife and three daughters." [1]

The widow Brown was indeed hard pressed. Thomas Wentworth

Higginson, visiting North Elba shortly after Brown's death, learned that she had for a time been unable to pay the annual tax bill of $10, having managed to put aside that amount by the exercise of the most rigid economies, but having lent it to a poor black woman whose prospects of repaying it were slim.[2]

One of the earliest black donors to Mary Brown was Frances Ellen Watkins who sent her "a few dollars" on November 14. Miss Watkins sent a warm, accompanying letter, assuring Mrs. Brown that "a republic that produces such a wife and mother may hope for better days."[3]

The meetings held by blacks throughout the North on Martyr Day, December 2, accounted for a good half of the funds raised for Mrs. Brown by colored donors. From collections taken on that day, Philadelphia blacks placed $100 in her hands before she left the city in company with her husband's body. At the meeting held at Shiloh Church in New York City on December 2, the sum of $54 was collected for the widow. Assembling in Detroit on that day, the Old Captain John Brown Liberty League announced a donation of $25. At the meeting held by the blacks in Pittsburgh, $16 was taken up for Mrs. Brown, the identical amount contributed by blacks in Columbus, Ohio, at their Brown memorial exercises.[4]

Later that month the widow received additional sums from blacks in various towns. Holding a festival, Elmira blacks raised $30 for her. Those in Boston sent her $59 "in token of their respect and love for the Hero of Harper's Ferry." On December 20 a group of black women in Detroit sent her $20, "not as an act of charity but as a heartfelt offering of gratitude from those for whose cause you are now so sadly bereaved." Mary's letter of reply expressed her gratitude and good will. Similar thank-you notes went out to other black contributors, including one to the "John Brown Relief Fund" of New Haven for a gift of $12.75.[5]

Blacks in Ontario shared this sense of obligation to Brown's widow. At the memorial services held in Montreal and Toronto on December 2, collections were taken up for the Brown family. At Chatham ten days later a "grand soiree" was held at the town hall, the roster of speakers including three participants of the Chatham convention of May 1858. Capped by a supper prepared by the women, the soiree raised $62, of which $31.66 was sent to Mrs. Brown.[6]

At Simcoe a former stagecoach driver, Harvey C. Jackson, made a financial appeal directed to blacks throughout the province. Having read Brown's letter to Lydia Maria Child, requesting assistance for his family, Jackson wrote her on November 29 expressing a desire to be of help. "I beg to state," he added, "that there are but few colored persons in Canada who would not give something for such a noble and praiseworthy object." Without waiting for Lydia's reply, Jackson issued a printed broadside, "An Address to the Colored People of Canada," urging them to hold fund-raising meetings in every locality and to send the proceeds to Samuel E. Sewall, 46 Washington Street, Boston. A long-time abolitionist, Judge Sewall was then heading one of the groups raising funds for the Brown family. Jackson ended his "Appeal" with words of high exhortation.[7]

Although Jackson had assured Mrs. Child that the blacks in Canada were "far from a starving state," it is not likely that many of them sent anything to Sewall. Their giving was generally done in a less formal and more spontaneous manner than by making use of the mails.

The Haitian people, predominantly of African descent, were eager to help the widow of one whom they so greatly admired. Their newspapers were so full of Brown that they had little space for anything else, wrote a New York daily. In commemoration of him, religious services were held in several cities and towns throughout the island on January 20, 1860. On that day the Haitian flags flew at half-mast, and the houses were hung in black. At Port-au-Prince, the capital, an African prelate, Abbe Moussa, officiated at the high mass for the repose of Brown's soul. With over 3000 in attendance, the National Chapel was lighted by "an infinity of candles." [8]

Not content with honoring Brown in ceremonial fashion, the Haitians conducted a fund-raising drive for the families of the "martyrs of Harper's Ferry." From the people of Haiti, Mary Brown received a total of not less than $2239.99. In a letter to President Fabre Geffrard on April 16, 1860, John Brown, Jr., assured him that the Brown family had a warm feeling for Haiti, particularly admiring Toussaint L'Ouverture, whose soul "visits the cabins of the slaves of the South when night is spread over the face of nature." [9]

Four years later, in February 1864, the citizens of Aux Cayes would give $562.52 to Mrs. Brown and a like amount to the families of the other Harpers Ferry casualties collectively. James Redpath, the key figure in transmitting this money to the recipients, reported that the Haitians had done no act which had gained so much respect for them abroad since their forebears expelled the French more than half a century earlier.[10]

The Haitians would not forget John Brown. In November 1877 when John Mercer Langston, newly appointed United States minister-resident and consul-general, arrived at the presidential palace at Port-au-Prince to present his credentials, he saw a picture of John Brown on the palace walls, possibly a photocopy of a sculptured bust of Brown which President Fabre Geffrard had purchased seventeen years earlier. This was not Langston's only reminder of the man on that occasion. When the reception had run its course, Langston was ushered down the palace steps to the strains of the John Brown song played by the national band.[11] It was an especially moving experience for one who had known John Brown personally.

Some blacks made financial contributions to Mary Brown through non-black agencies. A printed circular issued by the Pennsylvania Anti-Slavery Society, soliciting funds for the families of Brown and his men, was signed by Passmore Williamson, J. Miller McKim, and Robert Purvis. At Cleveland a committee of five, which included Charles H. Langston, published a sixty-two-page booklet, "A Tribute of Respect Commemorative of the Worth and Sacrifice of John Brown of Osawatomie," to be sold on behalf of the families of the fallen men. At Springfield, Massachusetts, on December 2, 1859, the $25 collected for Mary Brown came from an interracial gathering.[12]

In contributing funds to Mrs. Brown, blacks did not forget that there were other families whose breadwinners had lost their lives in the raid. At Siloam Presbyterian Church in Brooklyn, a collection was taken up on November 24 for the families of the Harpers Ferry fatalities. The women of the New York Liberty Fund raised $54 for the families of the martyrs, thanks to a rendition of the oratorio, "Joseph," by the children of Colored Grammar School No. 2. The blacks in Simcoe, Ontaro, raised $3 for the "families of Brown and his fellow sufferers." [13]

With Green and Copeland leaving no dependents and with Newby's slave family out of reach, Lewis S. Leary's wife and child, Mary and Lois respectively, became the chief recipients of monies raised in black circles. The meeting at Shiloh Church in New York on December 2, 1859, which gave $50 to Mrs. Brown, gave $14 to Mrs. Leary. Later that month two black churches in Troy, New York, sent $7.04 to the young widow. In January 1860 a group of colored adolescents in Boston sent her the sum of $40. The largest single amount she received from a group of black Americans was $60, the gift of a group of New York City women in the spring of 1860. From the "Haytian John Brown Fund" Mary Leary received $209.35.[14]

Just as Mrs. Brown received monies from blacks, so Mrs. Leary received money from whites. Thaddeus Hyatt, a former associate of Brown's in Kansas, had raised a "John Brown Family Fund" of $6150 by mid-July 1860 despite having spent some 13 weeks in a Washington jail for refusing to testify before the Senate committee appointed to investigate the Harpers Ferry affair. Nearly one-half of this amount came from the sale of a photograph of a bust of Brown which the Boston sculptor Edward A. Brackett had made following a visit to the Charlestown prison where he took Brown's measurements. Of the total $6150 which Hyatt raised, Mrs. Leary received $250.[15]

The young black widow received some financial help from James Redpath. After her husband's death she had gone to Cleveland to live with her foster parents, the John E. Pattersons, who had adopted her as an infant. In February 1861, Mrs. Leary wrote to James Redpath thanking him for a copy of *The Public Life of John Brown* and informing him of her efforts to purchase the house in Oberlin she occupied when her husband went to Harpers Ferry. The house was going for $500, she added, and if she could borrow that amount she was sure that she could take care of herself and her baby, earning money through her trade as a milliner.[16]

The white friends of Brown would not forget Leary's daughter even after his widow remarried. In the early 1870's Redpath and Wendell Phillips provided the tuition and fees to send Leary's daughter, Lois Sheridan Leary, to a private academy in Lawrence, Kansas. Redpath considered the money well spent. "Ever since I have sent her to school," he wrote in November 1874, "she has sent me regularly the reports of her teachers and her (report) cards show that she had been a very exemplary pupil." [17]

In the spring of 1860 Mrs. Leary received $50 from the John Brown Fund of Oberlin. Interracial in composition, this organization had been formed for the purpose of erecting a monument to the Oberlin blacks who had fought at Harpers Ferry. Leary and Copeland were the only Oberlinites who took part in the raid. Someone on the original planning committee, however, had assumed that Shields Green once lived in the town or had once been a familiar figure there. This notion was quickly dispelled, the *Oberlin* Evangelist for February 1, 1860, pointing out that Green had never put his foot in the town "so far as is known." A month earlier the fund committee, in an "Oberlin Monument Circular" issued on December 29, said that they had decided to retain Green's name anyhow, explaining that they did so in the light of his manly conduct at Harpers Ferry, his heroic endurance in prison, and his courageous deportment at the gallows.[18]

Headed by a committee of eleven, including John Mercer Langston, the group started off well, raising $175 on the occasion of the funeral exercises for Copeland on December 25. But raising money for the "stone memorial" proved to be much more difficult than its sponsors anticipated, especially since five other collections for the raiders had been held in the town within a month. By mid-February 1860, some seven weeks after the effort had been launched, the total amount on hand was only $350.25. Deducting the $50 donated to Mrs. Leary, and $105 for operating expenses, the group had a balance of less than $200.[19]

Hoping to raise at least $300, the Oberlin group decided to broaden its list of potential donors, making an appeal throughout the North. For mass distribution it produced a circular which pointed out that Copeland, Leary, and Green were not merely local figures but were, on the contrary, *"representative men,* of whom every colored man should be proud." Hence, ran the circular, the Oberlin group would not wish to withhold from Negroes elsewhere "and indeed from anyone," the privilege of sharing the honor with them.

In only a few cities did blacks respond to this appeal to erect a monument at Oberlin to commemorate the manly virtues of Copeland, Leary, and Green. A group of Boston blacks sent $10 for the proposed memorial, and at Albany two churches took collections of unspecified amounts for it, one of them the white Wesleyan Methodist Church and the other the Hamilton Street Baptist Church, whose pastor was T. Doughty Miller.[20]

Pledging $50 "as a starter," a group of Detroit Negroes formed a Monument Committee, which included William Lambert and George DeBaptiste. The Committee sponsored a musicale on February 23, 1860, the master of ceremonies, William Lambert, introducing a variety of black singers and instrumentalists. The Committee reported that the musicale had been a success artistically, but they were silent as to the amount raised.[21] Possibly the Detroit group never reached its starting goal of $50.

Falling somewhat short of their financial mark, the Oberlin committee settled on something less ambitious than a large-scale monument. They contracted for a modest shaft, 8 feet high and weighing half a ton, placing it in the Westwood Cemetery. One side of this memorial stone carried the inscription: "These colored citizens of Oberlin, the heroic associates of the immortal John Brown, gave their lives for the slave." A second side of the cenotaph bore the date of the death of Leary and his age at the time of his death, and third and fourth sides bore similar vital statistics concerning Copeland and Green.

The stone at Oberlin honored three of the four dead companions of Brown. The only surviving black Harpers Ferry raider, Osborne P. Anderson, came in for his share of concerned attention by Brown-oriented groups. The John Brown Family Fund earmarked $50 for Anderson and the Haytian John Brown Fund sent him

$209.34.[22] To raise money for his own support, among other reasons, Anderson hit upon the idea of publishing and selling his version of the Harpers Ferry affair.

In the spring of 1860 he busied himself with raising money for the printing expenses of his projected manuscript. In April 1860 he addressed a Negro audience at a Baptist church in Toronto, informing them of his intention to bring out a first-hand account of Harpers Ferry and the role of blacks therein. To repeated applause he asserted that the full story of the black man's role in the wars of the United States and of Canada had never been told and that it was his aim to snatch from oblivion "the heroism of the colored men who nobly seconded the efforts of the immortal John Brown." [23]

Two months later at a meeting called suddenly and in secret by the Fugitive Aid Society in Cleveland, Anderson described his project and his need for money to carry it out. Ever since Harpers Ferry, he said, he had been "housed up," afraid to make his presence known, and hence unable to work for a living. As Anderson told of his plight and of his hopes the audience was deeply stirred: "Old ladies cried 'à la mode' and stout-hearted men were not a little affected by the scene." Only $18 was collected for Anderson, his appearance having been unexpected. With this in mind he left a forwarding address in Chatham to which donations could be sent.[24]

By mid-October 1860 Anderson had made arrangements to have his manuscript published, although he still was short of cash, writing to Richard J. Hinton on October 13 soliciting a loan.[25] Three months later the work was published, its title page reading, *A Voice from Harper's Ferry: A Narrative of Events at Harper's Ferry with Incidents Prior and Subsequent to Its Capture by Captain John Brown and His Men.* Published in Boston and bearing the note, "Printed by the Author," it was a thin volume of only seventy-two pages, the last ten of which consisted of borrowed poetry. Not ghost-written, *A Voice from Harper's Ferry* revealed a vigorous and original style, if somewhat florid and redolent of doomsday. Its first ten pages concentrated on John Brown and his intentions, as Anderson viewed them. In his search for examples and analogies Anderson ranged widely throughout history, apparently as familiar with the battle fought at Hastings in 1066 as the one waged at Bunker Hill in 1775.

In January 1861, the month in which the book appeared, a group of Boston blacks assembled in the Twelfth Baptist Church to honor the new author and to bid him farewell after a short visit. Eulogistic speeches on the man and his book were delivered by the cream of Boston's black reformers, among them J. Sella Martin, Leonard A. Grimes, George T. Downing, Robert Morris, and William C. Nell. More than one speaker supplemented his own inspiration, and complimented the guest of honor, with passages from *A Voice from Harper's Ferry*. Speechmaking was followed by refreshments generously furnished by caterer Downing and served in the church vestry. This farewell benefit brought Anderson nearly $100. Before departing from the city he left a supply of his books at the anti-slavery headquarters where they might be purchased for 15¢ each or $10 a hundred.[26]

Anderson peddled his small book, going from city to city. In Rochester he "disposed of quite a number" of them.[27] But he would not have many weeks to engage in this occupation. During the spring of 1861 the sectional crisis between the North and the South was ·steadily escalating, obscuring all else, including interest in Anderson's account of the Harpers Ferry raid that had done so much to bring matters to a head.

The Harpers Ferry affair made for a sharply increased tension and hostility in the North, particularly among abolitionists. Their dislike of violence, previously one of their proudest boasts, now yielded to their stronger desire to see slavery brought low. Even before Brown went to the gallows, William Lloyd Garrison had done an about-face on pacifism. "Brand that man as a hypocrite and dastard, who, in one breath, exalts the deeds of Washington and Warren, and in the next, denounces Nat Turner as a monster for refusing longer to wear the yoke and be driven under the lash," he wrote on December 1, 1859. During the course of the same week, one of Garrison's staunch followers, Henry C. Wright, delivering an address at Natick, Massachusetts, "made a non-resistant speech in favor of resistance." [28]

Abolitionist literature, hitherto more reflective than incendiary, reflected this mood of physical force. In the spring of 1860 the American Anti-Slavery Society published a thirty-six-page tract, "An Account of Some of the Principal Slave Insurrections . . . During the Last Two Centuries." In its December 1859 issue, *The Anglo-African Magazine* reprinted "The Confessions of Nat Turner," prefacing it with an editorial comparing Turner's methods with those of John Brown. Thomas Wentworth Higginson wrote an article on conspirator Denmark Vesey and another insurrectionist, Nat Turner, both accounts appearing in the sedate pages of the *Atlantic Monthly*. Higginson's sketch on Turner asserted that his plan and that of John Brown were both "deliberately matured; each was in its way practicable." [29]

Symptomatic of the new tone in the abolitionist crusade was the formation in Albany of the Irrepressible Conflict Society for Human Rights, its motto, "Eternal hostility to slavery." Organized over the weekend following Brown's execution, the interracial group, with T. Doughty Miller as secretary, vowed to aid in ending slavery by whatever means possible. The Society proposed to publish tracts and to sponsor a series of lectures by black orators "who are universally conceded to be so far ahead of their Anglo-Saxon brethren, because so many of them speak from experience, not only from what they have seen, but from what their frames have *felt*." Speaking in June 1860 in the Common Council Chamber at Utica under the Society's auspices, William J. Watkins used "bold and fearless language." [30]

Meetings held in 1860 by black reformers revealed a militancy unmatched in general by anything in the 1850's. At a meeting held on March 5, 1860, celebrating the ninetieth anniversary of the Boston Massacre and sponsored by the city's black reformers, John S. Rock asserted that the John Brown of the second American revolution was but the Crispus Attucks of the first. Rock's listeners, one-third of them white, were told that the only events in United States history worthy of commemoration were the birth of the American Anti-Slavery Society and the bold strikes by Nat Turner and John Brown.[31]

At the annual meeting of that Society, held in New York in mid-May, Robert Purvis likewise called attention to the mulatto who fell at the Boston Massacre. Purvis reminded his Cooper Institute audience that "it was a black man's blood that was first to flow in behalf of American independence." At this gathering the number of blacks in attendance was many times that of any previous annual observance, according to a local reporter. And, he added, "they manifested their interest to a remarkable degree when the plates were passed." [32]

Six weeks later on July 4 at a meeting held at North Elba and arranged by Richard J. Hinton in honor of Brown's memory, Osborne P. Anderson said that Brown's sacrifice would be richly repaid. Anderson spoke from a rude platform which had been placed on the huge granite boulder a stone's throw from the Brown family farmhouse. He informed the audience of some 1000 that this was the first occasion he had ever felt like taking part in the Fourth of July observance. Hitherto that day had been to him a lie, he added, one observer taking note of his thoughtful face and sadly earnest eyes.[33]

Three other black militants who had been invited to the North Elba celebration—Frederick Douglass, J. Sella Martin, and H. Ford Douglas—had sent word expressing their deep regrets at not being able to attend. In his letter Frederick Douglass referred to Brown as "*the* man of the nineteenth century," adding that he had little hope that slavery could be abolished by peaceful means.[34]

On that holiday H. Ford Douglas was in Framingham, Massachusetts, the featured speaker at an anti-slavery gathering held in a beautiful grove. Only twenty-eight, of light complexion and with curly black hair, Douglas delivered a lengthy speech, his voice "musical but manly." His closing minutes were devoted to a eulogy of John Brown, whom he said had gone to join the company of "the just made perfect." [35]

If observing the Fourth of July was something out of the ordinary for black reformers, the same could not be said for August 1. On that day in 1834 the act of Parliament freeing the slaves in the British West Indies went into effect and since that year the abolitionists, particularly those who were black, had set the day aside for special observance. As Frederick Douglass put it, "the black man had no Fourth of July here so he makes the First of August serve the purpose." [36]

On the initial August 1 after Harpers Ferry, the celebrations by blacks were, according to one of their periodicals, more numerous and spirited than ever before. The colored people of West Chester County, Pennsylvania, observed the day by gathering in a grove. Nearly one-third of the audience of some 4000 was white, including Lucretia Mott and Thomas Garrett. The orator of the day, Jonathan C. Gibbs, pastor of the First Presbyterian Church of Philadelphia, said that John Brown had added a new glory to the martyr's crown, and that North Elba was "our Mecca." Inviting his audience to stand symbolically with him in the shadow of the great rock where Brown was buried, Gibbs asked them to pledge themselves anew to God and to man that America would be free.[37]

At New Bedford, Massachusetts, blacks likewise assembled out-of-doors, at Arnold's Grove, for their August 1 celebration. One of the resolutions they adopted was a panegyric to John Brown. The occasion was marked also by the presence of two black military units, the Liberty Guards of twenty-two muskets from Boston, and their hosts, the New Bedford Attucks.[38]

The presence of two black military units at this First of August observance could hardly have surprised anyone. As in other areas of black protest, the Harpers Ferry affair had given a new vitality to the movement to bear arms. Early in May 1860 the Detroit Military Guards was formed. The blacks in Boston, meeting at the Joy Street Church on May 30, 1860, pledged a renewal of their fight to repeal the state militia law excluding them. The mass meeting voted its thanks to four of its number, J. Sella Martin, William C. Nell, John S. Rock, and Robert Morris, for their appearance before the state legislature urging the repeal of the hated color restriction.[39]

In one instance, it may be noted, the John Brown incident worked against a colored volunteer unit. Early in 1859 the Pennsylvania state militia had furnished forty muskets to a colored military unit. Two days after Harpers Ferry the Adjutant General of the State, E. C. Wilson, repossessed the arms, citing the raid as his reason.[40]

This action reflected something of the widespread anti-Brown sentiment in the North, a mood which gave rise not only to anti-Brown meetings, moved by a sympathy for the South and proclaiming a "save the Union" theme, but also by an attempt to disrupt pro-Brown meetings.

A case in point was the so-called "Boston Mob" incident at Tremont Temple on December 3, 1860. A group of the city's anti-slavery crusaders had scheduled a meeting to commemorate the deaths of John Brown and his black followers. According to an unfriendly local daily, "the parties who got it up were all irresponsible—a large majority were Negroes." Before the meeting got under way, a group of hired rowdies had assembled, bent on breaking it up.[41]

The announced theme of the meeting was, "How Shall American Slavery Be Abolished?" One of the earlier-scheduled speakers, Frederick Douglass, said that he advocated "the John Brown way." He got no further. The mounting chorus of boos, shouts, catcalls, and epithets drowned out his voice, full-throated as it was. The disrupters now went into their second phase—physical action—a group of them storming on to the platform. Fist fights quickly followed, with Douglass comporting himself "like a trained pugilist." Despite his valor he was ejected from the building, although not dragged out by the neck as was Franklin B. Sanborn. The Deputy Chief of Police and his squads of men were unequal to the task of bringing order, and the meeting petered out, a triumph for rowdyism.[42]

The admirers of John Brown, not to be intimidated, called for a meeting that evening at J. Sella Martin's Joy Street Church. The anti-Brown forces sent out posters, calling on all who would to join them in halting the meeting. At eight o'clock the filled church was surrounded by a crowd of milling disrupters who could not gain entrance. They were kept at bay by the police while the meeting within the church proceeded, its speakers including Wendell Phillips, John Brown, Jr., Frederick Douglass, H. Ford Douglas, and J. Sella Martin. Two weeks later Samuel J. May, writing in his diary on December 17, 1859, observed that John Brown, Jr., meeting him at the Syracuse depot, "told me of a conspiracy against the lives of prominent colored men and abolitionists."[43]

Northern hostility to abolitionism had its repercussion even in the field of interracial marriage. In Detroit this practice had been "quite common," wrote one reporter: "On almost any Sunday well dressed colored men may be seen walking the streets with their white wives." After the Brown raid, however, the 1838 law against black-white marriages was reactivated, leading to the arrest and fining of a black clergyman, William Berry, for officiating at such a ceremony.[44]

Northern condemnation of the Harpers Ferry raid was largely obscured by the deep feeling of hostility it engendered in the South. The incident contributed markedly to the mounting racial apprehension of white Southerners, thus giving momentum to the gathering storm between the two sections.

Southern fears that Harpers Ferry was more than the work of less than half a hundred men led to the formation of a United States Senate committee of investigation. When the Senate convened three days after the raid James M. Mason of Virginia made it a first order of business to recommend the appointment of such a body. Ten days later "The Select Committee of the Senate appointed to inquire into the late invasion and seizure of public property at Harper's Ferry" came into being. Mason was named chairman of the five-man committee. He had drafted the Fugitive Slave Law of 1850 and had been one of the prominent figures who had conducted a three-hour interview with Brown on the day he was captured.

No black witnesses ever appeared before the Mason Committee. On January 11 the Committee authorized the chairman to issue a summons, among others, to Lewis Hayden of Boston and "George De Bapt" of Detroit. On the following day an official summons was made to Hayden and DeBaptiste, ordering them to appear before the Committee on January 23 and January 27, respectively.[45]

Before the subpoenas were served on the two black abolitionists, Mason learned of their racial identity. The United States Marshal at Detroit had sent him a letter informing him that "this De Baptiste is a Negro, though a smart, intelligent fellow." Learning, too, that Hayden was not white, Mason hastened to inform the United States Marshal at Boston to withhold the summons, "Hayden being a Negro acting as Messenger at the office of the Secretary of State of Massachusetts." On May 24, 1860, Mason officially informed the other members of the Committee that the summonses issued to DeBaptiste and Hayden had not been served inasmuch as they were Negroes.[46]

Seeking to establish the fact that the Harpers Ferry affair was primarily a sectional conspiracy, the Mason Committee preferred to ignore any role that blacks might have played. Men like Mason tended to see blacks in a passive, acquiescent role rather than those of agitators and militants. This attitude toward blacks as non-participants was illustrated by the manner in which the Mason Committee responded to a petition from such quarters.

Early in June 1860 a group of Massachusetts blacks sent a petition to the Senate, praying that body to suspend the labors of the Mason Committee. Charles Sumner, a long-time friend to the blacks, presented the petition to the Senate on June 5, which in turn and on the same day, referred the request to the Mason Committee. Barely deigning to notice it, the Committee, within a week, passed a resolution stating that "the paper purporting to be a petition from 'citizens of the Commonwealth of Massachusetts of African descent,' " be returned to the Senator who presented it.[47]

In mid-June the Mason Committee terminated its work, unable to prove that the Harpers Ferry affair implicated any sizable roster of accessories who had furnished the raiders with money, arms, or munitions. Reluctantly the Committee had to admit that the invasion was largely the work of a very small group with even fewer accomplices who really knew just what Brown was up to. But such a conclusion of non-complicity was lost on a white South to whom John Brown had become an obsession.

By many Southern leaders, Brown's raid was used for the purpose of more firmly establishing the power of slavery's defenders. To many Southerners in public life, among them Governor Wise, the raid could be employed to make personal, political, or party capital. But such men were the beneficiaries rather than the instigators of the South's fears and resentments over Harpers Ferry, the raid having unleashed the latent dread of slave insurrection and black equality.

This feeling of bitterness and apprehension was reflected in the tightening controls on blacks, slave and free, throughout the South. Slave patrols were strengthened, as in Mississippi where a succession of flaming cotton mills hinted ominously at a wave of arson. In some communities the patrols were required to make their rounds more often. Slave quarters were carefully searched for firearms. A slave in Clarke County, Virginia, "Negro Jerry," was sentenced to hang for conspiring with slaves to rebel. His accomplice, Joe, was ordered sold out of the state.[48]

The brunt of anti-Brown sentiment fell upon the free blacks, old restrictions on them being enforced and new ones being added. Because of their possible influence on slaves, particularly as their abettors in insurrections, free Negroes were watched even more closely during a time of peril, real or fancied. At Hagerstown, Maryland, a black Methodist clergyman, Thomas Henry, was accused by Edward W. Beatty of having "tampered with slaves" and having been an acquaintance of John Brown. Beatty aired these serious charges in a letter to Governor Wise, who in turn relayed them to Maryland authorities. Fortunately for Henry he had a champion in Judge John T. Mason who informed Governor Wise that Henry was innocent, in his opinion, having done nothing more than to arouse "the suspicion which usually attaches to all itinerant colored clergymen." [49]

For free blacks in general, however, it was a time of troubles. In the wake of Harpers Ferry some Southern communities withdrew licenses permitting free blacks to carry firearms. The Arkansas legislature voted to expel all free blacks, and some other Southern states seriously considered following suit. In Alabama, local vigilance committees posted notices ordering free blacks to leave the state within ten days "or they will be visited upon." In March 1860 the Maryland legislature prohibited the freeing of slaves, by deed as well as by last will and testament. Along with other states Maryland also passed a law authorizing its free Negroes to renounce their freedom and to select for themselves a master or mistress.[50]

Freedom of assembly for blacks, always reluctantly permitted, was further circumscribed. In Washington the police were "very vigilant in searching out and breaking up all public and private assemblies of colored persons," wrote a correspondent to the *Anglo-African*. The municipal authorities countermanded permits previously given to blacks to hold balls and festivals. In nearby Baltimore the African Methodist Episcopal Church was not allowed to hold its annual conference, the Police Board ruling it unlawful under an old statue prohibiting non-resident Negroes from entering the state. Local blacks were problem enough, as the city fathers would soon learn when, on December 12, 1859, the colored caulkers held their annual ball and a police patrol, entering the hall at 4 p.m., found a portrait of Governor Wise drawn in chalk on the floor and "near it one of a huge Ethiopian, with inscriptions unfit to print." In another part of the hall a chalk likeness of Brown bore the words, "The martyr—God bless him." [51]

Whites, particularly former Northerners, who condemned the new restrictions on blacks, met with harsh treatment. Wishing to furnish proof of this climate of repression, the American Anti-Slavery Society issued in the spring of 1860 a 144-page pamphlet entitled, "New 'Reign of Terror' in the Slaveholding States for 1859–60." This anti-slavery tract was made up of excerpts from newspapers, most of them in the South. Four months later the Society published a 72-page tract that was similar in character, "A Fresh Catalogue of Southern Outrages Upon Northern Citizens."

The sectional rift which these pamphlets symbolized grew wider with the coming of 1861. It was in this charged atmosphere that the crisis came to a head on April 15 of that year. President Abraham Lincoln issued a call for troops to put down a rebellion following the seizure of a federal garrison at Fort Sumter in the harbor at Charlestown, South Carolina. "The red flames of the burning arsenal at Harpers Ferry reflect back the light from Charleston harbor," intoned the *Anglo-African*.[52] The editor of this black weekly may have sensed the symbolic relationship between these two trouble spots, but neither he nor many of his contemporaries could have sensed that the ensuing Civil War would last four years and turn out to be unparalleled in magnitude.

The red flames of the Civil War did not extinguish the name of John Brown, especially in the black community. The song, "John Brown's Body," alone would have kept his memory alive. Improvised during the opening weeks of the war by a Massachusetts regiment, the song immediately became popular with other troops, soon sweeping throughout the civilian North.

Among blacks it took on an even stronger hold combined with a more fervent expression. "The John Brown song was always a favorite," observed Thomas Wentworth Higginson in writing of the black soldiers in his regiment. An associate of John Brown, Higginson had felt an inner glow of satisfaction when he was offered a command of colored troops. "I had known and loved John Brown too well," he wrote, "not to feel a thrill of joy at last on finding myself in a position where he only wished to be." At an interracial Emancipation Proclamation Day celebration in Rochester, at which the praying and the singing were in the charge of the blacks, the John Brown song "seemed to have a new meaning to the audience." [53]

When the First Regiment of Kansas Colored Volunteers observed Emancipation Proclamation Day on January 1, 1863, they had their share of barbecue and "strong drink," but they would not close the day without pausing to pay their respects to the memory "of the immortal hero whose grave is cradled among the Adirondack Mountains," capping their tribute with the John Brown song by the entire regiment. In the spring of 1863 the Philadelphia Supervisory Committee for Recruiting Negro Troops issued a striking, tinted poster which devoted half a page to the five stanzas of "John Brown's Body." [54]

When the Massachusetts Fifty-Fifth entered the fallen Charles-

ton in February 1865 the John Brown song was on their lips. A
newspaper reporter was deeply moved by the scene:

> Imagine, if you can, this stirring song, chanted with the most
> rapturous, most exultant emphasis, by a regiment of Negro
> troops who had been lying in sight of Charleston for nearly two
> years—as they trod with tumultuous delight the streets of this
> pro-slavery city, whose soil they had just touched for the first
> time.[55]

Newly freed blacks in the South had a similar reverence for the
song, a sentiment often fostered by their missionary-minded teachers
from the North. Within a day or two after she had begun teaching
in the Sea Islands of South Carolina in early November 1862,
young Charlotte Forten had her pupils singing the John Brown
song. A black herself who personally knew the leading abolitionists
in Massachusetts, Miss Forten felt the full significance of a group
of newly emancipated youngsters singing a song about a man
who died for their kind. "I wish their old 'secesh" masters could
hear their former chattels singing the praises of the brave old man
who died for their sake," wrote Charlotte to William Lloyd
Garrison.[56]

At other schools for the former slaves the John Brown song
topped all others in popularity, including "Marching Through
Georgia." A typical school for freedmen might well begin with
prayer, followed by the reading of a Bible passage and the singing
of "John Brown's Body." [57]

At the long but continuously inspiring services held on Emancipation Proclamation Day, January 1, 1863, at Port Royal in the
Sea Islands, the song received its meed of attention. "The meeting,"
wrote one who was present, "was closed by 'John Brown' (which
all the colored people know) thundered forth from a thousand
voices." The combined chorus of black civilians and black soldiers
rendering this particular song deeply moved the sensitive Miss
Forten. "It was grand," she confided to her diary. At near-by
Beaufort later that year the blacks would toll the old plantation
bell in observance of the anniversary of John Brown's death.[58]

The Brown song would not be forgotten when the blacks of

Charleston, celebrating the fall of the city to the Union troops, held a monstrous parade with over 10,000 in the line of march. Among their score of banners was one which read, "The spirit of John Brown still lives." The contingent of nearly 2000 black school children sang the John Brown song during the entire length of their two-and-a-half-hour march. On the last leg of their journey they insisted on adding a version which they had not learned at school, a familiar one, however, "We'll hang Jeff Davis on a sour apple tree." [59] Some of the more sensitive Northerners, including abolitionists, did not care for the sour apple tree stanza, but the rank and file, whether black or white, hardly shared so fastidious a feeling, however morally admirable.

Variant versions of the John Brown song were nothing new among its devotees, white or black. At a concert held at Shiloh Church, New York, in March 1862, featuring a chorus of colored children, one of the verses of the song retold the story of Brown gently kissing the black baby, the lowly mother weeping all the while. Thomas Wentworth Higginson heard his black regiment add a verse which was new to him, "We'll beat Beauregard on de clare battlefield." [60]

During the Civil War black leaders in their public addresses made some reference to John Brown more often than not. This was particularly likely to be so in the celebration of days which marked a set-back for slavery. At the meeting staged by Philadelphia abolitionists in the observance of Emancipation Proclamation Day, speaker Alfred M. Green expressed his profound regrets that Brown's "eyes beheld not this heavenly light, his ears heard not the joyful sound that our eyes and ears have been saluted with." Three weeks earlier T. Morris Chester, in an address at the twenty-ninth anniversary of The Philadelphia Library Company of Colored Persons, had made reference to the "intrepid Green and the undaunted Copeland . . . who cheerfully died for the good of the race." [61]

At a celebration at Cooper Institute on November 28, 1864, in observance of the abolition of slavery in Maryland, the predominantly black audience "sung with a will" the John Brown song, following an address by Frances Ellen Watkins Harper. During the course of the meeting Henry Highland Garnet announced that on December 2, the anniversary of Brown's hanging, appropriate exercises would be held in the Zion Baptist Church.[62]

Bent on creating anti-Southern sentiment during the war, black speakers in the British Isles evoked John Brown's name. For over a quarter of a century black leaders who visited England had sought to win sympathy for the slave and to arouse animosity toward his master. Blacks had also sought to influence Britishers who were visiting America. Upon his visit to Boston in October 1860, the Prince of Wales was presented with "An Address" by the city's leading blacks. They praised England as an asylum where so many runaway slaves had found safety and rest.[63]

One of the visiting blacks who spoke glowingly of John Brown was Sarah Parker Remond, of Salem, Massachusetts, who since her arrival in Liverpool in January 1859 had filled more than fifty lecture engagements to audiences impressed by her quiet sincerity and eloquence. At a meeting of the Leeds Anti-Slavery Society three weeks after Brown's death, Miss Remond referred to him at length. Having the honor, she said, of being identified with the ultra-fanatical Garrisonian school of abolitionists, she had no word of criticism for Brown "or for the means which he took to carry out his great idea." Interrupted by approving cries of "hear, hear," Miss Remond concluded with a eulogy to Brown. At Wakefield three weeks later Miss Remond said that the seeds sown by "dear old John Brown" would never perish.[64]

Sharing the platform with Miss Remond at Leeds and Wakefield was the ubiquitous Frederick Douglass, who had arrived in the British Isles late in November 1859. While at Halifax, Nova Scotia, awaiting passage abroad, Douglass had written a long letter to the secretary of the Sheffield Anti-Slavery Society reassuring her that during his forthcoming trip to England he would not espouse violence in making his pleas for the slave. But Douglass pointed out to his pacifist-minded correspondent that the slave was the victim of an ongoing insurrection, one by which his blood was drawn, drop by drop. And, added Douglass, it might not be fair to preach the rule of submission to the slave inasmuch as he had already been submitting for two hundred years.[65]

When Douglass reached the British Isles he did not openly preach violent revolution although he had nothing but kind words for John Brown. He told a Leeds audience that Harpers Ferry was a crime only in the sense that it might be a crime for one on board a pirate ship to strike down the captain and seize the vessel. Shifting his analogy Douglass said that Brown went to Harpers Ferry not as an insurgent against peace-loving men but rather as a rescuer against an armed band of insurgents. To the charge that Brown was imprudent, Douglass had a reply: "Would to God a little more imprudence in the United States!" [66]

At the Wakefield meeting Douglass explained that Brown's object was to lead the slaves out of bondage and that he took arms only to defend himself if attacked. His motives were as pure as those that took Moses to Egypt to bring out the Israelites. At a meeting at Newcastle-upon-Tyne a month later, Douglass asserted that in going to Harpers Ferry Brown had not entered a peaceful neighborhood. Rather, it was a community already in conflict, and he had gone there in order to put a stop to the war's atrocities.[67]

An editorial in the *New York Times,* entitled "Abolitionism Abroad," was not wide of the mark in stating that throughout his tour, Frederick Douglass "was vindicating the memory of John Brown, and holding him up to the admiration of his audiences as a saint and hero." The editorial offered Douglass as the prime example of "abolition's emissaries abroad" who were appealing to the people of Great Britain for sympathy and material assistance.[68]

Douglass stayed in the British Isles only five months—by the summer of 1860 the Mason Committee had disbanded, and it was safe for him to return to America. One of the other pro-Brown blacks speaking to the British public within months after Harpers Ferry was Jesse Ewing Glasgow, who early in 1860 brought out a slim book, *The Harper's Ferry Insurrection: Being an Account of the Late Outbreak in Virginia, and the Trial and Execution of John Brown Its Hero.* Then attending the University of Edinburgh, Glasgow had been a prize pupil at the Institute for Colored Youth,

located in his native Philadelphia. He had left the United States
in the 1840's and had returned for two weeks in the summer of
1859.[69]

His book, published at Edinburgh and modestly priced at one
shilling, was little more than a collection of newspaper articles and
other published accounts of the raid. The most praiseworthy thing
about the book was its motivation. It was designed, Glasgow
avowed, to impel its readers "to do something toward securing the
colored man's freedom and manhood in America." Interested
readers were advised to send donations to anti-slavery societies,
specifying that said contributions be earmarked for underground
railroad activities. Glasgow's book sold fairly well, going into a
fourth edition before the year was out.[70] It was never revised or
expanded, its author dying a year or so later, his studies at the
university uncompleted.

If during the war blacks evoked John Brown's name, his family
reciprocated by its interest in their welfare. Brown's wife and
offspring lacked his indomitable will and his intensity of feeling
as to racial equality. In their own ways, however, they bore witness
against slavery.

In the summer of 1860 John Brown, Jr., became an agent of
the Haytian Bureau of Emigration, working under his father's
former associate, James Redpath, the general agent of emigration
to Haiti. As an agent, Brown operated in Canada because, as he
told Redpath, he felt a deep interest in the runaway slaves there
who had proved themselves men but who still faced a deep-seated
color prejudice. Holding that opportunities beckoned to them in
Haiti, Brown urged black audiences to seek their fortunes in that
favored land.[71]

John, Jr., welcomed the outbreak of the Civil War, holding that
it would mark the end of slavery regardless of the North's motives
for getting into it. Brown soon resigned his post under Redpath
in order to join the Union Army. He felt, he said, that as a soldier
he could do more "to remove the disabilities against blacks." In

the opening days of the war Thomas Wentworth Higginson sought, without success, to raise a company to be led by John, Jr. By late 1861, however, Brown himself was engaged in enlisting a band of 100 recruits for a regiment which he would command. The son of his father, he let it be known that he had a strong preference for moral, temperate men who under no circumstances would return a runaway slave to his master.[72]

By October Brown held an officer's commission in one Kansas volunteer regiment and three months later was mustered in as captain of another. His military career, nonetheless, did not outlast the war. Writing to Franklin B. Sanborn in February 1864, however, he claimed to have lost none of his interest in the struggle between "liberty and despotism in America," and expressed his longing to see the ax of war laid at the roots of slavery.[73]

Another of John Brown's sons, Salmon, succeeded in raising a company at North Elba during the winter of 1861–62. But the recruits had second thoughts about going to Virginia under a son of John Brown. Receiving no commission for his efforts, Salmon did not sign on. A second disappointment awaited him a few months later when he was denied a promised lieutenancy in another company because "certain pro-slavery officers" were unwilling to serve with him. Salmon would remain a private citizen. Neither of Brown's other two sons, Owen, who had been a Harpers Ferry participant, or Jason, would bear arms in the war, although their expressed views remained decidedly anti-slavery. On December 4, 1859, two days after his father's hanging, Owen had hand-lettered a lengthy scroll, "A Declaration of Liberty By the Representatives of the Slave Population of the United States of America," a patchwork of quotations from his father's letters and the Declaration of Independence.[74]

Brown's daughter Annie shared the abolitionist sentiments of her brothers. Replying to an autograph seeker in February 1860, and obligingly sending him a signature of her father, she ended her letter, "Yours for the *good* of the *poor* Slave." [75]

In the late spring of 1863 Annie informed William Lloyd Garrison of her desire to go south to help teach the slaves who had been freed. She could not have gone before, she explained, because she had been attending school herself. A request from a daughter of John Brown would hardly be ignored in abolitionist circles. Annie soon received an invitation from the Friends' Freedman's Aid Society, and in the late summer of 1863 she began to teach former slaves, first at Portsmouth and then at Norfolk.[76]

Contrary to popular story, Annie never taught at the freedman's school on the plantation that once had belonged to Governor Wise but had been confiscated and occupied by the Union troops. Located on the Elizabeth River, the estate was only ten miles from Norfolk. On one occasion Annie did visit the colored school which had recently been started there. But when a newspaper reporter, sensing a good story, asked her to conduct one class at the school, she declined. The story, however, would persist. It is not unlikely that while on this visit Annie would learn that the first black baby to be born free on the Wise plantation was named after her father, bearing the somewhat incongruous label, John Brown Wise.[77]

Like the younger members of her family, Mary Brown, the widow, rejoiced in the social changes brought about by the Civil War. When the Emancipation Proclamation was issued she was as rhapsodic as her stoical nature would permit: "God bless Abraham Lincoln. And give God the glory for the day of Jubilee has come." When the Lincoln administration officially began to recruit Negroes as soldiers Mary was delighted. "I feel that that is just as it should be," she wrote.[78]

During the course of the war, blacks would inevitably link Brown's name more and more to that of Abraham Lincoln, the President who issued the proclamation of freedom and who signed into law the anti-slavery measures passed by Congress. At a meeting held in Shiloh Church, New York, in May 1862, to celebrate the abolition of slavery in the District of Columbia, three cheers were given for Brown and Lincoln. On the eve of the presidential election of 1864, blacks in Washington held a meeting at the Fifteenth Street Presbyterian Church to express their support of

Lincoln, ending the "grand jubilation" with the John Brown song.[79]

When Lincoln was assassinated in April 1865, his kinship with Brown was more firmly rooted in the mind of blacks. To them each of these figures had lost his life in the battle against slavery, one of them in delivering a summons against that outworn institution and the other in carrying it out. "Lincoln and John Brown are two martyrs whose memories will live united in our bosom," wrote the editor of a black New Orleans weekly.[80]

For nearly a century after the Civil War black Americans would honor highly the memories of both Lincoln and Brown. If for most of this time Lincoln's fame was the greater of the two, it would lose some of its lustre to present-day blacks. John Brown would fare considerably better.

VIII

A FIRE NOT FORGOTTEN

His coming started flames that still give light
Years after his dark noon at Calvary.
"John Brown," Herbert Clark Johnson,
Black World, September 1972 *

In the hundred years after the Civil War many things would change in black life, as in the life of the nation as a whole. Blacks went from the hopeful days right after the war, when they voted and held office in the South, to a low period characterized by disfranchisement, sharecropping, and socially condoned lynching. The turn of the century brought fresh hope with new organizations like the National Association for the Advancement of Colored People and the National Urban League. Two world wars had their profound impact on black life, bringing to the fore newer faces and newer programs.

But the basic issues at stake—social justice and racial equality—would not change. The quest of black people for their birthright as Americans remained the same. In this quest one of the constants was the image of John Brown.

His name would be evoked by a century of black protestors—civil rights spokesmen and other seekers of the new day they hoped was coming. If a national event called for a public celebration by blacks, such as the ratification of the Fifteenth Amendment, Brown's name was very likely to be brought up by one of the speakers or cited in one of the resolutions. If a protest were to

* Reprinted by permission of Mr. Johnson and *Black World.*

be lodged against some flagrant act of injustice, some editor of a colored newspaper was likely to observe, "All that is needed is a few Black John Browns." When thousands of black "exodusters" left the South in the late 1870's in search of better living conditions, they chose Kansas as their destination because, according to Senator John J. Ingalls, it had once been the scene of John Brown's labors in the cause.[1]

To post-Civil War blacks, his was a name to conjure with, almost a presence to be summoned. In many ways they showed their continuing high esteem for his memory. Their evocations of his name would contribute to the creation of the legendary Brown that would live in song and story. And, even more important, their numerous referrals to him, in their context and in their content, tell us much about the America of their times, particularly in its interracial aspects.

In perpetuating the name of John Brown, his only black follower to survive the Harpers Ferry raid was not destined to play the prominent role that might otherwise have been his. Osborne Perry Anderson led a life of obscurity after the publication of his small book, *A Voice from Harper's Ferry*. In the summer of 1861 he had considered going to Africa but had decided against it.[2] He would never marry.

After the outbreak of the Civil War he settled in Canada, his broken health ruling out a steady job. Occasionally he received a small sum of money from one of Brown's former acquaintances, such as Mrs. George L. Stearns. During his last years he was a tuberculosis victim. His final weeks were spent in Washington, D.C. Blacks in that city helped to pay his medical bills, and in October 1872 Franklin B. Sanborn sent him $10.[3]

Before the year was out Anderson was dead. At his funeral services held at the Fifteenth Street Presbyterian Church on December 10, 1872, the ten honorary pall-bearers included such prominent black figures as George T. Downing, Bishop J. T. Walls, Daniel A. Straker, Lewis H. Douglass, and Robert Purvis and his physician son, Charles. The aged father of Anderson listened as the elder Purvis eulogized Osborne, hailing him as "the last survivor of the only army of freedom ever recruited in the United States." [4]

Anderson was buried in the Columbia Harmony Cemetery, his admirers intending that this was to be a temporary interment. In Washington later that month a public meeting was held to raise money to remove the body to Westchester, Pennsylvania, the roster of speakers including Mary Ann Shadd Cary who had known Anderson in Ontario.[5] But his body would remain in Washington in an unmarked grave whose location faded with the passing years.

Writing to Annie Brown Adams in August 1908, Oswald Garrison Villard expressed his regrets that the grave of Anderson could not be found, efforts to that end being hopeless.[6] Just ten years prior to Villard's letter and forty years after the Harpers Ferry raid, the remains of two of Brown's other black followers, Dangerfield Newby and Lewis S. Leary, finally received a decent burial. The site of their final interment could hardly have been more appropriate—the John Brown farm at North Elba in the Adirondacks.

This took place after the Brown farm of 244 acres had come into possession of the state of New York. Mrs. Brown had sold the estate for $700 in 1863, moving to California. Seven years later the buyer, Alexis Hinckley, sold the property, then priced at $2000, to the John Brown Association, an organization founded and led by the popular journalist-lecturer, Kate Field. In 1896, the year of Kate's death, the Association transferred the ownership of the farm to New York State. At public exercises, held on July 21, 1896, the state officially accepted the gift. One of the highlights of the occasion was the singing of John Brown's favorite hymn by the Epps family, led by Lyman and his no longer youthful sons. "Above the rich blend of the quartet," wrote one chronicler, "floated the pure, sweet, tenor of old man Epps, in tones which might have come from the adolescent throat of a choir-boy." [7]

The second historic event at the state-owned farm was the public burial of ten of Brown's followers, among them Leary and Newby. Until then eight of the bodies had unobtrusively lain in two boxes on the right bank of the Shenandoah, a mile outside Harpers Ferry.

Of the ten men killed in action at Harpers Ferry, the bodies of two—Watson Brown and Jeremiah G. Anderson—were given to the Winchester Medical College to be used for anatomical purposes. In 1882 the prepared body of Watson was brought to North Elba and buried by the side of his father.[8]

The bodies of the eight other Brown followers killed in action, including those of Leary and Newby, had been wrapped in blankets and shawls, placed in two large boxes and buried at the water's edge, the man who interred them, James Mansfield, receiving $5.00 for his services. A more orderly burial was hardly possible in view of the deep resentments the raid had aroused in Harpers Ferry. The quiet, almost secret, mass burial made it possible for the gravesite to remain for forty years as unmolested as it was unmarked and unknown.

The long quiescence came to an end in the summer of 1899 when Thomas Featherstonhaugh, a staff member of the Medical Division of the Bureau of Pensions who had become a Brown collector and authority, decided that the time had come to rebury Brown's followers beside their leader, and with appropriate public ceremonies and military honors. Accompanied by E. P. Hall, a fellow Washingtonian, and O. G. Libby of the University of Wisconsin, Featherstonhaugh went to Harpers Ferry on July 29, 1899, and had the remains of Brown's men dug up, employing the services of the very man who had interred the bodies forty years previously. The three out of towners hastened to get out of Harpers Ferry before their mission became known, Libby personally conducting the remains to North Elba after having transferred them to an ordinary traveling trunk to avoid suspicion.

The bodies were so decomposed and the bones so jumbled together as to make it impossible to identify any individual one. It did not matter, however, the intention being to bury them in a single coffin, a handsome piece with silver handles and a silver name plate, a gift of the town of North Elba. Before the scheduled date of the ceremonies, August 30, 1899, the bodies of two other

Brown followers, Aaron D. Stevens and Albert Hazlett, were disinterred and brought from Perth Amboy, New Jersey, to be buried with their comrades.

The day of the burial ceremonies was hot but fair, luring some fifteen hundred spectators to the graveside. The casket with its ten bodies was wrapped in an American flag. The speakers included Richard J. Hinton, whose address consisted of a biographical sketch of each of the men, much of it based on personal acquaintance. The Epps family provided the hymns. A detachment of the Twenty-sixth United States Infantry then fired a parting salute over the empty plot, 200 feet from the farmhouse, that had been dug alongside the graves of John Brown and his son, Watson.[9]

Her first husband's body among the honored ten, Mary Leary Langston, writing from Lawrence, Kansas, to Joshua Young, who conducted the religious exercises at the ceremonies, expressed her keen interest in the reburials. "I am a widow and old and alone but I rejoice to know that the hero of Osawatomie and his followers are not forgotten," she wrote. "I remember them with pride and their brave struggle for the liberty of an oppressed race."[10]

Ruth Brown Thompson, Brown's daughter, was not present at the reburial exercises at North Elba. She sent word that she was so happy over the event that she couldn't sleep but that a lack of money kept her from making the trip. Like their father the Brown offspring were habitually lean in purse: "We Browns are all poor financiers," wrote Annie Brown Adams to F. B. Sanborn in 1893.[11]

The aging Brown children received some assistance from Sanborn and a few others, including black donors. In the summer of 1896 Annie received $15 from a group of blacks in St. Paul, following the news that her house in Petrolia, California, had burned down. The gift was "a great help," wrote Annie to George W. Cook, then Principal of the Normal Department at Howard University. Himself born a slave in Winchester, Virginia, Cook had written to Annie asking whether she was in need. Annie described her plight, invoking her father's name in closing: "May John Brown's God bless you all." [12]

Blacks in Albany formed an "Anna-Brown-Adams Relief Association," their avowed goal to send her $500. At a musical and literary benefit held in a local church on February 14, 1897, they raised $100, which they mailed to her. From the grateful recipient came a lengthy reply expressing heartfelt thanks for "this token of kindness for me and respect for my father." And like her father, Annie had words of advice for her colored friends:

> Let me entreat you to take care of your poor; the rich will take care of themselves. So imitate John Brown, by always holding out a helping and sympathetic hand to all the helpless and despised ones.[13]

The support blacks gave to Annie and her two sisters and two brothers fell far short of the expectations of Dr. Thomas Featherstonhaugh, ardent admirer of their father. Holding that for any member of the Brown family to suffer want was a disgrace to the Negroes, Featherstonhaugh decided to bestir them. "I got a bunch of darkies together on the 2nd inst., the 48th anniversary of John Brown's execution, and gave them a good raking over," he wrote to O. G. Villard on December 4, 1907.[14] At the meeting Featherstonhaugh's tone or manner may have displeased his listeners. At any rate little or nothing seems to have come of his urgings.

Brown's children apparently shared little of Featherstonhaugh's bitterness toward blacks for their alleged shortcomings in assisting them. John Brown, Jr., retained his friendly contacts with Negroes. In February 1878 he wrote to Frederick Douglass expressing his pleasure at having heard from him and saying that he hoped it would not be for the last time. During the migration of blacks to Kansas in 1879 Brown accepted contributions designed to help them get settled. In 1884 John received a cordial letter from Thomas Thomas, whom his father had met in Springfield nearly forty years previously.[15]

Every summer for a period John Jr., left his home at Put-in-Bay Island, Ohio, to go to Windsor, Ontario, to visit Samuel Harper, one of the Missouri slaves his father had led to freedom in the winter of 1858–59. Samuel had expressed the wish that he could pay John one-half of "what I owe your father." John and his brother, Owen, kept in touch with Lyman Epps, jointly writing to him in November 1885. Six months earlier they had greeted Epps when they came to North Elba to join in the exercises commemorating the eighty-fifth anniversary of their father's birth.[16]

Their brother Jason, living in a small settlement near Cleveland at the turn of the century, was often an overnight guest of Charles Waddell Chesnutt, the novelist, and his wife, when he came to the city. In 1891 Jason had written to the Roberts Company of Boston, publishers of books and pictures, stating that inasmuch as his father's likeness was in such great demand by the colored people, many of them poor, the company should produce such a picture to be sold to them a the very lowest price.[17]

To blacks the coming of a new century did not connote the forsaking of old heroes. During the first decade of the 1900's black Americans held John Brown observances in a number of cities, among them Pasadena, Akron, Albany, Springfield, Massachusetts, and Boston. The celebration at Pasadena, which included some blacks from Los Angeles, was held on May 9, 1900, the centennial of Brown's birth. At a similar meeting held in early June by blacks in Brooklyn, the featured speaker, T. Thomas Fortune, paid a lengthy tribute to John Brown, defending his use of retaliatory violence. Calling on blacks to follow their courageous leaders whether they led to Calvary or to a Virginia scaffold, Fortune asserted that without Harpers Ferry there would have been no Civil War. Stirred by Fortune's language, the presiding officer, W. A. Murphy, "advised the audience to learn how to make dynamite and other explosives in order to be prepared when the great crisis comes."[18]

In 1907 Brown's birthday was observed by blacks in Springfield, Massachusetts, where he had lived, the exercises featuring remarks by six former slaves. On the fiftieth anniversary of Brown's death, December 2, 1909, four of Boston's black civic groups combined to hold a "Boston John Brown Jubilee" at historic Faneuil Hall. With flags flying at half mast throughout the crowded building, exercises were held in the morning, afternoon, and evening, whites making up ten per cent of the audience. One speaker, a bit more direct than the others, asserted that "Brown stood for a feature of solving the problem that appears to many to be the only solution to our present-day problems." [19]

The most noteworthy Brown observance of the period was the John Brown Day held at Harpers Ferry in the summer of 1906, attended by delegates of the Niagara Movement, and highlighted by addresses from Reverdy C. Ransom and W. E. B. Du Bois, an episode treated in the opening chapter of this work. The militant Du Bois would find in Brown a stimulation that would far outlast the celebration of 1906. More than half a century later the aged black leader wrote that "John Brown not only regarded slavery as wrong, but Negroes as men." [20]

Du Bois' interest in Brown led him in 1907 to contract to write a biography of the man. In a letter to Oswald Garrison Villard, himself embarking on a life of Brown and seeking the help of Du Bois, the latter explained that he could be of little assistance inasmuch as his proposed work was "going to be an interpretation, 'and I am not trying to go very largely to the sources." [21]

Entitled simply *John Brown,* the Du Bois volume appeared in 1909. Its object, according to its preface, was to throw light on the "important inner development" of black Americans by showing Brown's personal identification with them and their plight. Du Bois admitted that he uncovered no new materials. But, he added, "the great broad truths are clear, and this book is at once a record of and a tribute to the man who of all Americans has perhaps come nearest to touching the souls of black folk." [22]

Du Bois regarded his *John Brown* as one of "my best written books," informing his friend and literary executor, Herbert Aptheker, that it was "his favorite volume." But the book was received somewhat coolly by historian William E. Dodd, reviewing it for the influential *American Historical Review*. Conceding that it was well written, Dodd said that it could be most aptly described by the terms, "hero worship, perhaps sensationalism." Reviewing the book in the *New York Evening Post,* of which he was editor, Villard was likewise lukewarm, finding little to praise. Du Bois, quite nettled and believing that his only sin was that of having "aroused the unfortunate jealousy of Villard," filed a protest with the latter. "We have another nasty note from Du Bois in which he says I deliberately ran down his book unjustly to put it out of the way of the arrival of mine," wrote Villard to Katherine Mayo, his research assistant.[23]

Villard's own book, *John Brown, 1800–1859: A Biography Fifty Years After,* and published in 1910, was a landmark in its careful approach to the man. It was based on sound evidence. Villard would, as he had informed Brown's daughter, write from the standpoint of an impartial historian yet one who had a deep sympathy for the abolitionists and their goals.[24]

Villard's biography won widespread praise, much of it from blacks. Upon reading it the budding young black poet, Leslie Pinckney Hill, sent to Villard a deeply moving sonnet, one of the finest things from his pen. Butler R. Wilson, a Boston attorney, wrote to Villard expressing the pleasure he and his wife, a niece of the fallen John A. Copeland, had derived from the book, "a superb piece of work." Wilson reported his wife as saying that in Villard's book justice was done for the first time to the memory of the colored men who were with Brown at Harpers Ferry.[25]

Daniel Alexander Payne Murray purchased a copy of Villard's volume after scanning it at the Library of Congress, where he was a staff employee. In 1900 the librarian, Herbert Putnam, had selected Murray to assemble a comprehensive collection of Negro-authored books and pamphlets to be displayed at the Paris exposition that year, a task for which Murray had won official commendation. Upon reading *John Brown,* Murray informed Villard that he regarded it as one might regard the Bible, "a case where nothing short of personal ownership and daily reading would suffice." Murray had previously informed Katherine Mayo that "after an extended perusal of the whole field of biography" he had come to regard John Brown as the greatest figure of them all.[26]

Not buying the book but receiving an autographed copy from the author himself was the most prominent Negro of his times, Booker T. Washington, the founder and principal of Tuskegee

Institute, in Alabama. The ever-busy Washington graciously acknowledged receipt of the book, saying that he promised himself the pleasure of reading it at the earliest opportunity.[27]

This was not the first time the two men had been in touch with each other concerning John Brown. In 1905 Villard had sent Washington several Brown letters he had received from Alfred Webb of Dublin, Ireland. Two years later Villard asked Washington to spearhead a nation-wide effort among blacks to observe the fiftieth anniversary of Brown's execution. Washington promised to ask the black churches to set the day aside for prayer and a celebration which would include an inventory of the progress the Negro had made since Brown "died for him." [28]

Washington sent letters to black newspapers calling attention to the anniversary and asking their support for a proper observance of it. The response from editors was disappointing, apparently, and Washington himself may have lacked a full measure of his boundless enthusiasm and energy for the project. The bulk of Washington's financial support came from sources not likely to approve of a John Brown. At any rate nothing came of the nation-wide plan of celebration. And as for Washington himself, he declined to appear at the centennial observance of Brown's birthday held by Albany blacks on May 9, 1909, although his reply was typically gracious. Nothing would have given him greater pleasure than to be present, he wrote, but it would not be possible inasmuch as he had just returned to Tuskegee after an absence of many weeks.[29]

Twentieth-century blacks honored Brown and kept his memory alive by making pilgrimages either to the scene of his raid at Harpers Ferry or the site of his tomb at North Elba. Both had the additional tourist attraction of being spots of great natural beauty.

"Full of the most thrilling memories in the history of our race," as Alexander Crummell pointed out in 1885 to the graduating class of Storer College, Harpers Ferry annually drew thousands of black excursionists. Black workingmen's groups chartered special trains thereto, such as Lodge #430 of the Brotherhood of Locomotive Firemen of Brunswick, Maryland, in September 1905. Black church groups arranged similar outings to Harpers Ferry via the Baltimore and Ohio Railroad, such as the First Baptist Church of Baltimore in September 1971. Such one-day trips, with the participants having the option of bringing their own lunches, generally provided for a period of at least three hours in the historic town.[30]

Brown admirers who visited Harpers Ferry after 1909 would inevitably make their way to Storer College, the location of the engine house in which Brown and his men had taken refuge. Supported by the American Baptist Home Missionary Society and designed to serve blacks, Storer had been founded in October 1867. In 1881 the peerless Frederick Douglass had come to the school to deliver a stirring address on John Brown, the manuscript of which he turned over to the college authorities so that they might publish it and use the proceeds to establish a John Brown Professorship.[31] At the Douglass residence in Washington, D.C., a favored visitor might be shown a brick from the fire-engine house, or John Brown's fort, as it was popularly called.

Storer came into possession of the fire-engine house in 1909. Nearly twenty years earlier, in 1892, the structure had been dismantled and moved to Chicago as an attraction to the World's Columbian Exposition. Two years later Kate Field raised enough money to bring it back to the Harpers Ferry region where it was rebuilt on an open lot three miles outside the town and not readily accessible to sightseers. Miss Field had hoped to use the fort as a nucleus for the establishment of a national park but upon her untimely death the property was sold for taxes, falling into the hands of a farmer with little interest in its historic significance.[32]

Learning that the owner had been neglecting the building and was planning to use it for storage purposes, the Storer trustees sought to raise the $2000 purchase price and appointed the Committee on the John Brown Fort. Its efforts successful, Storer had the building removed to its campus in 1910, to be used as a museum. The fort was now back in Harpers Ferry, a scant half-mile from its original site. Ten years later the Storer alumni placed a commemorative tablet on the building.[33]

The Storer trustees gladly accepted this gift. But such was not the case with another bronze marker that was designed for the engine house and was offered to the college by the National Association for the Advancement of Colored People in the spring of 1932. Following the formal conclusion of its twenty-third annual convention, held in Washington in May 1932, the N.A.A.C.P. had scheduled a pilgrimage to Harpers Ferry to unveil a commemorative tablet for the fort.

Storer's white president, Henry T. McDonald, had previously consented to receive it. McDonald was fully aware of the significance of Brown to black Americans and of the symbolic importance of the fort to all admirers of John Brown. In June 1908, nearly twenty-five years earlier, McDonald had proposed to have an impressive celebration at Storer College in commemoration of the fiftieth anniversary of the raid, pledging his own efforts to seek the attendance and participation of no less a personage than President Theodore Roosevelt. In 1923 Anna E. Murray, niece of both Lewis S. Leary and John A. Copeland, and wife of Daniel Alexander Payne Murray, had won the support of McDonald in her equally unsuccessful efforts to raise funds to place on the outer walls of the fort a tablet with a roster of Brown's raiders and also for the upkeep of the fort, including the hiring of a custodian.[34]

But on Saturday, May 21, 1932, when the five busloads of N.A.A.C.P. delegates arrived at Storer College they found that McDonald had changed his mind about accepting the tablet. His excuse was that its inscription contained "controversial matter." The Storer trustees had wanted the inscription to be confined to the words, "John Brown—His Soul Goes Marching On." The officers of the N.A.A.C.P. had other ideas.

Drafted by the outspoken W. E. B. Du Bois, editor of *The Crisis,* the official organ of the N.A.A.C.P., the inscription on the tablet was far more militant than McDonald and the white trustees were prepared to permit, reading as follows:

Here
John Brown
Aimed at Human Slavery

A Blow
That woke a guilty nation.
With him fought
Seven slaves and sons of slaves.
Over his crucified corpse
Marched 200,000 black soldiers
And 4,000,000 freedmen
Singing
"John Brown's body lies a-mouldering
in the grave
"But his Soul goes marching on !" [35]

But if he could not accept the tablet, McDonald made no effort to halt the commemorative exercises held in the college chapel. Indeed he extended an official welcome to the delegates, although to one journalist his remarks seemed to dwell upon the beauties of nature, touching upon the birds, flowers, and limpid streams. Then he took his leave, as if overcome in his desire to join them, although it is more likely that he wished to avoid the awkwardness of remaining on the platform where the rejected tablet sat conspicuously in a chair of its own. After the ceremonies the delegates, frustrated and indignant, refused to avail themselves of the meal Storer had prepared for them or to accept any other hospitalities from the college.[36]

The tablet would return to the national office of the N.A.A.C.P. in New York, and McDonald would remain at Storer another twelve years although many of the students condemned his action in refusing the tablet and talked of drafting a petition calling for his resignation. The N.A.A.C.P. hoped that the Storer trustees would eventually change their mind about accepting the tablet. But that had not taken place by the end of the summer term in 1955 when Storer had to close its doors due to the lack of funds. The fort itself would be moved back to within fifty feet of its original site fronting upon the confluence of the rivers.

In rejecting the N.A.A.C.P. tablet, the Storer trustees had been under some pressure from the local chapter of the United Daughters of the Confederacy. This organization had just honored a black who had fallen at Harpers Ferry, but he was not one of Brown's men—he was Hayward Shepherd who had been fatally shot on the bridge. In 1920 the United Daughters had appointed a committee to arrange for a memorial to Shepherd as a representative of the colored race who had given his all in faithful service.

Eleven years later, on October 10, 1931, a memorial tablet to Shepherd was unveiled at a spot near the original site of the fort, the dedication exercises under the joint sponsorship of the U.D.C. and the Sons of the Confederate Veterans. The stand was draped with Confederate colors and graced by a group of girls from the local junior chapter of the Daughters. Sharing the platform with them were two specially invited blacks with local ties—James Moten, who then filled the porter-custodian job that Shepherd once held, and James W. Walker, a Storer graduate and an independent farmer of Bunker Hill, West Virginia, but who was being honored as a lineal descendant of Shepherd.[37]

One of the two major addresses, "Heyward Shepherd: Victim of Violence," was given by Matthew Page Andrews, an authority on Maryland history, who expressed the hope that the memorial to the fallen black would make his name a symbol of "the happiest relationships" of the old order and an inspiration to the new. It was a well-written speech although its point of view that Southern slavery had been a training school for uncivilized blacks from Africa had an old-fashioned, antebellum flavor.[38]

The second memorial address, delivered by Mrs. Leopold Bashinsky of Troy, Alabama, President General of the United Daughters of the Confederacy, was in a similar vein. She received her loudest applause when she paid tribute to the faithfulness of the slaves and especially to the endearing qualities of the good old black mammies.[39]

This reference to the black mammies, however enthusiastically received by the largely white audience, did not go unchallenged. A dissenting note came from Pearl Tattem, a music teacher at Storer College. When she came forward to direct the Storer choir she first proceeded to identify herself as a descendant of one who had worn the Union blue during the Civil War, and then she announced that she was not of the black mammy type. The audience, taken aback by Miss Tattem's unscheduled remarks, remained silent, too well bred to openly express their disapproval.[40]

Between the two speeches came the unveiling of the marker. Its inscription described Shepherd as the first victim of an intended insurrection, and as one who exemplified the fidelity of thousands of blacks who throughout the Civil War conducted themselves in such a manner as to have left no stain on the record "which is the peculiar heritage of the American people, and an everlasting tribute to the best in both races." [41] The exercises came to an end with a benediction pronounced by black George F. Bragg, rector of Baltimore's St. James Episcopal Church.

The memorial to Hayward Shepherd aroused no enthusiasm among blacks. Many of them criticized the otherwise highly respected Father Bragg for his role, however pro forma its nature. Blacks were even more vexed when they learned that Bragg had hailed the address by Andrews as "simply magnificent." The whole affair, snapped *The Crisis,* "was a pro-slavery celebration." Sharply denouncing both the memorial and exercises, the *Baltimore Afro-American* carried a letter from Charles E. Hill, a Storer graduate and a Harpers Ferry resident, asserting that any program that honored Uncle Toms and glorified black mammies ran counter to black advancement.[42]

The interest that blacks had in Harpers Ferry as a historic spot included the Kennedy Farm where the raiders had lived and drilled immediately prior to their attack. In 1949 the Improved Benevolent and Protective Order of Elks of the World, a black uplift and fellowship organization, decided to purchase the farm and turn it into a shrine for the inspiration of Negro youth. At the on-site dedication ceremonies the speaker for the occasion was George W. Lee, a Republican politician and a wealthy businessman from Memphis, Tennessee. Famed for his oratory, Lee moved his audience by his comparison of the last days of John Brown with the last days of Jesus, stating that each had his Judas and each his Pontius Pilate. Lee himself resurrected the Brown kissing the black baby legend, with the gallows-bound martyr saying, "I'm dying today that you might be free." [43]

To highlight and publicize the acquisition of the farm, the Elks brought out a pamphlet, "The John Brown Reader," compiled and edited by Judge William C. Hueston, the fraternity's Commissioner of Education, and J. Finley Wilson, its Grand Exalted Ruler. Setting forth the familiar facts about Brown's career, the pamphlet devoted much of its attention to the history and activities of the Elks.[44]

In September 1952 the Elks dedicated the farm as a national shrine, their two-day exercises attracting more than 2000 lodge members and their friends. This gathering was surpassed in numbers at a Fourth of July weekend celebration in 1954 when a record crowd of 3000 journeyed to the farm, some of them doubtless attracted by a scheduled Saturday night dance. By that time the farm had been completely renovated, including the erection of an arch at its entrance and a large auditorium. By 1953 the Elks had expended a total of over $65,000 on a shrine. This included $30,000 for its purchase, a like sum for its improvements, and $5500 for equipment.[45]

The efforts of the Elks to make the farmhouse a national shrine did not prove to be successful, however. The Elks found it expedient to dispose of the property, which for a space of five years, from 1965 to 1970, was owned by James S. Julian, a black physician of Pikesville, Maryland. Julian bought the farmhouse in the hope that the road between the Antietam battlefield and the Harpers Ferry National Park would be improved shortly thereafter. With these hopes dimmed Julian sold the property to a real estate firm.[46]

Local Elks lodges did not forget Brown. On September 6, 1954, at New Richmond, Pennsylvania, fifty members of local and state lodges held wreath-laying ceremonies at the grave of John Brown's first wife, Dianthe Lusk. The Charlestown, West Virginia, lodge, No. 841, proudly took John Brown as its name.[47]

To admirers of John Brown the Harpers Ferry region was not the sole magnetic point. The homestead at North Elba where Brown

and his followers had been buried was likewise a place for pilgrimage, a spot to be venerated. Here on August 23, 1916, a tablet
with an engraved likeness of Brown at the rounded apex was
unveiled and affixed to the large boulder in the burial plot. After
touching on the highlights of Brown's career, the inscription listed
the names of the twelve followers buried beside him, followed by
separate columns for those who were hanged in December 1859 and
for those who escaped.

Although this was not a Negro-arranged affair, one of its featured
speakers was sociologist Kelly Miller, a prolific commentator on
black life and the dean of the College of Liberal Arts at Howard
University. Miller, magisterial in appearance, spoke at the pre-
unveiling exercises held that morning at the Happy Hour Theatre
in Lake Placid. In his oration that afternoon at the graveside in
North Elba he said that his presence at the unveiling was a tribute
from blacks to John Brown. He pledged that as long as the human
heart would continue to beat, "so long shall John Brown be enshrined in the love and esteem of the colored people." [48]

Organized annual pilgrimages to North Elba by blacks began
in 1922 with the founding of the John Brown Memorial Association. The key figure in the origin and subsequent career of this
organization was the handsome, well-built J. Max Barber. Turning
from a fitful career as editor of the monthly *Voice of the Negro,*
Barber had become a dentist, opening an office in Philadelphia in
1912. One of the founders of the Niagara Movement, Barber had
been at Harpers Ferry in August 1906 when that organization
held its inspiring "John Brown's Day" celebration.[49]

Addressing the Philadelphia branch of the N.A.A.C.P. early in
1922 Barber urged that a pilgrimage be made to North Elba to
lay a wreath on John Brown's grave in the name of Negro Americans. Swept by Barber's fervor, the meeting voted to send two
pilgrims, Barber himself and Dr. T. Spotuas Burwell. The two
men proceeded to North Elba in early May, armed with a letter
from the New York State Conservation Commission giving them
permission to hold services at the grave. When they arrived in
Lake Placid, they were met by a welcoming delegation from the
local Chamber of Commerce. The two visitors were even more

surprised when they learned that the public schools had been canceled for the day so that the children could witness the wreath-laying. The adult representation at the exercises included a good number of local professional men.

Standing at the top of the great rock that dominates the grave site, Barber gave a short speech, in essence a plea for a contemporary John Brown to combat lynching, disfranchisement, Jim Crow, and the Ku Klux Klan. Barber and Burwell then jointly laid the wreath—a bouquet of immortelles bound with red, white, and blue ribbons—on the grave. "Old soldiers embraced us," wrote Barber, and "men who knew John Brown wept for joy." [50]

That night memorial exercises were held at the Methodist Episcopal Church, with Burwell extolling the N.A.A.C.P. and likening it to John Brown's League of Gileadites. Shortly before adjournment the audience asked the two visitors to make the pilgrimage an annual affair.

The idea took root in Barber's mind. The following year, after making a trip to lay another wreath, he formed a pilgrimage committee. At Philadelphia, on July 1, 1924, the John Brown Memorial Association was organized, with Barber as president, Burwell as vice-president and the Reverend William Lloyd Imes of New York as secretary. Six weeks earlier a group of several hundred blacks had made a pilgrimage to the grave, where they listened to William Pickens, author-educator and at the time the N.A.A.C.P. field secretary and director of branches. Standing on the great rock, Pickens compared it to the spirit of John Brown in not yielding to the abrasiveness of time. "This jutting head of some cliff that descends to an unknown depth into the bowels of the earth seems to have been set there by Mother Nature as a fitting tombstone for the greatest Hero of Conscience." [51] That evening the Lincoln University quartette gave a program at the Town Hall.

The annual pilgrimage to North Elba under the auspices of the John Brown Memorial Association won general commendation in black circles. The influential *Pittsburgh Courier,* a nationally circulated weekly, editorialized that blacks who went to visit the grave would approach it with reverence and thanksgiving and that those who could not make the pilgrimage in person would accompany it in spirit.[52]

Although the highlight of the trip to North Elba was the laying of the wreath on the grave, the exercises also featured a guest speaker. The Association was able to attract such nationally famed figures as Clarence Darrow, John Haynes Holmes, A. Phillip Randolph, and Oswald Garrison Villard. Doubtless like the officers of the Association, these speakers received little or no money for their services.

Funds to support the work of the Association were derived from the membership fees of $1.00, later $2.00, a year and $100.00 for a life membership. Such memberships were obtained by local chapters, including those in Philadelphia, the oldest; New York; Brooklyn; Lake Placid; Kansas City, Missouri; Springfield, Massachusetts; Norristown, Pennsylvania; and Harpers Ferry. The Philadelphia chapter had the most life memberships, but the Frederick Douglass Chapter of New York, under the presidencies of James Egert Allen and Martha E. Johnson, was the most active, holding youth programs and annual "Pilgrimage Meetings" open to the public, and excursions to Harpers Ferry. Some chapters held musical recitals and John Brown Fashion Shows. The George Washington Carver Chapter in Brooklyn prided itself on the ownership of the lock and key to the Charlestown jail where the captured Brown and his men had lain.[53]

Incorporated in August 1927 in Pennsylvania, the activities of the Association, as one of its later presidents explained, were "somewhat less flamboyant than those of its hero." During its first decade the single most important goal of the Association was the erection of a monument to John Brown. This was not a new idea, one of Brown's black admirers, S. R. Scrotton, having suggested such an undertaking within a week after Martyr Day.[54]

Eight years later a black civil and naval engineer, B. De Villeroi of Philadelphia, formulated a plan whereby subscribers to a John Brown monument would give a minimum of $1.00, stipulating that those who gave $10 or more would have their names engraved on brass tablets at its base. De Villeroi promised that all monies collected would be placed in the hands of a Philadelphia banker.

Although the prospectus issued by De Villeroi held that gratitude was one of the inherent virtues of black people, apparently very few, if any, subscriptions were received. In 1872 a group of Negroes formed a short-lived John Brown Monument Association, receiving from James Redpath the copyright of his *Public Life of John Brown*. But this book, then in its fortieth printing, was no longer a bestseller. At Osawatomie in August 1877 black Charles H. Langston, who had known Brown fairly well, had the honor of delivering the dedicatory address at the unveiling of a thirteen-foot statue to his memory, but this affair had not been initiated by blacks.[55]

During the 1880's the idea of a black-sponsored monument was revived, a national committee being formed to raise from $10,000 to $12,000 to erect a granite shaft on the site occupied by the engine house at Harpers Ferry. This committee made little more than a beginning, although it was headed by Frederick Douglass, and its governing board included such prominent blacks as Blanche K. Bruce, John R. Lynch, Francis J. Grimké, and Robert H. Terrell, along with white Thomas Featherstonhaugh.[56]

Contributing possibly to the failure of this particular effort to erect a monument to Brown was the attitude of the militant and race-conscious T. Thomas Fortune, editor of the *New York Age*. If blacks proposed to erect a monument, said Fortune, it should be one to Nat Turner, a black hero. Far more than John Brown it was Nat Turner "who stands in need of our copper pennies to be melted down into a monument." Fortune said that he yielded to no one in his admiration for John Brown but that the character and sacrifices of Turner were dearer to him "because he was one of us and exhibited in the most abject condition the heroism and race devotion which have illustrated in all times the sort of men who are worthy to be free." [57]

With the approach of the fiftieth anniversary of Harpers Ferry, in 1909, Thomas Featherstonhaugh tried to interest blacks in erecting a Brown memorial at North Elba, just as he had tried to enlist their support in aiding Brown's children. The proposal that blacks erect such a monument was approved by the Brown offspring, wrote Featherstonhaugh to Oswald Garrison Villard on

October 20, 1907, but "the darkies have done nothing yet." Feather-stonhaugh persisted for nearly two years, writing to all the prominent blacks "I can hear of." The replies he received were uniformly disappointing, with each writer referring him to somebody else. Discouraged at not getting Negro support for the monument, Featherstonhaugh turned to his white friends, a step which proved to be equally unproductive.[58]

The president of the John Brown Memorial Association, undeterred by the failure of his predecessors, was determined to have a monument to Brown. This ambition was realized in the spring of 1935. On May 8 the citizens of Lake Placid gave a reception and banquet for the visiting members of the Association. At two o'clock the following afternoon, Brown's birthday, more than 1500 people gathered at his home site for the unveiling of a heroic bronze memorial. A platform had been erected for the speakers and the distinguished guests. With Dr. Burwell presiding, the visitors were welcomed by Lake Placid's mayor.[59]

Appropriately enough the statue was unveiled by Lyman Epps, who had sat on John Brown's knee and who had attended every annual pilgrimage of the Association. The infirm Epps, then 87, was assisted by Mrs. Anna Franklin, president of the Lake Placid chapter of the Association. The statue, more than eight feet tall and weighing six tons, the work of Joseph P. Pollia, a New York sculptor, shows Brown in pioneer garb, with one arm around a Negro boy. The boy's trousers and open shirt are frayed but his face is upturned and he is shown moving forward in step with Brown. The monument rested on a knoll close by the huge boulder just outside the burial grounds.[60]

The unveiling gave way to speech-making, the dedication address coming from J. Max Barber, the justly proud president of the Association. His discourse, although wide-ranging, was well constructed and it came from a full heart. "We rear this monument as our symbol of gratitude and as a token of our ideals." The money that had been raised for the statue, he continued, represented sacrifices but this was as it should be inasmuch as John Brown had "sacrificed to the last full measure for us." In his eloquent closing message Barber hailed Brown as a soldier, prophet, hero, and martyr. "Here was a man who put humanity above race, right above law, and freedom above everything." [61]

Barber's speech was followed by band music and the Lincoln University quartette. Then the monument was officially accepted by New York State, its Conservation Commissioner, Lithgow Osborne, extending the greetings of Governor Herbert H. Lehman, and pledging to give the monument the cherishing care it merited. The State Historian, Alexander G. Flick, also expressed the thanks and appreciation of his office. The program concluded with the singing of "America," the afternoon sunshine and the gentle breezes still lingering.[62]

The erection of the monument was the most ambitious Brown homesite project of the Association but by no means its only one. In 1930 the Association had erected a wooden frame protection, with windows front and back, for the gravestone that John Brown had prized so highly. Until then it had been exposed to vandals, souvenir hunters and the severe Adirondack winters. A three-foot high slab, twenty inches wide and three inches thick, it had originally lain at Canton, Connecticut, as a cenotaph for John Brown's grandfather, a captain in the Revolutionary War. Shortly after Brown's own death, and in accordance with his fervently expressed wishes, four names were added to the gravestone—his own, and those of his three slain sons, the two who fell at Harpers Ferry and the one who was killed at Osawatomie. In May 1941 the Association dismantled the gravestone's wooden protective shield, replacing it with one of bronze and plate glass.[63]

In the summer of 1946 the Association erected a plaque to the memory of the women of the Brown family. Five years later, on Brown's birthday, the Association placed a marker on the house he occupied.

The Association, however, had lost much of its momentum during World War II. Upon its outbreak the executive committee of the Association voted to suspend the annual North Elba trip for the duration of the war. A few members of the Philadelphia chapter would continue to make the pilgrimage during the war years, their avowed aim to keep the idea alive and to call attention to John Brown as a symbol of the goals of the Allied nations. But these trips to North Elba were on a small scale and little publicized.

Shortly before the war came to an end J. Max Barber resigned from the presidency of the Association. Its other co-founder, Dr. Burwell, had died, as had the aged Lyman Epps, the last link with the living Brown. Following the retirement of Barber, the Association never regained its pre-war solidarity. It continued a somewhat lessened existence, with four branches still active in 1973, the Shields Green Chapter in Philadelphia, the Frederick Douglass Chapter in New York, the George Washington Carver Chapter in Brooklyn, and the unit in Lake Placid, which in 1950 had changed its name to the Harry Wade Hicks Chapter, honoring a local white who had been a staunch supporter. But however reduced its momentum, the John Brown Memorial Association had over the years touched the heart and conscience of many, much like the man it commemorated.

If effective organized group action to honor Brown diminished somewhat, as it had begun, with the John Brown Memorial Association, this betokened no lessening of single or individual acts of commemoration. Down to the black power revolution of the mid-1960's, Brown continued to be a bright and morning star in the racial remembrance of Negro Americans. On September 24, 1938, twelve of the black organizations in Akron, Ohio, dedicated a memorial fountain in Perkins Park where Brown had once raised sheep. Colorful wreaths were laid at the base of the memorial, the ceremonies including musical selections by the Coleridge-Taylor Chorus.[64]

In October 1972 blacks and whites in Oberlin, Ohio, gathered to rededicate the monument that had been erected in 1860 to Lewis S. Leary, John A. Copeland, Jr., and Shields Green. In 1971 the City Council decided that the time had come to remove the cenotaph from its out-of-the-way spot in an obscure corner of the Westwood Cemetery. A park site on East Vine Street was selected, a location that had once boasted the home of John H. Scott, a black abolitionist who had taken part in the Oberlin-Wellington rescue in September 1858.

Treated with a chemical preservative and refurbished with a bronze plaque, the monument was officially dedicated on October 15. Among the more than casual onlookers was Dorothy Inborden Miller of Washington, D.C., grand-daughter of Sara Jane Leary, one of Leary's sisters. One of the speakers was Robert S. Thomas, black chairman of the Oberlin City Council, 1923 graduate of the college, and the key figure in the effort to relocate the monument. "As we dedicate this monument today," said Thomas, "may we not only pay tribute to three courageous men, and honor the accomplishments of a great race, but may this memorial also serve to recognize all, whatever their race, color, or religion, who are sincerely committed to justice and equality, and the brotherhood of man," [65] a sentiment to which John Brown would have subscribed.

Unaffected by any slackening of group efforts, individual blacks continued to take heed of John Brown. Black authors and artists found in him a worthy theme. Black playwrights, among them Theodore Ward and William Branch, re-created the man and his times. Ward's "John Brown" ran for a few weeks at an off-Broadway house in the spring of 1950. "To me," said Ward, "he is the first real American." Branch's "In Splendid Error," viewing afresh the relationship between Frederick Douglass and Brown, had a fifteen-week run at the Greenwich Mews in New York in late 1954. It was only the second dramatic piece from the twenty-six-year-old Branch.[66]

Of the black poets of this period who acclaimed Brown, the best known were Countee Cullen and Georgia Douglas Johnson. The latter, wife of the Recorder of Deeds under President Taft, and author of four volumes of lyric verse, wrote a sonnet to John Brown. Referring to him as "martyr of the freed," Mrs. Johnson viewed him as a figure not likely to fade away :

> And time still burgeoneth the fertile seed,
> Though he is crucified who wrought the deed.[67]

The gifted Countee Cullen, who matured early as a lyric poet, found his literary inspiration in John Keats but he dwelt upon racial themes. Following a visit to Brown's grave at North Elba, Cullen wrote, "A Negro Mother's Lullaby," a cradle song invoking the image and the spirit of John Brown, its opening and closing passages reading thus:

> Hushaby, hushaby, dark one at my knee,
> Slumber you softly nor pucker, nor frown;
> Though some may be bonded, you shall be free,
> Thanks to a man, Osawatomie Brown.
>
> (Rich counsel he's giving
> Close by the throne;
> Tall he was living,
> But now taller grown.
> His sons are high fellows;
> An Archangel is he;
> And they doff their bright halos
> To none but the Three.) [68]

The contemporary painter-sculptor, Henry W. Bannarn, fashioned a stone bust of the martyred hero ("Head of John Brown," 1941), although neither his Brown piece nor his reputation was as celebrated as those of Edmonia Lewis. In 1864 Miss Lewis had completed a medallion of Brown, modeled after the sculpture by Brackett. Exhibited during that year at the Boston Fair for the Soldier's Fund, it was Edmonia's maiden work in her chosen profession. Gerrit Loguen, artist son of Jermain Loguen, produced a lithographed drawing of his father's one-time associate.

Prominent twentieth century black painters who turned to Brown included Charles White, Horace Pippin, and Jacob Lawrence. White's was a single sketch and Pippin's was a trilogy—Brown reading his Bible, on trial, and going to his hanging. The last-named painting included one black figure, a woman with her arms folded and her face grimly set. Pippin undoubtedly had his mother in mind when he drew this individual, reflecting a family legend, however questionable its basis, that she had witnessed the execution.[69]

The deeply moving John Brown series of Jacob Lawrence, now in the permanent collection of the Detroit Museum of Fine Arts, comprises twenty paintings in gouache. The series was particularly well received at the month-long First World Festival of Negro Arts, held in Dakar, Senegal, in 1966, the rich and vivid colorings of the paintings seeming almost to outstare the city's brilliant April sun.

In expressing their high regard for John Brown, black artists and writers reflected the prevailing sentiment of their racial group at that time. Certainly as late as 1959, the centennial of his passing, Brown was still a canonical figure to black Americans. Their attitude found expression in an article by Langston Hughes, "John Brown's Centennial," in the *Chicago Defender,* October 17, 1959. Then a famed writer of both poetry and prose, Hughes had managed to retain the common touch, his themes the black rank and file. In his piece on the Harpers Ferry centennial, he asserted that the Civil War which freed the Negroes really began with the foray led by John Brown. His name was "one of the great martyr names of all history and the men who fought with him rank high on the scrolls of freedom."

Hughes mentions by name the five blacks who served with Brown, indicating the fate of each. Possibly in the back of his mind as he wrote the piece was the thought that his maternal grandmother, Mary Simpson Patterson, had been the wife of two of Brown's black associates—Lewis S. Leary, who fell at Harpers Ferry, and Charles H. Langston.

In the 1960's the question of equality for Negro Americans assumed a new urgency, brought on in part by younger black leaders whose posture was openly defiant. It was not so much that they were listening to a different drummer; it was rather that they were calling for a much faster beat, as befitted a more urgent hour.

Among these newer black leaders with their emphasis on black power and on raising the level of ethnic consciousness, how would John Brown fare?

Robert F. Williams, a leading figure in the Revolutionary Action Movement (R.A.M.), said that he always kept with him a copy of Henry David Thoreau's plea for Captain Brown, which was indeed a tribute of almost unrivaled eloquence and all the more noteworthy because Thoreau was accounted as an exponent of passive, nonviolent resistance. But the typical contemporary black militant's attitude toward John Brown was more likely to be phrased in somewhat negative terms—a regret that there were so few other whites like him. "From the beginning of the contact between blacks and whites," wrote Eldridge Cleaver, "there has been very little reason for a black man to respect a white, with such exceptions as John Brown and others lesser known." [70]

A similar lament that other whites were unlike John Brown was voiced by Ted Joans, a painter and a poet, in his "The Non-John Brown's," in which he identifies "the non-john brown WHITES" as the enemy the third world—Latin America, Africa, and Asia—must fight. Malcolm X, basically sharing this viewpoint, said that he had little regard for nonviolent white liberals. "If you are for me and my problems," he counseled, "then you must be willing to do as old John Brown did." The less sanguine H. Rap Brown narrowed his list of acceptable whites to John Brown himself, naming him "the only white man I could respect and he is dead." [71]

As a group the black militants of the late 1960's tended to concentrate on those movements which were black-conceived and black-led and hence have been inclined to devote less attention to Brown than was the case of their forebears. Some withheld praise from any white person, holding that all whites, individually and collectively shared a heavy burden of racial wrong-doing. Floyd McKissick, former national chairman of the Congress of Racial Equality, held that men like Brown were "exempt from the guilt of their people," on the ground that Brown "did as much for the defense of Black Men as he would have done in his own defense." [72] But from the black militant's point of view, even if an unusual white warranted absolution, he could hardly be worthy of commendation by blacks, such an accolade being reserved exclusively for their own.

The process of lumping all whites together in an adversary relationship could hardly prevail in the case of John Brown. For even the most race-conscious black could hardly quarrel with his unequivocal egalitarianism and his twin strategies of confrontation and direct action. However disenchanted with whites one might have become, he could hardly refute the assertion made in 1914 by Archibald H. Grimké, black lawyer and diplomat:

> John Brown was the white man who dared smite white men with the sword for oppressing black men and he was the white man who died to deliver his black fellow countrymen from this oppression.[73]

And even beyond these considerations of his personal behavior and his methods, Brown possessed one towering trait that would command the respect of the most militant black today, as it endeared the man to the preceding generations of black Americans. This was his love of freedom, a principle by which he lived and for which he died.

But whether he fared well or ill with one segment of the population at any given juncture, John Brown would remain a timeless figure, one who in his day had transcended the accidents of color, status, or antecedents. Lerone Bennett, Jr., noted historian and perceptive interpreter of the black experience, points out that "it is to John Brown we must go, finally, if we want to understand the limitations and possibilities of our situation. He was of no color, John Brown, of no race or age." The gifted contemporary young black poet, Michael S. Harper, in his lengthy lyrical eulogy, "History as Cap'n Brown" views the man in his more inclusive context. "Come to the crusade," he has Brown crying out, "not Negroes, *brothers.*" [74]

Given to moral absolutism, John Brown was flawed, one in whose bosom there was a subtle interflow of good and ill. But he would survive because he was the embodiment of first principles. Warped in many ways, he nonetheless had a liberal vision of the brotherhood of man. And it was this vision that so stirred his conscience that he could not hold his peace.

Hence if devotion to Brown was likely to remain a racial heritage to black Americans, it was also likely to endure as an expression of man's common humanity in search of its most satisfying self. John Brown's body might be grave-bound in North Elba but it carried its own seeds of regeneration, to be scattered abroad with the periodic arrival of a rising wind.

BIBLIOGRAPHICAL NOTE

A figure both historical and legendary, the enigmatic John Brown has been of enduring interest to his fellow Americans. The Brown literature has been enormous, including poetry, fiction, and drama as well as essays, history, and biography. Of the last named, there are three that stand out for their original scholarship, their authors Oswald Garrison Villard, Stephen B. Oates, and Richard O. Boyer.

Villard's *John Brown, 1800–1859, A Biography Fifty Years After* (1910) was a landmark in its careful approach to the man. Although himself one of the founders of the National Association for the Advancement of Colored People, Villard did not let his liberal sympathies influence his analysis of Brown. His biography does not gloss over Brown's defects of character or errors of judgment. Villard was respectful of sound evidence, pointing out (in *The Nation*, February 12, 1914) that "undocumented recollections are a trap a wary historian must usually shun, particularly if recorded by one well on in years."

For a pioneer scholarly biography, Villard's work stood the test of time admirably. But in its five subsequent reprintings up to 1943 its text was never updated. This needed task went unfilled until 1970 with the appearance of Oates' *To Purge This Land with Blood*. Oates used sources not available to Villard for all his spadework, such as the massive manuscript collection of the recently deceased Boyd B. Stutler of Charlestown, West Virginia. Oates succeeded in his attempt to re-create Brown's life on the basis of contemporary sources, no mean feat since such sources were often shot with partisanship. In a full-bodied, widely ranging study, *The Legend of John Brown: A Biography and a History* (1973), Richard O. Boyer, defining a legend as "the story of a people at a time of peril," views Brown as the central figure in the long sectional war over slavery. The first of two projected volumes, this carefully researched work takes Brown and his times down to the autumn of 1855 when Brown arrived in Kansas. Jules Abels, *Man on Fire: John Brown and the Cause of Liberty* (1971), well written and fast-paced, was aimed at the general reader. Outstripping all other of the above biographies in its uncritical admiration, Truman Nelson's *The Old Man: John Brown at Harper's Ferry* (1973), holds that the raid "was a classic coup, as distinguished from both insurrection and revolution." Nelson makes liberal use of the flashback technique; he dispenses with footnotes and index.

The bibliographies listed in Villard, Oates, and Boyer, particularly the last-named, are most helpful to those wishing to study Brown. Oates' bibliography gives brief appraisals of previous Brown biographers, a theme on which he expands considerably in an article, "John Brown and His Judges: A Critique of the Historical Literature," in *Civil War History,* March 1971. An additional sidelight on many of these authors, along with others, may be found in Ernest Kaiser's "John Brown's Legacy," a review essay on W. E. B. Du Bois' *John Brown* (the centennial edition), appearing in *Freedomways,* Summer 1963. For those seeking a general anthology of the man, *A John Brown Reader,* edited by Louis Ruchames, is highly recommended.

As might be expected, scores of articulate blacks have expressed themselves on the subject of John Brown, dating from his times to ours. *Blacks on John Brown,* edited by Benjamin Quarles (1972), brings together a cross-section of these writings, which include personal letters, eulogies, resolutions, sermons, essays, and newspaper articles.

Primary source materials dealing with the raid and its aftermath and designed primarily to develop the critical discernment of college students may be found in the following well-edited compilations: Edward Stone, ed., *Incident at Harper's Ferry* (Englewood Cliffs, N.J., 1956), and Richard Scheidenhelm, ed., *The Response to John Brown* (Belmont, Cal., 1972). Much the same in general approach and in editorial competence, *John Brown,* a compilation assembled by Jonathon Fanton and Richard Warch (Englewood Cliffs, N.J., 1973), is ostensibly designed for a wider audience, making up one of the titles in the Prentice-Hall "Great Lives Observed" series.

NOTES

1
John Brown's Day

1. J. Max Barber, "The Niagara Movement at Harpers Ferry," *The Voice of the Negro* (Atlanta, Ga.), Oct. 1906, pp. 409–10.

2. *The Washington Bee,* Aug. 25, 1906. Mary White Ovington, *The Walls Came Tumbling Down* (New York, 1947), 101.

3. Mary White Ovington, New York *Evening Post,* Aug. 18, 1906.

4. *Ibid.*

5. Frederick Douglass, *Life and Times of Frederick Douglass* (Hartford, 1884), 452.

6. New York *Evening Post,* Aug. 17, 1906.

7. *New York Age,* Aug. 2, 1906. *Alexander's Magazine* (Boston), Sept. 15, 1906, p. 18.

8. *The Afro-American Ledger* (Baltimore), May 5, 1906.

9. Barber, "Niagara Movement," 410.

10. *New-York Tribune,* Jan. 6, 1860.

11. *Washington Bee,* Aug. 25, 1906.

12. Among other of Brown's actions against slavery, Du Bois mentions him as having left his business in 1854 to help free the fugitive slave Anthony Burns. This was the only factual error in the Du Bois address and one that he would not repeat in the biography of Brown he published three years later.

13. *Boston Guardian,* Aug. 26, 1906. Herbert Aptheker. *Documentary History of the Negro People in the United States* (New York, 1951), 907–10. New York *Evening Post,* Aug. 20, 1906.

14. *Washington Bee,* Aug. 25, 1906.

15. Barber, "Niagara Movement," 412–15. *The Colored American Magazine* (New York), Aug. 1906, p. 78.

16. Barber, "Niagara Movement," 408. New York *Evening Post,* Aug. 20, 1906. Watson, "Recalling 1906," *The Crisis* (New York), Apr. 1934, p. 100.

17. Reverdy C. Ransom, *The Pilgrimage of Harriet Ransom's Son* (Nashville, Tenn., 1950?), 197.

18. *Guardian,* Aug. 25, 1906.

19. *Boston Globe,* Dec. 2, 1909, in "Boston John Brown Jubilee" (Boston, 1909), 41.

20. John to Mary, Mar. 7, 1844, in Boyd B. Stutler Collection of John Brown Papers, 8 reels, The Ohio Historical Society (hereafter cited as Stutler Coll.). Franklin B. Sanborn, "John Brown and His Friends," *Atlantic Monthly,* July 1872. Brown to his children, Nov. 22, 1859, in Louis Ruchames, ed., *A John Brown Reader* (London, New York, 1959), p. 142 (hereafter cited as Ruchames, ed., *Brown Reader*).

21. *The Principia* (New York), Nov. 26, 1859. Brown to John, Jr., Aug. 26, 1853, in Ruchames, ed., *Brown Reader,* 81. *Frederick Douglass' Paper* (Rochester, N.Y.), Jan. 27, 1854. New York *Herald,* Oct. 21, 1859.

22. "John Brown's Autobiography, Written by Him to Henry L. Stearns, Son of George L. Stearns, and Bearing date Red Rock, Iowa, July 7, 1857," in Richard J. Hinton, *John Brown and His Men* (New York, 1894), 651 (hereafter cited as Hinton, *John Brown*). Frank L. Stearns, "John Brown and His Eastern Friends," *New England Magazine* (Boston), July 1910, p. 590. Eleanor Atkinson, "The Soul of John Brown: Recollections of the Great Abolitionist by his Son," *The American Magazine,* Oct. 1909, p. 636. Osborne Perry Anderson, *A Voice from Harper's Ferry* (Boston, 1861), 24 (hereafter cited as Anderson, *Harper's Ferry*).

23. *New-York Tribune,* Oct. 17, 1886.

24. James Redpath, *The Public Life of John Brown* (Boston, 1860), 105 (hereafter cited as Redpath, *Public Life*). *New York Times,* Nov. 20, 1859.

25. Redpath to William F. Poole, Feb. 27, 1864, in Walter Muir Whitehill, "John Brown of Osawatomie in Boston," *Proceedings of the Massachusetts Historical Society, October 1947–May 1950,* p. 269.

2
Brown's Black Orientation

1. George Washington Williams, *The Negro Race in America from 1619–1880* (2 vols., New York, 1883), II, 217.

2. For this letter, see Ruchames, ed., *Brown Reader,* 34–41.

3. For this often-reprinted letter, see Franklin B. Sanborn, *The Life and Letters of John Brown* (Boston, 1885), 40–41 (hereafter cited as Sanborn, *Life and Letters*).

4. Mary Land, "John Brown's Ohio Environment," *The Ohio State Archeological and Historical Quarterly,* Jan. 1948, p. 28.

5. The account of this incident by John Brown, Jr., is in Sanborn, *Life and Letters,* 52–53, and for Ruth Brown Thompson's version, see the same work, 37.

6. Justus Newton Brown, "Lovejoy's Influence on John Brown," *The Magazine of History,* Sept.–Oct. 1916, p. 101. *Hudson of Long Ago: Reminiscences of Lora Case, Written in 1897* (Hudson, Ohio, 1963), 54.

7. John Brown, Jr., to F. B. Sanborn, Dec. 12, 1890, in *The Nation,* Dec. 25, 1890, p. 500. For an earlier, more richly detailed and slightly variant version of this incident, see Brown, Jr., to Sanborn, Feb. 16, 1885, in Miscellaneous Papers of John Brown. Manuscripts Division, New York Public Library. The "colored theological student," of whom John, Jr., speaks, could have been John Sykes Fayette, who was graduated from Western Reserve College in 1836. "There is nothing in the records that would indicate his race but I know from oral tradition that he was black," writes Mrs. Ruth E. Helmuth, University Archivist, to the author (May 16, 1972). For corroborative evidence, see Carroll Cutler, *A History of Western Reserve College During Its First Half Century, 1826–1876* (Cleveland, 1876), 43.

8. Brown to Mary, in John Brown Letters, Henry E. Huntington Library, San Marino, California.

9. Brown to Thomas Wentworth Higginson, Mar. 12, 1858, in Thomas Wentworth Higginson Papers, Boston Public Library.

10. James Foreman to James Redpath, Dec. 28, 1859, in Ruchames, ed., *Brown Reader,* 167. John, Jr., to Sanborn, Jan. 8, 1884, in Stutler Coll. Ernest C. Miller, "John Brown's Ten Years in Northwestern Pennsylvania," *Pennsylvania History,* Jan. 1948, p. 25. George B. Delamater, in Ruchames, ed., *Brown Reader,* 173.

11. Brown to John, Jr., Apr. 24, 1848, in Stutler Coll.

12. Brown to John, Jr., May 15, 1847, in Brown Letters, Huntington Library.

13. F. B. Sanborn, "John Brown in Massachusetts," *Atlantic Monthly,* Apr. 1872, p. 423. Brown to John, Jr., May 15, 1847, in Brown Letters, Huntington Library. Sanborn tells the hardly credible story that Brown "sent Thomas to 'look up' Madison Washington, leader of the slaves who seized the *Creole* but that Washington, when found, proved an unfit person for such a position." Sanborn, "John Brown in Massachusetts," p. 423.

14. *Springfield Republican,* Feb. 3, 1848. On May 15, 1847, less than

a month after Douglass had returned from the British Isles, Brown wrote that he was "in hourly expectation of a visit from him." Brown to John, Jr., May 15, 1847, in Brown Letters, Huntington Library.

15. *North Star,* Feb. 11, 1848.

16. Douglass, *Life and Times,* 273–75.

17. "Sambo's Mistakes," Maryland Historical Society, Baltimore.

18. *Springfield Republican,* Apr. 20, 1848. *North Star,* Dec. 8, 1848. Brown to Owen Brown, Jan. 10, 1849, in Ruchames, ed., *Brown Reader,* 67.

19. Ruth Brown Thompson, in Sanborn, *Life and Letters,* 100.

20. Mary Lee, "John Brown Rests Amid the Mountains," *New York Times Magazine,* Oct. 20, 1929, pp. 7, 23.

21. Robert F. Lucid, ed., *The Journal of Richard Henry Dana, Jr.* (3 vols., Cambridge, Mass., 1968), I, 364. See also "How We Met John Brown," *Atlantic Monthly,* July 1871, pp. 1–9.

22. Brown to Willis A. Hodges, Oct. 28, 1848, in New York *Evening Post,* Dec. 20, 1859. Brown to Hodges, Jan. 22, 1849, *ibid.*

23. Brown to Smith, June 30, 1849, in Stutler Coll.

24. Brown to "Dear Sons John, Jason, Frederick, and Daughters," Dec. 4, 1850, in Sanborn, *Life and Letters,* 77. Brown to Ruth and Henry Thompson, Oct. 6, 1851, in Miscellaneous Papers of John Brown, New York Public Library. Brown to Thompson, May 10, 1853, in Stutler Coll.

25. Brown to Willis A. Hodges, Jan. 22, 1849, in New York *Evening Post,* Dec. 20, 1859. Brown to his wife, Dec. 27, 1852, in Sanborn, *Life and Letters,* 108–9.

26. Brown to his wife, Jan. 17, 1851, in Ruchames, ed., *Brown Reader,* 75.

27. Henry Andrew Wright, "John Brown in Springfield," *New England Magazine,* May 1894, pp. 276–80. Ruchames carries this document, although without the "Resolutions" and the list of signatories (Ruchames, ed., *Brown Reader,* 76–78).

28. Ruth Brown Thompson, in Sanborn, *Life and Letters,* 131–32. *Frederick Douglass' Paper,* Dec. 25, 1851.

29. *Ibid.,* Jan. 27, 1854. *Utica Morning Herald,* in *Boston Advertiser,* Nov. 9, 1859.

30. Lyman E. Epps to Frederick Douglass, July 12, 1854, *Douglass' Paper,* July 21, 1854. Edwin N. Cotter, Jr., "John Brown in the Adirondacks," *Adirondack Life,* Summer 1972, p. 10. "Unfortunately there are no materials in the Timbucto settlement in the Essex County Historical Society," wrote the librarian of the Society, Dorothy A. Plum, to the author, Sept. 20, 1971.

31. Lougen to Douglass, Mar. 7, 1854, *Douglass' Paper,* Apr. 14, 1854.

32. *The Pennsylvania Freeman,* Mar. 30, 1854.

33. Brown to Thompson, Sept. 30, 1854; Brown to "Dear Children," Nov. 2, 1854, in Stutler Coll.

34. Annie Brown Adams to F. G. Adams (then secretary of the Kansas Historical Society), Sept. 5, 1886, in New-York Historical Society, John Brown Miscellaneous Folder.

35. *Douglass' Paper,* Sept. 7, 1855.

36. *Ibid.,* Sept. 14, 1855.

37. Editorial, *ibid.,* July 25, 1856.

38. *Report, The Select Committee of the Senate appointed to inquire into the late invasion and seizure of the public property at Harper's Ferry.* Report of Committee, No. 278, 36th Congress, 1st Session, "Testimony," p. 197. This report is comprised of two parts, the first entitled, "Invasion at Harper's Ferry," and running to 71 pages, and the second entitled, "Testimony," and running to 255 pages (hereafter cited as *Mason Report*).

39. Brown to "Dear Wife and Children," June 28, 1855, in Sanborn, *Life and Letters,* 194. *Douglass' Paper,* July 6, 1855.

40. John Brown, Jr., to F. B. Sanborn, Mar. 27, 1885, in Stutler Coll. Sanborn, *Life and Letters,* 194, note 1.

41. Brown to "Dear Wife and Children, Every One," Oct. 14, 1855, in Sanborn, *Life and Letters,* 201. Brown to his father, Oct. 14, 1855, in Ruchames, ed., *Brown Reader,* 88. Brown to "Dear Wife and Children, Every One," Nov. 2, 1855, in Sanborn, *Life and Letters,* 204.

42. *Douglass' Paper,* Jan. 11, 1856. Brown to his wife and children, Oct. 14, 1855, in Sanborn, *Life and Letters,* 201.

43. Brown wrote two accounts of the Wakarusa War, one to Douglass (see above) and the other to his wife and children, the latter dated Dec. 16, 1855, and in John Brown Manuscripts, Kansas Historical Society (hereafter referred to as Brown Papers, Kansas Hist. Soc.), and carried in Oswald Garrison Villard, *John Brown: A Biography Fifty Years Later* (Boston, 1910), 118–20 (hereafter cited as Villard, *Brown*). Brown's commission, dated Nov. 27, 1855, is found in John Brown Papers Collected by Ferdinand J. Dreer, Historical Society of Pennsylvania (hereafter cited as Dreer Papers). Villard, *Brown,* 122.

44. "John Brown and His Sons in Kansas Territory," *Indiana Magazine of History,* June 1935, p. 146.

45. Brown to "Dear Wife and Children, Every One," Apr. 7, 1856, in Sanborn, *Life and Letters,* 229.

46. John, Jr., to Douglass, Apr. 4, 1856, in *Douglass' Paper,* May 2, 1856. Charles H. Robinson, *The Kansas Conflict* (Lawrence, Kans., 1898), Appendix, "Correspondence About Brown," 485.

47. Brown to "Dear Wife and Children, Every One," June (no day of month) 1856, in Ruchames, ed., *Brown Reader*, 97.

48. Villard, *Brown*, 248.

49. *Douglass' Paper*, Sept. 12, 1856.

50. Jeremiah R. Brown quotation from undated clipping in John W. Cromwell Collection of Newspaper Clippings, Howard University. Brown to Giddings, June (no date of month) 1848, Ruchames, ed., *Brown Reader*, 65. "Old Browns Farewell to the Plymouth Rocks, Bunker Hill Monuments, Charter Oaks, and Uncle Thoms Cabbins," in Ruchames, ed., *Brown Reader*, 106.

3
Rehearsal Pattern

1. "In Idea of Things in Kansas," in Sanborn, *Life and Letters*. *New-York Tribune*, Mar. 4, 1857.

2. Narcissa May Smith, "Reminiscences of John Brown." *Midland Monthly*, Sept. 1895, p. 233.

3. Watson to "Dear Mother, Brother and Sister," Oct. 30, 1856, in Sanborn, *Life and Letters*, 341. Douglass to Brown, Dec. 7 (1856?), in Dreer Papers. Brown to John, Jr., Mar. 24, 1857, in Stutler Coll.

4. Brown to John, Jr., Feb. 4, 1858, in Stutler Coll.

5. During the early months of 1858 Brown kept a combination diary-memorandum book, its skeletal entries containing little more than a record of his correspondence. Charles R. Douglass to Oswald Garrison Villard, July 27, 1908, in John Brown Manuscript Materials Used by Oswald Garrison Villard in Preparing the Life of John Brown, Columbia University Library (hereafter cited as Villard Ms.).

6. Gloucester to Brown, Feb. 19, 1858, in Brown Papers, Kansas Hist. Soc.

7. Brown to his wife, Mar. 2, 1858, in Sanborn, *Life and Letters*, 443.

8. Gloucester to Brown, Mar. 9, 1858; Loguen to Brown, Mar. 4, 1858; in Brown Papers, Kansas Hist. Soc.

9. Brown, Mar. 6, 1858, entry in diary-memorandum book, Boston Public Library.

10. Brown to Gloucester, Mar. 26, 1858; entry of Mar. 26, 1858, in diary-memorandum book, Boston Public Library.

11. Benjamin Drew, *A Northside View of Slavery* (Boston, 1856), 11. Loguen statement made to T. W. Higginson, *Liberator*, May 28, 1858.

12. Brown to John, Jr., Apr. 8, 1858, in Stutler Coll.

13. For Delany's role in planning the convention and in its deliberations, see Victor Ullman, *Martin R. Delany: The Beginnings of Black Nationalism* (Boston, 1971), 195–200.

14. Richard Realf in *Mason Report,* "Testimony," 95. For a slightly different version, see George B. Gill's account in Sanborn, *Life and Letters,* 731.

15. Fred Landon, "From Chatham to Harper's Ferry," *The Canadian Magazine,* Oct. 1919, p. 442. Benjamin Drew, *A Northside View of Slavery,* 165. William Wells Brown, *Pine and Palm,* Sept. 28, 1861.

16. Hinton says that Brown stayed at the home of Isaac Holden (*John Brown,* 175), but other accounts list his host as Israel D. Shadd. Interview with James M. Bell, *St. Louis Globe-Democrat,* Apr. 29, 1888.

17. Alexander M. Ross, *Memoirs of a Reformer* (Toronto, 1893), 84. John E. Cook surmised that "some twenty-five or thirty of these circulars were sent." "Confession of John E. Cook" (Charlestown, Va., 1859), 8.

18. Brown diary-memorandum book, Boston Public Library. Cook, "Confession," 8.

19. Loguen to Brown, May 6, 1858, in Brown Papers, Kansas Hist. Soc.

20. Richard Realf, in *Mason Report,* "Testimony," 96–97.

21. James C. Hamilton, "John Brown in Canada," *The Canadian Magazine,* Dec. 1894, p. 132.

22. *Mason Report,* "Invasion of Harper's Ferry," 46.

23. Brown's April 8 reference in Brown diary-memorandum book, Boston Public Library. Day to Brown in Boyd B. Stutler, "John Brown's Constitution," *Lincoln Herald,* Dec. 1948–Feb. 1949, p. 24.

24. Stutler, "John Brown's Constitution," p. 22.

25. On August 1, 1958, the Archeological and Historic Sites Board of Ontario unveiled a bronze plaque at the First Baptist Church in commemoration of the centennial of the Chatham convention. For a diagram of the convention sites, see Hamilton, "John Brown in Canada," 126. The Dreer Papers has a copy of the printed commission forms to be signed by the "Pres. of the Convention."

26. William Wells Brown in *Pine and Palm,* Sept. 28, 1861. Realf, in *Mason Report,* "Testimony," 99.

27. Anderson, *Harper's Ferry,* 10, 9.

28. Odell Shepherd, ed., *The Journals of Bronson Alcott* (Boston, 1938), 316.

29. In the Stutler Collection.

30. Lee to Col. S. Cooper, Adjutant General of the United States, Oct. 19, 1859, in "John Brown Letters found in the Virginia State Library Archives in 1901," in *Virginia Magazine of History,* July 1902, p. 123.

31. Entries dated May 28 and June 3, 1858, in Brown diary-memorandum book, Boston Public Library.

32. *Ibid.,* Apr. 14, 1858.

33. Brown to "Dear Wife and Children, Every One," May 25, 1858, in Sanborn, *Life and Letters,* 456.

34. Sanborn to Brown, Jan. 13, 1858, in John Brown Manuscripts, Trevor Arnett Library, Atlanta University (hereafter cited as Brown Ms., Trevor Arnett Library).

35. Douglass, *Life and Times,* 316–17.

36. Hinton, *John Brown,* 163. Anderson, *Harper's Ferry,* 17.

37. Realf to Brown, May 31, 1858, in Sanborn, *Life and Letters,* 481. Gill, in Hinton, *John Brown,* 732.

38. Brown to his Children in Ohio, in Sanborn, *Life and Letters,* 481.

39. *New-York Tribune,* Jan. 22, 1859.

40. Hinton, *John Brown,* 220.

41. *New-York Tribune,* Mar. 17, 1859.

42. Villard, *Brown,* 371.

43. *New-York Tribune,* Jan. 22, 1859.

44. *Ibid.*

45. Sanborn, *John Brown,* 485, 487.

46. Hamilton, "John Brown in Canada," 123.

47. Hinton, *John Brown,* 226.

48. J. B. Grinnell, *Men and Events of Forty Years* (Boston, 1891), 207–10.

49. Gill to Hinton, June 18, 1860, in Villard Ms.

50. While at Ingersoll, Ontario, earlier that year Brown had directed his family to write him care of John Jones, Box 764, Chicago. Brown to his family, Apr. 16, 1858, in John Brown Papers, 1842–1928, Chicago Historical Society (hereafter referred to as Brown Papers, Chicago Hist. Soc.).

51. Kagi to Charles P. Tidd, Mar. 13, 1859, in *Calendar of Virginia State Papers,* 308.

52. Ruth to T. W. Higginson, Dec. 27, 1859, in Higginson Papers, Boston Public Library.

53. *Detroit Free Press,* Mar. 19, 1859.

54. *Douglass' Paper,* Nov. 17, 1854. *Detroit Advertiser and Tribune,* Dec. 21, 1867. For a lengthy and revealing obituary of DeBaptiste, see *Detroit Advertiser and Tribune,* Feb. 23, 1875. Another sketch of DeBaptiste may be found in David M. Katzman, *Before the Ghetto: Black Detroit in the Nineteenth Century* (Urbana, Ill., 1973), 14–15.

56. *Detroit Post,* in *Anti-Slavery Standard,* Apr. 9, 1870.

57. Redpath, *John Brown,* 239.

4
The Recruitment of Blacks

1. Realf in *Mason Report,* "Testimony," 97.

2. Brown to his Children, Jan. 23, 1852, and Jan. 9, 1856, in Brown Papers, Chicago Hist. Soc.

3. *The Ram's Horn,* in *Liberator,* Aug. 3, 1849.

4. W. A. Phillips, "Three Interviews with Old John Brown," in Ruchames, ed., *Brown Reader,* 218.

5. Brown to wife, Jan. 7, 1853, in Stutler Coll.

6. Redpath, *Public Life,* 46. Higginson in *Liberator,* May 28, 1858.

7. Loguen to Douglass, Aug. 5, 1853, in *Douglass' Paper,* Aug. 12, 1853.

8. Brown to Douglass, Aug. 18, 1853, *ibid.*

9. For this address, see *A Memorial Discourse by Rev. Henry Highland Garnet . . . with an Introduction by James McCune Smith* (Philadelphia, 1865), 45–51.

10. *Ibid.,* 52.

11. Douglass in *Liberator,* June 8, 1849.

12. New York *Herald,* Aug. 12, 1852. *Radical Abolitionist,* June 1857.

13. *Liberator,* Aug. 13, 1841. Brown to John, Jr., Sept. 18, 1849, in Stutler Coll.

14. *Liberator,* July 9, 1847. *Anti-Slavery Standard,* Aug. 7, 1858.

15. *Proceedings of the Colored National Convention Held in Rochester, July 6, 7, 8, 1853* (Rochester, 1853), 9.

16. For this address in full, see Dorothy Porter, ed., *Negro Protest Pamphlets* (New York, 1969).

17. William C. Nell, *Colored Patriots of the American Revolution* (Boston, 1855), 11.

18. *Patriot and Union,* Oct. 28, 1859. *Ibid.,* Oct. 20, 1859.

19. *Liberator,* Apr. 5, 1850. *Anti-Slavery Standard,* Oct. 10, 1859.

20. *Standard,* Dec. 5, 1850. *Proceedings of the Colored National Convention of 1855* (Salem, N.J., 1856), 25.

21. Thomas Drew, *The John Brown Invasion: An Authentic History of the Harper's Ferry Tragedy* (Boston, 1860), 21. *Calendar of Virginia State Papers,* XI, 346.

22. Mary Land, "John Brown's Ohio Environment," 41. Clayton S. Ellsworth, *"Oberlin and the Anti-Slavery Movement up to the Civil War,"* doctoral dissertation, Cornell U., 1930, p. 173. *Pine and Palm,* Oct. 19, 1861.

23. Brown's diary-memorandum book, New York *Herald,* Oct. 25, 1859.

24. Sanborn, *Life and Letters,* 549.

25. Delany to Kagi, Aug. 16, 1858, in *Calendar of Virginia State Papers,* XI, 292.

26. Annie Straith Jamieson, *William King: Friend and Champion of Slaves* (Toronto, 1925), 159. Issac Holden, interview in *Chatham Planet,* Apr. 28, 1881.

27. Bell to John, Jr., Sept. 14, 1859, in *Baltimore Sun,* Oct. 26, 1859.

28. Victor Ullman, *Look to the North Star: A Life of William King* (Boston, 1969), 250–53.

29. John, Jr., to Kagi, Aug. 27, 1859, in *Calendar of Virginia State Papers,* IX, 121. Bell to John, Jr., Sept. 14, 1859, in *Baltimore Sun,* Oct. 26, 1859. John, Jr., to Kagi, Aug. 27, 1859, in *Baltimore American and Commercial Advertiser* (hereafter cited as *Baltimore American*), Oct. 26, 1859.

30. John, Jr., to Kagi, Aug. 27, 1859, in *Calendar of Virginia State Papers,* IX, 317. Same to same, Oct. 5, 1859, in New York *Herald,* Oct. 25, 1859.

31. Ambush to Tod, Aug. 7, 1862, in Herbert Aptheker, *A Documentary History of the Negro People in the United States* (New York, 1951), p. 462.

32. *Liberator,* Dec. 9, 1859.

33. E. A. Gloucester to Brown, Aug. 18, 1859, in Dreer Papers.

34. *Baltimore American,* Oct. 25, 1859.

35. Douglass, *Life and Times,* 317–20.

36. Webb to O. G. Villard, Dec. 10, 1907, in Villard Ms. J. G. Anderson to J. B. Anderson, June 17, 1859, in Hinton, *John Brown,* 239, note.

37. Katherine Mayo interview with Annie Brown Adams, Oct. 2 and 3, 1908, Villard Ms. Mrs. Russell to Katherine Mayo, undated interview in 1909, in Ruchames, ed., *Brown Reader,* 235.

38. Boteler to newspaper reporter, *Philadelphia Enquirer,* May 2, 1883. John, Jr., to Sanborn, Apr. 21, 1885, in Alfred William Anthony Papers, New York Public Library.

39. Charles Remond Douglass to O. G. Villard, July 27, 1908, in Villard Ms.

40. Sanborn to Higginson, June 4, 1859, in Higginson Papers. Edward Morton to Brown, June 1, 1859, in Sanborn, *Life and Letters,* 468. Sanborn to Brown, Aug. 27, 1859, in Dreer Papers.

41. Sanborn to Higginson, Sept. 14, 1859, in Higginson Papers. Same to same, Sept. 23, 1859, in *Baltimore American,* Oct. 26, 1859.

42. Hayden to Brown, Sept. 16, 1859, in *Boston Evening Transcript,* Oct. 26, 1859.

43. Harris to Kagi, Aug. 22, 1859, in *Calendar of Virginia State Papers,* XI, 335.

44. On disagreements between white and black abolitionists, see Jane H. Pease and William H. Pease, "Ends, Means and Attitudes: Black-White Conflict in the Anti-Slavery Movement," *Civil War History,* June 1972, pp. 117–28. Katherine Du Pre Lumpkin, "The General Plan Was Freedom: A Negro Secret Order of the Underground Railroad," *Phylon,* First Quarter, 1967, p. 70.

45. Potter, *The South and Sectional Conflict* (Baton Rouge, La., 1968), 218.

46. Hinton to *Boston Evening Transcript,* Dec. 3, 1859. Wattles, in *Mason Report,* "Testimony," 225.

47. Statement to Gileadites in Ruchames, ed., *Brown Reader,* 76. Brown to John, Jr., Feb. 5, 1858, in C. R. Galbreath, "John Brown: Additional Notes," *Ohio Archeological and Historical Quarterly,* 1921 (vol. 30), 338. Brown to Kagi, Aug. 11, 1859, in *Calendar of Virginia State Papers,* XI, 338.

48. J. Ewing Glasgow, *Insurrection: Being an Account of the Late Outbreak in Virginia, and of the Trial and Execution of John Brown, Its Hero* (Edinburgh, 1860), p. 9. Realf, in *Mason Report,* "Testimony," 44. *Cleveland Plain Dealer,* Nov. 3, 1859. Stearns, in *Mason Report,* "Testimony," 244.

49. Franklin B. Sanborn, *Recollections of Seventy Years* (2 vols., Boston, 1909), I, 184. Sanborn, "The Virginia Campaign of John Brown," *Atlantic Monthly,* Apr. 1875, p. 453. Hinton, "Old John Brown and the Men of Harper's Ferry," *Time* (London), Aug. 1890, p. 828.

50. John, Jr., to Kagi, Sept. 27, 1859, in New York *Herald,* Oct. 25, 1859. John, Jr., to John Cochrane, Feb. 28, 1878, in *New-York Tribune,* Mar. 23, 1878.

51. Anderson, *Harper's Ferry,* 27. Kagi to John, Jr., Oct. 10, 1859, in John Brown Diary, 1838–45, and 1855–59, and other Papers, Boston Public Library. Anderson, *Harper's Ferry,* 20.

52. On the whole topic see Steven H. Shiffrin, "The Rhetoric of Black Violence in the Antebellum Period: Henry Highland Garnet," *Journal of Black Studies,* Sept. 1971, pp. 45–54, and Ernest G. Bormann, ed., *Forerunners of Black Power: The Rhetoric of Abolition* (Englewood Cliffs, N.J., 1971).

53. On this point, see John Demos, "The Antislavery Movement and the Problem of Violent 'Means,'" *New England Quarterly,* Dec. 1964, pp. 501–26.

54. Higginson to Spooner, Nov. 30, 1858, in Lysander Spooner Papers, 1835–1886, Boston Public Library. *Anti-Slavery Standard,* Oct. 10, 1850.

55. Hinton, *John Brown,* 449.

56. *Pine and Palm,* July 27, 1861.

56. *Rochester Democrat,* Oct. 21, 1859, in *New-York Tribune,* Oct. 22, 1859.

58. Lucy N. Colman, *Reminiscences of Lucy Colman* (Buffalo, 1891), 86.

59. Writing to his wife on September 16, 1859, Watson Brown said that Newby had seven children (*Anti-Slavery Standard,* Mar. 24,

1860). The generally accepted number, however, is six. For a sketch of Newby, see Thomas Featherstonhaugh, "John Brown's Men: The Lives of Those Killed at Harper's Ferry," *Publications of the Southern Historical Association,* III, 1899, p. 294.

60. Verbatim from letter from Harriet to "Dear Husband," *Calendar of Virginia State Papers,* XI, 310.

61. Same to same, Aug. 16, 1859, in *Calendar of Virginia State Papers,* XI, 310.

62. Annie to Higginson, Nov. 29, 1859, in Brown Letters, Boston Public Library.

63. Katherine Mayo interview with Henrietta Evans, Mar. 5, 1908, in Villard Ms. See also Rose Leary Love, "A Few Facts About Lewis Sheridan Leary Who Was Killed at Harper's Ferry in John Brown's Raid," *Negro History Bulletin,* June 1943, pp. 198, 215.

64. William C. Nell, "Lewis S. Leary," *Pine and Palm,* July 27, 1861.

65. Mary Leary Langston to Houghton Mifflin, Oct. 10, 1910, in Villard Ms. W. E. Bigglestone (Oberlin College Archives) to author, Sept. 7, 1971.

66. Leary to Kagi, Sept. 8, 1859, in Dreer Papers.

67. William C. Nell, "John A. Copeland," *Pine and Palm,* July 20, 1861. John Mercer Langston, *From the Virginia Plantation to the National Capitol* (Hartford, 1894), 195.

68. Dauphin Thompson to "Dear Brother and Sister," in Hinton, *John Brown,* 277. Villard, *Brown,* 418. "Statements of Annie Brown, Daughter of John Brown, Written November 1886," handwritten, thirty-eight-page document, in Chicago Hist. Soc.

69. Annie Brown to Sanborn, undated letter, in Sanborn, *Recollections,* 179. Luke Sharp (on Anderson), *Detroit Free Press,* in *Chatham Weekly Planet,* Apr. 28, 1881. Annie Brown (on Newby) to Sanborn, in his *Recollections,* 179.

70. John E. Cook, *Confession,* 64. Douglass said later that Anderson told him that Brown's announcement that he was going to Harpers Ferry "caused loud talk of deserting." Douglass to John Cochrane, Feb. 4, 1878, in *New-York Tribune,* Feb. 9, 1878. Douglass makes the point again in his autobiography (see *Life and Times,* 321.).

71. Anderson, *Harper's Ferry,* 15.

72. *Ibid.,* 31.

5
Harpers Ferry: Scene and Sequel

1. Oswald Garrison Villard, "How Patrick Higgins Met John Brown," *Harper's Weekly,* Jan. 26, 1909, p. 7.

2. Phelps to W. R. Smith, Oct. 17, 1859, in *Correspondence Relating to the Insurrection at Harper's Ferry,* Oct. 17, 1859, Senate Document Y (Annapolis, 1860).

3. Starry's testimony may be found in *Mason Report,* 23–24. Villard, "How Patrick Higgins Met John Brown," 8.

4. Washington, in *Mason Report,* "Testimony," 35.

5. *Ibid.,* 34.

6. *Mason Report,* 34.

7. Joseph Barry, *The Strange Story of Harper's Ferry* (Martinsburg, West Va., 1903), p. 58. William H. Moore, "Incidents & Developments of Osowatomy Brown's Insurrectionary Movements at Harper's Ferry . . ." (Baltimore, 1859), p. 46.

8. Alexander R. Boteler, 'Recollections of the John Brown Raid," *Century Magazine,* July 1883, p. 406. Cecil D. Eby, "The Last Hours of the John Brown Raid: the Narrative of David H. Strother," *Virginia Magazine of History and Biography,* Apr. 1967, pp. 172–73. Edwin Coppoc said that Newby "fell on the street by my side, whilst we were running to the aid of some of our friends who were surrounded by the enemy." Hinton, *John Brown,* 488. Joseph Barry, who was on the scene, says that Newby's body lay in the streets from 11 a.m. Monday to Tuesday afternoon. Barry, *The Strange Story of Harper's Ferry,* p. 95.

9. *Maryland Herald,* in *Liberator,* Nov. 11, 1859.

10. Boteler, "Recollections of the John Brown Raid," 407.

11. Copeland to Addison W. Halbert, Dec. 10, 1859, in Executive Papers, Brown Raid, Virginia State Library.

12. This account is based on Cook's *Confession* and the testimonies of Terence Byrne and Lind F. Currie, in *Mason Report.*

13. Lee to Colonel S. Cooper, Oct. 19, 1859, in *Letters Received by the Office of the Adjutant General, 1822–1860,* in National Archives Microfilm Publications, Roll 618. Redpath, *John Brown,* 328. Allstadt, in *Mason Report,* "How the Slaves Received John Brown's Proposition," *Shepherdstown Register,* Nov. 12, 1859.

14. Lee's Diary, Oct. 17, 1859, in *Robert E. Lee's Diary, July 10, 1855 to March 1, 1861,* Virginia Historical Society. John E. P. Daingerfield, "John Brown at Harper's Ferry," *Century Magazine,* June 1885, p. 267.

15. Lee to Secretary of War, Oct. 18, 1859, in *Mason Report,* "Invasion," 45.

16. Daingerfield, "John Brown at Harper's Ferry," 266. Lee to S. Cooper, Oct. 19, 1859, in *Letters Received . . . by . . . Adjutant General.*

17. *Mason Report,* "Invasion," 24. Wise to Virginia legislature, in *New York Express,* Dec. 8, 1859. *Baltimore American,* Oct. 21, 1859.

18. *Congressional Globe,* Dec. 6, 1859. Virginia Mason, *The Public Life and Diplomatic Correspondence of James M. Mason* (Roanoke, Va., 1903), 148. *Richmond Whig,* Oct. 26. 1859. Green to Andrew, Dec. 30, 1859, in George Green Shackelford, ed., "Attorneys Andrew

of Boston and Green of Richmond Consider the John Brown Case,"
Virginia Magazine of History and Biography, Jan. 1952, p. 103.

19. Benjamin Tucker to Wise, Oct. 5, 1859, in Executive Papers,
Brown Raid, Virginia State Library. Barry, *The Strange Story
of Harper's Ferry,* 61.

20. *Weekly Anglo-African,* Nov. 5, 1859. *Baltimore Sun,* Nov. 22,
1859. New York *Herald,* Jan. 7, 1860.

21. *Sun.,* Nov. 26, 1859. *Enquirer,* Dec. 20, 1859. *Richmond Whig,*
in *National Era,* Dec. 22, 1859.

22. *Sun,* Oct. 23, 1859. See Chapter 8 below for honors given to
Shepherd by whites of a later generation.

23. Mason to editor of *Constitution,* Oct. 21, 1859, in *Washington
Evening Star,* Oct. 25, 1859. Boteler, "Recollections of the John Brown
Raid," 401. D. H. Strother ("Porte Crayon"), "The Late Invasion at
Harpers Ferry," *Harper's Weekly,* Nov. 5, 1859.

24. *Times,* Oct. 27, 1859.

25. *Liberator,* Dec. 9, 1859.

26. Boyle to Wise, Oct. 21, 1859, in Executive Papers, Brown Raid,
Virginia State Library. *Evening Star,* Nov. 9, 1859.

27. T. W. Higginson, "Conversation with C. P. Tidd, Feb. 10,
1860," in Higginson Papers. *National Era,* Nov. 17, 1859. Wise to
legislature, in *New York Express,* Dec. 8, 1859.

28. Sennott, in *New York Times,* Mar. 14, 1860. Anderson, *Harper's
Ferry,* 62.

29. *Baltimore American,* Nov. 18, 1859. *Liberator,* Dec. 2, 1859.
New York Times, Apr. 23, 1860. *Evening Post,* Oct. 25, 1859.

30. *Cleveland Plain Dealer,* Nov. 18, 1859.

31. *Weekly Anglo-African,* Dec. 10, 1859.

32. *Republican,* Dec. 5, 1859. Hicks to George W. Mumford, Secretary of the State of Virginia, Nov. 14, 1859, in Dreer Papers. Hicks
to Colonel Joseph P. Warner, Nov. 28, 1859, in "Governor Hicks and
the John Brown Raid" (seven letters from Hicks concerning Harpers
Ferry), *Maryland Historical Magazine,* Sept. 1911, p. 279. For the
effect of Harpers Ferry on military preparations throughout the
South, see John Hope Franklin, *The Militant South, 1800–1861*
(Cambridge, Mass., 1956), 189.

33. New York *Herald,* Nov. 1, 1859. *Baltimore Daily Exchange,*
Oct. 18, 1859.

34. Chambers, "What a School Girl Saw of John Brown's Raid,"
Harper's Magazine, Jan. 1902, p. 14. Rayburn S. Moore, ed., "John
Brown's Raid at Harper's Ferry: An Eyewitness Account by Charles
White," *Virginia Magazine of History and Biography,* Oct. 1959,
p. 390. *New-York Tribune,* Nov. 12, 1859. *Ibid.,* Nov. 21, 1859.

35. *Enquirer,* Nov. 19, 1859. Redpath, *Public Life,* 371.

36. Davis to Wise, in Wise Family Papers. Murat Halstead, "The Execution of John Brown," *Ohio Archeological and Historical Quarterly*, July 1921, p. 291. *Boston Daily Advertiser*, Dec. 3, 1859. Lee to Henry Carter Lee, Dec. 6, 1859, in Robert Carter Lee Papers, Virginia Historical Society.

37. Redpath, *Public Life*, 341. Thomas Wentworth Higginson, "John Brown at Osawatomie," *Alexander's Magazine*, Aug. 15, 1906.

38. New York *Herald*, Nov. 17, 1859.

39. For contemporary comments on Copeland's "Confession," see *Daily Cleveland Herald*, Nov. 5, 1859, *Cleveland Daily Democrat*, Oct. 31 and Nov. 3, 1859, and the *Cleveland Plain Dealer*, Nov. 5, 1859, the last named containing a letter to the editor from Mrs. Issac Sturtevant.

40. Brown to his family, Oct. 31, 1859, in Sanborn, *Life and Letters*, 580. In a letter written to Lydia Maria Child on the same day, Brown referred to Avis as a "most humane gentleman." *Ibid.*, 581. Thornton T. Perry, Jr. "Martin R. Delany: Charles Town's Most Famous Negro," *Magazine of the Jefferson County Historical Society*, Dec. 1950, p. 43.

41. William Fellows, Charlestown guard, to newspaper reporter, New York *Sun*, Feb. 13, 1898.

42. Phillips, in *The Principia*, Dec. 24, 1859. *Baltimore American*, Nov. 21, 1859.

43. *Liberator*, Dec. 2, 1859.

44. Gibbs to Mrs. Spring, Nov. 11, 1859, in Villard Ms.

45. Stutler Coll. Letter of Nov. 30, in Sanborn, *Life and Letters*, 613.

46. Brown to Miss Sterns, Nov. 27, 1859, in Stutler Coll. Brown to the son of Thomas Musgrave, Nov. 17, 1859, in *Liberator*, Dec. 23, 1859. Brown to Ross, Dec. 1, 1859, in Thomas E. Champion, "The Underground Railroad and One of its Operators," *The Canadian Magazine*, May 1895, p. 15. Brown to Vaill, Nov. 15, 1859, in New York Public Library.

47. Ruth to John Brown, Nov. 27, 1859, in letters on John Brown presented to the Massachusetts Historical Society by Josiah P. Quincy, *Massachusetts Historical Society Proceedings*, Feb. 1908, p. 329. H. O. Wagoner and others to Brown, Nov. 17, 1859, cited in Redpath, *Echoes*, 391. Colored Women of Brooklyn to Brown, Nov. 23, 1859, *ibid.*, 419.

48. *Ibid.*, 418. Annie Brown to Mrs. Spring, May 28, 1860, in Villard Ms. Mrs. Spring to Redpath, July 1861 (no day of month), in *Pine and Palm*, Nov. 30, 1861. Hinton says that Frances was a constant and cheering correspondent, sending Brown "several very pretty lyrics of her own." Hinton, *John Brown*, 498.

49. Douglass in *Douglass' Monthly,* Nov. 1859.

50. *Weekly Anglo-African,* Oct. 29, 1859.

51. *Ibid.,* Dec. 31, 1859. *New York Times,* Nov. 8, 1859. For Douglass' previously announced intentions of going abroad see Maria Weston Chapman to Sarah P. Remond, Sept. 4, 1859, in John B. and Mary Estlin Papers, 1840–1844. Douglass to John Robert Kinnicut, Oct. 9, 1859, in A. A. Schomburg Collection, New York; *Weekly Anglo-African,* Sept. 10, 1859. Douglass to John W. Hurn, June 13, 1883, in Frederick Douglass Ms.

52. Wise to Hunter, Nov. 6, 1859, in "Letters on John Brown presented by Josiah P. Quincy," 330. Wise to Barnard, Nov. 15, 1859, in Executive Papers, Brown Raid, Virginia State Library.

53. *Liberator,* Jan. 6, 1860. J. P. Hughston to Wise, Nov. 16, 1859, in Dreer Papers.

54. *Anglo-African Magazine,* Dec. 1859, pp. 381–82.

55. *Boston Advertiser,* Nov. 1, 1859.

56. *New York Express,* Oct. 19, 1859.

57. *Weekly Anglo-African,* Nov. 12, 1859.

58. *Baltimore Sun,* Oct. 25, 1859. *Herald,* Nov. 2, 1859. *Times,* Nov. 2, 1859.

59. *Herald,* Nov. 3, *Times,* Nov. 3, *Evening Post,* Nov. 3, 1859.

60. *Herald,* Nov. 16, 1859.

61. *Ibid.,* Nov. 19, 1859. *Anglo-African,* Nov. 19, 1859.

62. *Ibid.,* Dec. 10, 1859.

63. *Cincinnati Daily Gazette,* Nov. 15, 1859. *Plain Dealer,* Nov. 18, 1859. William F. Cheek, "John Mercer Langston: Black Protest Leader and Abolitionist," *Civil War History,* June 1971, p. 119.

64. Dated November 6, this report from the *New-York Tribune* may be found in Redpath, *Public Life,* 228.

65. *Douglass' Monthly,* Nov. 1859. *Liberator,* Dec. 9, 1859.

6
Hanging Days in Virginia

1. Taliaferro to Wise, Dec. 1, 1859, Henry A. Wise Papers.

2. *Baltimore Daily Exchange,* Dec. 5, 1860.

3. Taliaferro's proclamation in Stutler Coll. Wise to Taliaferro, Nov. 24, 1859, in Executive Papers, Brown Raid, Virginia State Library.

4. Brent references in *Leavenworth Times* (Kansas), Nov. 2, 1911. *Baltimore American,* Dec. 5, 1859. Seventy-five years later a Jefferson County black would relate that he had been present when "they broke John Brown's neck," adding, "Oh, I was happy to see a hanging; I never seen one before." *Unwritten History of Slavery: Autobiographical Account of Negro Ex-slaves,* Social Sciences Source Documents, No. 1, Fisk University (Nashville, Tenn., 1945).

5. *Tribune,* Dec. 5, 1859.

6. Brown to Mrs. George L. Stearns, Nov. 29, 1859, in Ruchames, ed., *Brown Reader,* 155.

7. Carl D. Eby, Jr., "Whittier's 'Brown of Ossawatomie,' " *New England Quarterly,* Dec. 1960, p. 458. Child to Whittier, Nov. 16, 1859, in Stutler Coll. *Anti-Slavery Standard,* Dec. 31, 1859.

8. Richard D. Webb, *The Life and Letters of John Brown* (London, 1861), pp. 317–18. See also Lydia Maria Child, *The Freedmen's Book* (Boston, 1865), pp. 241–42, in which the poem bears the title, "John Brown and the Colored Child."

9. Cecil D. Eby, "John Brown's Kiss," *Virginia Cavalcade,* Autumn 1961, p. 45.

10. Robert S. Fletcher, "Ransom's John Brown Painting," *Kansas Historical Quarterly,* Nov. 1940, p. 344. See also James C. Malin, "The John Brown Legend in Pictures: Kissing the Negro Baby," 339–42. Malin's article carries uncolored reproductions of the paintings.

11. Along with other contemporary opinions on the painting, these appear in a sixteen-page pamphlet, "The 'Last Moments of John Brown,' painted by Thomas Hovenden, N. A., 1884, and etched by Thomas Hovenden, N. A., 1885"[1] (Philadelphia, 1885). (New York Public Library.) *Harper's Weekly,* Jan. 31, 1885 (p. 74), carries a reproduction of the Hovenden painting.

12. *Liberator,* May 18, 1860. Boyd B. Stutler, "Captain John Brown and Harper's Ferry" (pamphlet, Harpers Ferry, 1930), 9. Eby, "John Brown's Kiss," 47.

13. For a facsimile of this statement, see Villard, *Brown,* 555.

14. *Baltimore American,* Dec. 6, 1859.

15. *New York Times,* Mar. 14, 1860.

16. *New York Journal of Commerce,* in *Baltimore American,* Dec. 8, 1859.

17. *Baltimore Sun,* Dec. 2, 1859. *Herald,* Dec. 5, 1859.

18. *Hampshire Gazette and Courier* (Northampton, Mass.), Dec. 6, 1859, Stutler Coll *Liberator,* Dec. 9, 1859.

19. *Herald.* Dec. 3. 1859. *Anglo-African.* Dec. 17. 1859.

20. Child to Mrs. S. M. Parsons, Dec. 1859 (no date of month), in *Letters of Lydia Maria Child,* 138.

21. *Principia,* Dec. 3, 1859. *Liberator,* Dec. 16, 1859.

22. *Anglo-African,* Dec. 17, 1859. *Boston Post,* Dec. 3, 1859. *Providence Daily Journal,* Dec. 17, 1859. See also John Michael Ray, "Rhode Island Reactions to John Brown's Raid," *Rhode Island History,* Oct. 1961, pp. 97–108.

23. *Philadelphia Daily News,* Dec. 10, 1859.

24. *Dollar Weekly Pennsylvanian,* Dec. 10, 1859.

25. *Anglo-African,* Dec. 3, 1859.

26. *Ibid.,* Dec. 10, 1859.

27. Annie Brown to Still, Dec. 20, 1859, in Dreer Papers. Mary to J. Miller McKim. Feb. 12, 1861, in Miscellaneous Papers of John Brown, New York Public Library.

28. *Anglo-African,* Dec. 10, 1859.

29. *Herald,* Dec. 3, 1859.

30. *New York Express,* Dec. 7, 1859.

31. *Ibid.,* Dec. 17, 1859.

32. *Scottsville Register,* in *Liberator,* Dec. 30, 1859.

33. *Liberator,* Jan. 6, 1960. Fred Landon, "Canadian Negroes and the John Brown Raid," *Journal of Negro History,* Apr. 1921, p. 177.

34. *Baltimore Sun,* Dec. 5, 1859. Ralph E. Weber, "Riots in Victoria, 1860," *Journal of Negro History,* Apr. 1971, p. 141.

35. Medical staff to Wise, Nov. 27, 1859, in Wise Papers. Peticolas to Andrew Hunter, Nov. 1, 1859, in letters on John Brown presented to Josiah P. Quincy, *loc. cit.,* p. 329. Mary to Wise, Nov. 21, 1859, Dreer Papers. Wise to Mary, Nov. 26, 1859, in Dreer Papers.

36. *Philadelphia Daily News,* Dec. 5, 1859. *Philadelphia Evening Bulletin* in *New York Times,* Dec. 5, 1859.

37. *Standard,* Dec. 17, 1859.

38. Joshua Young, "The Funeral of John Brown," *New England Magazine,* Apr. 1904, p. 239. Joshua Young, "God Greater than Man: A Sermon Preached June 11th, After the Rendition of Anthony Burns," pamphlet, Burlington, 1854. Ruth to T. W. Higginson, Dec. 27, 1859, in Higginson Papers.

39. *New-York Tribune,* Oct. 17, 1886. Watkins to Still, Dec. 17, 1859, in William Still, *The Underground Rail Road* (Philadelphia, 1872), p. 791.

40. Watkins to unnamed friend, Dec. 9, 1859, in *Standard,* Jan. 14, 1860.

41. Lee to Mary Anna Randolph Lee, Dec. 1, 1859, Lee Papers, Virginia Hist. Soc. *Letters of Lydia Maria Child,* 138.

42. *Baltimore American,* Nov. 21, 1859.

43. *Frank Leslie's Illustrated Newspaper,* Dec. 10, 1859. *Baltimore American,* Nov. 27, 1859. *Ibid.,* Dec. 10, 1859. *New-York Tribune,* Dec. 13, 1859.

44. Strother, "Trial of the Conspirators," *Harper's Weekly,* Nov. 12, 1859.

45. *St. Louis Globe-Democrat,* Apr. 8, 1888. Andrew Hunter, "John Brown's Raid," *Publications of the Southern History Association,* July 1897, p. 32.

46. Copeland to Henry, Dec. 10, 1859, in Robert S. Fletcher, ed., "John Brown and Oberlin," *The Oberlin Alumni Magazine,* Feb. 1932, p. 138.

47. Johnson to John Copeland, Sr., Oct. 29, 1859; Copeland Sr., to

his son, Oct. 31, 1859, in Villard Ms. Copeland to his parents, Nov. 26, Fletcher, *loc. cit.,* 137.

48. Copeland to "Friend Halbert," Dec. 10, 1859; Copeland to "Dear Elias," Dec. 10, 1859, in Executive Papers, Brown Raid, Virginia Hist. Soc.

49. Copeland to "Dear Friends and Brothers of the Oberlin Anti-Slavery Society," Dec. 11, 1859, in Villard Ms.

50. Copeland to his family, Dec. 2, 1859, in Fletcher, *loc. cit.,* 138–39. *Cleveland Weekly Leader,* Dec. 21, 1859. For broadside, see Mary Ann Shadd Cary Papers, Howard University.

51. *Baltimore Sun,* Dec. 19, 1859.

52. Charles Thomas Price, "A War Time Reminisce," undated manuscript in Massachusetts Historical Society.

53. *Independent Democrat,* Dec. 17, extra edition. *Baltimore Sun,* Dec. 17, *New York Times,* Dec. 17. *Baltimore Amer. and Com. Appeal,* Dec. 17. *Virginia Free Press,* Dec. 22, 1859.

54. *Washington Star,* Dec. 17, 1859.

55. Letters to Wise, in Wise Papers.

56. Stearns to McKim, Dec. 15, 1859, in Villard Ms. *Perth Amboy Chronicle,* Aug. 28, 1899.

57. *Liberator,* Dec. 16, 1859. *New-York Tribune,* Dec. 16, 1859.

58. *Weekly Anglo-African,* Dec. 31, 1859, and Feb. 4, 1860.

59. *New-York Tribune,* Dec. 17, 1859. *Anglo-African,* Dec. 24, 1859, Feb. 4, 1860. The lengthy letter itself, the body in the handwriting of Green and the postscript in the handwriting of Campbell, is in Executive Papers, Brown Raid, Virginia State Library.

60. Copeland to Wise, Dec. 4, 1859, in Wise Papers.

61. Copeland to Wise, Dec. 12, 1859; Wise to Copeland, Dec. 12, 1859; Copeland to Wise, Dec. 14, 1859; in Wise Papers.

62. *Independent Democrat,* Jan. 17, 1860.

63. Beecher to Wise, Dec. 17, 1859, in Wise Papers.

64. *Independent Democrat,* Jan. 17, 1860. For this full story as Monroe remembered it see his "A Journey to Virginia in December, 1859," *Oberlin Thursday Lectures, Addresses and Essays* (Oberlin, 1897), 158–84.

65. Mason to Wise, Dec. 12, 1859; Wise to Mason, Dec. 14, 1859, in Executive Papers, Brown Raid. In nineteenth-century America there was ample precedent for the use of black cadavers for medical dissection, such corpses generally comprising a disproportionate quota of the total. See David C. Humphrey, "Dissection and Discrimination: The Social Origins of Cadavers in America, 1760–1915," *Bulletin of the New York Academy of Medicine,* Sept. 1973, pp. 819–27.

66. "Oberlin Monument Circular," Oberlin, Dec. 29, 1859, in *Liberator,* Jan. 13, 1860.

67. *Anglo-African,* Jan. 14, 1860.
68. Monroe, *op. cit.,* 184.
69. Stevens to Watkins, Jan. 3. 1860, in *Anti-Slavery Standard,* Jan. 21, 1860.
70. Annie Brown to Mrs. Spring, May 29, 1860, in Villard Ms.
71. Stevens to Mrs. Spring, Mar. 8, 1860, *ibid.* Mrs. Spring to James Redpath, July (no date of month) 1861, in *Pine and Palm,* Nov. 30, 1861.

7
The Noose's Black Shadow

1. Brown to his wife and children, Nov. 8, 1859, in Sanborn, *Life and Letters,* 586. *New-York Tribune,* Nov. 12, 1859.
2. Redpath, *John Brown,* 71, also T. W. Higginson, *Contemporaries* (Boston, 1899), 242.
3. Watkins to Mrs. Brown, Nov. 14, 1859, in Still, *Underground Railroad,* 791.
4. *Weekly Anglo-African,* Jan. 7, 1860. *Ibid.,* Dec. 17, 1859. *Liberator,* Feb. 10, 1859.
5. *Ibid.* Wendell Phillips to Joshua B. Smith, Dec. 29, 1859, in Stutler Coll. *Weekly Anglo-African,* Feb. 11, 1860. For Mary's letters to blacks in Detroit and New Haven, respectively, see *New York Times,* Jan. 23, 1860, and *Anglo-African,* Mar. 10, 1860.
6. *Baltimore Sun.* Dec. 5. 1859. Robin Winks, *The Blacks in Canada: A History* (New Haven, 1971), p. 269. *Chatham Tri-Weekly Planet,* Dec. 15, 1859.
7. Jackson to Mrs. Child, *New-York Tribune,* Dec. 7, 1859. "An Address to the People of Canada," dated Dec. 7, 1859, in Stutler Coll.
8. *New-York Tribune,* Feb. 14, 1860. *New York Times,* Mar. 3, 1860. *Anglo-African,* Mar. 3, 1860. W. P. Newman in *Anti-Slavery Standard,* Mar. 24, 1860.
9. For these donations from Haiti to Mary, see James Redpath, "The Haytian John Brown Fund," in *Anti-Slavery Standard,* Oct. 4, 1862, and Redpath to Garrison, Feb. 12, 1864, in *Liberator,* Feb. 19, 1864.
10. Redpath to Garrison, Feb. 12, 1864, in *Liberator,* Feb. 19, 1864.
11. *Weekly Anglo-African,* Apr. 14, 1860. John Mercer Langston, *From the Virginia Plantation to the National Capitol,* 372.
12. A copy of the Pennsylvania Anti-Slavery Society circular may be found in the Higginson Papers. "A Tribute of Respect . . .," Cleveland, 1859. *Springfield Republican,* Dec. 3, 1859.
13. *Weekly Anglo-African,* Nov. 26, 1859. *Ibid.,* Dec. 17, 1859. *Liberator,* Dec. 31, 1859.
14. In his broadside to his fellow Canadians urging them to raise funds for Mrs. Brown, Harvey C. Jackson advised them to earmark a portion of their contributions for the relatives of Green and Copeland if they had any relatives in need. "An Address to the People of

Canada," *Weekly Anglo-African,* Feb. 11, 1860. *Liberator,* Feb. 24, 1860. *Anglo-African,* June 2, 1860. James Redpath, "The Haytian John Brown Fund: A Card," in *Anti-Slavery Standard,* Oct. 4, 1862.

15. *New-York Tribune,* July 26, 1860. Hyatt, "To the Friends of John Brown," July 16, 1860, in *Douglass' Monthly,* Oct. 1860.

16. Mary to Redpath, Feb. 2, 1861, in Stutler Coll. See also Mary to Samuel E. Sewall, Aug. 13, 1860, and John E. Patterson to Sewall, Aug. 9, 1860, *ibid.*

17. Mary Leary Langston to Joshua Young, Sept. 9, 1899, in Villard Ms. Redpath to F. B. Sanborn, Nov. 30, 1874, in Stutler Coll.

18. *Oberlin Evangelist,* Feb. 1, 1860. For a copy of the "Oberlin Monument Circular," see *Liberator,* Jan. 13, 1860. When the fund committee decided to retain Green's name after finding that he was no Oberlinite, they might have logically added the name of Dangerfield Newby, but perhaps no one raised such a question.

19. *Weekly Anglo-African,* Jan. 14, 1860. J. M. Fitch to Higginson, Feb. 13, 1860, in Higginson Papers.

20. *Liberator,* Feb. 24, 1860. *Anglo-African,* Mar. 6, 1860.

21. *Ibid.,* Mar. 31, 1860.

22. *New-York Tribune,* July 26, 1860. Redpath, "The Haitian John Brown Fund." in *Anti-Slavery Standard,* Oct. 4, 1862.

23. *Weekly Anglo-African,* Apr. 28, 1860.

24. *Ibid.,* July 7, 1860.

25. Anderson to Hinton, Oct. 13, 1860, in Brown Ms., Kansas Hist. Soc.

26. W. C. ·Nell to the *Liberator,* Jan. 8, 1861, in *Liberator,* Jan. 11, 1861.

27. *Douglass' Monthly,* Feb. 1861.

28. Garrison to Redpath, Dec. 1, 1860, in *Liberator,* Dec. 9, 1859. Henry Wilson in *Congressional Globe,* Dec. 6, 1859.

29. "An Account of Some of the Principal Slave Insurrections . . .," New York, 1860. T. W. Higginson, *Atlantic Monthly,* June 1861, pp. 728–44, and Aug. 1861, pp. 173–87. Brown reference in latter issue, p. 175.

30. *Weekly Anglo-African,* Dec. 24, 1859. *Ibid.,* June 30, 1860.

31. *Liberator,* Mar. 16, 1860.

32. *New-York Tribune,* May 9, 1860.

33. *Liberator,* July 27, 1860.

34. Douglass to Redpath, June 29, 1860, *ibid.*

35. *Anti-Slavery Standard,* July 14, 1860.

36. *Douglass' Monthly,* Sept. 1860.

37. *Anti-Slavery Standard,* Aug. 11, 1860.

38. *Douglass' Monthly,* Sept. 1860.

39. *Pine and Palm,* Oct. 5, 1861. *Liberator,* June 15, 1860. For Rock's speech at the legislative hearing, see *Liberator,* Mar. 2, 1860.

40. *Harrisburg Patriot and Union,* Oct. 24, 1859. *New York Times,* Oct. 24, 1859. *New-York Tribune,* Oct. 24, 1859.

41. *Boston Courier,* Dec. 4, 1860.

42. *New-York Tribune,* Dec. 4, 1860. *Liberator,* Dec. 7, 1860.

43. *New-York Tribune,* Dec. 4, 1860. *Liberator,* Dec. 7, 1860. Diary of Samuel J. May, Cornell University Library.

44. *Weekly Anglo-African,* Dec. 31, 1860. Katzman, *Before the Ghetto,* 92.

45. These summonses may be seen in "Select Committee to Inquire into the Facts Attending the Invasion and Seizure of the United States Armory at Harper's Ferry by John Brown and his Companions," in the National Archives, Washington, D.C.

46. John S. Bagg to Jeremiah S. Black, Jan. 16, 1859 (letter sent to Mason although addressed to Black) ; Mason to Watson Freeman, undated, "Select Committee to Inquire into the Facts. . . ." *Mason Report,* "Invasion," 38.

47. *Journal of the Senate,* 1st sess., 36th Cong., p. 665. *Mason Report,* "Invasion," 20.

48. Donald B. Kelley, "Harper's Ferry: Prelude to Crisis in Mississippi," *Journal of Mississippi History,* Nov. 1965, p. 355. *Charlestown Independent Democrat,* Jan. 10, 1860.

49. Beatty to Wise, Nov. 12, 1859; Mason to Wise, Nov. 12, 1859; Mason to Wise, Nov. 16, 1859, in Wise Papers.

50. *New-York Tribune,* Jan. 7, 1860. *New Orleans Daily Free Delta,* Nov. 24, 1860. *Laws of the State of Maryland* (Annapolis, 1860), Chapter 322, sections I and II.

51. "Box" to *Weekly Anglo-African,* Nov. 28, 1859, in *Weekly Anglo-African,* Dec. 10, 1859. *Anti-Slavery Standard,* Oct. 29, 1859.

52. *Anglo-African,* Apr. 27, 1861.

53. Higginson, *Army Life in a Black Regiment* (New York, 1960), 29.. *Ibid.,* 45. *Anti-Slavery Standard,* Jan. 10, 1863.

54. *Anti-Slavery Standard,* Jan. 24, 1863. A copy of this colored lithograph may be found in the Dreer Papers.

55. *New-York Tribune,* Feb. 22, 1865.

56. Nov. 10, 1862, entry in Ray A. Billington, ed., *The Journal of Charlotte Forten* (New York, 1971), 132. Charlotte to Garrison, Nov. 27, 1862, in *Liberator,* Dec. 19, 1862.

57. Luther P. Jackson, "The Educational Efforts of the Freedmen's Bureau and Freedmen's Aid Societies in South Carolina, 1862–1872," *Journal of Negro History,* Jan. 1923, p. 30. Henry Lee Swint, *The Northern Teacher in the South, 1862–1870* (Nashville, Tenn., 1941), 80.

58. *New-York Tribune,* Jan. 5, 1863. *Journal of Charlotte Forten,* 173. Thomas P. Knox to William Lloyd Garrison, Dec. 5, 1863, in *Liberator,* Jan. 29, 1864.

59. *New-York Tribune,* Mar. 27, 1865.

60. *Weekly Anglo-African,* Mar. 8, 1862. Higginson, *Army Life in a Black Regiment,* 45. For other variant versions of the song, plus a historical analysis of it, see Boyd B. Stutler, "John Brown's Body," *Civil War History,* Sept. 1958, pp. 751–60.

61. *Standard,* Jan. 24, 1863. T. Morris Chester, "Negro Self-Respect and Pride of Race," in "Twenty-Ninth Anniversary of the Philadelphia Library of Colored Persons" (Philadelphia, 1863), 4.

62. *Liberator,* Dec. 9, 1864.

63. *Ibid.,* Dec. 31, 1860.

64. *Leeds Mercury,* Dec. 24, 1859. *Wakefield Express,* in New York *Herald,* Feb. 12, 1860.

65. Douglass to Helen Doucaster, Dec. 7, 1859, in the John Rylands Library, Manchester, England.

66. *Leeds Mercury,* Dec. 24, 1859.

67. *Frederick Douglass' Paper,* Feb. 17, 1860. *Douglass' Monthly,* Apr. 1860.

68. *Times,* Jan. 16, 1860.

69. Fanny Jackson-Coppin, *Reminiscences of School Life and Hints on Teaching* (Philadelphia, 1913), 21, 157.

70. Ewing, *The Harper's Ferry Insurrection,* 5. A copy of the fourth edition is owned by the Virginia Historical Society (Richmond).

71. Brown to Redpath, July 20, 1861, in *Pine and Palm,* Aug. 3, 1861.

72. Brown to Isaac Cary, Mar. 14, 1862, *ibid.* Brown to Redpath, July 20, 1861, *ibid.,* Aug. 3, 1861. Brown to "My dear Friend," July 29, 1861, in Stutler Coll. ("My dear Friend" was undoubtedly F. B. Sanborn.)

73. Brown to Sanborn, Feb. 17, 1864, in Stutler Coll.

74. Editor's Foreword in "John Brown and Sons in Kansas Territory," *Indiana Magazine of History,* June 1935, p. 142. *Standard,* May 29, 1862. Owen Brown to Redpath, May 20, 1861, in *Pine and Palm,* May 25, 1861. Jason Brown to James W. Weld, July 7, 1861, in Villard Ms. The Owen Brown scroll is at the Historical Society of Pennsylvania.

75. Annie Brown to "Dear Sir," Feb. 7, 1860, in Brown Papers, Chicago Hist. Soc.

76. Annie to Garrison, June 9, 1863, in Stutler Coll. Annie to O. G. Villard, Oct. 2 and 3, 1908, in Villard Ms.

77. "Annie was supposed to have taught in your father's house. Her statement knocks out that statement altogether," wrote O. G. Villard to John S. Wise on Dec. 1, 1908, Villard Ms. Lucy Chase to Dear Ones at home, June 14, 1863, in Henry L. Swint, ed., *Dear*

Ones at Home: Letters from Contraband Camps (Nashville, Tenn., 1966), 79.

78. Mary to Mrs. George L. Stearns, Jan. 7, 1863; Mary to Mrs. George L. Stearns, Mar. 3, 1863, in Stutler Coll.

79. *Liberator,* May 23, 1862. *Washington Daily Morning Chronicle,* Nov. 2, 1864.

80. *New Orleans Tribune,* Apr. 20, 1865.

8
A Fire Not Forgotten

1. Note, for example, the meeting held by blacks at Cooper Union, New York, on Apr. 8, 1870, in *New-York Tribune,* April 9, 1870. "A few black John Browns" quotation from *The Colored Citizens,* Fort Scott, Kansas, Jan. 4, 1879, in Martin E. Dann, ed., *The Black Press, 1827–1890* (New York, 1971), 101.

2. *Pine and Palm,* July 27, 1861.

3. Mary Brown to Mrs. G. L. Stearns, Mar. 3, 1863, in Stutler Coll. *New National Era,* Dec. 19, 1872. Sanborn to Gerrit Smith, Oct. 19, 1872, in Sanborn, *Recollections,* I, 232.

4. *New National Era,* Dec. 19, 1872.

5. *Ibid.,* Dec. 26, 1872.

6. Villard to Mrs. Adams, Aug. 14, 1908, in Villard Ms.

7. Alfred L. Donaldson, *A History of the Adirondacks* (2 vols., New York, 1921), II, 19. Albert Shaw, "John Brown in the Adirondacks," *Review of Reviews,* Sept. 1896, p. 312.

8. A. W. Macy, "Buried After Twenty-Three Years: A Sequel to the Fight at Harper's Ferry," *The Independent,* June 20, 1895.

9. Thomas Featherstonhaugh, "The Final Burial of the Followers of John Brown," *The New England Magazine,* Apr. 1901, pp. 129–34. Donaldson, *History of the Adirondacks,* 20–22.

10. Mrs. Langston to Young, Sept. 9, 1899, in Villard Ms.

11. Donaldson, *Adirondacks,* 22. Mrs. Adams to Sanborn, Sept. 24, 1893, in Stutler Coll.

12. Mrs. Adams to Cook, Dec. 14, 1896, in Stutler Coll.

13. Mrs. Adams to Messrs. Wm. H. Johnson, E. B. Irving, and J. E. Bruce, Mar. 24, 1897, in *The Autobiography of Dr. William Henry Johnson* (Albany, N.Y., 1910), 212.

14. Letter in Villard Ms.

15. Brown to Douglass, Feb. 26, 1878, in Douglass Manuscripts, Library of Congress. John, Jr., to former Governor Robinson, Feb. (no day of month), 1884, in Brown Ms., Kansas Hist. Soc. John, Jr., to Sanborn, Jan. 10, 1884, in Alfred William Anthony Papers, New York Public Library.

16. Hamilton, "John Brown in Canada," *loc. cit.,* 122.

17. John and Owen to Epps, Nov. 1, 1885, in Stutler Coll. John, Jr., to Sanborn, May 31, 1885, in Anthony Ms. Helen M. Chesnutt, *Charles Waddell Chestnutt: Pioneer of the Color Line* (Chapel Hill, N.C., 1952), 282. Jason to Roberts Brothers, Mar. 19, 1891, in Villard Ms.

18. Broadside, "Celebrate Brown's Birthday, Colored Citizens of Pasadena and Los Angeles, at Raymond Hill, South Pasadena, May 9, 1900," in Stutler Coll. Murphy quote from *New York Times,* June 4, 1900. For the manner in which the white press criticized Fortune's remarks, see Emma Lou Thornbrough, *T. Thomas Fortune: Militant Journalist* (Chicago, 1972), pp. 198–200.

19. *Springfield Republican,* May 16, 1907. For the Boston occasion, see the pamphlet "Boston John Brown Jubilee, Faneuil Hall, Boston, Mass., December 2, 1909." (Howard University.)

20. Du Bois review of Truman Nelson's *The Surveyor,* in *The National Guardian,* June 6, 1960.

21. Du Bois to Villard, Nov. 15, 1907, in Villard Ms.

22. *John Brown* (Philadelphia, 1909), 7–8.

23. *The Autobiography of W. E. B. Du Bois* (New York, 1968), p. 259. Herbert Aptheker, *Afro-American History: The Modern Era* (New York, 1971), 58. *American Historical Review,* Apr. 1910, p. 633. New York *Evening Post,* Oct. 30, 1909. Du Bois, *Autobiography,* 259. Villard to Mayo, Nov. 22, 1909, in Villard Ms.

24. Villard to Annie Brown Adams, Feb. 25, 1908, in Villard Ms.

25. Hill's sonnet, in the Villiard manuscripts, appears in Quarles, ed., *Blacks on John Brown,* 104. Wilson to Villard, Jan. 16, 1911, in Villard Ms.

26. Dorothy B. Porter, *The Negro in the United States: A Selected Bibliography* (Washington, D.C., 1970), p. v. The Historical Society of Pennsylvania has a copy of this eight-page pamphlet: Daniel Murray, compiler, "Preliminary List of Books and Pamphlets by Negro Authors for Paris Exposition and Library of Congress," Washington, D.C., 1900. Murray to Villard, Nov. 17, 1910; Murray to Mayo, May 2, 1908, in Villard Ms.

27. Washington to Villard, Oct. 27, 1910, in Villard Ms.

28. Villard to E. J. Scott, Dec. 28, 1908, Villard to Sanborn, Nov. 30, 1907; Villard to Annie Brown Adams, Dec. 13, 1907; Villard to Stephen S. Wise, Apr. 1, 1909, in Villard Ms.

29. Washington to Johnson, May 3, 1909, in *Autobiography of William Henry Johnson,* 144.

30. Crummell, *Africa and America: Addresses and Discourses* (Springfield, Mass., 1891), 13. *Afro-American Ledger,* Sept. 9, 1905. *Baltimore Afro-American,* Sept. 14, 1971.

31. For this speech, see Quarles, *Blacks on John Brown,* 54–64. The

brick from the engine house, along with many other Douglass mementoes, are on display at his Cedar Hill home, now operated by the National Park Service.

32. Undated one-page broadside in Villard Ms.

33. Boyd B. Stutler, "Captain John Brown and Harper's Ferry" (Harpers Ferry, 1930), 28

34. McDonald to Villard, June 19, 1908; Murray to Villard, July 25, 1903, in Villard Ms. On August 29, 1923, Villard sent $10 to Mrs. Murray for her project but apparently there were very few additional donors.

35. *The Crisis,* July 1932, p 219.

36. *Pittsburgh Courier,* June 4, 1932. *Baltimore Afro-American,* June 4, 1932.

37. *Shepherstown Register,* Oct. 15, 1931.

38. Matthew Page Andrews, "Heyward Shepherd: Victim of Violence," thirty-two-page pamphlet published under the auspices of the Heyward Shepherd Memorial Association, n.d., n.p.

39. *New York Times,* Oct. 11, 1931.

40. *Ibid.*

41. Taken from the tablet itself, at Harpers Ferry.

42. Andrews, "Heyward Shepherd: Victim of Violence," p. 3. *Crisis,* Jan. 1932, p. 467. *Afro-American,* Oct. 31, 1931.

43. David M. Tucker, *Lieutenant Lee of Beale Street* (Nashville, Tenn., 1971), pp. 201–2.

44. "The John Brown Reader," Washington, D.C., 1949.

45. Charles H. Wesley, *History of the Improved Benevolent and Protective Order of Elks of the World* (Washington, D.C., 1955), pp. 381–83, 406.

46. J. William Joynes, "John Brown's Hideaway Faces New Threat," *Baltimore News American,* Mar. 18, 1973. See also Lee Flor, "Preservation of John Brown House is Urged," *Washington Evening Star and Daily News,* Mar. 7, 1973.

47. *Meadville* (Pa.) *Tribune,* Sept. 4, 1954. Wesley, *Elks,* 464.

48. For this occasion, see *Lake Placid News,* Aug. 25, 1916; *Adirondack Enterprise* (Saranac Lake, N. Y.), Aug. 26, 1916; *Springfield Republican,* Aug. 24, 1916, and *The Crisis,* Oct. 1916, p. 297.

49. For a picture and a brief sketch of Barber in 1912, when he was thirty-two, see *The Crisis,* Nov. 1912, p. 16.

50. J. Max Barber, "A Pilgrimage to John Brown's Grave," *ibid.,* Aug. 1922, p. 169.

51. William Pickens, "John Brown's Day," *ibid.,* July 1924, p. 127.

52. *Courier,* Apr. 30, 1932.

53. For copies of the printed announcements issued by the Frederick Douglass Chapter, I am indebted to James Egert Allen. For copies

of the annual pilgrimage programs for 1952 and 1970, plus other useful mimeographed and printed materials relating to the Association, I am indebted to Samuel E. Blount, its official historian.

54. Nelson C. Reid to author, Feb. 26, 1973. *Weekly Anglo-African,* Dec. 10, 1859.

55. "Subscription for the Erection of a Monument to the Memory of the Brave and Unfortunate John Brown, who Perished on the Scaffold for the Emancipation of the Colored Race on the Sixteenth[*sic*] of December 1859" (Philadelphia, 1867), 8. James Redpath, *The Public Life of Capt. John Brown* (Sandusky, Ohio, 1872), 6. James C. Malin, *John Brown and the Legend of Fifty-six* (Philadelphia, 1942), 354.

56. Undated printed announcement in Douglass Ms., Library of Congress.

57. *New York Age,* Jan. 12, 1889. *Ibid.,* Jan. 29, 1889.

58. Featherstonhaugh to Villard, Oct. 20, 1907; Featherstonhaugh to Villard, Aug. 17, 1909; Featherstonhaugh to Villard, Jan. 28, 1909, in Villard Ms.

59. *New York Herald-Tribune,* May 10, 1935. *New York Times,* May 10, 1935. "John Brown in Bronze, 1800–1859, containing Program and Addresses of the Dedicatory Ceremony and Unveiling of the Monument of John Brown, May 9, 1935, at the Farm Bearing His Name at Lake Placid, New York," Lake Placid, 1935, and Alexander C. Flick, "John Brown Memorial Statue," *New York History,* July 1935, pp. 329–32.

60. *Ibid.*

61. "John Brown in Bronze," 19.

62. Flick, "John Brown Memorial Statue," 332.

63. Clarence S. Gee, "The Stone on John Brown's Grave," *New York History,* Apr. 1961, p. 166. For a picture of the members of the John Brown Memorial Association gathered around the gravestone on May 9, 1930, see *New York History,* Apr. 1961., 164. (For Brown's keen interest in acquiring this stone, see his letter to his family, Mar. 12, 1857, in Sanborn *Life and Letters,* 375.)

64. *Akron Beacon-Journal,* Sept. 25, 1938

65. For the story of the rededication, see Robert S. Thomas, "They Gave Their Lives for the Slaves," *Oberlin Alumni Magazine,* Jan.–Feb. 1973, pp. 31–33. For a copy of the speech by Thomas, I am indebted to Dorothy Inborden Miller.

66. Ward's remark is found in Doris Abramson, *Negro Playwrights in the American Theatre* (New York, 1969), 257, which also has an analysis of the play by Branch.

67. *The Crisis,* Aug. 1922, p. 89.

68. *Opportunity,* Jan. 1942, p. 7.

69. Selden Rodman, *Horace Pippin: A Negro Painter in America* (New York, 1947), 17, 18.

70. Robert F. Williams, *Negroes with Guns* (New York, 1962), 122. Eldridge Cleaver, *Soul on Ice* (New York, 1968), 82–83.

71. Ted Joans, *Black Pow-wow: Jazz Poems* (New York, 1969). 61. George Breitman, ed., *Malcolm X Speaks: Selected Speeches and Statements* (New York, 1965), p. 241. H. Rap Brown, *Die Nigger Die!* (New York, 1969), 116.

72. Floyd McKissick, *Three-fifths of a Man* (New York, 1969), 147–48.

73. "John Brown and the New Slavery," typewritten address in Archibald H. Grimké Papers, Howard University.

74. Lerone Bennett, Jr., *The Negro Mood and Other Essays* (Chicago, 1964), 100. Michael S. Harper, "History as Cap'n Brown," in Quarles, ed., *Blacks on John Brown*, 146.

INDEX

BLACKS ON JOHN BROWN

John Brown Going to His Hanging, Horace Pippin (1888–1946). The
Pennsylvania Academy of the Fine Arts

BLACKS ON
JOHN BROWN

Edited by
Benjamin Quarles

To Blanche and William Stuart Nelson

CONTENTS

INTRODUCTION

LOST in the Adirondack hills with two companions one day in late June 1849, Richard Henry Dana, Jr., noted author of *Two Years before the Mast,* sighted a one-story log house on a freshly cleared farm. Its owner, as the three lost campers soon learned, was a recently arrived settler named John Brown. He "received us with kindness," wrote Dana, inviting them to stay for supper. Seated at the long table were a black man and a black woman. Somewhat taken aback by this display of social equality, Dana was even more surprised when his host introduced the blacks by their last names, with the prefixes of Mr. and Mrs. In his diary Dana duly underscored these courtesy titles given to the black diners, *"Mr.* Jefferson" and *"Mrs.* Wait." At John Brown's family board, as Dana quickly found out, blacks neither sat below the salt nor were addressed as unequals.

Brown is best known in history for his hostility to slavery. But, as the Dana episode would suggest, his personal behavior toward blacks with whom he came in contact was well out of the ordinary. Other white abolitionists subscribed to the theories of man's essential brotherhood as did Brown, but they shared the racial prejudices commonly held. Hence to them, despite their high-principled hostility to slavery, anything smacking of social equality with blacks was distasteful and painful when it was not indeed deemed as an offense to nature's laws.

Brown was of a different mold. To him the color of a man's skin was no measure of his worth. Whites were not innately superior, blacks innately inferior. By the time he reached manhood Brown had divested himself of color prejudice, if indeed he had ever harbored any.

In typical proof-of-the-pudding fashion, Brown translated his theories into action. Feeling no strain in the presence of blacks, he sought them out. In the spring of 1849 Brown moved from Springfield, Massachusetts, to North Elba, New York, in order to settle among the Negroes who had located there as a consequence of land grants they had received from the philanthropist-reformer Gerrit Smith. North Elba was a bleak spot in the Adirondacks but to Brown it spelled an opportunity to be a guide and friend to a group of blacks in need. Typical of the advice he would give black people for the next ten years, Brown, in a letter to Willis A. Hodges on January 22, 1849, urged the settlers at North Elba to sustain "the very best character for honesty, truth and faithfulness," and not to be content with merely conducting themselves "as well as the whites, but to set them an example in all things." [1]

Always treating blacks on a peer basis, Brown did not ignore their faults as one might condescendingly gloss over the shortcomings of those assumed to be one's inferiors. In an article "Sambo's Mistakes," contributed in 1848 to a short-lived Negro weekly, *Ram's Horn,* Brown criticized blacks for "getting up expensive parties, and running after fashionable amusements," while tamely submitting to injustice and dodging manly responsibilities.

In his travels Brown sought out black acquaintances for overnight lodgings. More often than not, the mail-forwarding addresses he gave were black residences. Should the occasion arise, "please drop me a line enclosed to Stephen Smith, Esq., Lombard Street, Philadelphia," wrote Brown to Theodore Parker on March 7, 1858.

On more than one occasion Brown was a house guest at the home in Rochester, New York, of abolitionist Frederick Douglass. He spent three weeks there in February 1858, devoting much of his time to the drafting of a constitution for a new framework of government. Later in that month Brown went to Brooklyn, where he spent a week at the home of the Reverend and Mrs. James Newton Gloucester. While at Chatham, Ontario, two months later, presiding

[1] New York *Post,* December 20, 1859.

at a predominantly black convention to ratify his constitution, Brown stayed at the home of Isaac Holden, a black merchant and surveyor.

Two weeks prior to the Chatham convention Brown demonstrated another aspect of his essential egalitarianism, that of not accepting a service denied to blacks. Arriving in Chicago one morning in late April, Brown and nine of his followers, including former runaway slave Richard Richardson, went to the Massasoit House for breakfast. Brown was told that Richardson could not be seated with the others. Muttering angrily to the proprietor, Brown left the dining room, his party following suit. Nearby they found a place, the Adams House, which paid no attention to Richardson's color.

Brown's indignation over Jim Crow practices would leave no doubt as to his attitude toward slavery. Moreover it would suggest that Brown's hatred of human bondage was based in part upon a fellow feeling, if not an affection, for the slave. On November 21, 1834, twenty-five years before Harpers Ferry, Brown, then in Randolph, Pennsylvania, had written to his brother Frederick: "Since you left I have been trying to devise some means whereby I might do something in a practical way for my poor fellow-men . . . in bondage." [2]

As a matter of course Brown supported what he called "railroad business," the assisting of runaway slaves in their dash for freedom. Taking the initiative himself, Brown, late in 1858, led a raid into Bates and Vernon counties in Missouri, seizing eleven slaves and conducting them to the Canadian border. One of Brown's men killed a slaveowner, the whole affair prompting President Buchanan to offer a reward for Brown's capture.

The passage of the Fugitive Slave Law of 1850, facilitating the capture of runaway slaves, had fanned Brown's abolitionism. A number of alarmed blacks had come to him, saying that they could not sleep with this new threat to their safety and that of their

[2] Oswald Garrison Villard, *John Brown, 1800–1859: A Biography Fifty Years After* (New York, 1943), p. 43.

families. Brown told them to "trust in God, and keep their powder
dry," as he informed his wife, Mary, in a letter from Springfield,
Massachusetts, on November 28, 1850.[3]

As if to implement this advice, Brown, while in Springfield in
January 1851, organized the United States League of Gileadites.
Forty-four black men and women pledged their support to this
semimilitaristic organization, whose basic aim was to protect and
rescue runaways, by armed force if necessary. Little came of the
League, perhaps because Brown soon left for Ohio and perhaps
because no appropriate incident arose.

The Gileadite project, however, had guerrilla-war elements that
were to characterize Brown's most fearful and dramatic undertaking, the raid on Harpers Ferry, Virginia, in October 1859, designed
to free the slaves. But, more important, this raid symbolized Brown's
dual relationship with the people of color—his closeness to the free
blacks in the North and his activist concern for their slave brothers
in the South.

In planning for Harpers Ferry, Brown had sought to recruit
blacks, particularly prominent figures. Those to whom he made
overtures included Frederick Douglass, lumberman Stephen Smith,
clergyman Jermain W. Loguen, underground railroad operator
William Still, and John Mercer Langston, a lawyer and member of
the Oberlin town council. No black of prominence, however,
showed up at Harpers Ferry. Of the twenty-one Harpers Ferry
comrades of John Brown, five were blacks. In the quickly crushed
raid, two of the five blacks were killed, Dangerfield Newby and
Lewis S. Leary; two were captured, John A. Copeland and Shields
Green; and one made his escape, Osborn Perry Anderson.

However much of a military fiasco, the Harpers Ferry raid left
a deep impression on the country. It angered the South and made
southerners apprehensive. In the North, too, Brown's raid was
widely and strongly condemned. But in that section of the country

[3] Boyd B. Stutler Collection of the John Brown Papers, Ohio Historical
Society (Columbus), Roll No. 1.

such denunciation was by no means universal, thousands of northerners regarding Brown as candidate for a halo.

The view that Brown was a martyr reached its strongest intensity among blacks. To them he was a man of moral courage, a benchmark figure whose social resolve had not waited upon taking a poll or achieving a consensus. A symbol, he conferred worth upon his followers. Black Americans regarded Brown as a deeply religious being to whom slavery was the sin of sins.

A week before her husband's hanging Mrs. Brown informed an interviewer, Theodore Tilton, that the "religious element of his character was always the ruling motive of his life." [4] The orator Wendell Phillips put it a bit more dramatically, saying that Brown carried letters of marque from God. The haunting lines, so familiar in black religious folksong, "Way down yonder by myself, / And I couldn't hear nobody pray," hardly sprang from anybody in the company of John Brown. Black people were deeply impressed by Brown's obvious and intense religious commitment, coming to share his belief that he was an instrument of the Almighty to free the slaves. Viewing Brown as God-sent, blacks tended to discern the hand of Providence in Harpers Ferry.

Obviously his black contemporaries did not subscribe to the widespread belief that Brown was mentally unbalanced. They held that society, rather than Brown, was deranged. They tended, moreover, to ignore or gloss over any of his shortcomings—his assertive self-righteousness, his unwillingness to give praise or credit to others, and his dictatorial type of leadership. Brown was also reticent to the point of secrecy, but this trait hardly bothered his black followers. They realized that if one were engaged in work considered seditious by many and hence fraught with personal peril, secrecy must be the order of the day. Trusting Brown, it did not matter to them if he were tight-lipped. Moreover, living in a land in which their basic rights were so often flouted, black Americans often deemed it advisable not to know too much.

[4] *The Principia* (New York), November 26, 1859.

Like his black followers at Harpers Ferry, Brown's black admirers did not debate his plan of action. Two weeks after the raid, Henry Highland Garnet found fault with the operation, holding that the only thing needed "was a box of matches in the pocket of every slave, and then slavery would be set right." This was hardly tongue-in-cheek talk since arson by slaves was not uncommon. But aside from this kind of passing comment, blacks did not enter into analysis of Brown as a military tactician or field commander.

Similarly blacks did not debate as to whether the Brown of the Kansas years had blood on his hands, being guilty of ordering the cold-blooded killing of five proslavery men at Pottawatomie Creek in May 1856. Blacks took Brown on his own terms—to them he was his own morality. Consistently they divorced his actions from his motives, preferring to dwell upon the latter. "To the outward eye of men, John Brown was a criminal, but to their inward eye he was a just man and true," said Frederick Douglass in an address at Storer College in 1881. "His deeds might be disowned, but the spirit which made those deeds possible was worthy of highest honor." To black Americans the leader at Harpers Ferry was primarily a symbol that gave them dignity.

If blacks were as one in their general appraisal of Brown and if, as a rule, they avoided controversy as to his methods, why such a volume as this, one might ask. Blacks, historically the most individualistic of Americans, found different things to admire in Brown. They certainly found a rich variety of deeply evocative ways in which to express their sentiments toward him. Moreover, in the course of their appraisal of Brown, they tell us much about the America of their day, particularly in its black-white relationships.

And finally the image of Brown projected by his black admirers was, in no small measure, a factor in creating the John Brown that has lived in song and story. John Brown, however flawed, did not turn out to be a passing phenomenon, a temporary catharsis, but rather a new peaking in a continuing process—that of a nation coming to grips with its conscience, a microcosm of man in his unceasing moral pilgrimage. The documents in this volume provide a first-hand view of this image-making John Brown of the blacks.

A word might be in order as to any deletions made in these documents. The poems, letters, and reports of meetings have not been cut. The chapter from George Washington Williams and the one from W. E. B. Du Bois, along with the speeches of others, have been abridged, however, the deletions averaging from one-quarter to one-third of their lengths. In most instances the material deleted was repetitious, either in the document itself or in its relationship to others. In some instances the deleted passage consisted of a speaker's leisurely introduction. The opening remarks of some speakers, turn-of-the-century figures particularly, tended to be of a wide-ranging, stage-setting type, as if to give the audience time to settle down. Deletions are indicated by ellipses and, unless otherwise indicated, all deletions are the editor's, not the authors'.

These readings are arranged chronologically, an arrangement which would seem to be supportable. For although black people then and now share basically similar views on John Brown, it is to be borne in mind that history is continuity no less than change. Certain ideas live on, certain figures are timeless. It hardly need be added, however, that the best of these constants are themselves forces for change, goading us to face up to the more painful realities of our own times.

PART I

BLACK SEED (1858–1861):
CONTEMPORARY VIEWPOINTS

The black contemporaries of John Brown held him in
high esteem from their first acquaintance with him. After
his capture and execution, their admiration reached new
heights. On December 2, 1859, the "Day of Mourning,"
these expressions of affection were interspersed with
reverence for the man and a new determination to
match his zeal. These contemporary blacks did not regard their tributes to Brown as being overdone or ful-
some. "I never thought that I should ever join in doing
honor to or mourning any *American* white man," said
Charles H. Langston in a eulogy delivered in Cleveland
on the day of Brown's hanging. In extolling Brown,
however, Langston and his black contemporaries felt
that they were but doing a simple needed thing—giving
honor where honor was due.

James Newton Gloucester

Of the blacks who exchanged letters with Brown none spoke in more militant tones or sent him more money than clergyman James Newton Gloucester, whose donations were supplemented by those of his wife, Elizabeth, a successful businesswoman. Brown's belief that the peaceful emancipation of the slaves was not an impossibility was shared by Gloucester, and it is not surprising that in his diary Brown had jotted down Gloucester's home address in Brooklyn, 265 Bridge Street, to which he had a standing invitation. Gloucester, himself an admirer of Brown, in a letter of February 19, 1858, put Brown in a class with the legendary Davy Crockett, frontiersman and folk hero. In another letter, written three weeks later, Gloucester expressed his regret that he would not be able to attend a meeting between Brown and a group of black leaders, scheduled at Philadelphia in mid-March 1858, but enclosing $25 and reaffirming his approval of Brown's proposals. The two letters are part of the John Brown Papers, collection of the Kansas Historical Society, Topeka.

Philadephia Feb. 19, 1858

Most Esteemed Friend

Being called away from home by death—to Philadelphia—I have not as yet sent any answer to your first communication. I do so now. I was pleased to hear from you at last after so long [a] silence. I thought perhaps you might have passed to your more immediate field of Premeditated Labour—having not seen or heard anything from you for so long a time—but I rejoice that you are still in life and health—with the same vigorous hopes as formerly. Your very commendable measures to deliver the slave has yet my heartiest consent and cooperation. I have never as yet faltered in my previous asserted interest to you in the matter—all I need is

3

the clear intelligent watchword of that Gallant Hero—distinguished in former triumphs and those in David Croket style. I can go ahead but you speak in your letter of the people. I fear there is little to be done in the masses. The *masses* suffer for the want of intelligence and it is difficult to reach them in a matter like you propose. So far as is necessary to secure their cooperation the Colored People are *impulsive*—but they need *Sagacity—Sagacity* to distinguish their proper course.

They are like a bark at sea without a *commander* or *rudder* ready to catch port—or no port as it may be—and it is so difficult to strike a line to meet them. No one knows better than Mr. [Frederick] Douglass the truth of this. But however I do not despair, I only note it as it may form a part of the history of your undertaking and that it may not otherwise damp ardor.

I wish you Godspeed in your Glorious work—may nothing arise to prevent accomplishing your intended visit to this city. . . . Please to make my house your home. I am not at home now but will be in a few days.

Your sincere Friend,

JAMES N. GLOUCESTER

Brooklyn March 9 1858

Captain Brown

Esteemed Sir I regret that I cannot at this time be with you and friends convened in Philadelphia but you have my heartiest wish, with all the true friends here, for your success.

I hope sir, you will find in that city a large response—both in *money* and *men*—prepared at you command to do battle to that *ugly foe*.

I am more and more convinced that now the day and now the hour, and that the proper mode is at last suggested, *practically*.

Long enough have we had this great evil in our land discussed in all its possible aspects. Long have we applied to it, as we have thought, all the moral means that enlightened men are capable, but yet this evil as a system remains the same; they have not phased it as yet in one material point.

What then shall we do is the only sensible question to every true lover of God and man. Shall we go on and still prosecute under these means and thus as we have done for years dismally fail, or shall we in the language of that noble patriot of his country (Patrick Henry) now use these means that God and nature has placed within our power. I hope Sir to this sentiment in Philadelphia there is but one response—for in that city reside some noble men and women whose hearts are always warmed and cheered at every rising hope for the slave. But Sir your measure anticipates not only for the abject slave but to those colored men, north and south, who are but virtually slaves. There is in truth no *black man,* north or south of Mason and Dixon Line—a freeman whatever be his wealth, position or worth to the world. This is but the result of that *hellish system,* against which every honest man and woman in the land should be combined. I hope Sir you will be able, assisted by those eminent gentlemen who accompany you, to make these things plain and take their hold upon the Philadelphia mind, and join with you in holy energy and combat against the all damnable foe. Let them see the little book you presented to me and so dissipate their doubts and fears.

Please to put me down for (25) more to begin with.

Yours for struggling universal rights.

J. N. GLOUCESTER

Jermain Wesley Loguen

Jermain Wesley Loguen, a runaway slave turned clergyman, had won Brown's attention for his resourceful leadership in underground railroad activities in Syracuse. In early April 1858 Loguen had accompanied Brown to Chatham, Ontario, where Brown met the legendary Harriet Tubman and where he forwarded his plans to hold a convention to ratify a constitution he had drafted. Held on May 8 and 10, 1858, this Chatham Convention attracted twelve whites and thirty-four blacks. Loguen, however, was not among them, having written to Brown on May 6 saying that he would not be present, but bidding him Godspeed. The letter is part of the John Brown Papers, collection of the Kansas Historical Society, Topeka.

Syracuse, May 6, 1858

My dear Friend & Bro—

I have your last letter from Canada. I was glad to learn that you & your brave men had got on to Chatham. I have see[n] our man Gray, & find it with him as I feared we should—that he was not ready yet. I do not think he will go to war soon—others that would go have not the money to get there with. And I have conclud[ed] to let them all rest for the present. Have you got Isaac Williams with you or not? Have you got Harriet Tubman of St. Catherines? Let me hear from you soon or whenever you can. As I think I cannot get to Chatham, I should like much to see you & your men before you go to the mountains. My wife & all unite in wishing you all the great success in your *Glorious undertaken.* May the *Lord* be with you is our prayer.

Your friend in the cause.

J. W. LOGUEN

Frederick Douglass

The black orator-spokesman Frederick Douglass (1817–1895)
had known Brown since 1847, when he had made a visit to
Brown's home in Springfield. Their friendship ripened after
Brown moved to upstate New York in 1849; it was at the
Douglass home in Rochester in 1858 that Brown drafted the
constitution designed to usher in the new day of freedom. On
the eve of Harpers Ferry, Brown had sought earnestly, but
vainly, to enlist Douglass's support. Shortly after the raid
Douglass fled the country, fearing that he might be seized as
an accomplice. Safe on Canadian soil, Douglass realized that
his flight was hardly heroic, even if sensible. He was given
an opportunity to explain his role when John E. Cook, one of
Brown's captured followers, charged him with having failed to
keep his promises to supply the raiders with men and weapons.
Making the most of this palpably false accusation, Douglass
sent a letter to a Rochester newspaper. Widely reprinted, as
he had hoped, it was a skillful blending of slavery condemnation
and self-absolution, with Brown coming in for direct mention
only twice. But the letter throws light upon the relationship
of the two reformers and it foreshadows the unstinted praise
which, from then on, Douglass showered upon the fallen
champion. The following is the letter as it appeared in *Douglass'
Monthly,* November 1859.

Canada West, Monday, Oct. 31, 1859.
To the Editor of the Rochester Democrat:

I notice that the telegram makes Mr. Cook (one of the unfortunate insurgents at Harpers Ferry, and now a prisoner in the hands
of the thing calling itself the Government of Virginia, but which is
but an organized conspiracy by one party of the people against the
other and weaker) denounce me as a coward—and so assert that I

promised to be present in person at the Harpers Ferry insurrection. This is certainly a very grave impeachment, whether viewed in its bearings upon friends or upon foes, and you will not think it strange that I should take a somewhat serious notice of it. Having no acquaintance whatever with Mr. Cook, and never having exchanged a word with him about the Harpers Ferry insurrection, I am disposed to doubt that he could have used the language concerning me which the wires attributed to him. The lightning, when speaking for itself, is among the most direct, reliable and truthful of things; but when speaking for the terror-stricken slave-holders at Harpers Ferry it has been made the swiftest of liars. Under their nimble and trembling fingers it magnified seventeen men into seven hundred—and has since filled the columns of the New York Herald for days with interminable contradictions. But assuming that it has told the truth as to the sayings of Mr. Cook in this instance, I have this answer to make to my accuser: Mr. Cook may be perfectly right in denouncing me as a coward. I have not one word to say in defense or vindication of my character for courage. I have always been more distinguished for running than fighting—and tried by the Harpers Ferry insurrection test, I am most miserably deficient in courage—even more so than Cook, when he deserted his brave old Captain and fled to the mountains. To this extent Mr. Cook is entirely right, and will meet no contradiction from me or from anybody else. But wholly, grievously and most unaccountably wrong is Mr. Cook, when he asserts that I promised to be present in person at the Harpers Ferry insurrection. Of whatever other imprudence and indiscretion I may have been guilty, I have never made a promise so rash and wild as this. The taking of Harpers Ferry was a measure never encouraged by my word or by my vote, at any time or place. My wisdom, or my cowardice, has not only kept me from Harpers Ferry, but has equally kept me from making any promise to go there. I desire to be quite emphatic here—for of all guilty men he is the guiltiest who lures his fellow men to an undertaking of this sort, under promise of assistance, which he afterwards fails to render. I therefore declare that there is no man living, and no man dead, who, if living, could truthfully say that I ever promised him or anybody else, either conditionally or otherwise, that I would be present in person at the Harpers Ferry insurrection. My field of labor for the abolition of Slavery has not extended to an attack upon the United States Arsenal. In the teeth of the documents already published, and of those which may hereafter be published, I affirm that no man connected with that insurrection, from its noble and heroic leader down, can connect my name with a single broken promise of any sort whatever. So much I may deem it proper to say negatively.

The time for a full statement of what I know, and of all I know, of this desperate but sublimely disinterested effort to emancipate the slaves of Maryland and Virginia from their cruel task-masters has not yet come, and may never come. In the denial which I have now made my motive is more a respectful consideration for the opinions of the slave's friends than from my fear of being made an accomplice in the general *conspiracy* against Slavery. I am ever ready to write, speak, publish, organize, combine, and even to conspire against Slavery, when there is a reasonable hope of success. Men who live by robbing their fellow-men of their labor and liberty, have forfeited their right to know anything of the thoughts, feelings, or purposes of those whom they rob and plunder. They have, by the single act of slave-holding, voluntarily placed themselves beyond the laws of justice and honor, and have become only fitted for companionship with thieves and pirates—the common enemies of God and of all mankind. While it shall be considered right to protect one's self against thieves, burglars, robbers, and assassins, and to slay a wild beast in the act of devouring his human prey, it can never be wrong for the imbruted and whip-scarred slaves, or their friends, to hunt, harass, and even strike down the traffickers in human flesh. If anybody is disposed to think less of me on account of this sentiment, or because I may have had a knowledge of what was about to occur, and did not assume the base and detestable character of an informer, he is a man whose good or bad opinion of me may be equally repugnant and despicable. Entertaining this sentiment, I may be asked why I did not join John Brown—the noble old hero whose one right hand has shaken the foundation of the American Union, and whose ghost will haunt the bed-chambers of all the born and unborn slaveholders of Virginia through all their generations, filling them with alarm and consternation! My answer to this has already been given, at least impliedly given. "The tools to those who can use them." Let every man work for the abolition of Slavery in his own way. I would help all and hinder none. My position in regard to the Harpers Ferry insurrection may be easily inferred from these remarks, and I shall be glad if those papers which have spoken of me in connection with it, would find room for this statement.

I have no apology for keeping out of the way of those gentlemanly United States Marshals, who are said to have paid Rochester a somewhat protracted visit lately with a view of an interview with me. A Government recognizing the validity of the Dred Scott decision, at such a time as this, is not likely to have any very charitable feelings towards me, and if I am to meet its representatives I prefer to do so at least upon equal terms. If I have committed any offense against society I have done so on the soil of the State of New York, and I should be perfectly willing *there* to be arraigned before an impartial jury; but I have quite insuperable objections to be caught in the hands of Mr. Buchanan, and *"bagged"* by Gov. Wise. For this appears to be the arrangement—Buchanan does the fighting and hunting, and Wise *"bags"* the game.

Some reflections may be made upon my leaving on a tour to England just at this time. I have only to say that my going to that country has been rather delayed than hastened by the insurrection at Harpers Ferry. All knew that I intended to leave here in the first week of November.

Charles H. Langston

Charles H. Langston had served a twenty-day jail sentence in the spring of 1859 for assisting in the freeing of a runaway slave, John Price, in an action that became known as the Oberlin-Wellington rescue. John Brown had attended the court trial in Cleveland at which Langston had made an impassioned plea, with the spectators breaking out in cheers. Brown sought to enlist Langston for Harpers Ferry, not giving up until two weeks prior to the raid. Langston was suspected of complicity in the abortive effort, a charge he felt called upon to deny for safety's sake. Langston was not alone in taking this protective step—he had been preceded, as he pointed out, by Joshua R. Giddings, John P. Hale, Gerrit Smith (all widely known) and the brothers Ralph and Samuel Plumb of Oberlin, Ohio. The *Cleveland Plain Dealer,* the journal to which Langston addressed his "card," or denial, found it a "curious document," charging that "in his zeal to fire off an abolition lecture, he came nigh forgetting the object of the card altogether." This allegation meant nothing to Langston. Two weeks later he was scheduled for a formal address on Brown but this prior opportunity to eulogize the hero awaiting his hanging was too good to be missed. The following letter is from the *Cleveland Plain Dealer,* November 18, 1859.

Mr. Editor—Card writing seems to be the order of the day, particularly with reference to Capt. John Brown and his insurrectionary movements at Harper's Ferry. We have heard through the public journals from many of the great men and some of the great women too who are said to be connected with the "bloody attempt to dissolve the Union," "to subvert and overturn the Government," "to push forward the irrepressible conflict," "and to incite the

11

slaves of Virginia and Maryland to cut their masters' throats." Giddings, Hale, Smith, the Plumbs, and others have denied any knowledge of, or connection with the "mad scheme or its crazy perpetraters." Why the hasty denial? Why all this hot haste to throw off the imaginary disgrace or danger, which may grow out of complicity with this daring friend of Liberty and lover of mercy? Were the noble old hero and his brave and faithful followers, engaged in a mean, selfish, and dastardly work? Were they "plotting crime" against the rights or liberties of any human being? Were they in Virginia to take the property or lives of men who respect the rights of life, liberty or property in others? Capt. Brown was engaged in no vile, base, sordid, malicious or selfish enterprise. His aims and ends were lofty, noble, generous, benevolent, humane and Godlike. His actions were in perfect harmony with, and resulted from the teaching of the Bible, of our Revolutionary fathers and of every true and faithful anti-slavery man in this country and the world.

Does not the holy Bible teach that it is the duty of the strong and powerful to assist the weak and helpless, that the rich should succor the poor and needy? Does it not command us to remember those in bonds as being bound with them? Does it not tell us to loose the bonds of wickedness, undo the heavy burdens and let the oppressed go free? Does not the Bible plainly say, "whatsoever ye would that man shall do to you, do ye even so to them?" and further: "he that stealeth a man and selleth him or if he be found in his hand, he shall surely be put to death."

Did not Capt. Brown act in consonance with these Biblical principles and injunctions? He went into Virginia to aid the afflicted and the helpless, to assist the weak and to relieve the poor and needy. To undo the heavy burdens, to let the oppressed go free, to do to others as he would have them to do to him. And above all to put to death, as the papers tell us, those who steal men and sell them, and in whose hands stolen men are found. His actions then are only the results of his faithfulness to the plain teaching of the word of God.

The renowned fathers of our celebrated revolution taught the world that "resistance to tyrants is obedience to God," that all men are created equal, and have the inalienable right to life and liberty. They proclaim *death* but not *slavery*, or rather "give me liberty or give me death." They also ordained and established a constitution to secure the blessings of liberty to themselves and their *posterity*. (It is to be remembered that they have a large colored posterity in the Southern States). And they further declared that when any government becomes destructive of these ends, namely, life, liberty, justice and happiness, it is the right of the people to abolish it and to institute a new government.—On these pure and holy principles they fearlessly entered into a seven years war against the most powerful nation of the earth, relying on a just God, whom they believed would raise up friends to fight their battles for them. Their belief was more than realized. The friends of freedom came to their assistance.

Did not Capt. Brown act in accordance with the foregoing revolutionary principles? Did not he obey God by resisting tyrants? Did he not in all things show his implicit faith in the equality of all men? and their unalienable right to life and liberty? When he saw that the governments of the South were destructive of these ends, did he not aim to abolish them and to institute a new government laying its foundation on such principles as to him seemed most likely to secure the happiness and safety of the people?

Some will say no doubt that the teaching of the renowned fathers had no reference to Negroes, for, says Judge Taney, the prevalent opinion at the time of the revolution was that "black men had no rights which white men were bound to respect." In sober earnestness did the "great and good men of those days which tried men's souls," have no higher idea of liberty and the rights of man than that? Did they believe in one-sided, selfish, partial, sectarian freedom? Liberty for proud "Anglo Saxon" and chains and fetters for "all the world and the rest of mankind." I think they must have had a higher, a nobler idea of man and his inalienable rights. But be this as it may, the Abolitionists, the true friends of God and humanity, are applying both the doctrines of the Bible and the teaching of the fathers to every human being, whether white or black, bond or free. We Abolitionists profess to propagate no new doctrines in politics or morals, but to urge all men to practice the old well-defined and immutable principles "of the fatherhood of God and the universal brotherhood of man." Liberty and equality belong naturally to the entire brotherhood; and the man who takes from his brother his liberty, becomes a tyrant and thus forfeits his rights to *live*.

Now it is plain to be seen that Capt. Brown only carried out in his actions the principles emanating from these three sources, viz: First—The Bible. Second—The Revolutionary Fathers. Third— All good Abolitionists.

If, then, Brown acted on these pure and righteous principles, why are the friends of justice, liberty and right so hasty in denying all connections with him or sympathy with his ends and aims? Perhaps they see the bloody gallows of the "affrighted chivalry" rising before them in awful horror. Or more probably they see a political grave yearning to receive them.

But to speak of myself I have no political prospects and therefore no political fears! for my black face and curly hair doom me in this land of equality to political damnation and that beyond the possibility of redemption. But I have a neck as dear to me as Smith's, Hale's or Giddings', and therefore I must like them publish a card of denial. So here it is. But what shall I deny? I cannot deny that I feel that the very deepest sympathy with the Immortal John Brown in his heroic and daring efforts to free the slaves.—To do this would be in my opinion more criminal than to urge the slaves to open rebellion. To deny any connection with the "daring and fiendish plot" would be worse than nonsense. The *fearless chivalry* of the old dominion would move me guilty without the least difficulty. For their heroic imaginations now convert every harmless pillow into an infernal machine, behold the veritable Capt.

Brown in every peaceable non-resistant northern abolitionist, and see in every colored man the dusky ghost of Gen. Nat Turner, the hero of Southampton. So their testimony against me would be imaginary, their trial a farce, but their rope halter would be a stern and binding reality.

. . . With these explanations and denials, I hope the Marshal of the Northern District of Ohio, the Federal Administration generally, and all slave holders and particularly all official "smelling committees," will be fully satisfied.

C. H. LANGSTON

Cleveland, Nov. 1859.

Black Women to Mrs. Mary A. Brown

A week before Brown's scheduled hanging a group of black women in New York sent a letter to Mary Brown, wife of the jailed leader. Here the correspondents express their sentiments toward Brown and their intentions toward his stricken helpmeet. The black women did not overstate their sentiments, even if, as later proved true, they could not live up to their intentions. Their letter was carried in *The Weekly Anglo-African* (New York), December 17, 1859.

LETTER TO THE WIFE OF JOHN BROWN

The following is the letter alluded to in our report, found elsewhere, of the sympathy meeting in Brooklyn, on the 21st inst., as being sent by the ladies of New York, Brooklyn and Williamsburgh, to the wife of the martyr, Brown:

> No. 62 East Sixteenth St., N.Y.
> November 23, 1859.

Dear Mrs. Brown: A few weeks since some colored ladies of this city met at the house of the Rev. Henry Highland Garnet, an old and, I doubt not, highly valued friend of your husband's, to supplicate our common Father in behalf of one whom they felt had offered up his life, and the lives of those dearer to him than his own, in the effort to obtain for their oppressed race their "God given rights." It was a time of strong supplication, of weeping, and of wrestlings with God, and some of us felt we had, through Him, who had been our beloved brother's Exampler, obtained an answer of peace, and I think I may say, from our united experience, "Be comforted."

16

Till that meeting for prayer I, and I know many of them, had labored, as it were, under a horror of great darkness. Before the gray dawn had broken over a sleeping world, through the busy hours of the day, at evening tide, and in the mid-watches of the night, the cry had gone up unceasingly from our sorrowful and burdened spirits: "Lord, send deliverance to our brother from the hands of fierce and cruel men who seek his blood!" We could get no rest—we could give but little comfort to each other; but since then the burden has been taken from my heart individually, and strange to say, *I cannot feel* troubled about him. Ah, you weepingly say, "he is not their husband." Yet, dear friend, he is our honored and dearly-loved brother, and we are satisfied that there is One who cares for him more tenderly than we, or than even his sorrowing and desolate companion. We know he is dear to our God as the apple of his eye. Do you doubt it? We do not, and we are sure you do not. Can not our Heavenly Father quickly send ten legions of Angels to strike terror into the hearts of these men? Can he not send *one* bright visitant, as in the days of old, when his faithful servant, chained and manacled, lay sleeping between his keepers, and yet at that light touch, and in obedience to that angel voice, arose and went forth, not knowing but "that it was a vision?" Yes, surely. Our God changes not; and if your husband be delivered, to sorrow a few more years those scenes of cruelty which have so wrung his noble spirit for more than thirty years; and if it be his Master's will to whisper now to him, "Come up higher!" would you hold back the chariot wheels, though they be wheels of fire. No, my dear sorrowing sister—we are assured, from what we gather of your like-mindedness with your noble champion, your motto is: "It is my God—my covenant God—who doeth all things well." Well, we wanted to tell you how we have met again and again in prayer for you, and those who are still in bonds, and how, in offering this word of sympathy to you now we desire to express our deep, undying gratitude to him who has given his life so freely to obtain for us our defrauded rights, and whose bereaved ones we accept, according to his suggestion in "The Tribune" of November 12, as a solemn legacy at his hands—if indeed it be our Master's will to give him now the Crown of Glory, which awaits all those to whom it will be said at that day: "Inasmuch as ye have done it unto the least of these ye have done it unto me."

Tell your dear husband then, that henceforth you shall be our own! We are a poor and despised people—almost forbidden, by the oppressive restrictions of the Free States, to rise to the higher walks of lucrative employments, toiling early and late for our daily bread; but we hope—and we intend, by God's help—to organize in every Free State, and in every colored church, a band of sisters, to collect our weekly pence, and pour it lovingly into your lap. God will help us, for he is the Judge of the widow and the Father of the fatherless. And you have all been made widows, and your children fatherless, because your husbands, and your children's fathers, counted not their lives as dear, so that they might fulfill this command of our God's: "Therefore I say unto you, whatsoever ye would that others should do unto you, do ye even so unto them, for this is the law and the prophets." (The Mosaic as well as the Christian dispensation.)

Fear not, beloved sister. Trust in the God of Jacob. He who of old sent his prophet forth with this word to the tyrant who oppresses, and woe, woe, woe, is theirs if, instead of honoring the word of the Lord, they slay the prophet. Trust then in this same God, and if you will cast your fatherless ones upon Him, and if you and they will, as your beloved husband has done, deal justly, love mercy, and walk humbly with your God, and it shall be well with you in time and in eternity.

We hope soon to send you the first fruits of our offering of love. Many will doubtless minister to you; but in our ministration we trust to make a fund to minister to you and yours till you shall say it is enough, and until you yourselves shall say to us: "Clothe the naked, feed the hungry, shelter the homeless ones, who are daily fleeing from the oppressor."

We do not ask you to write now. We know, we cannot be un-
mindful of the loneliness, and we fear the agony of these solemn
days. The one who is privileged to write these words for her sisters
unto you, knows well the heart of the widow and all its desola-
tions; but we pray that He whose you are, whom you serve, who
has said that not a cup of cold water shall be given to a disciple
in His name, without receiving a disciple's reward, will cause His
face to shine upon you, will speak peace to your troubled spirit,
will send the strong consolations of the Gospel, which have the
voices in his counsel and the guide of the life of your husband and
our brother into your heart. May a Triune Jehovah shed life, light
and peace around your dwelling,

                                                    Pray your loving sisters.

Sentiments on Martyr Day (December 2, 1859): Newspaper Reports from *The Weekly Anglo-African* and an Address by J. Sella Martin

On the day that Brown was hanged there was an outpouring of sympathy in many northern communities. Mournful blacks took solemn note of the day, sometimes in conjunction with white groups. Detroit and Pittsburgh were two of the many cities whose black residents held meetings of their own, as reported in *The Weekly Anglo-African*. In Boston on the night of December 2, 1859, abolitionist stalwarts held a standing-room-only meeting at Tremont Temple, with 3,000 gathered outside. The meeting had been organized by whites and was conducted by them, but, as one reporter put it, "All the colored people of Boston and its vicinity were present." One of the more eloquent speakers was J. Sella Martin, who for six months had held the pulpit at Tremont Temple, a precedent for a black, and was then the pastor of Joy Street Baptist Church. In his address, Martin, a former slave himself, upbraided the master class and defended the slaves against the charge of having failed to rally to Brown. The two reports following are from *The Weekly Anglo-African* (New York), December 17, 1859. Martin's speech appeared in *The Liberator* (Boston), December 9, 1859.

MEETING IN DETROIT

On Friday evening, December 2d, 1859 pursuant to previous notice, a densely crowded meeting of colored citizens convened at the Second Baptist Church, Croghan Street.

The meeting was called to order by Wm. Lambert, who briefly referred to the solemn event of the day as the cause of the meeting.

He then introduced the evening's exercises, according to the following programme:

Prayer, by Rev. Wm. Webb.

Reading of the 9th Psalm, by Rev. A. P. Green.

Music—Ode to Old Capt. John Brown by Profs. Martin and Brown's Liberty Songsters.

Religions and Anti-Slavery Character of Brown, by Revs. Messrs. Anderson and Green.

Music—Daughters of Zion, by Liberty Songsters.

Brown's Christian Fortitude, by Rev. Wm. Webb.

Music—Might Speed the Right, by Liberty Songsters.

The religious exercises being over; Mr. George Hannibal Parker, President of the Old Capt. John Brown Liberty League ascended the platform and took the chair. The meeting then assumed a more deliberative and revolutionary character, whereupon Wm. Lambert presented and read the following declaration of sentiment and resolves, which were enthusiastically received:

Whereas, We, the oppressed portion of this community, many of whom have worn the galling chains and felt the smarting lash of slavery, and know by sad experience its brutalizing effects upon both the body and the mind, and its damaging influence upon the soul of its victim, and

Whereas, We, by the help of Almighty God and the secret abolition movements that are now beginning to develop themselves in the southern part of this country, have been enabled to escape from the prison-home of slavery, and partially to obtain our liberty; and having become personally acquainted with the life and character of our much beloved and highly esteemed friend, Old Capt. John Brown, and his band of valiant men, who, at Harper's Ferry, on the 16th day of October, 1859, demonstrated to the world this sympathy and fidelity to the cause of the suffering slaves of this country, by bearding the hydra headed monster, Tyranny, in his den, and by his bold, effective, timely blow is now causing the South to tremble with a moral earthquake as he totally and freely delivered up his life to lay as a ransom for our enslaved race and thereby, "solitary and alone," he has put a liberty ball in motion which shall continue to roll and gather strength until the last vestige of human slavery within this nation shall have been crushed beneath the ponderous weight, Therefore,

Resolved, That we hold the name of Old Capt. John Brown in the most sacred remembrance, now the first disinterested martyr for our liberty, whereupon the true Christian principle of his Divine Lord and Master, has freely delivered up his life for the liberty of our race in this country. Therefore will we ever vindicate his character through all coming time, as our temporal redeemer whose name shall never die,

Resolved, That, as the long lost rights and liberties of an oppressed people are only gained in proportion as they act in their own cause, therefore are we now loudly called upon to arouse to our own interest, and to concentrate our efforts in keeping the Old Brown liberty-ball in motion and thereby continue to kindle the fires of liberty upon the altar of every determined heart among men and continue to fan the same until the proper time, when a revolutionary blast from liberty's trump shall summon them simultaneously to unite for victorious and triumphant battle.

Resolved, That we tender our deepest and most heart felt sympathy to the family of Capt. John Brown in their sad bereavement, and pledge to them that they shall ever be held by us as our special friends, in whose welfare we hope ever to manifest a special interest.

After the reading of this declaration, the "Marsellaise Hymn" with the able and eloquent speeches of the Revs. Messrs. Anderson, Green, Webb, and Mr. John D. Richards, who responded so ably and eloquently to the declaration that the fire of liberty was kindled in the hearts of the whole assembly, in whose remembrance the name of Old John Brown will never die.

After a general expression upon the declaration, it was resolved that the several colored churches be dressed in mourning for thirty days, and that an appointment be made for the preaching of the funeral sermon of our much beloved friend within that period.

Rev. Mr. Webb, from the Finance Committee, reported that the "League" had twenty-five dollars in hand, ready to send to Mrs. Brown, which would be forwarded to her as soon as her mind becomes a little composed from the effects of her sad bereavement.

On motion, it was resolved that the proceedings of this meeting be presented to the city papers for publication, and that copies be sent to the several anti-slavery papers throughout the country, requesting them to publish the same.

On motion, the meeting then adjourned, to meet again on Friday evening the 16th inst., and the assemblage arose under the soul-stirring strains of the patriotic song, "On on to battle—we fear no foe."

MEETING IN PITTSBURGH

Mr. Editor:—On Tuesday evening, the 29th ult., a public meeting was held at the Wylie street A.M.E. Church, to give expression to sentiments in relation to Captain John Brown.

The meeting was organized by calling Charles Jones to the chair, and appointing Rufus S. Jones as Secretary, after which a committee was appointed consisting of Messrs. John Peck, Benjamin T. Tanner, Austin B. Lloyd, Lewis Woodson, Jr., and Harvey G. Webb, in connection with S. A. Neal, Samuel Lindsay, and Thomas Beach, as a conferring committee on the part of the colored residents of Allegheny City. While the committee withdrew to prepare resolutions, several warm speeches were made.

The committee reported the following preamble and resolutions, which were discussed and adopted:

We, the colored people of Pittsburgh and vicinity, assembled in Wylie street Church Nov. 29, 1859, acknowledge in the person of John Brown a hero, patriot, and Christian—a hero because he was fearless to defend the poor; a patriot because he loves his country-men; and a Christian because he loves his neighbor as himself, and remembered those in bonds as bound with them, Therefore, be it

Resolved, That in his death we feel that, with Caiphas, "it needs be that one man die for the people."

Resolved, That we sincerely believe in the old maxim, that "the blood of the martyrs is the seed of the church."

Resolved, That we see in the Harper's Ferry affair what Daniel Webster saw when speaking of Crispus Attucks, the black Revolutionary martyr who fell in Boston—viz. the severance of two antagonistic principles.

Resolved, That John Brown, in taking up arms to liberate the slaves, only acted upon the maxim that "resistance to tyrants is obedience to God."

Resolved, That upon next Friday, December 2d, the day upon which he is to be executed, we close our places of business between the hours of ten and three o'clock; that a sermon be preached at 11 o'clock a.m., in the A.M.E. Church, and that appropriate services be held in the evening of the same place at which time a collection shall be raised in behalf of Capt. Brown's family.

Resolved, That the teachers of our public schools be requested to suspend service on that day.

Resolved, That, in the event of the execution of John Brown upon the 2d of December, the anniversary of that day be hereafter perpetually observed among us as a day of humiliation and prayer.

According to resolution, a sermon was preached last Friday, at 11 o'clock by the Rev. Nelson U. Turpin, pastor of the Wylie street Church. His text was the first clause of the twenty-second verse of the seventy-fourth psalm. After he had concluded, Rev. John Gibbs, pastor of Brown's chapel, Allegheny City, arose, and made a few fitting remarks, which had a tendency to make one feel that more than [an] ordinary man had fallen a prey to tyranny.

In the evening there was a meeting at the same place, at which Rev. Mr. Turpin presided, and B. T. Tanner acted as Secretary.

Addresses were delivered by Prof. George B. Vashon, M. H. Freeman, Saml. A. Neal, and Rev. J. R. V. Morgan, after which a collection was made in behalf of the family of the martyred Brown
amounting to sixteen dollars.

SPEECH OF REV. J. S. MARTIN

Mr. President, Ladies and Gentlemen,—To-day, a solemn question has been asked this nation. The Pilate of Providence has asked
America—"Whom will you that I deliver unto you—the Barabbas
of Slavery, or the John Brown of Freedom?" And, intimidated by
the false majesty of despotic enactments, which have usurped the
place of Christianity, corrupted by a false policy, and stung to
phrenzy by the insinuations of our political high priests, we have
cried out, as a nation—"Release unto us the Barabbas of slavery,
and destroy John Brown." And, true to this horrible, this atrocious
request, John Brown has been offered up. Thank God, he said, "I
am ready to be offered up."

Men say that his life was 'a failure.' I remember the story of
one of the world's moral heroes, whose life was just such a 'failure.'
I remember one who, having retired to the deserts of Judea, to
wring from the hard, stony life of those deserts the qualifications
of a moral hero, by living an ascetic life, had subjugated the lower
desires of his nature, and who, with all those qualifications, and
with all this purity, was brought into a corrupt and voluptuous
court. I remember, too, that in that court, notwithstanding he was
its favorite, notwithstanding the corruption and luxury of the times,
he preserved himself the same stern man, and said to the King—
"It is not lawful for you to live with your brother Phillip's wife.'
These were the stern words of John the Baptist and John Brown—
for John Brown, like John the Baptist, retired into the hard and
stony desert of Kansas, and there, by the weapons of heroism, by
the principles of freedom, and the undaunted courage of a man,

wrung from that bloody soil the highest encomiums of Freedom, and the most base acknowledgements of slavery, that the one was right and the other wrong. (Applause.) I know that John Brown, in thus rebuking our public sin, in thus facing the monarch, has had to bear just what John the Baptist bore. His head to-day, by Virginia,—that guilty maid of a more guilty mother, the American Government, (cheers, mingled with a few hisses, which were at once drowned in an outburst of vehement applause)—has been cut off, and it has been presented to the ferocious and insatiable hunger, the terrible and inhuman appetite, of this corrupt government. To-day, by the telegraph, we have received the intelligence that John Brown has forfeited his life—all this honesty, all this straight-forwardness, all this self-sacrifice, which has been mani-fested in Harper's Ferry.

My friends, his life was just such a "failure" as all great move-ments have been. The physical failure has been the death of the seed, externally, which has given life to the germ, which has sprung forth to spread its moral boughs all over this corrupt nation. (Ap-plause.) I have not the slightest doubt that this will be the result . . . John Brown has died, but the life of Freedom, from his death, shall flow forth to this nation.

I know that there is some quibbling, some querulousness, some fear, in reference to an out-and-out endorsement of his course. Men of peace principles object to it, in consequence of their reli-gious conviction; politicians in the North object to it, because they are afraid that it will injure their party; pro-slavery men in the South object to it, because it has touched their dearest idol; but I am prepared, my friends, (and permit me to say, this is not the language of rage,) I am prepared, in the light of all human history, to approve of the *means;* in the light of all Christian principle, to approve of the *end.* (Applause.) I say this is not the language of rage, because I remember that our Fourth-of-July orators sanc-tion the same thing; because I remember that Concord, and Bunker Hill, and every historic battlefield in this country, and the celebration of those events, all go to approve the means that John Brown has used; the only difference being, that in our battles, in America, means have been used for *white* men and that John Brown has used his means for *black* men. (Applause.) And I say, that so far as principle is concerned, so far as the sanctions of the Gospel are concerned, I am prepared to endorse his end; and I endorse it because God Almighty has told us that we should feel with them that are in bonds as being bound with them. I endorse his end, because every single instinct of our nature rises and tells us that it is right. I find an endorsement of John Brown's course in the large assembly gathered here this evening; I find an endorsement of the principles that governed him in going to Virginia, in the presence of the men and women who have come here to listen to his eulogy, and sympathize with his suffering family. I know that all have not come for that purpose, but I know there are seven thousand still in Israel who have not bowed the knee to the political Baal. (Loud applause.)

Now, I bring this question down to the simple test of the Gospel; and, agreeing with those men who say the sword should not be used, agreeing with them in that principle, and recognizing its binding obligation upon us all, yet I believe in that homeopathic principle which operates by mercury when mercury is in the system, and that that which is supported by the sword should be overthrown by the sword. I look at this question as a peace man. I say, in accordance with the principles of peace, that I do not believe the sword should be unsheathed. I do not believe the dagger should be drawn, until there is in the system to be assailed such terrible evidences of its corruption, that it becomes the *dernier resort.* And my friends, we are not to blame the application of the instrument, we are to blame the disease itself. When a physician cuts out a cancer from my face, I am not to blame the physician for the use of the knife; but the impure blood, the obstructed veins, the disordered system, that have caused the cancer, and rendered the use of the instrument necessary. The physician has but chosen the least of two evils. So John Brown chose the least of two evils. To save the country, he went down to cut off the Virginia cancer. (Applause.)

I say, that I am prepared to endorse John Brown's course fully. He has said that he did not intend to shed blood. In my opinion, speaking as a military critic, this was one of the faults of his plan. In not shedding blood, he left the slaves uncertain how to act; so that the North has said that the Negroes there are cowards. They are not cowards, but great diplomats. When they saw their masters in the possession of John Brown, in bonds like themselves, they would have been perfect fools has they demonstrated any willingness to join him. They have got sense enough to know, that until there is a perfect demonstration that the white man is their friend —a demonstration bathed in blood—it were foolishness to cooperate with them. They have learned this much from the treachery of white men at the North, and the cruelty of the white men at the South, that they cannot trust the white man, even when he comes to deliver them. So it was not their cowardice, nor their craven selfishness, but it was their caution, that prevented them from joining Brown. I say this because I think it is necessary to vindicate the character of the Negro for courage. I know very well that in this country, the white people have said that the Negroes will not fight; but I know also, that when the country's honor has been at stake, and the dire prejudice that excludes the colored man from all positions of honor, and all opportunities for advancement, has not interfered to exclude him from the military, he was gone with the army, and there displayed as much courage as his white brother.

To some extent, I sympathize with the suggestions of the *Boston Journal,* that we should consider the state of excitement among the people of Virginia; for I know what that state of excitement is. I know that if a rat should happen to strike his tail against the lathes, they would all be up, looking through the house—taking good care always to make a Negro go before. (Laughter.) I am ready to say, if he has violated the law, if he has taken an improper course, if he has been the traitor that the South brands him as having been, and the madman that the North says he has been, John Brown is not to be blamed. I say that the system which violates the sacredness of conjugal love, the system that robs the cradle of its innocent treasure—the system that goes into the temple of manhood, and writes upon the altar its hellish hieroglyphics of slavery—the system that takes away every God-given right, and tramples religion under foot—I say that that system is responsible for every single crime committed within the borders where it exists. (Applause.) It is the system, my friends. I hold that that is a false logic which talks about good slaveholders. I hold that it is folly on the part of the slaveholder himself when he attempts to keep his slaves by mild means. The more a man learns, the more kindly he is treated, the more he aspires for liberty, the more restive he becomes under the yoke.—Hence it is not an accident, but a necessity of the system of slavery, that it should be cruel; and all its devilish instrumentality, and enginery, and paraphernalia must be cruel also. It is folly for us to talk about the slaveholders being kind. Cruelty is part and parcel of the system. If slavery is right at all, then all its terrors and horrors,—the whip, the manacle, the thumbscrew, the paddle, the stake, the gibbet—are right also; if it is not right, then all these are wrong. The people of the North have said John Brown was a madman—I suppose mostly because it is on the eve of an election: but if he was mad, his madness not only had a great deal of "method" in it, but a great deal of philosophy and religion. I say, my friends, that no man ever died in this country as John Brown has died to-day. I say it because John Brown was a praying man. I remember hearing an incident in reference to his praying, from the lips of a man in whose presence and in whose house it occurred, and I loved him the more when I heard it. Coming to Henry Highland Garnet, of New York, some two years ago, he said to him, after unfolding all his plans, "Mr. Garnet, what do you think of it?" Said Mr. Garnet, who is at once a Christian, a gentleman, and a scholar,—"Sir, the time has not come yet for the

success of such a movement. Our people in the South are not sufficiently apprised of their rights, and of the sympathy that exists on
the part of the North for them; our people in the North are not
prepared to assist in such a movement, in consequence of the prejudice that shuts them out from both the means and the intelligence
necessary. The breach between the North and the South has not
yet become wide enough." Mr. Brown, looking him in the face as
his keen eye was lit up with its peculiar fire, and his soul seemed to
come forth with all its intellectual energy to look out and scan, if
possible, the whole horizon of Providence, said, "Mr. Garnet, I
will ask God about it"; and he got down upon his knees, and there
poured out his heart to that God who is peculiarly the God of the
bondman. He then showed the depth of his religious feeling—the
intense interest that he had in the emancipation of mankind, and
the heroism of his soul. Mr. Garnet says that never in his life has
he been so moved by a prayer as he was by that prayer of John
Brown's. When such a man as this dies as he has died to-day, with
the prayers of five millions of people going up to Heaven in his
behalf—for I know that at least that number of Christians have
prayed for him—when such a man dies, I am sure that his death
under such circumstances affords us a great, an almost demon-
strable evidence of the success of the movement that he has inau-
gurated and of the final accomplishment of the great object of his
soul. (Applause.) I say that no man has ever died in this country
as John Brown has died. While his soul has gone up to God, and his
body has been taken down a lifeless corpse, thank God all over the
country, meetings are being held-to-night to give expression to that
great feeling of sympathy which is to swell the great tornado.—Let
Virginia thank herself for it! In her guilty planting she has sown
the wind; let her thank herself if in her terrible harvest she reaps
the whirlwind of destruction. (Applause.)

Go down to Virginia, and see that firm old man as he comes out
from his prison, leaning upon the arm of the sheriff and with his
head erect, ascends the dreadful steps of the gibbet. We see as he

goes his way to the top, and every step he takes seems to be inspired with that feeling which the poet Longfellow describes as animating the heart of the young man climbing to the top of the mountain—"Excelsior"—until planting himself on the top, he is ready for his martyrdom. Though his body falls, the spirit of slavery and despotism falls with it, while John Brown goes up to heaven. Thank God! thank God! (Applause.)

I have detained you long enough. This is not the time to vindicate his cause. I have made these remarks only because they seem to be suggested here. I close by saying, my friends, that John Brown . . . shall slay more in his death than he ever slew in all his life. It is thought by the slaves—and it is a beautiful conceit, though coming from slaves—that the meteors from the heavens are sparks that . . . strike upon the craters of volcanoes, and that is the cause of their eruption. From the firmament of Providence today, a meteor has fallen. It has fallen upon the volcano of American sympathies, and though, for awhile, it may seem to sleep, yet its igneous power shall communicate . . . to the slumbering might of the volcano, and it shall burst forth in one general conflagration of revolution that shall bring about universal freedom. (Applause.) I feel, my friends and fellow-citizens, tonight, that courage, the adamantine courage, which has today been blasted by the terrible enginery of slavery will serve as the grit in the grindstone upon which the slave shall sharpen his weapon . . . I believe that every drop of blood shed today will be gathered up by the ever vigilant spirit of freedom . . . by whose resplendent light the darkest hovels of slavery shall be penetrated until the chains shall be melted from every limb, and the slave stand forth "regenerated and disenthalled by the irresistible Genius of Universal Emancipation." (Loud Applause.)

Harvey C. Jackson:
The Response of Blacks in Canada

Blacks in Canada, particularly in the cities and towns just above the Great Lakes—the haven area for runaway slaves—were deeply moved by the Harpers Ferry episode. To these blacks Brown was no stranger, his fame among them stemming in large measure from the predominantly black-attended Chatham convention, which he had called in May 1858, combined with his seizure later the same year of eleven Missouri slaves, who, after a hazardous three months in his company, were landed on Canadian soil. A broadside issued by Harvey C. Jackson of Simcoe, Ontario, and dated five days after Brown's hanging, illustrates the typical sentiment of Canadian blacks toward him and toward his bereaved family. The broadside is part of the Boyd B. Stutler Collection of the John Brown Papers, Ohio Historical Society (MSS. No. 42, Roll No. 5), used by permission of the Ohio Historical Society.

Fellow Citizens:—You are all aware of the excitement recently created at Harper's Ferry, in the State of Virginia, in consequence of the bold and heroic attack upon Slavery, made by Captain John Brown and a few others, whose object was to break the chains of that accursed institution. You are also aware that their attempt was a failure, so far as the immediate emancipation of our kindred were concerned. But that bold attempt to liberate the slaves will be attended with the most important results. It has already enlightened public opinion more than all the anti-slavery speeches made for the last ten years; it has caused anti-slavery newspapers and letters to penetrate the very *centre* of those despotic states. Even the New Orleans *Picayune* is frightened at the influx of those "inflammatory" articles and documents. Some persons may brand Brown's effort

32

as "rash, futile, and wild," but they must acknowledge that it will be productive of much good, or renounce their judgement. Christianity never spread so fast at any other period as it did when the earth was made gory with the blood of the Martyrs. Brown and his confederates are martyrs to the cause of Liberty, and their blood will cry out from the earth and gain many advocates to Freedom. But even supposing the contrary was the case; the intent, the aim was good, in behalf of our oppressed race, and we should do our duty,—show the world that we appreciate such noble and philanthropic actions. By the martyrdom of Capt. Brown, that brave, undaunted, heroic spirit, and his noble confederates, a parcel of widows and orphans, sharing the same sympathy towards our race, are left without means to meet the necessities of life, and it is for you to say whether you will assist in providing for the widows and in educating the orphans. I *know* you will assist. Coming ages will appreciate Capt. Brown's worth, his greatness of soul.

Let there be a meeting called in every locality where any colored persons reside. Let the "whites" be solicited to aid in the glorious and heavenly enterprise; let each locality remit what is collected, to Mr. Samuel E. Sewall, 46 Washington St., Boston. Mr. Sewall, a gentleman of great integrity, has been appointed to receive the funds collected for the benefit of the relations of the Harper's Ferry Martyrs. Friends, let the world see that we appreciate a disinterested and generous deed—let us manifest it by *action,* as well as by word.

Have Copeland and Green relations who will suffer pecuniarily by their being murdered by the Virginians? If so, request Mr. Sewall when you send your contributions, to *give them a proportionate amount.*

Yours, for the cause of humanity.
HARVEY C. JACKSON.
Simcoe, Canada West, Dec. 7th, 1859.

John Anthony Copeland

A resident of Oberlin, Ohio, John A. Copeland (1834–1859)
had attended the college there, had belonged to the Oberlin
Anti-Slavery Society, and had been among those indicted in the
famous Wellington-Oberlin slave-rescue case. While in jail at
Charlestown awaiting execution for complicity in the Harpers
Ferry raid, Copeland wrote at least five letters. Although these
letters deal mainly with such eternal verities as man's freedom
and God's omniscience, they occasionally mention personal
names, one letter making two brief references to John Brown.
In this letter, written on December 10, he also refers to Crispus
Attucks, the first to die in the Boston Massacre on March 5,
1770. The letter was included by Robert S. Fletcher in "John
Brown and Oberlin," *The Oberlin Alumni Magazine*, February
1932, pp. 137–38.

Charlestown, Va. Dec. 10, 1859.
My Dear Brother:—I now take my pen to write you a few lines to
let you know how I am, and in answer to your kind letter of the
5th instant. Dear Brother, I am, it is true, so situated at present
as scarcely to know how to commence writing; not that my mind is
filled with fear or that it has become shattered in view of my near
approach to death. Not that I am terrified by the gallows which I
see staring me in the face, and upon which I am so soon to stand
and suffer death for doing what George Washington, the so-called
father of this great but slavery-cursed country, was made a hero
for doing, while he lived, and when dead his name was immortal-
ized, and his great and noble deeds in behalf of freedom taught by
parents to their children. And now, brother, for having lent my aid
to a General no less brave, and engaged in a cause no less honorable and glorious, I am to suffer death. Washington entered the

field to fight for freedom of the American people—not for the white man alone, but for both black and white. Nor were they white men alone who fought for the freedom of this country. The blood of black men flowed as freely as that of white men. Yes, the *very first* blood that was spilt was that of a Negro. It was the blood of that heroic man, (though black he was) Cyrus Attuck. And some of the *very last* blood shed was that of black men. To the truth of this, history, though prejudiced, is compelled to attest. It is true that black men did an equal share of the fighting for American Independence, and they were assured by the whites that they should share equal benefits for so doing. But after having performed their part honorably, they were by the whites most treacherously deceived—they refusing to fulfill their part of the contract. But this you know as well as I do, and I will therefore say no more in reference to the claims which we, as colored men, have on the American people.

It was a sense of the wrongs which we have suffered that prompted the noble but unfortunate Captain Brown and his associates to attempt to give freedom to a small number, at least, of those who are now held by cruel and unjust laws, and by no less cruel and unjust men. To this freedom they were entitled by every known principle of justice and humanity, and for the enjoyment of it God created them. And now dear brother, could I die in a more noble cause? Could I, brother, die in a manner and for a cause which would induce true and honest men more to honor me, and the angels more readily to receive me to their happy home of everlasting joy above? . . .

You may think I have been treated very harshly since I have been here, but it is not so. I have been treated exceedingly well—far better than I expected to be. My jailer is a most kind-hearted man, and has done all he could consistent with duty to make me and the rest of the prisoners comfortable. Capt. John Avis is a gentleman who has a heart in his bosom as brave as any other. He met us at the Ferry and fought us as a brave man would do.

But since we have been in his power he has protected us from insult and abuse which cowards would have heaped upon us. He has done as a brave man and gentleman only would do. Also one of his aids, Mr. John Sheats, has been very kind to us and has done all he could to serve us. And now, Henry, if fortune should ever throw either of them in your way and you can confer the least favor on them, do it for my sake. Give my love to all my friends. And now my dear brothers, one and all, I pray God we may meet in Heaven.

Good bye. I am now and shall remain your affectionate brother,
JOHN A. COPELAND.

Brown and Nat Turner:
An Editor's Comparison

Inevitably the Harpers Ferry affair reminded many people, white and black, of the Nat Turner insurrection in Southampton County, Virginia, in August 1831. Thomas Hamilton, editor of *The Monthly Anglo-African,* was no exception. In this periodical he reproduced "The Confessions of Nat Turner" (a statement taken down by attorney Thomas R. Gray immediately before the court trial), along with an accompanying editorial comparing and contrasting John Brown and Nat Turner. To reach a wider audience, Hamilton carried the "Confessions" and this editorial, both under the title "The Nat Turner Insurrection," in *The Weekly Anglo-African,* a companion periodical he edited, on December 31, 1859.

There are two reasons why we present our readers with the "Confessions of Nat Turner." First, to place upon record this most remarkable episode in the history of human slavery, which proves to the philosophic observer that in the midst of this most perfectly contrived and apparently secure system of slavery, humanity will out, and engender from its bosom forces that will contend against oppression, however unsuccessfully; and secondly, that the two methods of Nat Turner and of John Brown may be compared. The one is the mode in which the slave seeks freedom for his fellows, and the other mode in which the white man seeks to set the slave free. There are many points of similarity between these two men: they were both idealists; both governed by their views of the teachings of the Bible; both had harbored for years the purpose to which they gave up their lives; both felt themselves swayed as by some divine, or at least, spiritual impulse; the one seeking in the air, the earth, and the heavens for signs which came at last; and the

37

other, obeying impulses which he believes to have been fore-
ordained from the eternal past; both cool, calm, and heroic in
prison and in the prospect of inevitable death; both confess with
child-like frankness and simplicity the object they had in view—
the pure and simple emancipation of their fellow men; both win
from the judges who sentenced them, expressions of deep sympathy—and here the parallel ceases. Nat Turner's terrible logic
could only see the enfranchisement of one race, compassed by the
extirpation of the other; and he followed his gory syllogism with
rude exactitude. John Brown, believing that the freedom of the
enthralled could only be effected by placing them on an equality
with the enslavers, and unable in the very effort at emancipation
to tyrannize himself, is moved with compassion for tyrants, as
well as slaves, and seeks to extirpate this formidable cancer, without spilling one drop of Christian blood.

These two narratives present a fearful choice to the slaveholders,
nay, to this great nation—which of the two modes of emancipation
shall take place? The method of Nat Turner, or the method of
John Brown?

Emancipation must take place, and soon. There can be no long
delay in the choice of methods. If John Brown's be not soon
adopted by the free North, then Nat Turner's will be by the enslaved South.

Had the order of events been reversed—had Nat Turner been
in John Brown's place at the head of these twenty-one men, governed by his inexorable logic and cool daring, the soil of Virginia
and Maryland and the far South would by this time be drenched
in the blood and the wild and sanguinary course of these men, no
earthly power could stay.

The course which the South is now frantically pursuing will engender in its bosom and nurse into maturity a hundred Nat Turners, whom Virginia is infinitely less able to resist in 1860, than she
was in 1831.

So, people of the South, people of the North! men and brethren, choose ye which method of emancipation you prefer—Nat Turner's or John Brown's?

Osborn Perry Anderson

Osborn[e] Perry Anderson (1830–1872), one of the five blacks at Harpers Ferry, had met John Brown at a convention at Chatham, Ontario, in May 1858, designed to ratify a constitution which Brown had drafted. After the Harpers Ferry fiasco, Anderson lived alternately in Canada or the northern states, although much more circumspectly in the latter. Originally a Pennsylvanian, he served in the Union army during the Civil War. He died, unmarried, on December 14, 1872, in Washington, D.C. His thin book, *A Voice from Harper's Ferry,* published in Boston in 1861, was designed in part to raise money for his support. Its first ten pages, selections from which are given here, concentrate on John Brown and his intentions, as Anderson saw them.

    The idea underlying the outbreak at Harper's Ferry is not peculiar to that movement, but dates back to a period very far beyond the memory of the "oldest inhabitant," and emanated from a source much superior to the Wises and Hunters, the Buchanans and Masons of to-day. It was the appointed work for life of an ancient patriarch spoken of in Exodus, chap. ii., and who, true to his great commission, failed not to trouble the conscience and to disturb the repose of the Pharaohs of Egypt with that inexorable, "Thus saith the Lord: Let my people go!" until even they were urgent upon the people in its behalf. Coming down through the nations, and regardless of national boundaries or peculiarities, it has been proclaimed and enforced by the patriarch and the warrior of the Old World, by the enfranchised freeman and the humble slave of the New. Its nationality is universal; its language every where understood by the haters of tyranny; and those that accept its mission, every where understand each other. There is an unbroken chain

of sentiment and purpose from Moses of the Jews to John Brown
of America; from Kossuth, and the liberators of France and Italy,
to the untutored Gabriel, and the Denmark Veseys, Nat Turners
and Madison Washingtons of the Southern American States. The
shaping and expressing of a thought for freedom takes the same con-
sistence with the colored American—whether he be an independent
citizen of the Haytian nation, a proscribed but humble nominally
free colored man, a patient, toiling, but hopeful slave—as with the
proudest or noblest representative of European or American civilization and Christianity. Lafayette, the exponent of French honor
and political integrity, and John Brown, foremost among the men
of the New World in high moral and religious principle and magnanimous bravery, embrace as brothers of the same mother, in
harmony upon the grand mission of liberty; but, while the French-
man entered the lists in obedience to a desire to aid, and by invitation from the Adamses and Hamiltons, and thus pushed on the
political fortunes of those able to help themselves, John Brown,
the liberator of Kansas, the projector and commander of the Harper's Ferry expedition, saw in the most degraded slave a man and
a brother, whose appeal for his God-ordained rights no one should
disregard; in the toddling slave child, a captive whose release is as
imperative, and whose prerogative is as weighty, as the most famous in the land. When the Egyptian pressed hard upon the Hebrew, Moses slew him; and when the spirit of slavery invaded the
fair Territory of Kansas, causing the Free-State settlers to cry out
because of persecution, old John Brown, famous among the men
of God for ever, though then but little known to his fellow-men,
called together his sons and went over, as did Abraham, to the unequal contest, but on the side of the oppressed white men of Kansas
that were, and the black men that were to be. To-day, Kansas is
free, and the verdict of impartial men is, that to John Brown, more
than any other man, Kansas owes her present position.

I am not the biographer of John Brown, but I can be indulged
in giving here the opinion common among my people of one so

eminently worthy of the highest veneration. Close observation of
him, during many weeks, and under his orders at his Kennedy-
Farm fireside, also, satisfies me that in comparing the noble old
man to Moses, and other men of piety and renown, who were
chosen by God to his great work, none have been more faithful,
none have given a brighter record. . . .

To go into particulars, and to detail reports current more than
a year before the outbreak, among the many in the United States
and Canada who had an inkling of some "practical work" to be
done by "Osawattomie Brown," when there should be nothing to
do in Kansas,—to give facts in that connection, would only forestall future action, without really benefitting the slave, or winning
over to that sort of work the anti-slavery men who do not favor
physical resistance to slavery. Slaveholders alone might reap benefits; and for one, I shall throw none in their way, by any indiscreet
avowals; they already enjoy more than their share; but to a clear
understanding of all the facts to be here published, it may be well
to say, that preliminary arrangements were made in a number of
places,—plans proposed, discussed and decided upon, numbers invited to participate in the movement, and the list of adherents increased. Nine insurrections is the number given by some as the
true list of outbreaks since slavery was planted in America; whether
correct or not, it is certain that preliminaries to each are unquestion-
able. Gabriel, Vesey, Nat Turner, all had conference meetings; all
had their plans; but they differ from the Harper's Ferry insurrection in the fact that neither leader nor men, in the latter, divulged
ours, when in the most trying of situations. Hark and another met
Nat Turner in secret places, after the fatigues of a toilsome day
were ended; Gabriel promulged his treason in the silence of the
dense forest; but John Brown reasoned of liberty and equality in
broad daylight, in a modernized building, in conventions with
closed doors, in meetings governed by the elaborate regulations

laid down by Jefferson, and used as their guides by Congresses and Legislatures; or he made known the weighty theme, and his comprehensive plans resulting from it, by the cosy fireside, at familiar social gatherings of chosen ones, or better, in the carefully arranged junto of earnest, practical men. Vague hints, careful blinds, are Nat Turner's entire make-up to save detection; the telegraph, the post-office, the railway, all were made to aid the new outbreak. By this, it will be seen that Insurrection has its progressive side, and has been elevated by John Brown from the skulking, fearing cabal, when in the hands of a brave but despairing few, to the highly organized, formidable, and to very many, indispensable institution for the security of freedom, when guided by intelligence.

So much as relates to prior movements may safely be said above; but who met—when they met—where they met—how many yet await the propitious moment—upon whom the mantle of John Brown has fallen to lead on the future army—the certain, terribly certain, many who must follow up the work, forgetting not to gather up the blood of the hero and his slain, to the humble bondman there offered—these may not, must not be told! Of the many meetings in various places, before the work commenced, I shall speak just here of the one, the minutes of which were dragged forth by marauding Virginians from the "archives" at Kennedy Farm; not forgetting, however, for their comfort, that the Convention was one of a series at Chatham, some of which were of equally great, if not greater, importance.

The first visit of John Brown to Chatham was in April, 1858. Wherever he went around, although an entire stranger, he made a profound impression upon those who saw or became acquainted with him. Some supposed him to be a staid but modernized Quaker; others, a solid business man, from "somewhere," and without question a philanthropist. His long white beard, thoughtful and reverent brow and physiognomy, his sturdy, measured tread, as he circulated about with hands, as portrayed in the best lithograph, under the pendant coat-skirt of plain brown Tweed, with other garments to match, revived to those honored with his acquaintance and knowing to his history, the memory of a Puritan of the most exalted type.

After some important business, preparatory to the Convention, was finished, Mr. Brown went West, and returned with his men, who had been spending the winter in Iowa. The party, including the old gentleman, numbered twelve,—as brave, intelligent and earnest a company as could have been associated in one party. There were John H. Kagi, Aaron D. Stevens, Owen Brown, Richard Realf, George B. Gill, C. W. Moffitt, Wm. H. Leeman, John E. Cook, Stewart Taylor, Richard Richardson, Charles P. Tidd and J. S. Parsons—all white except Richard Richardson, who was a slave in Missouri until helped to his liberty by Captain Brown. At a meeting held to prepare for the Convention and to examine the Constitution, Dr. M. R. Delany was Chairman, and John H. Kagi and myself were the Secretaries.

When the Convention assembled, the minutes of which were seized by the slaveholding "cravens" at the Farm, and which, as they have been identified, I shall append to this chapter, Mr. Brown unfolded his plans and purpose. He regarded slavery as a state of perpetual war against the slave, and was fully impressed with the idea that himself and his friends had the right to take liberty, and to use arms in defending the same. Being a devout Bible Christian, he sustained his views and shaped his plans in conformity to the Bible; and when setting them forth, he quoted freely from the Scripture to sustain his position. He realized and enforced the doctrine of destroying the tree that bringeth forth corrupt fruit. Slavery was to him the corrupt tree, and the duty of every Christian man was to strike down slavery, and to commit its fragments to the flames. He was listened to with profound attention, his views were adopted, and the men whose names form a part of the minutes of that in many respects extraordinary meeting, aided yet further in completing the work.

PART II

IN FLOWER (1870–1925): REAFFIRMATION

The black leaders of the post-Reconstruction period and the turn-of-the-century years viewed Brown as a continuing source of inspiration. In the darkening racial skies of the late nineteenth century his memory was one of the few bright stars. Black civic organizations and labor locals sponsored group excursions to Harpers Ferry. On December 2, 1909, the fiftieth anniversary of his death, Boston Negroes held a John Brown Jubilee at Faneuil Hall, with hundreds turned away.

The new century brought new organizations, such as the National Association for the Advancement of Colored People, and a fresh hope. A related sense of self-worth led to a revitalized interest in the black past, signalized by the founding in 1915 of the Association for the Study of Negro Life and History. In this mounting appreciation of their role in the making of America the black people did not lose sight of John Brown. He retained his place of eminence, his glory hardly diminished by having henceforth to share it with an increasing host of black movers and shakers.

Of the seven evaluations of Brown in this section, one comes from a familiar figure, Frederick Douglass. Delivered nearly a quarter of a century after Harpers Ferry, this expression measures something of the continuity of sentiment toward Brown as reflected by a single individual as well as by a succeeding generation.

William Wells Brown

Nearly a dozen years after the Harpers Ferry outburst William
Wells Brown (1814–1884), a former abolitionist crusader
who had won a reputation on both sides of the Atlantic as a
man of letters, wrote an essay, "John Brown and the Fugitive
Slave Law." A former runaway slave himself, Brown found
a congenial topic in the militant response of John Brown and the
blacks in Springfield, Massachusetts, to the Fugitive Slave Law
of 1850. Wells Brown's treatment of the Gileadites is, of
course, wholly factual, an assurance one can hardly attach to
his account of the eight black women in the "hot room," Brown
having an uncritical fondness for a good story. Moreover,
Wells Brown places the date of the episode as "during the week
following the rendition of Anthony Burns," which took place
in May 1854, whereas he did not return to the United States
until September 26 of that year, after a long sojourn in the
British Isles. The essay appeared in *The Independent* (New
York), March 30, 1870.

When the Fugitive Slave Act of 1850 became the law of the
land, it found a large number of escaped slaves in the Northern
States, who, on their flight from the South, had temporarily taken
up their abode in towns through which they were passing, instead
of going to Canada, as they had at first intended. Many of these
had been years from slavery, had accumulated property, raised up
families, and were considered a part of the resident population. In
some places they had churches of their own, where a sufficient
number warranted a separate organization. The announcement of
the passage of the law created a profound sensation throughout
the country, both amongst the whites and blacks; and especially the
latter. So great was their feeling and the fear of recapture that

47

a large number fled to Canada, without waiting to dispose of
their property; others sold out at an enormous sacrifice; while
many laborers and domestics left without stopping to settle with
employers. Thus families were suddenly broken up, and every railroad train toward the British Provinces was a bearer of these
people. In one town in the State of New York the whole of the
members of a Methodist church, with their pastor, fled to Canada.
In Springfield, Mass., where a large number of fugitives had taken
up their residence, the excitement appeared intense. The blacks
left their employment, and were seeking more secluded hiding-
places in the surrounding towns, or preparing to leave the country.
At this period John Brown, who had formerly resided at Springfield, hearing of the state of affairs, returned, called the fugitives
together, organized them into a body for mutual defense, inspired
them with hope and self-reliance, and thus saved these frightened
and helpless people from suffering and poverty.

The advice, agreement, and code of laws that bound this little
band together was written out by John Brown, and is now for the
first time put in print, and is as follows:

"WORDS OF ADVICE.

Branch of the United States League of Gileadites. Adopted January 15th, 1851. As written and recommended by John Brown.

'UNION IS STRENGTH.'

"Nothing so charms the American people as personal bravery.
The trial for life of one bold and to some extent successful man,
for defending his rights in good earnest, would arouse more sympathy throughout the nation than the accumulated wrongs and
sufferings of more than three millions of our submissive colored
population. We need not mention the Greeks struggling against the
oppressive Turks, the Poles against Russia, nor the Hungarians
against Austria and Russia combined, to prove this. No jury can
be found in the Northern States that would convict a man for de-

fending his rights to the last extremity. This is well understood by Southern Congressmen, who insisted that the right of trial by jury should not be granted to the fugitive. Colored people have more fast friends amongst whites than they suppose, and would have ten times the number they now have were they but half as much earnest to secure their dearest rights as they are to ape the follies and extravagances of their white neighbors, and to indulge in idle show, in ease, and in luxury. Just think of the money expended by individuals in your behalf in the past twenty years. Think of the number who have been mobbed and imprisoned on your account. Have any of you seen the Branded Hand? Do you remember the names of Lovejoy and Torrey? *

"Should one of your number be arrested, you must collect together as quickly as possible, so as to outnumber your adversaries who are taking an active part against you. Let no able-bodied man appear on the ground unequipped or with his weapons exposed to view; let that be understood beforehand. Your plans must be known only to yourself, and with the understanding that all traitors must die, wherever caught and proven to be guilty. 'Whosoever is fearful or afraid, let him return and depart early from Mount Gilead.'—Judges, vii chap., 3 verse; Deut., xx. chap., 8 verse. Give all cowards an opportunity to show it on condition of holding their peace. Do not delay one moment after you are ready; you will lose all your resolution if you do. Let the first blow be the signal for all to engage, and when engaged do not do your work by halves; but make clean work with your enemies, and be sure you meddle not with any others. By going about your business quietly, you will get the job disposed of before the number that an uproar would bring together can collect; and you will have

* Elijah Lovejoy was killed by proslavery sympathizers in Alton, Illinois, in 1837. For helping slaves to escape Charles T. Torrey had been sentenced to six years of hard labor, dying in prison. Caught trying to transport slaves to the Bahamas, ship captain Jonathan Walker was branded on the hand.—B.Q.

the advantage of those who come out against you, for they will be wholly unprepared with either equipments or matured plans—all with them will be confusion and terror. Your enemies will be slow to attack you after you have once done up the work nicely; and, if they should, they will have to encounter your white friends as well as you, for you may safely calculate on a division of the whites, and may by that means get to an honorable parley.

"Be firm, determined, and cool; but let it be understood that you are not to be driven to desperation without making it an awful dear job to others as well as to you. Give them to know distinctly that those who live in wooden houses should not throw fire, and that you are just as able to suffer as your white neighbors. After effecting a rescue, if you are assailed, go into the houses of your most prominent and influential white friends with your wives, and that will effectually fasten upon them the suspicion of being connected with you, and will compel them to make a common cause with you, whether they would otherwise live up to their profession or not. This would leave them no choice in the matter. Some would, doubtless, prove themselves true of their own choice; others would flinch. That would be taking them at their own words. You may make a tumult in the court-room where a trial is going on by burning gunpowder freely in paper packages, if you cannot think of any better way to create a momentary alarm, and might possibly give one or more of your enemies a hoist. But in such a case the prisoner will need to take the hint at once and bestir himself; and so should his friends improve the opportunity for a general rush.

"A lasso might possibly be applied to a slave-catcher for once with good effect. Hold on to your weapons, and never be persuaded to leave them, part with them, or have them far away from you. Stand by one another, and by your friends, while a drop of blood remains; and be hanged, if you must, but tell no tales out of school. Make no confession."

This closes John Brown's advice to the fugitives, as written out.

Then comes the

"AGREEMENT.

"As citizens of the United States of America, trusting in a Just and Merciful God, whose spirit and all-powerful aid we humbly implore, we will ever be true to the Flag of our beloved Country, always acting under it. We whose names are hereunto affixed do constitute ourselves a Branch of the United States League of Gileadites. That we will provide ourselves at once with suitable implements, and will aid those who do not possess the means, if any such are disposed to join us. We invite every colored person whose heart is engaged for the performance of our business, whether male or female, old or young. The duty of the aged, infirm, and young members of the League shall be to give instant notice to all members in case of an attack upon any of our people.

"We agree to have no officers except a Treasurer and Secretary *pro tem* until after some trial of courage and talent of ablebodied members shall enable us to elect officers from those who shall have rendered the most important services. Nothing but wisdom and undaunted courage, efficiency, and general good conduct shall in any way influence us in electing our officers."

Following this are the names of forty-four men and women, all in the handwriting of John Brown, who seems to have presided over the meeting as well as to have been its master spirit.

A code of laws which we found in the MS., and which we omit, followed this agreement. During the week following the rendition of Anthony Burns the writer was passing through Springfield, and learned that the colored people of the place were in a state of great excitement owing to the report that the slave-hunters were there and intended to arrest some of the fugitives and return them to the South. As night drew near, the excitement among the blacks became more intense; and a feeling of despair and revenge seemed depicted upon the countenances of the colored people, which feeling was shared by many of the whites, who deeply sympathized

with the intended victims. With a friend, we visited the locality
where most of the colored people resided, a little after eight o'clock
in the evening, and when the excitement was at its h[e]ight. The
clear moonlight enabled us to see the black sentinels stationed at
the corners of the streets and alleys approaching the dusky neighborhood, in the midst of which stood a large two-story house,
occupied exclusively by colored families. After submitting to an
examination that satisfied the outposts that we were of the right
stripe, we were permitted to pass, and one of their number was
sent in advance of us to prevent our being disturbed. By special
invitation, we were conducted to the "hot room," as it was called,
of the large building. On entering, we found this to be a room of
about thirty by forty feet square, in the center of which stood an
old-fashioned cook-stove, the top of which seemed filled with boil-
ers, and all steaming away completely filling the place with a dense
fog. Two lamps, with dingy chimneys, and the light from the fire,
which shone brightly through the broken doors of the stove, lighted
up the room. Eight athletic black women, looking for all the world
as if they had just returned from a Virginia cornfield, weary and
hungry, stood around the room.

Each of these Amazons was armed with a tin dipper, apparently
new, which had no doubt been purchased for the occasion. A
woman of exceedingly large proportions—tall, long-armed, with a
deep scar down the side of her face and with a half grin, half
smile—was the commander-in-chief of the "hot room." This
woman stood by the stove, dipper in hand, and occasionally taking
the top from the large wash-boiler, which we learned was filled
with boiling water, soap, and ashes.

In case of an attack, this boiler was to be the "King of Pain."
As we saw the perspiration streaming down the faces of these
women, we ventured a few questions. "Do you expect an attack?"
we asked. "Dunno, honey; but we's ready ef dey comes," was the
reply from the aunty near the stove. "Were you ever in slavery?"
we continued. "Yes; ain't bin from dar but little while." "What

state?" Bred and born in old Virginny, down on de Pertomuc."
"Have you any of your relations in Virginia now?" "Yes; got six
chillens down dar somewhar, an' two husbuns—all sole to de spec-
laturs afore I run away." "Did you come off alone?" "No; my las
ole man bring me way." "You don't mean to be taken back by the
slave-catchers, in peace?" "No; I'll die fuss." "How will you manage if they attempt to come into this room?" "We'll all fling hot
water on 'em, and scall dar very harts out." "Can you all throw
water without injuring each other?" "Oh, yes, honey; we's bin
practicin' all day." And here the whole company joined in a hearty
laugh, which made the old building ring.

The intense heat drove us from the room. As we descended the
steps and passed the guards, we remarked to one of them: "The
women seem to be prepared for battle." "Yes," he replied; "dem
wimmens got de debil in em to-night, an' no mistake. Dey'll make
dat a hot hell in dar fur somebody, ef de slave-catchers comes here
to-night; dat dey will." And here the guards broke forth in a hearty
laugh, which was caught up and joined in by the women in the
house, which showed very clearly that these blacks felt themselves
masters of the situation. Returning to the depot to take the train
for Boston, we found there some ten or fifteen blacks, all armed
to the teeth and swearing vengeance upon the heads of any who
should attempt to take them.

True, the slave-catchers had been there. But the authorities,
foreseeing a serious outbreak, advised them to leave the city; and,
feeling alarmed for their personal safety, these disturbers of the
peace had left in the evening train for New York. No fugitive
slave was ever afterward disturbed at Springfield.

Frederick Douglass

In 1881 Douglass came to Storer College at Harpers Ferry to deliver an oration on Brown, the manuscript of which he would turn over to the college authorities so that they might publish it and use the proceeds to establish a John Brown Professorship. One of the platform guests was the state's attorney who had prosecuted the case against Brown, Andrew J. Hunter, who was most cordial in greeting Douglass. Douglass's oration provides sidelights on Brown as a person and an assessment of his role. Approaching classic proportions in the nineteenth-century mold, and studded with historical references, the address was carefully written and well organized. The following selections are from "John Brown: An Address at the Fourteenth Anniversary of Storer College" (Dover, N.H., 1881), pp. 1, 9–12, 14–18, 25–28.

Not to fan the flame of sectional animosity now happily in the process of rapid and I hope permanent extinction; not to revive and keep alive a sense of shame and remorse for a great national crime, which has brought its own punishment, in loss of treasure, tears and blood; not to recount the long list of wrongs, inflicted on my race during more than two hundred years of merciless bondage; nor yet to draw, from the labyrinths of far-off centuries, incidents and achievements wherewith to rouse your passions, and enkindle your enthusiasm, but to pay a just debt long due, to vindicate in some degree a great historical character, of our own time and country, one with whom I was myself well acquainted, and whose friendship and confidence it was my good fortune to share, and to give you such recollections, impressions and facts, as I can, of a grand, brave and good old man, and especially to promote a better understanding of the raid upon Harper's Ferry of which he was the chief, is the object of this address. . . .

54

It is said that next in value to the performance of great deeds ourselves, is the capacity to appreciate such when performed by others; to more than this I do not presume. Allow me one other personal word before I proceed. In the minds of some of the American people I was myself credited with an important agency in the John Brown raid. Governor Henry A. Wise was manifestly of that opinion. He was at the pains of having Mr. Buchanan send his Marshals to Rochester to invite me to accompany them to Virginia. Fortunately I left town several hours previous to their arrival.

What ground there was for this distinguished consideration shall duly appear in the natural course of this lecture. I wish however to say just here that there was no foundation whatever for the charge that I in any wise urged or instigated John Brown to his dangerous work. I rejoice that it is my good fortune to have seen, not only the end of slavery, but to see the day when the whole truth can be told about this matter without prejudice to either the living or the dead. I shall however allow myself little prominence in these disclosures. Your interests, like mine, are in the all-commanding figure of the story, and to him I consecrate the hour. His zeal in the cause of my race was far greater than mine—it was as the burning sun to my taper light—mine was bounded by time, his stretched away to the boundless shores of eternity. I could live for the slave, but he could die for him. The crown of martyrdom is high, far beyond the reach of ordinary mortals, and yet happily no special greatness or superior moral excellence is necessary to discern and in some measure appreciate a truly great soul. Cold, calculating and unspiritual as most of us are, we are not wholly insensible to real greatness; and when we are brought in contact with a man of commanding mold, towering high and alone above the millions, free from all conventional fetters, true to his own moral convictions, a "law unto himself," ready to suffer misconstruction, ignoring torture and death for what he believes to be right, we are compelled to do him homage.

In the stately shadow, in the sublime presence of such a soul I find myself standing to-night; and how to do it reverence, how to do it justice, how to honor the dead with due regard to the living, has been a matter of most anxious solicitude.

Much has been said of John Brown, much that is wise and beautiful, but in looking over what may be called the John Brown literature, I have been little assisted with material, and even less encouraged with any hope of success in treating the subject. Scholarship, genius and devotion have hastened with poetry and eloquence, story and song to this simple altar of human virtue, and have retired dissatisfied and distressed with the thinness and poverty of their offerings, as I shall with mine.

The difficulty in doing justice to the life and character of such a man is not altogether due to the quality of the zeal, or of the ability brought to the work, nor yet to any imperfections in the qualities of the man himself; the state of the moral atmosphere about us has much to do with it. The fault is not in our eyes, nor yet in the object, if under a murky sky we fail to discover the object. Wonderfully tenacious is the taint of a great wrong. The evil, as well as "the good that men do, lives after them." Slavery is indeed gone; but its long, black shadow yet falls broad and large over the face of the whole country. It is the old truth oft repeated, and never more fitly than now, "a prophet is without honor in his own country and among his own people." Though more than twenty years have rolled between us and the Harper's Ferry raid, though since then the armies of the nation have found it necessary to do on a large scale what John Brown attempted to do on a small one, and the great captain who fought his way through slavery has filled with honor the Presidential chair, we yet stand too near the days of slavery, and the life and times of John Brown, to see clearly the true martyr and hero that he was and rightly to estimate the value of the man and his works. Like the great and good of all ages—the men born in advance of their times, the men whose bleeding footprints attest the immense cost of reform, and show us the long and dreary spaces, between the luminous points in the progress of mankind,—this our noblest American hero must wait the polishing wheels of after-coming centuries to make his glory more manifest, and his worth more generally acknowledged. Such instances are abundant and familiar. If we go back four and twenty centuries, to the stately city of Athens, and search among her architectural splendor and her miracles of art for the Socrates of today, and as he stands in history, we shall find ourselves perplexed and disappointed. In Jerusalem Jesus himself was only the "carpenter's son"—a young man wonderfully destitute of worldly prudence—a pestilent fellow, "inexcusably and perpetually interfering in the world's business,"—"upsetting the tables of the money-changers"—preaching sedition, opposing the good old religion—"making himself greater than Abraham," and at the same time "keeping company" with very low people; but behold the change! He was a great miracle-worker, in his day, but time has worked for him a greater miracle than all his miracles, for now his name stands for all that is desirable in government, noble in life, orderly and beautiful in society. That which time has done for other great men of his class, that will time certainly do for John Brown. The brightest gems shine at first with subdued light, and the strongest characters are subject to the same limitations. Under the influence of adverse education and hereditary bias, few things are more difficult than to render impartial justice. Men hold up their hands to Heaven, and swear they will do justice, but what are oaths against prejudice and again inclination! In the face of high-sounding professions and affirmations we know well how hard it is for a Turk to do justice to a Christian, or for a Christian to do justice to a Jew. How hard for an Englishman to do justice to an Irishman, for an Irishman to do justice to an Englishman, harder still for an American tainted by slavery to do justice to the Negro or the Negro's friends. "John Brown," said the late Wm. H. Seward, "was justly hanged." "John Brown," said the late John A. Andrew, "was right." It is easy to perceive the sources of these two opposite judgments: the one was the verdict of slaveholding and panic-stricken Virginia, the other was the verdict of the best heart and brain of free old Massachusetts. One was the heated judgment of the passing and passionate hour, and the other was the calm, clear, unimpeachable judgment of the broad, illimitable future.

There is, however, one aspect of the present subject quite worthy of notice, for it makes the hero of Harper's Ferry in some degree an exception to the general rules to which I have just now adverted. Despite the hold which slavery had at that time on the country, despite the popular prejudice against the Negro, despite the shock which the first alarm occasioned, almost from the first John Brown received a large measure of sympathy and appreciation. New England recognized in him the spirit which brought the pilgrims to Plymouth rock and hailed him as a martyr and saint. True he had broken the law, true he had struck for a despised people, true he had crept upon his foe stealthily, like a wolf upon the fold, and had dealt his blow in the dark whilst his enemy slept, but with all this and more to disturb the moral sense, men discerned in him the greatest and best qualities known to human nature, and pronounced him "good." Many consented to his death, and then went home and taught their children to sing his praise as one whose "soul is marching on" through the realms of endless bliss. One element in explanation of this somewhat anomalous circumstance will probably be found in the troubled times which immediately succeeded, for "when judgments are abroad in the world, men learn righteousness. . . ."

Another feature of the times, worthy of notice, was the effect of this blow upon the country at large. At the first moment we were stunned and bewildered. Slavery had so benumbed the moral sense of the nation, that it never suspected the possibility of an explosion like this, and it was difficult for Captain Brown to get himself taken for what he really was. Few could seem to comprehend that freedom to the slaves was his only object. If you will go back with me to that time you will find that the most curious and contradictory versions of the affair were industriously circulated, and those which were the least rational and true seemed to command the readiest belief. In the view of some, it assumed tremendous proportions. To such it was nothing less than a wide-sweeping rebellion to overthrow the existing government, and construct another upon its ruins, with Brown for its President and Commander-in-Chief; the proof of this was found in the old man's carpet-bag in the shape of a constitution for a new Republic, an instrument which in reality had been executed to govern the conduct of his men in the mountains. Smaller and meaner natures saw in it nothing higher than a purpose to plunder. To them John Brown and his men were a gang of desperate robbers, who had learned by some means that government had sent a large sum of money to Harper's Ferry to pay off the workmen in its employ there, and they had gone thence to fill their pockets from this money. The fact is, that outside of a few friends, scattered in different parts of the country, and the slave-holders of Virginia, few persons understood the significance of the hour. That a man might do something very audacious and desperate for money, power or fame, was to the general apprehension quite possible; but, in face of plainly-written law, in face of constitutional guarantees protecting each State against domestic violence, in face of a nation of forty million of people, that nineteen men could invade a great State to liberate a despised and hated race, was to the average intellect and conscience, too monstrous for belief. In this respect the vision of Virginia was clearer than that of the nation. Conscious of her guilt and therefore full of suspicion, sleeping on pistols for pillows, startled at every unusual sound, constantly fearing and expecting a repetition of the Nat Turner insurrection, she at once understood the meaning, if not the magnitude of the affair. It was this understanding which caused her to raise the lusty and imploring cry to the Federal government for help, and it was not till he who struck the blow had fully explained his motives and object, that the incredulous nation in any wise comprehended the true spirit of the raid, or of its commander. Fortunate for his memory, fortunate for the brave men associated with him, fortunate for the truth of history, John Brown survived the saber gashes, bayonet wounds and bullet holes, and was able, though covered with blood, to tell his own story and make his own defense. Had he with all his men, as might have been the case, gone down in the shock of battle, the world would have had no true basis for its judgment, and one of the most heroic efforts ever witnessed in behalf of liberty would have been confounded with base and selfish purposes. . . .

To the outward eye of men, John Brown was a criminal, but to their inward eye he was a just man and true. His deeds might be disowned, but the spirit which made those deeds possible was worthy [of] highest honor. It has been often asked, why did not Virginia spare the life of this man? why did she not avail herself of this grand opportunity to add to her other glory that of a lofty magnanimity? Had they spared the good old man's life—had they said to him, "You see we have you in our power, and could easily take your life, but we have no desire to hurt you in any way; you have committed a terrible crime against society; you have invaded us at midnight and attacked a sleeping community, but we recognize you as a fanatic, and in some sense instigated by others; and on this ground and others, we release you. Go about your business, and tell those who sent you that we can afford to be magnanimous to our enemies." I say, had Virginia held some such language as this to John Brown, she would have inflicted a heavy blow on the whole Northern abolition movement, one which only the omnipotence of truth and the force of truth could have overcome. I have no doubt Gov. Wise would have done so gladly, but, alas, he was the executive of a State which thought she could not afford such magnanimity. She had that within her bosom which could more safely tolerate the presence of a criminal than a saint, a highway robber than a moral hero. All her hills and valleys were studded with material for a disastrous conflagration, and one spark of the dauntless spirit of Brown might set the whole State in flames. A sense of this appalling liability put an end to every noble consideration. His death was a foregone conclusion, and his trial was simply one of form. . . .

Slavery was the idol of Virginia, and pardon and life to Brown meant condemnation and death to slavery. He had practically illustrated a truth stranger than fiction,—a truth higher than Virginia had ever known,—a truth more noble and beautiful than Jefferson ever wrote. He had evinced a conception of the sacredness and value of liberty which transcended in sublimity that of her own Patrick Henry and made even his fire-flashing sentiment of "Liberty or Death" seem dark and tame and selfish. Henry loved liberty for himself, but this man loved liberty for all men, and for those most despised and scorned, as well as for those most esteemed and honored. Just here was the true glory of John Brown's mission. It was not for his own freedom that he was thus ready to lay down his life, for with Paul he could say, "I was born free." No chain had bound his ankle, no yoke had galled his neck. History has no better illustration of pure, disinterested benevolence. It was not Caucasian for Caucasian—white man for white man; not rich man for rich man, but Caucasian for Ethiopian —white man for black man—rich man for poor man—the man admitted and respected, for the man despised and rejected. "I want you to understand, gentlemen," he said to his persecutors, "that I respect the rights of the poorest and weakest of the colored people, oppressed by the slave system, as I do those of the most wealthy and powerful." In this we have the key to the whole life and career of the man. Than in this sentiment humanity has nothing more touching, reason nothing more noble, imagination nothing more sublime; and if we could reduce all the religions of the world to one essence we could find in it nothing more divine. It is much to be regretted that some great artist, in sympathy with the spirit of the occasion, had not been present when these and similar words were spoken. The situation was thrilling. An old man in the center of an excited and angry crowd, far away from home, in an enemy's country—with no friend near—overpowered, defeated, wounded, bleeding—covered with reproaches—his brave companions nearly all dead—his two faithful sons stark and cold by his side—reading his death-warrant in his fast-oozing blood and increasing weakness as in the faces of all around him—yet calm, collected, brave, with a heart for any fate—using his supposed dying moments to explain his course and vindicate his cause: such a subject would have been at once an inspiration and a power for one of the grandest historical pictures ever painted. . . .*

With John Brown, as with every other man fit to die for a cause, the hour of his physical weakness was the hour of his moral strength—the hour of his defeat was the hour of his triumph—the moment of his capture was the crowning victory of his life. With the Alleghany mountains for his pulpit, the country for his church and the whole civilized world for his audience, he was a thousand times more effective as a preacher than as a warrior, and the consciousness of this fact was the secret of his amazing complacency. Mighty with the sword of steel, he was mightier with the sword of the truth, and with this sword he literally swept the horizon. . . .

Nothing should postpone further what was to him a divine command, the performance of which seemed to him his only apology for existence. He often said to me, though life was sweet to him, he would willingly lay it down for the freedom of my people; and on one occasion he added, that he had already lived about as long as most men, since he had slept less, and if he should now lay down his life the loss would not be great, for in fact he knew no better use for it. During his last visit to us in Rochester there appeared in the newspapers a touching story connected with the horrors of the Sepoy War in British India. A Scotch missionary and his family were in the hands of the enemy, and were to be massacred the next morning. During the night, when they had given up every hope of rescue, suddenly the wife insisted that relief would come. Placing her ear close to the ground she declared she heard

* Ellipses in original.

the Slogan—the Scotch war song. For long hours in the night no
member of the family could hear the advancing music but herself.
"Dinna ye hear it? Dinna ye hear it?" she would say, but they
could not hear it. As the morning slowly dawned a Scotch regiment was found encamped indeed about them, and they were saved
from the threatened slaughter. This circumstance, coming at such
a time, gave Capt. Brown a new word of cheer. He would come
to the table in the morning his countenance fairly illuminated, saying that he had heard the Slogan, and he would add, "Dinna ye
hear it? *Dinna* ye hear it?" Alas! like the Scotch missionary I was
obliged to say "No." Two weeks prior to the meditated attack,
Capt. Brown summoned me to meet him in an old stone quarry on
the Conecochequi river, near the town of Chambersburgh, Penn.
His arms and ammunition were stored in that town and were to
be moved on to Harper's Ferry. In company with Shields Green
I obeyed the summons, and prompt to the hour we met the dear
old man, with Kagi, his secretary, at the appointed place. Our
meeting was in some sense a council of war. We spent the Saturday and succeeding Sunday in conference on the question, whether
the desperate step should then be taken, or the old plan as already described should be carried out. He was for boldly striking
Harper's Ferry at once and running the risk of getting into the
mountains afterwards. I was for avoiding Harper's Ferry altogether. Shields Green and Mr. Kagi remained silent listeners
throughout. It is needless to repeat here what was said, after what
has happened. Suffice it, that after all I could say, I saw that my
old friend had resolved on his course and that it was idle to parley.
I told him finally that it was impossible for me to join him. I could
see Harper's Ferry only as a trap of steel, and ourselves in the
wrong side of it. He regretted my decision and we parted.

Thus far, I have spoken exclusively of Capt. Brown. Let me say
a word or two of his brave and devoted men, and first of Shields
Green. He was a fugitive slave from Charleston, South Carolina,
and had attested his love of liberty by escaping from slavery and

making his way through many dangers to Rochester, where he had lived in my family, and where he met the man with whom he went to the scaffold. I said to him, as I was about to leave, "Now Shields, you have heard our discussion. If in view of it, you do not wish to stay, you have but to say so, and you can go back with me." He answered, "I b'l'eve I'll go wid de old man;" and go with him he did, into the fight, and to the gallows, and bore himself as grandly as any of the number. At the moment when Capt. Brown was surrounded, and all chance of escape was cut off, Green was in the mountains and could have made his escape as Osborne Anderson did, but when asked to do so, he made the same answer he did at Chambersburg, "I b'l'eve I'll go down wid de ole man." When in prison at Charlestown, and he was not allowed to see his old friend, his fidelity to him was in no wise weakened, and no complaint against Brown could be extorted from him by those who talked with him.

If a monument should be erected to the memory of John Brown, as there ought to be, the form and name of Shields Green should have a conspicuous place upon it. It is a remarkable fact, that in this small company of men, but one showed any sign of weakness or regret for what he did or attempted to do. Poor Cook broke down and sought to save his life by representing that he had been deceived, and allured by false promises. But Stephens, Hazlett and Green went to their doom like the heroes they were, without a murmur, without a regret, believing alike in their captain and their cause.

For the disastrous termination of this invasion, several causes have been assigned. It has been said that Capt. Brown found it necessary to strike before he was ready; that men had promised to join him from the North who failed to arrive; that the cowardly Negroes did not rally to his support as he expected, but the true cause as stated by himself, contradicts all these theories, and from his statement there is no appeal. Among the questions put to him by Mr. Vallandingham after his capture were the following: "Did you expect a general uprising of the slaves in case of your success?" To this he answered, "No, sir, nor did I wish it. I expected to gather strength from time to time and then to set them free." "Did you expect to hold possession here until then?" Answer, "Well, probably I had quite a different idea. I do not know as I ought to reveal my plans. I am here wounded and a prisoner because I foolishly permitted myself to be so. You overstate your strength when you suppose I could have been taken if I had not allowed it. I was too tardy after commencing the open attack in delaying my movements through Monday night and up to the time of the arrival of government troops. It was all because of my desire to spare the feelings of my prisoners and their families."

But the question is, Did John Brown fail? He certainly did fail to get out of Harper's Ferry before being beaten down by United States soldiers; he did fail to save his own life, and to lead a liberating army into the mountains of Virginia. But he did not go to Harper's Ferry to save his life. The true question is, Did John Brown draw his sword against slavery and thereby lose his life in vain? and to this I answer ten thousand times, No! No man fails, or can fail who so grandly gives himself and all he has to a righteous cause. No man, who in his hour of extremest need, when on his way to meet an ignominious death, could so forget himself as to stop and kiss a little child, one of the hated race for whom he was about to die, could by any possibility fail. Did John Brown fail? Ask Henry A. Wise in whose house less than two years after, a school for the emancipated slaves was taught. Did John Brown fail? Ask James M. Mason, the author of the inhuman fugitive slave bill, who was cooped up in Fort Warren, as a traitor less than two years from the time that he stood over the prostrate body of John Brown. Did John Brown fail? Ask Clement L. Vallandigham, one other of the inquisitorial party; for he too went down in the tremendous whirlpool created by the powerful hand of this bold invader. If John Brown did not end the war that ended slavery, he did at least begin the war that ended slavery. If we look over the dates, places and men, for which this honor is claimed, we shall find that not Carolina, but Virginia—not Fort Sumter, but Harper's Ferry and the arsenal—not Col. Anderson, but John Brown, began the war that ended American slavery and made this a free Republic. Until this blow was struck, the prospect for freedom was dim, shadowy and uncertain. The irrepressible conflict was one of words, votes and compromises. When John Brown stretched forth his arm the sky was cleared. The time for compromises was gone—the armed hosts of freedom stood face to face over the chasm of a broken Union—and the clash of arms was at hand. The South staked all upon getting possession of the Federal Government, and failing to do that, drew the sword of rebellion and thus made her own, and not Brown's, the lost cause of the century.

George Washington Williams

"The first major Negro American historian," as John Hope
Franklin calls him, George Washington Williams (1848–1891)
had a richly varied career which included military service in
the Civil War, the practice of law, the pastorate of a church,
and membership in the Ohio legislature. While a student at
Newton Theological Seminary, from which he was graduated
in 1874, he showed an interest in history, leading nine years
later to the publication of his two-volume *History of the Negro
Race in America from 1619 to 1880*. In this work he devotes
a chapter to John Brown. Half of the chapter is made up a
long passage contributed by the widow of George L. Stearns,
one of Brown's financial backers. This passage is omitted here
although a short one from Mrs. Stearns is retained. Williams's
work indicates that he knew the value of original source materials. But from the title of this chapter, "John Brown—Hero
and Martyr," (Vol. II, pp. 214–15, 221–27) the reader must
expect the general tone to be judgmental on occasion and warm
with feeling throughout.

On the 9th of May, 1800, at Torrington, Connecticut, was born
a man who lived for two generations, but accomplished the work
of two centuries. That man was John Brown, who ranks among
the world's greatest heroes. Greater than Peter the Hermit, who
believed himself commissioned of God to redeem the Holy Sepul-
chre from the hands of infidels; greater than Joanna Southcote,
who deemed herself big with the promised Shiloh; greater than Ig-
natius Loyola, who thought the Son of Man appeared to him, bearing His cross upon His shoulders, and bestowed upon him a Latin
commission of wonderful significance; greater than Oliver Cromwell, the great Republican Protector; and greater than John Hampden,—he deserves to rank with William of Orange.

67

John Brown was nearly six feet high, slim, wiry, dark in complexion, sharp in feature, dark hair sprinkled with gray, eyes a dark gray and penetrating, with a countenance that betokened frankness, honesty, and firmness. His brow was prominent, the centre of the forehead flat, the upper part retreating, which, in conjunction with his slightly Roman nose, gave him an interesting appearance. The crown of his head was remarkably high, in the regions of the phrenological organs of firmness, conscientiousness, self-esteem, indicating a stern will, unswerving integrity, and marvellous self-possession. He walked rapidly with a firm and elastic tread. He was somewhat like John Baptist, taciturn in habits, usually wrapped in meditation. He was rather meteoric in his movements, appearing suddenly and unexpectedly at this place, and then disappearing in the same mysterious manner.

When Kansas lay bleeding at the feet of border ruffians; when Congress gave the free-State settlers no protection, but was rather trying to drag the territory into the Union with a slave constitution,—without noise or bluster John Brown dropped down into Osage County. He was not a member of the Republican party; but rather hated its reticency. When it cried Halt! he gave the command *Forward, march!* He was not in sympathy with any of the parties, political or anti-slavery. All were too conservative to suit him. So, as a political orphan he went into Kansas, organized and led a new party that swore eternal death to slavery. The first time he appeared in a political meeting in Kansas, at Osawatomie, the politicians were trimming their speeches and shaping their resolutions to please each political faction. John Brown took the floor and made a speech that threw the convention into consternation. He denounced slavery as the curse of the ages; affirmed the manhood of the slave; dealt "middle men" terrible blows and said he could "see no use in talking." "Talk," he continued, "is a national institution; but it does no good for the slave." He thought it an excuse very well adapted for weak men with tender consciences. Most men who were afraid to fight, and too honest to be silent, deceived themselves that they discharged their duties to the slave by denouncing in fiery words the oppressor. His ideas of duty were far different; the slaves, in his eyes, were prisoners of war; their tyrants, as he held, had taken up the sword, and must perish by it. This was his view of the great question of slavery. . . .

That John Brown intended to free the slaves, and nothing more, the record shows clearly. His move on Harper's Ferry was well planned, and had all the parties interested done their part the work would have been done well. As to the rectitude of his intentions he gives the world this leaf of history:

"And now, gentlemen, let me press this one thing on your minds. You all know how dear life is to you, and how dear your lives are to your friends: and in remembering that, consider that the lives of others are as dear to them as yours are to you. Do not, therefore, take the life of any one if you can possibly avoid it; but if it is necessary to take life in order to save your own, then make sure work of it."— John Brown, before the battle at Harper's Ferry.

"I never did intend murder, or treason, or the destruction of property, or to excite or incite slaves to rebellion, or to make insurrection. The design on my part was to free the slaves."—John Brown, after the battle at Harper's Ferry.

Distance lends enchantment to the view. What the world condemns to-day is applauded to-morrow.

We must have a "fair count" on the history of yesterday and last year. The events chronicled yesterday, when the imagination was wrought upon by exciting circumstances, need revision to-day.

The bitter words spoken this morning reproach at eventide the smarting conscience. And the judgments prematurely formed, and the conclusions rapidly reached, may be rectified and repaired in the light of departed years and enlarged knowledge.

John Brown is rapidly settling down to his proper place in history, and "the madman" has been transformed into a "saint." When Brown struck his first blow for freedom, at the head of his little band of liberators, it was almost the universal judgment of both Americans and foreigners that he was a "fanatic." It seemed the very soul of weakness and arrogance for John Brown to attempt to do so great a work with so small a force. Men reached a decision with the outer and surface facts. But many of the most important and historically trustworthy truths bearing upon the motive, object, and import of that "bold move," have been hidden from the public view, either by prejudice or fear.

Some people have thought John Brown—*"The Hero of Harper's Ferry"*—a hot-headed, blood-thirsty brigand; they animadverted against the precipitancy of his measures, and the severity of his invectives; said that he was lacking in courage and deficient in judgment; that he retarded rather than accelerated the cause he championed. But this was the verdict of other times, not the judgment of to-day.

John Brown said to a personal friend during his stay in Kansas: "Young men must learn to wait. Patience is the hardest lesson to learn. I have waited for twenty years to accomplish my purpose." These are not the words of a mere visionary idealist, but the mature language of a practical and judicious leader, a leader than whom the world has never seen a greater. By greatness is meant deep convictions of duty, a sense of the Infinite, "a strong hold on truth," a "conscience void of offence toward God and man," to which the appeals of the innocent and helpless are more potential than the voices of angry thunder or destructive artillery. Such a man was John Brown. He was strong in his moral and mental nature, as well as in his physical nature. He was born to lead; and he led, and made himself the pro-martyr of a cause rapidly perfecting. All through his boyhood days he felt himself lifted and quickened by great ideas and sublime purposes. He had flowing in his veins the blood of his great ancestor, Peter Brown, who came over in the "Mayflower"; and the following inscription appears upon a marble monument in the graveyard at Canton Centre, New York: "In memory of Captain John Brown, who died in the Revolutionary army, at New York, September 3, 1776. He was of the fourth generation, in regular descent, from Peter Brown, one of the Pilgrim Fathers, who landed from the 'Mayflower,' at Plymouth, Massachusetts, December 22, 1620." This is the best commentary on his inherent love of absolute liberty, his marvellous courage and transcendent military genius. For years he elaborated and perfected his plans, working upon the public sentiment of his day by the most praiseworthy means. He bent and bowed the most obdurate conservatism of his day, and rallied to his standards the most eminent men, the strongest intellects in the North. His ethics and religion were as broad as the universe, and beneficent in their wide ramification. And it was upon his "religion of humanity," that embraced our entire species, that he proceeded with his herculean task of striking off the chains of the enslaved. Few, very few of his most intimate friends knew his plans—the plan of freeing the slaves. Many knew his great faith, his exalted sentiments, his ideas of liberty, in their crudity; but to a faithful few only did he reveal his stupendous plans in their entirety. . . .

"Of men born of woman," there is not a greater than John Brown. He was the forerunner of Lincoln, the great apostle of freedom. . . .

The news of his battle and his bold stand against the united forces of Virginia and Maryland swept across the country as the wild storm comes down the mountain side. Friend and foe were alike astonished and alarmed. The enemies of the cause he represented, when they recovered from their surprise, laughed their little laugh of scorn, and eased their feelings by referring to him as the "madman." Friends faltered, and, while they did not question his earnestness, doubted his judgment. "Why," they asked, "should he act with such palpable rashness, and thereby render more difficult and impossible the emancipation of the slaves?" They claimed that the blow he struck, instead of severing, only the more tightly riveted, the chains upon the helpless and hapless Blacks. But in the face of subsequent history we think his surviving friends will change their views. . . . May it not be believed that the good old man was right, and that Harper's Ferry was just the place, and the 17th of October just the time to strike for freedom, and make the rock-ribbed mountains of Virginia to tremble at the presence of a "master!"—the king of freedom?

He was made a prisoner on the 19th of October, 1859, and remained until the 7th of November without a change of clothing or medical aid. Forty-two days from the time of his imprisonment he expiated his crime upon the scaffold—a crime against slave-holding, timorous Virginia, for bringing liberty to the oppressed. He was a man, and there was nothing that interested man which was foreign to his nature. He had gone into Virginia to save life, not to destroy it. The sighs and groans of the oppressed had entered into his soul.

He had heard the Macedonian cry to come over and help them. He went, and it cost him his life, but he gave it freely. . . .

South Carolina, Missouri, and Kentucky sent a rope to hang him, but, the first two lacking strength, Kentucky had the ever-lasting disgrace of furnishing the rope to strangle the noblest man that ever lived in any age.

The last letter he ever wrote was written to Mrs. Geo. L. Stearns, and she shall give its history:

This letter requires the history which attaches to it, and illustrates the consideration which the brave martyr had for those in any way connected with him. It was written on a half sheet of paper, the exact size of the pages of a book into which he carefully inserted it, and tied up in a handkerchief with other books and papers, which he asked his jailer (Mr. Avis) to be allowed to go with his body to North Elba, and which Mrs. Brown took with her from the Charlestown prison. Her statement to me about it is this: She had been at home some two weeks, had looked over the contents of the handkerchief many times, when one day in turning the leaves of that particular book, she came upon this letter, on which she said she found two or three blistered spots, the only *tear drops* she had seen among his papers. They are now yellow with time. On the back of the half sheet was written: "Please mail this to her," which she did, and so it reached my hand, seeming as if from the world to which his spirit had fled. It quite overwhelmed my husband. Presently he said: "See, dear, how careful the old man has been, he would not even direct it with your name to go from Virginia to Boston through the post-offices; and altho' it contains no message to me, one of those '*farewells!*' is intended for me, and also the 'Love to *All* who love their neighbors.'"

"CHARLESTOWN, JEFFERION Co VA. 29th Nov. 1859.

"MRS. GEORGE L. STEARNS
"Boston, Mass.

"My Dear Friend:—No letter I have received since my imprisonment here, has given me more satisfaction, or comfort, than yours of the 8th inst. I am quite cheerful: and never more happy. Have only time to write you a word. May God forever reward you *and all yours*.

"*My love to* ALL *who love their neighbors*. I have asked to be *spared* from having any *mock, or hypocritical prayers made over me* when I am publicly *murdered;* and that my only *religious attendents* be *poor, little, dirty, ragged, bareheaded and barefooted, Slave Boys; and Girls,* led by some old *gray-headed slave Mother.*

"Farewell. Farewell.
"Your Friend,
"JOHN BROWN." [1]

The man who hung him, Governor Wise, lived to see the plans of Brown completed and his most cherished hopes fulfilled. He heard the warning shot fired at Sumter, saw Richmond fall, the war end in victory to the party of John Brown; saw the slave-pen converted into the school-house, and the four millions Brown fought and died for, elevated to the honors of citizenship. And at last he has entered the grave, where his memory will perish with his body, while the soul and fame of John Brown go marching down the centuries!

Galileo, Copernicus, Newton, and John Brown have to wait the calmer judgments of future generations. These men believed

---

[1] This letter is printed for the first time, with Mrs. Stearns's consent. [Footnote in original.]

that God sent them to do a certain work—to reveal a hidden truth; to pour light into the minds of benighted and superstitious men. They completed their work; they did nobly and well, then bowed to rest—

> "With patriachs of the infant world—with kings,
> The powerful of the earth,"

while generation after generation studies their handwriting on the wall of time and interprets their thoughts. Despised, persecuted, and unappreciated while in the flesh, they are honored after death, and enrolled among earth's good and great, her wise and brave. The shock Brown gave the walls of the slave institution was felt from its centre to its utmost limits. It was the entering wedge; it laid bare the accursed institution, and taught good men everywhere to hate it with a perfect hatred. Slavery received its death wound at the hands of a "lonely old man." When he smote Virginia, the non-resistants, the anti-slavery men, learned a lesson. They saw what was necessary to the accomplishment of their work, and were now ready for the "worst." He rebuked the conservatism of the North, and gave an example of adherence to duty, devotion to truth, and fealty to God and man that make the mere "professor" to tremble with shame. "John Brown's body lies mouldering in the clay," but his immortal name will be pronounced with blessings in all lands and by all people till the end of time.

Brown Versus Nat Turner:
An Editorial Exchange on Rank

In 1889 Frederick Douglass, Jr., son of the prominent public figure by that name, proposed that black people raise funds to build a statue in honor of John Brown. The suggestion, although hardly new in black circles, drew the fire of the editor of the *New York Age,* T. Thomas Fortune. Widely regarded as the ablest as well as the most race-conscious and militant of the 120 black editors of the period, Fortune held that blacks would be more logically advised to erect a memorial to Nat Turner. This spirited exchange (which follows) did not result in a statue to either Brown or Turner but it reminded black readers anew of the sacrificial role of both. The two editorials by Fortune, entitled "John Brown and Nat. Turner" and "Nat. Turner," appeared in *New York Age* on January 12 and 29, 1889, respectively. The editorial by Frederick Douglass, Jr., which bore no heading, appeared in *The National Leader* (Washington, D.C.) on January 19, 1889.

JOHN BROWN AND NAT. TURNER

The *Washington National Leader,* of which Mr. Frederick Douglass, Jr., is associate editor, recently wanted to know if it was not almost time that the colored people were doing something to perpetuate the memory of John Brown.

We think not. We think John Brown's memory is strong enough to perpetuate itself even if all the Negroes in the universe were suddenly to become extinct. His memory is a part of the history of the government. It is embalmed in a thousand songs and stories. Your own father, Mr. Douglass, has written a lecture on the life of John Brown, which will help along the perpetuation of that great and good man. A German scholar [Hermann Von Holst] has just given a brochure to the world, which competent critics declare the most judicial and thorough study of the character of John Brown ever produced.

No; John Brown's memory stands no immediate prospect of vanishing into oblivion.

But there is another, a fore-runner of John Brown, if you please, who stands in more need of our copper pennies to be melted down into a monument to perpetuate his memory than John Brown. We refer of course to Nat Turner, who was executed at Jerusalem, Northampton [*sic*] County, Virginia, for inciting and leading his fellow slaves to insurrection long before John Brown invaded Kansas and planned an unfortunate raid on Harper's Ferry.

Nat. Turner was a black hero. He preferred death to slavery. He ought to have a monument. White men care nothing for his memory. We should cherish it.

It is quite remarkable that whenever colored men move that somebody's memory be perpetuated, that somebody's memory is always a white man's.

Young Mr. Douglass should mend his ways in this matter. His great father will some day have a monument which he will have eminently deserved, and it will have to be built by the pennies of colored people. White people build monuments to white people.

[Response by Frederick Douglass, Jr.]

The editor of the New York *Age* draws the color line over our proposition to erect a monument to the memory of the life and character of John Brown, and suggests that Nat. Turner stands more in need of one. We have no fault to find with his suggestion; but when he slurringly remarks "that whenever colored men move that somebody's memory be perpetuated, that somebody's memory is always a white man's," he helps to sustain the charge made against us by the whites of the South, "that it is the colored people who draw the color line." We have always been of the opinion that the character and good acts of a man were worthy of emulation and perpetuation, and not his color. But the young gentleman who edits the *Age* makes color the condition of action toward erecting a monument in honor of one who broke the chains from about his [Fortune's or the Negro's] neck and made him free to act for himself. . . .

Nat. Turner has been dead for many years, and the editor of the *Age* has never found time to suggest a monument for him until now, and he only suggests it now in opposition to the one being erected in honor of John Brown, because he was so fortunate or unfortunate as to be born white. Prejudice among the white people of this country is dying out; but the editor of the *Age* would encourage it among the blacks. This is not wise nor just, but what does the *Age* care? We trust you will get straight on this matter. If you wish to slur at the proposer of a monument for John Brown, do so: but don't set up such a ridiculous strain of reasoning as an objection based on color.

NAT. TURNER

Fred Douglass, Jr., in the *National Leader,* exhibits too much temper in replying to our editorial suggesting a monument to Nat. Turner instead of one to John Brown. It indicates that we touched the Achillean weak spot in his armor.

"That Nat. Turner has been dead many years" is almost equally true of John Brown. John Brown lost his life in urging and leading an insurrection of slaves. Nat. Turner at an earlier date did the same. The conduct of the one was no more heroic than that of the other. The whites have embalmed the memory of John Brown in marble and vellum, and Fred. Douglass, Jr., now wants colored people to embalm it in brass; while the memory of the black hero is preserved neither in marble, vellum nor brass.

What we protest against is Negro worship of white men and the memory of white men, to the utter exclusion of colored men equally patriotic and self-sacrificing. It is the absence of race pride and race unity which makes white men despise black men all the world over.

We do not draw the color line. Fred. Douglass, Jr., knows that his insinuation in this regard is a baseless invention. We simply insist that in theory "do unto others as you would have them do unto you" is splendid, but that in practice the philosophy of conduct is "do unto others as they do unto you," the sooner to make them understand that a dagger of the right sort has two edges, the one as sharp of blade as the other.

We yield to none in admiration of the character and sacrifices of John Brown. The character and sacrifices of Nat. Turner are dearer to us because he was of us and exhibited in the most abject condition the heroism and race devotion which have illustrated in all times the sort of men who are worthy to be free.

Reverdy C. Ransom

Reverdy C. Ransom (1861–1959) was selected as the concluding orator for the observance of John Brown Day at Harpers Ferry on August 17, 1906. The occasion was the highlight of the second annual convention of the Niagara Movement, a black civil rights organization. Then pastor of the Charles Street African Methodist Episcopal Church in Boston, and later elevated to the bishopric, Ransom had early gained a reputation for fluency in public address, for preaching a social gospel, and for church leadership in community welfare activities. One-third of his John Brown Day oration, entitled "The Spirit of John Brown," was devoted to a castigation of public officials and political parties for their indifference to the wrongs inflicted upon blacks. The excerpts below, however, are largely confined to the speaker's evaluation of Brown, whom he viewed as unique, a Mt. Blanc among men. They are from the monthly *The Voice of the Negro* (Atlanta), October 1906, pp. 412–15, 417.

Great epochs in the world's history are hinged upon some spot of land or sea, which become historic and sacred forever more. There are Mt. Sinai and Calvary, the Jordan, the Euphrates, the Nile and Rubicon, Thermopylae, Runnymede, Waterloo, Gettysburg, Appomattox, Port Arthur and Manila Bay; while John Brown has made Harper's Ferry as classic as Bunker Hill.

The leonine soul of this old hero saint and martyr proves how impotent and defenseless are tyranny, injustice and wrong, even when upheld by the sanction of the law, supported by the power of money and defended by the sword.

If modern history furnishes a solitary example of the appearance of a man who possessed the spirit of the prophets of ancient Israel, it is John Brown. The sublime courage with which he met the Goliath of slavery in mortal combat, was not surpassed by that of David, who went forth to meet the Philistine who had defied the armies of the living God. He was commissioned by the same authority, and bore the same credentials as did Moses, who left his flocks in the Midian Desert to go and stand before Pharoah and demand in the name of "I AM THAT I AM" that he should free his slaves.

John Brown left his flocks and fields at Mt. Elba, New York, and fought at Osawatomie to make the soil of Kansas free; at Harper's Ferry where his brave followers fought and fell, he delivered a blow against slavery in the most vital part, and fired the gun whose opening shot echoed the sound of the death knell of slavery.

This old Puritan whose steel grey eyes gleamed with the spirit of courage that possessed Cromwell at the battle of Dunbar, took literally "the sword of the Lord and of Gideon" as both battle cry and watch word. Men like John Brown appear only once or twice in a thousand years. Like Mt. Blanc, the king of the mountains, he towers high above the loftiest figure of his time. The place he occupied in the affairs of men is unique. He is the Melchizidek of the modern world. He had no predecessors and can have no successors. Any picture of him which does not have its proper setting amid the back-ground of his time, makes him appear Quixotic, rather than the heroic figure that he was.

Like Moses, Joshua, Cromwell and Touissant L'Overture, he defies classification. He belonged to no party, was a disciple of no school, he was swayed neither by precedent nor convention. He was a man of achievement, of action. Garrison may write and Beecher may preach, while the silver toned voice of Phillips pleads; this man will perform the doing of it. He could not choose his course, the hand of the Almighty was upon him. He felt the breath of God upon his soul and was strangely moved. He was imbued with the spirit of the Declaration of Independence, and clearly saw that slavery was incompatible with a free republic.

He could not reconcile the creed of the slave-holder with the word of God. . . .

God sent him to Harper's Ferry to become a traitor to the government in order that he might be true to the slave. This nation was established by men who took up arms to fight against a tax on tea, and the universal verdict of mankind approves their action. When John Brown fought at Harper's Ferry, he commanded his immortal band with the sword of Frederick the Great, which had been presented to George Washington, and posterity has given him a fame no less secure than that of these two great captains who unsheathed it in no worthier a cause. . . .

The true value and merit of a man lie embalmed and treasured up in the life he lived, and the character of the service he rendered to mankind. The whole life of John Brown was serious and purposeful. He was a descendant of one of the company who landed from the Mayflower at Plymouth Rock, and from ancestors who fought in the Revolutionary War. He had all of the moral uprightness and strict religious character of the Puritan, as well as his love of liberty and hatred of oppression and tyranny.

From a child he loved to dwell beneath the open sky. The many voices of the woods, and fields, and mountains, spoke to him a familiar language. He understood the habits of plants and animals, of birds, and trees and flowers, and dwelt with them upon terms of familiarity and friendship. His heredity and environment were just such a school as was needed to shape his character and prepare him for his God appointed task. For he believed himself to be sent upon a mission under the authority of Heaven. When he wrought like a mighty man of valor, whether in Kansas or at Harper's Ferry, he believed with all the modesty of his truly great and heroic soul, that he was only doing his duty. He proved the sincerity of his motives, the unselfishness of his purpose, and his entire devotion, by sacrificing upon the altar of human freedom his money, goods, wife and children. When God's clock struck the hour he acted. . . .

The distinctive act which has given the name of John Brown to immortality, was his attempt to organize and arm the slaves to arise and strike for their freedom. This deed aroused the nation and startled the world. His was not an attempt to assist them to break their chains, in order to flee to Canada, but to forcibly assert and maintain their freedom in the Southland where they had been held as slaves.

The Negro will never enjoy the fruits of freedom in this country until he first demonstrates his manhood and maintains his rights, here in the South, where they are the most violently protested and most completely denied.

What is to be the final status of the Negro in this country can not be settled in New England, nor settled in the North. There will be no rest, or peace, or harmony upon this question until it is settled, and settled justly, on Southern soil, where the great majority of the Negro Americans make their homes.

In the days of John Brown a handful of slaves found freedom in flight to Canada and the North. But this did not change the condition of the enslaved millions, or the attitude of their cruel oppressors, while it did cause the Supreme Court of the United States to make every white man of the North a detective and agent of the South in the detection, capture and surrender of fugitive slaves.

Today Negroes are coming North in increasing numbers. But this does not change or modify a revised constitution in any Southern state, abolish one Jim Crow car, or stop a single lynching. In the days of slavery the Negro had a few devoted friends in the North and also in the South, but those in the South dare not speak or act; while some in the North were outspoken, they were backed by no public opinion which should support radical action. So today, the Negro has sympathetic friends and helpers, but public opinion nowhere sustains agitation or action against the conditions that prevail. . . .

It is indeed paradoxical that a nation which has erected monuments of marble and bronze to John Brown, Frederick Douglass, William Lloyd Garrison, Charles Sumner, and other abolitionists; a nation which proclaims a holiday that all classes, including school children, may decorate with flowers the graves of the men who fought to preserve the union, and to free the slaves, a nation which has enacted into organic law the freedom and political status of a race which has been bought with blood; now sits supinely down, silent and inactive, while the work of the liberators is ignored, while those who fought to destroy the government, regain in the halls of congress the victories they lost on the field of battle, while the constitution is flouted and the Fifteenth Amendment brazenly trampled under foot. . . .

Like the ghost of Hamlet's father, the spirit of John Brown beckons us to arise and seek the recovery of our rights, which our enemy, "with the witchcraft of his wit, with traitorous gifts," has sought forever to destroy. John Brown was thought by many, even among his friends, to be insane. But an exhibition of such insanity was required to arouse the nation against the crime of slavery and to bring on the civil war. No weak and ordinary voice can call the nation back to a sense of justice. A commonplace movement or event cannot influence or change the present attitude and current of the public mind. The rifle shot at Harper's Ferry received answer from the cannon fired upon Fort Sumter. This nation needs again to be aroused. The friends of truth and justice must be rallied. But men cannot be rallied without a rallying cry; and even with this upon their lips, there must be a lofty standard to which they may resort. Cannot the hearts of men warm as earnestly to the cry of the rights of an American citizen as they did to that of the freedom of the slave? Will the nation which could not tolerate the enslavement of human beings, sanction the dis[en]franchisement of its citizens?

Abraham Lincoln set before this nation in its darkest hour the preservation of the union as the standard for all loyal men. Can the men of the present take higher ground than to make secure the life and liberty of the black men who helped to sustain it when it was tottering to its fall?

The gage of battle has been thrown down. The lines are clearly drawn; the supremacy of the constitution has been challenged. In fighting for his rights the Negro defends the nation. His weapons are more powerful than the pikes and Sharps rifles which John Brown sought to place in his hands at Harpers Ferry. He has the constitution, the courts, the ballot, the power to organize, to protest and to resist.

The battle before us must be fought, not on the principle of the inferiority of one race, and the superiority of the other, but upon the ground of our common manhood and equality.

Socrates drained the cup of hemlock to its dregs, Jesus Christ suffered crucifixion on the cross; Savonarola was burned in the streets of Florence, and John Brown was hung from a gallows. But the cause for which they willingly became martyrs, the principles they advocated, and the truths they taught, have become the richest and most glorious heritage of mankind.

Before the strife and hatred of race and class have vanished, many will be called upon to wear the martyr's crown. A new birth of freedom within a nation is always accompanied with great suffering and pain. How much greater then the travail through which humanity must pass, to bring forth its last and highest birth, for which all preceding ages have worked and waited until now.

We see it in the tyrant's face, in the oppressor's cruel wrongs, we read it in the statute books of every unjust law, we hear it in the strife of human conflict, we feel it in the universal aspiration of the soul, it comes to earth by many signs from heaven. The spirit of human brotherhood is unbarring the gates of life to admit a civilization in which it can reign incarnate, while out of the many threads of human life upon this planet, we are weaving the royal garments it shall wear.

W. E. B. Du Bois

William Edward Burghardt Du Bois (1868–1963), pioneer
black historian and sociologist, critic of Booker T. Washington,
founder of the Niagara Movement, and exponent of the
"talented tenth" concept of black leadership, would naturally
find in John Brown a congenial spirit. Already a prolific writer,
Du Bois was asked in 1907 by G. W. Jacobs and Company to
do a life of Brown. In a letter to Oswald Garrison Villard on
November 15, 1907, Du Bois wrote that his projected Brown
biography was "going to be an interpretation, and I am not
trying to go very largely to the sources" (John Brown Manuscript Sources, compiled by O. G. Villard, Columbia University). Nearly two years later Du Bois published *John Brown*
(Philadelphia: G. W. Jacobs, 1909), designing it as "a record
of and a tribute to the man who of all Americans has perhaps
come nearest to touching the real souls of black folk." The
book's concluding chapter, "The Legacy of John Brown," from
which the following passages are taken (pp. 365–67, 372–76,
383–86, footnotes omitted), is a combination summary and
afterword, ending on the kind of messianic note which became
the hallmark of the Du Bois style.

"I, JOHN BROWN, am quite certain that the crimes of this guilty
land will never be purged away but with blood. I had, as I now
think vainly, flattered myself that without very much bloodshed
it might be done."

These were the last written words of John Brown, set down the
day he died—the culminating of that wonderful message of his
forty days in prison, which all in all made the mightiest Abolition
document that America has known. Uttered in chains and solemnity,
spoken in the very shadow of death, its dramatic intensity after
that wild and puzzling raid, its deep earnestness as embodied in

the character of the man, did more to shake the foundations of slavery than any single thing that ever happened in America. Of himself he speaks simply and with satisfaction: "I should be sixty years old were I to live to May 9, 1860. I have enjoyed much of life as it is, and have been remarkably prosperous, having early learned to regard the welfare and prosperity of others as my own. I have never, since I can remember, required a great amount of sleep; so that I conclude that I have already enjoyed full an average number of working hours with those who reach their three-score years and ten. I have not yet been driven to the use of glasses, but can see to read and write quite comfortably. But more than that, I have generally enjoyed remarkably good health. I might go on to recount unnumbered and unmerited blessings, among which would be some very severe afflictions and those the most needed blessings of all. And now, when I think how easily I might be left to spoil all I have done or suffered in the cause of freedom, I hardly dare wish another voyage even if I had the opportunity."

After a surging, trouble-tossed voyage he is at last at peace in body and mind. He asserts that he is and has been in his right mind: "I may be very insane; and I am so, if insane at all. But if that be so, insanity is like a very pleasant dream to me. I am not in the least degree conscious of my ravings, of my fears, or of any terrible visions whatever; but fancy myself entirely composed, and that my sleep, in particular, is as sweet as that of a healthy, joyous little infant. I pray God that He will grant me a continuance of the same calm but delightful dream, until I come to know of those realities which eyes have not seen and which ears have not heard. I have scarce realized that I am in prison or in irons at all. I certainly think I was never more cheerful in my life". . . .

Against slavery his face is set like flint: "There are no ministers of Christ here. These ministers who profess to be Christian, and hold slaves or advocate slavery, I cannot abide them. My knees will not bend in prayer with them, while their hands are stained with the blood of souls." He said to one Southern clergyman: "I will thank you to leave me alone; your prayers would be an abomination to God." To another he said, "I would not insult God by bowing down in prayer with any one who had the blood of the slave on his skirts." . . .

This was the man. His family is the world. What legacy did he leave? It was soon seen that his voice was a call to the great final battle with slavery.

In the spring of 1861 the Boston Light Infantry was sent to Fort Warren in Boston harbor to drill. A quartette was formed among the soldiers to sing patriotic songs and for them was contrived the verses, "John Brown's body lies a-mouldering in the grave, His soul is marching on," etc. This was set to the music of an old camp-meeting tune—possibly of Negro origin—called, "Say, Brother, Will You Meet Us?" The regiment learned it and first sang it publicly when it came up from Fort Warren and marched past the scene where Crispus Attucks fell. Gilmore's Band learned and played it and thus "the song of John Brown was started on its eternal way!"

Was John Brown simply an episode, or was he an eternal truth? And if a truth, how speaks that truth to-day? John Brown loved his neighbor as himself. He could not endure therefore to see his neighbor, poor, and unfortunate or oppressed. This natural sympathy was strengthened by a saturation in Hebrew religion which stressed the personal responsibility of every human soul to a just God. To this religion of equality and sympathy with misfortune, was added the strong influence of the social doctrines of the French Revolution with its emphasis on freedom and power in political life. And on all this was built John Brown's own inchoate but growing belief in a more just and a more equal distribution of property. From this he concluded,—and acted on that conclusion —that all men are created free and equal, and that the cost of liberty is less than the price of repression.

Up to the time of John Brown's death this doctrine was a growing, conquering, social thing. Since then there has come a change and many would rightly find reason for that change in the coincidence that the year in which John Brown suffered martyrdom was the year that first published the *Origin of Species*. Since that day tremendous scientific and economic advance has been accompanied by distinct signs of moral retrogression in social philosophy. Strong arguments have been made for the fostering of war, the utility of human degradation and disease, and the inevitable and known inferiority of certain classes and races of men. While such arguments have not stopped the efforts of the advocates of peace, the workers for social uplift and the believers in human brotherhood, they have, it must be confessed, made their voices falter and tinged their arguments with apology.

Why is this? It is because the splendid scientific work of Darwin, Weissman, Galton and others has been widely interpreted as meaning that there is essential and inevitable inequality among men and races of men, which no philanthropy can or ought to eliminate; that civilization is a struggle for existence whereby the weaker nations and individuals will gradually succumb, and the strong will inherit the earth. With this interpretation has gone the silent assumption that the white European stock represents the strong surviving peoples, and that the swarthy, yellow and black peoples are the ones rightly doomed to eventual extinction.

One can easily see what influence such a doctrine would have on the race problem in America. It meant moral revolution in the attitude of the nation. Those that stepped into the pathway marked by men like John Brown faltered and large numbers turned back. They said: He was a good man—even great, but he has no message for us to-day—he was a "belated Covenanter," an anachronism in the age of Darwin, one who gave his life to lift not the unlifted but the unliftable. We have consequently the present reaction—a reaction which says in effect, Keep these black people in their places, and do not attempt to treat a Negro simply as a white man with a black face; to do this would mean the moral deterioration of the race and the nation—a fate against which a divine racial prejudice is successfully fighting. This is the attitude of the larger portion of our thinking people. . . .

This is the situation to-day. Has John Brown no message—no legacy, then, to the twentieth century? He has and it is this great word: the cost of liberty is less than the price of repression. The price of repressing the world's darker races is shown in a moral retrogression and an economic waste unparalleled since the age of the African slave-trade. What would be the cost of liberty? What would be the cost of giving the great stocks of mankind every reasonable help and incentive to self-development—opening the avenues of opportunity freely, spreading knowledge, suppressing war and cheating, and treating men and women as equals the world over whenever and wherever they attain equality? It would cost something. It would cost something in pride and prejudice, for eventually many a white man would be blacking black men's boots; but this cost we may ignore—its greatest cost would be the new problems of racial intercourse and intermarriage which would come to the front. Freedom and equal opportunity in this respect would inevitably bring some intermarriage of whites and yellows and browns and blacks. This might be a good thing and it might not be. We do not know. Our belief on the matter may be strong and even frantic, but it has no adequate scientific foundation. If such marriages are proven inadvisable, how could they be stopped? Easily. We associate with cats and cows, but we do not fear intermarriage with them, even though they be given all freedom of development. So, too, intelligent human beings can be trained to breed intelligently without the degradation of such of their fellows as they may not wish to breed with. In the Southern United States, on the contrary, it is assumed that unwise marriages can be stopped only by the degradation of the blacks—the classing of all darker women with prostitutes, the loading of a whole race with every badge of public isolation, degradation and contempt, and by burning offenders at the stake. It this civilization? No.

The civilized method of preventing ill-advised marriage lies in the training of mankind in the ethics of sex and child-bearing. We cannot ensure the survival of the best blood by the public murder and degradation of unworthy suitors, but we can substitute a civilized human selection of husbands and wives which shall ensure the survival of the fittest. Not the methods of the jungle, not even the careless choices of the drawing-room, but the thoughtful selection of the schools and laboratory is the ideal of future marriage. This will cost something in ingenuity, self-control and toleration, but it will cost less than forcible repression.

Not only is the cost of repression to-day large—it is a continually increasing cost: the procuring of coolie labor, the ruling of India, the exploitation of Africa, the problem of the unemployed, and the curbing of the corporations, are a tremendous drain on modern society with no near end in sight. The cost is not merely in wealth but in social progress and spiritual strength, and it tends ever to explosion, murder, and war. All these things but increase the difficulty of beginning a régime of freedom in human growth and development—they raise the cost of liberty. Not only that but the very explosions, like the Russo-Japanese War, which bring partial freedom, tend in the complacent current philosophy to prove the wisdom of repression. "Blood will tell," men say. "The fit will survive; stop up the tea-kettle and eventually the steam will burst the iron," and therefore only the steam that bursts is worth the generating; only organized murder proves the fitness of a people for liberty. This is a fearful and dangerous doctrine. It encourages wrong leadership and perverted ideals at the very time when loftiest and most unselfish striving is called for—as witness Japan after her emancipation, or America after the Civil War. Conversely, it leads the shallow and unthinking to brand as demagogue and radical every group leader who in the day of slavery and struggle cries out for freedom.

For such reasons it is that the memory of John Brown stands to-day as a mighty warning to his country. He saw, he felt in his soul the wrong and danger of that most daring and insolent system of human repression known as American slavery. He knew that in 1700 it would have cost something to overthrow slavery and establish liberty; and that by reason of cowardice and blindness the cost in 1800 was vastly larger but still not unpayable. He felt that by 1900 no human hand could pluck the vampire from the body of the land without doing the nation to death. He said, in 1859, "Now is the accepted time." Now is the day to strike for a free nation. It will cost something—even blood and suffering, but it will not cost as much as waiting. And he was right. . . .

Francis J. Grimké

Francis J. Grimké (1850–1937), civic-minded pastor of the Fifteenth Street Presbyterian Church in Washington, D.C., somehow found time to cultivate his taste for reading, reflection, and writing. He turned out a formidable collection of sermons and addresses, plus letters to public figures, including chastising dispatches to the Chief Executive himself. In an address, "John Brown," delivered on December 5, 1909, Grimké struck an insistently instructive note, stressing lessons to be learned and examples to be followed. The following selections from the address are from Carter G. Woodson, ed., *The Works of Francis J. Grimké* (4 vols., Washington, D.C., 1942), I, 124–27, 132–41; copyright by the Association for the Study of Negro Life and History, Inc., and by Associated Publishers, Inc. Used by permission.

This boasted land of the free, in many respects, has been and now is one of the most despicable countries in the world. Its treatment of the Negro as a slave, and since, as a freeman; the cold-blooded and heartless manner in which he has been shut out of nearly all the avenues of making an honest living; and the brutal manner in which he has been shot down and is still being shot down by lawless mobs in the South without redress, constitute one of the darkest, if not the darkest chapter, in its history, and reflect very seriously upon its character as a Christian nation. On the other hand, it may be said with equal truthfulness, in other respects, it is one of the most glorious countries in the world. In spite of its record of injustice and oppression and mob violence against a helpless and defenseless people, it has produced a set of men and women that will challenge comparison with the very finest specimens that the race has produced in any age of the

world. Go where you will you will find nowhere a more magnificent set of men and women than was produced during the great
struggle for freedom in this country. I do not undervalue the
character or the services of the men who gave shape and direction
to the movement which resulted in the Declaration of Independence and the birth into the family of nations of our great Republic; but I do not hesitate to say, I believe that the men and
women who shed greatest luster upon the Republic, who furnish
the materials for the most glorious chapter in its history, are those
who arrayed themselves on the side of freedom during the great
Anti-slavery struggle. In that magnificent crusade there was more
real character shown, more manhood and womanhood of the
highest type developed,—more of all those qualities we call divine,
than in any other struggle that has ever taken place on this continent. The biggest crop of morally great men and women,—the
highest kind of greatness,—which this country has produced came
out of that struggle. And therefore of all the men and women who
go to make up its history, they are the ones, above and beyond
all others, who ought to be held in grateful and everlasting remembrance. When I think of these noble specimens of humanity:
—of their lofty patriotism; of their noble daring in behalf of
human rights,—in behalf of the weak and oppressed, and compare
them with some of the miserable hypocrites in high places,—with
the cowards and sycophants and time-servers with which our land
is infested today, the more am I impressed with the importance
of holding up their example, of directing special attention to them.

It is of one of these princely sons of the Republic, one of these
heaven-born heroes, one of earth's great martyrs to liberty, to
human rights, that I desire to speak of this morning, John Brown.

My purpose is to recall briefly the salient points of his life, and
to draw a few lessons from them. He was born in the State of
Connecticut, May 9, 1800, a little over a century ago. At eight
years of age he lost his mother.

At ten, through the influence of a friend, he began for the first

time to read a little history; and in this way, "By reading the lives
of great and good men, by making himself familiar with their
thoughts and sentiments, grew to dislike, we are told, frivolous
conversation and persons." Would that our young men and women
of to-day possessed more largely than they do something of the
same spirit. There is entirely too much frivolity among us. There
is a lack of seriousness which is not a promising sign. No race
can hope to amount to very much whose young people are given
up mainly or largely to the pleasures and frivolities of life. John
Brown began early to take a serious view of life. The thought
expressed by the poet,—

> A sacred burden is the life ye bear,
> Look on it, lift it, bear it solemnly,
> Stand up and walk beneath it steadfastly,
> Fail not for sorrow, falter not for sin,
> But onward, upward, till the goal ye win.

This thought began very early to take possession of him, and
to exert a controlling influence over him.

He began also very early to show an ambition to excel in whatever he undertook, a quality which continued to characterize him
all through his life. Even as a boy he aimed to do well whatever
he undertook, and knew no such word as fail. Hence success almost always crowned his efforts. If failure came it was not because he hadn't done his best to succeed.

In his fifteenth year he became a Christian, and a firm believer
in the Bible as the Word of God. This old book became his daily
companion; he loved it and studied it as he did no other book.
During the five years following his conversion he felt a very strong
desire to improve his mind; but was prevented from doing very
much in the way of reading and studying, owing to pressure of
business and an inflammation of the eyes from which he was suffering. He managed, however, in spite of these obstacles, to
acquire a knowledge of arithmetic and of surveying.

In his twenty-first year he took to himself a wife; and was most fortunate in his selection of a companion. She was not only a woman of most excellent character, but also profoundly sympathized with him in his desire to help the slave, to be of service to the oppressed blacks in this country. In 1833, death having deprived him of this excellent lady, he was married a second time to a no less worthy helpmeet, by whom he had thirteen children, and who was loyal to him and the cause which lay so near his heart, to the very end.

In 1846 he moved to New England, and took up his abode at Springfield, Massachusetts. In 1849 he changed his residence to North Elba, N.Y. Gerrit Smith had set aside a hundred thousand acres of land in that part of the state, which he offered free to any colored families who would come and occupy them. This invitation was accepted by quite a number, and John Brown, who was anxious to help the colored people, and who felt that he could be of help to them, went to see Mr. Smith with a view of settling among them.

The substance of what he said to Mr. Smith was, "I am something of a pioneer; I grew up among the woods and wild Indians of Ohio; and am used to the climate and way of life that your colony finds so trying. I will take one of your farms myself, clear it up and plant it, and show my colored neighbors how such work should be done; will give them work as I have occasion, look after them in all needful ways, and be a kind of father to them."

How beautiful is the spirit which these words reveal! how Christ-like! His desire was not to be ministered unto, but to minister, to be of service to others, and especially to this poor race of ours. The little that he could do to help these colored families, in the region of North Elba, exposed as they were to the rigors of a northern climate, he was glad to do; but it was the condition of the millions of this race all over the country—enslaved, degraded, brutalized, reduced to the level of mere chattels, beasts of burden —that weighed most heavily upon his heart and mind. Others might be indifferent to the wrongs that were being perpetrated upon these oppressed millions, but he was not: he felt that it was his duty, his divinely appointed mission to strike a blow for the liberation of the slave. And this was the thought which now filled him; which dominated his soul; which stirred him to the very depths of his being. . . .

John Brown had very little faith in moral suasion in dealing with slavery. He believed that severer measures were necessary; that it would yield to violence, and violence only. This was his remedy, his method of attack from the first. He saw no hope for [the] slave; no hope of purging the nation of the sin of slavery except by an appeal to arms,—through the shedding of blood. And it was under this conviction that his plans were made which culminated at Harpers Ferry.

How the old hero was wounded; how he was struck several times over his head with a saber, and bayoneted twice after he was down on the ground; how for the space of thirty hours he lay on the floor of the guardhouse weltering in his blood, without a bed, and without receiving any attention; how he was finally lodged in the jail at Charles Town, tried, condemned, and executed, we are all familiar with, and therefore I will not take the time to recount these events in detail. Suffice it to say,—in attempting to serve others, his own life was sacrificed.

After he was pronounced dead, his body was lowered from the scaffold; loving friends received it, and conveyed it to his home at North Elba; and on the eighth of the month, with appropriate ceremonies, all that was mortal of the old hero was laid to rest, where his ashes still repose.

His body was laid to rest, but not his spirit. They had shattered the earthly tabernacle, but the dauntless, irrepressible, liberty-loving spirit of John Brown was still alive, and was destined to play a still more important part in the great struggle for freedom, to exert a still more potent influence. It is Byron who says,—

> They never fail who die
> In a great cause. The block may soak their gore;
> Their heads may sodden in the sun; their limbs
> Be strung to city gates and castle walls;
> But still their spirit walks abroad. Though years
> Elapse and others share as dark a doom,
> They but augment the deep and sweeping thoughts
> Which overpower all others and conduct
> The world, at last, to freedom.

And this was the higher mission upon which John Brown had now entered. By his death and seeming failure, the cause was to be greatly strengthened: a new impulse was to be given to the movement: and large accessions were to be made to the ranks of freedom. To destroy the institution of slavery and let the oppressed go free was the crowning ambition of this man's life; and God, who knew the desire of his heart, permitted him to be executed at Charles Town as the most effective means to that end. Great as were his services in life, they were vastly greater in death. This was the view which he himself took of it, and which subsequent events showed to be true. . . .

The part which his death was destined to play, in the great struggle, became more and more apparent to John Brown himself as the hour of his execution approached. As early as February 24, 1858, he had said,—"I expect nothing but to endure hardship; but I expect to effect a mighty conquest, even though it be like the last victory of Samson."

To his brother, Nov. 12, 1859, he wrote,—"I am gaining in health slowly, and am quite cheerful in view of my approaching end, being firmly persuaded that I am worth more for hanging than for any other purpose." He closes his letter to his sister of the same date with words: "Say to all my friends that I am waiting cheerfully and patiently the day of my appointed time, fully believing that for me now to die will be an infinite gain and of untold benefit to the cause we love, wherefore be of good cheer and let not your heart be troubled." And in his last letter addressed to his family he says, "I am waiting the hour of my public murder with great composure of mind and cheerfulness, feeling the strong assurance that in no other possible way could I be used to so much advantage to the cause of God and humanity; and that nothing that either I or all my family have sacrificed or suffered will be lost. . . ."

It is impossible to overestimate the importance of the part which John Brown played in the great struggle for freedom in this country. He has placed the whole nation, and especially our race, under a lasting debt of gratitude to him. Only here and there, as we run down the long annals of history, do we find a man of his stamp. God doesn't send a great many such men into this world; but occasionally he does send us a man of his stripe,—a man of courage, of convictions, of moral earnestness, of unswerving loyalty to the right, a man who isn't afraid to die in the path of duty. . . .

Such was this old hero; this martyr to liberty, to the rights of man; this friend of the weak, of the oppressed, of the downtrodden; this friend of the slave, of the brother in black, when friends were few. Others may forget him, but the members of this race can never, will never. As long as one representative of the enslaved millions in this country and their descendants remain, will his memory be cherished.

And now in closing, there are a few lessons, as a race, which we should learn from this noble record:—We need to be dominated by a great purpose, as John Brown was. John Brown had a mark towards which he was ever pressing. He could say, and say from the bottom of his heart,—This one thing I do; and that one thing was the freedom of the slave. As a race we are suffering in this land from great wrongs; the purpose is to keep us down, to deprive us of our rights, civil and political, to rivet upon us chains that are more galling than those which bound the slave. Are we going to submit to it? Are we going quietly to acquiesce in this renewed effort of the Slave Power to neutralize the great Amendments to the Constitution, or are we going to stand up for our rights as men, and as citizens of the Republic? John Brown had a purpose,—let it be our purpose, a purpose which nothing shall be able to shake,—to stand up squarely and uncompromisingly for what belongs to us, for what we are entitled to. The heathen may rage, the people may imagine a vain thing, bloody riots may be incited, red-handed murder, in the shape of mobs, may continue to stalk through the land; but let us not be driven from our purpose. God is greater than presidents, or Senates, or Houses of Representatives,—greater than political parties, greater than all the hoards of Negro-haters, North and South, in high places and in low places, who are seeking to hound us down. If we are right we are bound, sooner or later, to triumph. Tenacity of purpose,—the purpose to "sink or swim, live or die, survive or perish,"—is what you need, and what I need, and what the race needs; and what we must have if we are to succeed, if we are to hold our own in the great struggle in which we are engaged. The fact that John Brown was willing to die that we might be free, willing to die, that we might become citizens of this Republic, with all that that implies, should lead us to hold sacred our rights. Rights purchased at such a time should not be lightly esteemed. The memory of John Brown, of the greatness of the sacrifice which he made, should fix forever in the breast of every Negro in this land, the purpose never to surrender the rights which he helped to make possible to us,—rights that have been so dearly bought.

We need the spirit of self-sacrifice which John Brown possessed. He lived in the plainest kind of a house, he lived on the plainest kind of food, he dressed in the plainest kind of clothes, and his family did the same,—and all for the sake of the cause in which he was interested and to which he had given his life. John Brown was willing to deny himself of a great many things, a great many of the comforts of life,—to say nothing of the luxuries, in order that he might help the slave. And that is the spirit that we need, as a race, but which we haven't got, I am sorry to say, in any large measure. We have yet to learn this great lesson of self-denial for the sake of the cause in which we are engaged. In contending for our rights, among other things, we have got to have money if the fight is to be properly made. If it is only a campaign of education, we must have money; and, if we are to carry matters into the courts, we have got to have money,—the lawyers are to be paid, and there are other expenses incident to such proceedings that must be met. You can't take a step without money. And this money ought not to come from white men. We ourselves ought to furnish the sinews of war; we ought to be sufficiently interested in our own rights to be willing to make some sacrifices in order to maintain them. Until, as a people, we are willing to deny ourselves for the cause, we are not going to make much headway. As long as we think more of a dollar, and of what that dollar will bring to us in the way of personal material comforts, than we do of our rights, the cause will languish. It shows that while we are prating about our wrongs, and pretending to be chafing under them, it is only talk. These wrongs haven't yet taken hold of us as they ought to, otherwise we would be willing to make sacrifices to have them righted, or, at least, to make a manly effort to do so. It is well enough to love the almighty dollar, but we ought not to be willing to hold on to it at the expense of our rights. The spirit of self-sacrifice, of self-denial for the cause is what we need, more largely than we have, as a race.

We need the noble daring, the sublime courage which John Brown possessed. John Brown was no coward. He had convictions, and he was not afraid to let men know what he thought. And we need brave men in this battle which we are waging,—men who are physically brave, men who are morally brave. There are things that only brave men can say; there are times when only brave men dare speak. Frederick Douglass was such a man. He looked like a lion, and he had the heart of a lion. "John Brown's body lies mouldering in the grave, His soul is marching on," we sometimes sing. God grant that the spirit of this old battled-scarred hero, this man of dauntless courage, while it is marching on, may take possession of some of us. It is impossible to wage successfully any warfare, physical or moral, with cowards; you have got to have brave men to lead, and brave men in the ranks. And this is the kind of men that we need and must have, if we are to succeed,—men who are not afraid to speak; men who are not afraid to act; men who are not afraid to die, if it becomes necessary.

We need the tireless, sleepless energy of John Brown. He was alive, wide awake in every fiber of his being. He knew how to work, and how to work long and hard for the object which he had in view.

We need to catch the spirit of this old hero,—his passion for work. For there is so much to be done, in so many directions in working out this great problem of our elevation. We need all the energy and push that we can possibly muster up. Those that are sleeping, must be waked up; those that are sitting with folded hands, must be stirred to action. Everywhere, within the race, among old as well as young, there must be generated a sense of the importance of active, earnest work on the part of all. Whatever our hands find to do we must be made to realize the importance of doing with our might. If we don't we will be sure to be left behind in the race of life. It is the man who has push and energy and pluck that is going to succeed; and the same is true of a race. There must be no folding of the hands; no calling for a little more sleep, a little more slumber. We must all be active and earnest; we must all be up and doing.

We need John Brown's faith in God, and in the old book of God. The Psalmist says,—

"Great peace have they that love thy law."

And again,

> Except the Lord build the house,
> They labor in vain that build it:
> Except the Lord keep the city,
> The watchman waketh but in vain.

It is important for us, as a race, to remember this, and to hold on to God, and to make his Word the man of our counsel, and the guide of our lives. We may think that we can get along without God, that we can work out the problem of our elevation without him; but we are mistaken. Let us live ourselves, to the glory of God and train our children to do the same. This is what John Brown did; and this is what we must do if we are to come out all right. In noble qualities of this man we have a splendid example for the imitation of our race. May his inspiring example, the example of a great purpose, steadily adhered to; of a spirit of self-sacrifice, of sublime courage, of noble daring, of tireless, sleepless energy, of implicit faith and trust in God and in his Word, not be lost upon us, and upon our children, and our children's children. Let it be to us a constant spur and stimulus to all high endeavor, to all noble action. There yet remains a great deal to be done; but with faith in God, and faith in ourselves, and the purpose to do the right, we cannot fail. If John Brown were permitted to speak to us today from heaven, where he has been now for fifty years, he would say to us, I believe, ["]Never despair! Never give up! The forces that are for you are greater than those that are against you. Be patient; be earnest; be aggressive. In spite of Atlanta riots; in spite of the official lynching, or the unjust dismissal of Negro soldiers, and the Negro-hating spirit which it exhibits, and all the other brood of evils that seem to be threatening you, keep a stout heart. Out of the darkness, and the seeming triumph of the forces of oppression and injustice in 1859 when I was executed, there came the Emancipation Proclamation, and the great Amendments to the Constitution. Be assured of one thing, God did not strike the shackles from your limbs, and lift you to the plane of American citizenship, that he might desert you and leave you in the hands of your enemies. The same power that was with you in the dark days of slavery, and that stood behind you when the great Amendments were being put through, is still with you, and will continue to be with you to the end.

["]Back of all the forces that have been put in operation for the uplift of your race, from the beginning to the present, God has been, and still is. He it was who stirred the Anti-slavery leaders to action, and brought on the war, and inspired the men in Congress,—men like Sumner, and Stevens, and Wade,—and that moved upon the heart of Lincoln himself. It was the power of God, working through human agencies, that brought about emancipation, and that lifted you to the plane of citizenship, and clothed you with the sacred right of the ballot. And will he now desert you? Will he leave you naked to the tender mercies of your enemies? Never. God doesn't work that way; that is not his way of doing things. These great landmarks in your history,—slavery, emancipation, citizenship, the ballot, are the evidences that there is to be no backward step. God never would have brought you thus far unless he meant to stand by you, and to see that the rights guaranteed to you under the Constitution, are yours in reality as well as in name. In spite of discouragements; in spite of the gathering gloom, God is leading you on."

> God's ways seem dark: but, soon or late
> They reach the shining hills of day.

That is what John Brown would say to us today, I believe, if he were permitted to speak to us. Ours is not a hopeless fight, but one that is sure to eventuate in victory.

As we go to our homes this afternoon, with the memory of this old hero fresh upon us, let us remember what God hath wrought since the raid on Harpers Ferry and since the great sacrifice at Charles Town, and let us rejoice, and lift up our hearts and voices in praise and thanksgiving to Him. Not unto us; not unto us; but unto His great and holy Name be all the glory. Amen.

Leslie Pinckney Hill

In 1909 Oswald Garrison Villard, newspaper editor and publisher, produced a path-breaking book on John Brown,
based on prodigious investigation, much of it by a
secretary-researcher, Katherine Mayo. Among the many who
acclaimed the work was a budding poet, Leslie Pinckney Hill
(1880–1960), who later became president of Cheyney State
Teachers College, Cheyney, Pennsylvania. Earner of two
degrees at Harvard, Hill was a man of considerable literary
gifts. Villard's carefully wrought portrait of Brown stimulated
Hill to one of his best efforts, a soaring sonnet of reverent commitment. The manuscript is owned by the Columbia University
Libraries.

ON READING VILLARD'S
"JOHN BROWN FIFTY YEARS AFTER"

In the deep silence of the midnight hour
I close the book, and leave the finished tale
In reverent awe. Logic doth not avail.
Too moving are the pathos and the power
Of the weird soul that never learned to cower
In life or death—but deemed it sweet to fail,
If so the will of God might yet prevail—
To ask what were our boon or what his dower.
   I only know the heritage that falls
To me, a scion of his dreadful sowing:
The troubled voice of all my kinsmen calls—
"O brother, while our night towards day is growing,
Gird round you stoutly, counting not the price,
His ashen raiment of self-sacrifice."

PART III

HARDY PERENNIAL (1925–1972):
THE ENDURING BROWN

The middle decades of the twentieth century witnessed sweeping changes in American life, including the New Deal of the 1930's, America's participation in the war against Germany and Japan, and the ensuing cold war tension between America and her former ally, Russia. During the twenty-five years following Pearl Harbor the role of the black American, whether on the battlefront or the domestic scene, increasingly demanded the attention of the president and the Congress. It was the Supreme Court, however, that took the most momentous step in black-white relations. Ruling in May 1954 that segregation in the public schools was contrary to the Constitution, the Court gave new life to the movement for racial equality, prompting the Congress three years later to pass the first civil rights bill in over eighty years.

Although many things in black life had changed from the days of President Harding to those of President Nixon, one thing remained constant—the esteem that black Americans had for John Brown. In black circles some of the luster had gone from Lincoln's name but Brown obviously had weathered well. Black poets wrote sonnets to his memory and

black playwrights like Theodore Ward and William Branch re-created the man and his times. Black
painters, including Horace Pippin, Jacob Lawrence,
and Charles White, found in Brown a worthy
theme. The black sculptor Henry Bannard fashioned
a stone bust of Brown.

During this period a leading civil rights organization
and a prominent black fraternal organization honored
John Brown. At its twenty-third annual meeting, held
in Washington in May 1932, the National Association
for the Advancement of Colored People sent five
busloads of delegates to Harpers Ferry to present to
Storer College a bronze tablet in honor of Brown (a
gift the college board of trustees, allegedly at the
strong urging of the United Daughters of the Confederacy, refused to accept because, they said, its
inscription contained "controversial matter"). In 1949
the Improved Benevolent and Protective Order of
Elks of the World purchased the John Brown Farm, a
place (the former Kennedy Farm) near Harpers
Ferry where Brown had assembled his small band.
The Elks acquired the site to make "a shrine of historical significance so that it would serve as an
inspiration to youth as they recalled the life of John
Brown," wrote official historian Charles H. Wesley.

Certainly in 1959, the hundredth anniversary of
his passing, Brown was still revered among blacks.
Whether he would fare as well with them during the
next 100-year period was less certain but quite probable. The black militants of the 1960's varied a little
in their response to Brown. Robert F. Williams, a
leading figure in the Revolutionary Action Movement
(RAM), said that he always kept with him a copy of
Thoreau's plea for Captain Brown (in *Negroes with*

Guns, 1962, p. 122). But the typical black militant's attitude toward Brown was more likely to be phrased in somewhat negative terms—a regret that so few other whites were of his stripe. "From the beginning of the contacts between blacks and whites," writes Eldridge Cleaver, "there has been very little reason for a black man to respect a white, with such exceptions as John Brown and others lesser known" (*Soul on Ice,* 1968, pp. 82–83).

H. Rap Brown shared this viewpoint, noting that "John Brown was the only white man I could respect and he is dead" (*Die, Nigger, Die,* 1969, p. 116). Malcolm X was somewhat more inclusive, if equally brief, in reference to John Brown. "I don't go for any nonviolent white liberals," he said in January 1965. "If you are for me and my problems—when I say me I mean *us,* our people—then you have to be willing to do as old John Brown did" (George Breitman, ed., *Malcolm X Speaks,* 1965, p. 241). Floyd McKissick, former national chairman of the Congress of Racial Equality, held that men like John Brown were "exempt from the guilt of their people," on the ground that Brown "did as much in defense of Black Men as he would have done in his own defense" (*Three-Fifths of a Man,* 1969, pp. 147–48).

As a group the black militants of the 1960's have tended to concentrate on movements that were black-conceived and black-led and hence they have tended to devote less attention to Brown than was the case of their forebears. Some have withheld praise from any white person, holding that all whites, individually and collectively, share a heavy burden of racial guilt. Moreover, runs this school of thought, even if an occasional white warranted absolution, he would

hardly be worthy of commendation by blacks—a
tribute that should be reserved for nonwhites exclusively.

This process of lumping all whites together in an
adversary relationship may not prevail in John Brown's
case. For even the most race-conscious black could
hardly quarrel with Brown's unequivocal egalitarianism, his direct-action approach, his strategy of
confrontation, eyeball to eyeball. And beyond the
considerations of his personal behavior and his methods
there are about Brown one towering characteristic
that must needs endear him to the most uncompromising black militants of today, as to the generations of
blacks that preceded them. This was Brown's love of
freedom, a principle by which he lived and for which
he died.

J. Max Barber

J. Max Barber (1878–1945), one of the founders of the
Niagara Movement, had turned from a fitful career as editor
of the monthly *Voice of the Negro* to become a dentist, opening
an office in Philadelphia in 1912. Ten years later he became
the co-founder of the John Brown Memorial Association. At
North Elba in May 1935 a dream came true for Barber and
his co-workers when they unveiled a six-ton bronze statue
depicting Brown with his arm around a Negro boy. At the
dedication exercises Barber, as president of the Association,
gave an address, a somewhat wide-ranging discourse but well
constructed and coming unmistakably from a full heart. It was
printed in *John Brown in Bronze, 1800–1859, Containing
Program and Addresses of the Dedicatory Ceremony and
Unveiling of the Monument of John Brown, May 9, 1935* (Lake
Placid, N.Y., 1935), pp. 19–25.

We have gathered here today for the purpose of dedicating this
monument to John Brown, the herald of freedom, the great fore-
runner of emancipation. This statue in bronze will not do John
Brown the slightest bit of good or harm. John Brown's life has
been closed and his work is done. The pebble of his influence
which he tossed into the sea of time goes rippling on through peoples and nations to the end of the world.

We rear this monument as our symbol of gratitude and as a
token of our ideals. We erect this statue here as our finger on the
milepost of this age pointing the future traveler on the way we
thought and dreamed. It is our signpost to the generations to come.
They must know by this that we reverenced heroism for justice and
that we were grateful for martyrdom for freedom.

Today my heart thrills with joy. Thirteen years ago two lone pilgrims, Dr. Burwell and I, came up here to place a wreath on this grave. We came in the name of the American Negro to show to the world that we were grateful for God's gift of John Brown to mankind. Since then I have talked John Brown everywhere. In pulpits, on lecture platforms, in private conferences—everywhere.

The money which has gone into the making of this monument represents sacrifices. It ought to be so. John Brown sacrificed to his last full measure for us.

We take great pleasure in presenting this monument to the State of New York in the name of the American Negro. New York has always appreciated John Brown. Gerrit Smith, one of its great governors, was one of John Brown's backers. When John Brown was hanged the bell on the capitol at Albany was tolled for three hours as a symbol of the sorrow of the Empire State and cannon were slowly fired to honor his passing.

Some of those who worked to raise the money for this monument have passed on from labor to reward. If it is given to the departed spirits to revisit and to view the scenes of their former activities here below, some of our friends join John Brown in watching these exercises here today. We salute you who have gone on ahead of us! To those of the early colonials who fought slavery in its infancy, who saw then that it was an alien thing to our soil and our ideals, hail! All hail to the Abolition Society and to men like Ben Franklin and Thomas Jefferson! Hail to that great galaxy of noble spirits who met the ugly monster of slavery when it was full panoplied and fought. Lovejoy and Lundy and Garrison and Phillips; Harriet Beecher Stowe, Prudence Crandall and Sojourner Truth; Frederick Douglas[s], John Brown and his gallant little band of crusaders: Freedom's Rosary, I call them, Hail! And hail to you who were baptized in fire and blood at Chancellorsville, at Gettysburg and in that awful carnage in the Wilderness! And to the Sainted Lincoln thrice hail! We salute all of you who crowd around this mystic circle which separates the living from the dead.

We are trying to keep aloft the torch of liberty and idealism so as to hand it on.

A lot of men bulk big in the little minute of their lives who are never heard of again after they have died. The coming centuries will hear of but three names of our Civil War period—Abraham Lincoln, the great emancipator; Ulysses S. Grant, the great general; and John Brown, the great forerunner of emancipation.

Unquestionably Lincoln's name will dominate the age because he was indeed a towering character, a great philosopher, a statesman, a really great man for any age, and because he happened to be the head of the nation at this time. Grant will be known as the dogged commander who took the disorganized Union forces and welded them into a mighty army which brought the conflict to a successful conclusion. He was the rod of iron Lincoln used to flail the forces of slavery into submission.

Pushing up beside Lincoln must always appear the name of John Brown. He was the voice crying in the wilderness. He it was who kindled the beacon fires of freedom on a thousand hills. He was the grim, grey herald of that awful conflict which robed the nation in fire and blood. It was a conflict which had to come in order that we might have a new birth of freedom, a real birth of freedom. After John Brown there could be no peace with slavery in the land.

We stand on an historic spot. If the clock of time were turned back seventy-six years, we should now see John Brown setting out on that journey which was to take him to Harper's Ferry and immortal glory. He had gone to Kansas and wrestled with the demon of slavery there. And his name was known and dreaded from the Swamp of the Swan to Osawatomie as the nightmare of slavery. He had gone into Missouri and snatched a band of slaves from the greedy claws of the slave power and taken them through Kansas and Iowa to Canada. The patrols of several states and the deputies of the United States were looking for him with a price on his head. In Canada he had conferred with free Negroes and organized them. He had gone before the Massachusetts Legislature and pleaded our cause. The newspapers had letters from him denouncing slavery. And now he had come back here to set his house in order as much as he could, and to take tender farewell of the women folk of his family.

He had confided in his wife something of his plans and then, as was his wont, he bowed his hoary head in prayer to God for guidance. He arose and gave each one a tender word. Then he emerged from yonder door. Mary Brown followed him to the porch. He looked around and sighed. Of all of his labors this little frame house begirt with stumps was all he could call home. And how little time he had spent here! It was heartbreaking to think that a man had spent so much time and money and suffering for others and his own family stood in need. "Good-bye, Mary. Do the best you can," he said. He embraced and kissed her and went out across these hills to his fate. Perhaps at the turn in the road he looked back and waved farewell, for I believe the premonition of his fate was on him.

The next time Mrs. Brown saw her husband he was behind the bars in Charlestown jail. As you all know, he was hanged on the gallows December 2, 1859, and a few days later Mrs. Brown brought his broken body back to these windswept hills and laid him here to rest in this sacred spot.

What was it that made the soul of John Brown so restless in life? What was it that lured him to Kansas, to Missouri and finally to Harper's Ferry and his death? What was it that would not let him peacefully tend his flocks, tap his sugar maples and till his lands here in these hills? You will have to go to Virginia and hear him answer the angry forces who arrested him. "The cry of distress of the oppressed called me," he told them when they demanded who sent you here.

He had looked abroad in the land and had seen the most monstrous, the foulest system of slavery the world had ever known. And it was his land, his country, the soil his fathers had helped to conquer and dedicate to liberty and equality which sheltered this living death. Slavery made him sick with shame. It was a crime-stained, brutish thing which encrusted the land with filth. Bloody and cruel and heartless, its insatiable appetite was devouring the idealism of the nation.

All that elevates and adorns life was beyond the reach of the slave. When Brown was a boy, man-stealing was the chief commercial industry of the civilized world. And yet we are amazed at a few kidnappings today. By the time Brown grew to middle age three million Negroes were chained down in manure pits of slavery. The preachers of the Gospel, supposed to be the vicars of Christ, justified slavery from their pulpits. The courts of the land hovered over it and protected it as a holy thing. The very Congress of the nation constituted itself a deputy of the slave power and undertook to return to the owners runaway slaves. Matrimony was a mockery where Negroes were concerned, even more than among the rich today. An ambitious Negro's head was crushed as is a serpent's when it wriggles into the parlor. Civilization was taught to hold its nose when it passed us by. Unborn Negro children were already mortgaged to this infamous system before they even got a glimpse of God's golden sunlight. Negro women were forced to become the cloaca for the lechery of diseased white men in order that white womanhood might be protected. A prisoner on Devil's Island might escape and be free but Negroes crawled to the gates of hope and found them barred.

And this reptilian, crime-stained thing was tightening its coils around the soul of the nation tighter than the sea serpents tightened around the far-framed Laocoon and his sons.

Ay! The conscience of the nation was frozen with apathy. It had stood for every evil, every encroachment, from the defiant slave ships increasing their cargoes to the frightful Dred Scott decision. The iron-lipped vampire of slavery sucked all the honey out of the life of a whole race and all of the morality out of the life of the white man. The Declaration of Independence was like

the dry bones Ezekiel saw in the valley of Esdraelon. It was dead.
Some prophet had to speak to these dry bones and make them
live again.

It was into this abattoir of sin, into this lair of the damned, into
this valley of death that John Brown burst with the passionate
intensity of an avenging knight of God. And it was due to his raid
at Harper's Ferry, his letters while in jail and his death that freedom leaped like an epidemic across the land.

From the standpoint of the sneering materialist and to those
lacking in vision and idealism John Brown's life was a failure. He
failed in his tanning business in Ohio. He met failure in his plans
to settle at Oberlin. He failed at Akron, he failed in his wool business at Springfield. Everywhere—disaster after disaster. He failed
in his business undertakings because he subordinated them to the
cause of freedom. Finally he failed at Harper's Ferry. Here was,
indeed, a boulevard of broken dreams.

And yet, was this life a failure? Lives are judged by the motives
animating them and by the influences that follow. Is there anyone who will assert that John Brown's life is of no moral value to
this country? All of his motives were pitched in a high altitude—
in the stratosphere of motives, if you please. The example of his
unselfish devotion to freedom ought to lift and illumine our life
today. He proved that there still lived unselfish men, men capable
of dying for an ideal. Where can one find such zeal for righteousness, such hatred of injustice and such disinterested bravery as we
find in John Brown? Whose life and death had any more to do
with emancipation?

Not since paleolithic man crossed the rim of Asia into Europe,
not even during the Crusades or the so-called age of chivalry
has the world seen a truer, nobler knight. And not since that special star blazed in the black Syrian night 2,000 years ago leading
the three wise men of the East to the manger in the stable has a
truer savior of mankind appeared on earth.

The Sanhedrin of slavery hanged him as a traitor but the world would be infinitely better if it had more men like John Brown. He believed that it was right to resist even law when it violates the principles of natural justice. The brave who fell at Lexington did that. The ragged, barefoot continentals at Valley Forge did it. Emmett did it in Ireland, Wallace in Scotland and Garibaldi in Italy. Leonidas did it at Thermopylæ and Toussaint in Haiti. And we honor them. John Brown did the same thing at Harper's Ferry and we hanged him.

What men of this type do is not personal, not local, not even national, but *human*. Here was a man who put humanity above race, right above law, and freedom above everything. He appealed from the sanctions of the law to the higher laws of humanity. He was big enough and bold enough to defy a nation for the right. He was a traitor to his country in order to be true to his conscience and his God. Such men leap beyond the ramparts of common laws and common men and set the standards of the race on higher ground.

John Brown was as truly a prophet as was Moses and his trembling soul thrilled at the voice of God commanding him to forsake his sheep and lands here even as did Moses' soul in the Midian desert when commanded to go down into Egypt.

Soldier, prophet, hero, martyr! A grateful people bring garlands here to your grave today and dedicate this monument to you and your comrades. You have not died in vain. Your life shines on with the light of eternal right and men will yet learn that in the shifting phantasmagoria of time nations and races rise and splutter and boast and perish but that God and justice and the human race live on.

John Brown's citizenship is now registered in Heaven. His dust rests here beneath the spice and balm of these enchanted hills. His memory is forever enshrined in history's golden urn. And glory, glory hallelujah! His immortal soul goes marching on.

Approval of the *Pittsburgh Courier*

The practice of making an annual pilgrimage to John Brown's grave site at North Elba, begun by the John Brown Memorial Association in 1922, won the commendation of the *Pittsburgh Courier,* an influential, nationally circulated black weekly. A reflective and gracefully written editorial, "John Brown," conveying a sense of gratitude and high regard, appeared on April 30, 1932 (used by permission of the *New Pittsburgh Courier*).

It is time for spring cleaning. We are dusting the shelves, rearranging the furniture and, one by one, we take out our favorite volumes, dust them off and put them back in their accustomed places. We come across the "Life of John Brown," a familiar volume, and we thumb the leaves and, ere we are aware, the dust cloth drops to the floor and we are enmeshed in the story of Negro slavery and the sacrifices of the one and only John Brown. We come across his birth; we follow his pioneering against the greatest curse known to man, and as we close the book we are reminded that this is the time of year when the pilgrimage wends its way to Lake Placid, near where lies the body of the martyr.

Those of us who can go will approach the scene of the last resting place of our friend with reverence and thanksgiving. Those of us who cannot go will follow the pilgrimage mile by mile with as much reverence as though we, ourselves, were a part of the caravan.

It was but yesteryear that John Brown raised his voice against slavery. The story is still fresh in the minds of a grateful people. The freedom we enjoy crowds out wars, politics, state papers and even presidents, and there looms large and permanently in our minds the one and only John Brown. The pilgrimage is but a faint

116

expression of our gratitude. The blessings we have in life, liberty, and a somewhat retarded pursuit of happiness, are all a part of the life of John Brown. We can as easily forget the one as the other. It is hoped we shall never forget either.

Georgia Douglas Johnson

Georgia Douglas Johnson (1886–1965), wife of the Recorder of Deeds under President Taft, produced four volumes of lyric verse. Her recurring themes were love, life, and race, touched upon in mixed tones of resignation and hope. Her voice, generally calm, takes on a more passionate stress in this sonnet to Brown, appearing in her volume *Bronze* and also, although with slightly altered punctuation, in *The Crisis,* August 1922 (p. 89). In her closing lines Mrs. Johnson makes reference to the Alleghenies, doubtless deliberately (for poetic reasons) but conceivably confusing them with the Adirondacks. The poem is used by permission of *The Crisis*.

TO JOHN BROWN

We lift a song to you across the day
Which bears through travailing the seed you spread
In terror's morning, flung with fingers red
In blood of tyrants, who debarred the way
To Freedom's dawning. Hearken to the lay
Chanted by dusky millions, soft and mellow-keyed,
In minor measure, Martyr of the Freed,
A song of memory across the day.

Truth cannot perish though the earth erase
The royal signals, leaving not a trace,
And time still burgeoneth the fertile seed,
Though he is crucified who wrought the deed:
O Alleghanies, fold him to your breast
Until the judgment! Sentinel his rest!

Countee Cullen

Countee Cullen (1903–1946) matured early as a lyrical poet, publishing his first volume of verse before graduating Phi Beta Kappa from New York University in 1925, and bringing out two additional volumes before he reached thirty. "He was a true poet and wrote brave and beautiful things," said a fellow practitioner, William Rose Benét. His literary inspiration was John Keats and his technique was traditional, so Cullen could hardly be called a protest poet. But he dwelt on racial themes and, in this poem, he numbered John Brown in the company of the saints. The poem appeared in *Opportunity,* January 1942, p. 7, and is reprinted with permission of the National Urban League, Inc.

A NEGRO MOTHER'S LULLABY

(After a visit to the grave of John Brown)

Hushaby, hushaby, dark one at my knee,
Slumber you softly, nor pucker, nor frown;
Though some may be bonded, you shall be free,
Thanks to a man, Osawatamie Brown.
      (His sons are high fellows;
      An Archangel is he;
      They doff their bright halos
      To none but the Three.)
Hushaby, hushaby, sweet darkness at rest,
Two there have been who their lives laid down
That you might be beautiful here at my breast:
Our Jesus and . . . Osawatamie Brown.
      (His sons are high fellows;
      An Archangel is he;

They doff their bright halos
To none but the Three.)
Hushaby, hushaby; when a man, not a slave,
With freedom for wings you go through the town,
Let your love be dew on his evergreen grave.
Sleep in the name of Osawatamie Brown.
(Rich counsel he's giving
Close by the throne;
Tall he was living,
But now taller grown.
His sons are high fellows;
An Archangel is he;
And they doff their bright halos
To none but the Three.)

Langston Hughes

On the centennial of Harpers Ferry, Langston Hughes (1902–
1967), in a weekly column appearing under his name, turned
his thoughts to John Brown. A man of multiple literary gifts
—poetry, biography, autobiography, fiction, and journalism,
plus musical comedy and opera lyrics, Hughes had been one
of the bright lights of the Harlem Renaissance of the 1920's.
Educated at Lincoln and Columbia universities, Hughes always
retained the common touch, his style unembellished and his
themes the rank and file—"the Negro who is holding up the
lamp post, scrubbing door knobs, cleaning floors, or banging on
the ebony keys of a piano in the back of a cabaret," as one
writer puts it. The following article, "John Brown's Centennial,"
illustrating the author's concrete style and direct approach,
confirmed its appeal to black readers by its strong feeling for
the men at Harpers Ferry. Possibly in the back of Hughes's
mind as he wrote this column was the thought that his maternal
grandmother, Mary Simpson Patterson, had been married to
two of Brown's black associates, first Lewis S. Leary, who fell at
Harpers Ferry, and later Charles H. Langston. The article
appeared in the Chicago Defender, October 17, 1959 (reprinted by permission of the Chicago Defender).

Just as the War for Independence that freed America from
English domination actually commenced with the death of the
Negro, Crispus Attucks, in 1770, and the Boston Tea Party in
1773, so the Civil War that freed the slaves really began with
John Brown's Raid.

At that point, however, there was yet no formal declaration of
war between the states. But the first shot had been fired, the first
blood shed, and both whites and Negroes died on the banks of
the Potomac for the sake of freedom.

Frederick Douglass, Harriet Tubman, Sojourner Truth and many other brave black men and women had already escaped from slavery into the North, but many thousands still remained in bondage.

It occurred to old John Brown, who had already fought for freedom in Kansas, that armed revolt might be precipitated in one place and from there spread throughout the slave population of the South.

With this thought in mind, Brown gathered together a secret band of 21 faithful followers, Negro and white, and planned to seize by force the federal arsenal at Harpers Ferry and then rally to his cause the slaves of Virginia and surrounding states.

In John Brown's party there were five Negroes. Dangerfield Newby, a freed slave, wanted to free his wife and seven children still held in bondage. Shields Green had learned of freedom from Frederick Douglass and left Douglass to join John Brown.

From their college classes at Oberlin had come young Lewis Sheridan Leary and John Armstrong Anderson. And Osborn Perry Anderson, a printer, had come from Pennsylvania. These men knew that they might never see their families again. And they did not tell their loved ones where they were going when they left home, or what they intended to do. But they were willing to die for freedom.

On the night of Sunday, Oct. 16, 1859, John Brown, his sons, and his little band of dedicated men successfully attacked and captured the arsenal full of arms at Harpers Ferry. But the massed might of the federal government was called out against them. At Washington President Buchanan ordered the marines and the cavalry into action.

Hundreds of troups under the leadership of no less a personage than Col. Robert E. Lee, moved into action against Brown's little band. Brown was of course defeated, taken prisoner, and hanged on the gallows, as were John Copeland and Shields Green. Of the other men of color, Sheridan Leary and Dangerfield Newby were slain in the early fighting. But Osborn Anderson escaped, to fight again later in the Civil War. Brown's two sons were killed and he himself wounded.

But he lived to march erect up the steps of the gallows on which the government had sentenced him to die on Dec. 2, 1859, a little less than two years before the Civil War, which was to accomplish what Brown's objectives began.

John Brown's name is one of the great martyr names of all history and the men who fought with him rank high on the scrolls of freedom. Even today, the old Civil War song repeats, "John Brown's Body lies a-mouldering in the grave, but his soul goes marching on." When Brown was captured, he said, "You may dispose of me very easily . . . but this question is still to be settled—this Negro question, I mean—the end of that is not yet."

Ralph Waldo Emerson called him a "new saint who will make the gallows glorious like the cross." And when he died, the great Negro leader, Douglass, said of Brown, "To his own soul he was right, and neither 'principalities nor powers, life nor death, things present nor things to come,' could shake his dauntless spirit or move him from his ground."

This month marks one hundred years since John Brown struck his blow for freedom. On Oct. 15, 16, 17, and 18 the town of Harpers Ferry, West Virginia, is commemorating John Brown's Raid with a re-enactment of the storming of the arsenal, with a pageant, "The Prophet," and an exhibition including the photographs of the 21 men who followed Brown.

I hope that a great many Afro-Americans will attend this commemoration. Those of us who cannot attend will remember with reverence this white man, John Brown, who laid down his life that his brothers might be free.

Chicago Defender Editorial

Two weeks after the centennial of the Harpers Ferry raid the *Chicago Defender,* a leading weekly, carried a thoughtful editorial, "The Forgotten John Brown." The piece was judicious in tone, although its assertion that Brown was an almost un-remembered figure was hardly borne out by its closing lines, a paraphrasing of the John Brown song. The editorial appeared November 7, 1959, and is reprinted by permission of the *Chicago Defender.*

The centennial of John Brown's raid on the federal arsenal at Harpers Ferry, Va., passed almost without notice. Except for a mild, silent observance of that momentous day in October 1859, by a few faithfuls, there would have been nothing to point to that landmark in American history.

Yet the raid and Brown's execution set off the powder keg of emotion which rendered the moral dispute over the status of the Negro and the political conflict over states' rights insoluble by anything short of civil war.

The attack on the arsenal was the first step in Brown's plan to set up a sovereign state in the mountains of Maryland and Virginia as a haven in which Negro slaves could find refuge.

The paradox of Brown's idealistic goals and his fearless methods are still being argued in college seminars a century later. Some would exonerate him on grounds of congenital insanity; others see him as a fanatic whose passions knew no bounds. Only a conspicuous few see him in the true perspective of history, as a martyr to a cause—human freedom.

History books are not replete with instances in which men have mounted the scaffold and placed their necks in the hangman's noose, forfeiting their lives for impersonal principles, for freedom, freedom of black men at that.

If Brown was belligerent, it was a belligerency motivated by his hatred of slavery. His deep convictions led him to work for Negro emancipation as part of his Christian duty. He was willing to free the slaves at the point of the gun. And he risked life and limb in a bold attempt to bring this resolve to pass.

This is the man whose sacrificial offering upon the altar of social justice and right earned him only a marginal place in the annals of his country. In short, history almost forgot him. Yet, John Brown's death so stirred the soul of America that a civil war was inescapable consequence. He had anticipated the course and verdict of history.

He was convinced that the slave owners would never willingly abolish an institution which was to their material benefit, and that it was necessary to fight force with force. And he was right. Now latter-day historians tell us that the Civil War was fought because many things went wrong, and that the whole conflict was a tragic mistake that could easily have been avoided if the men of the 1860's had the serene wisdom of the present-day generation.

This is quite possibly true; and yet the point does remain that the war somehow had its beginning in the simple fact that one race held another race in slavery, and beyond that there lies the fact that the owning race considered itself infinitely superior to the race that was owned. This was a rather expensive attitude, since it led to the loss of some 600,000 lives.

Even Abraham Lincoln's extraordinary judgment on Brown fell short of the mark when he said: "An enthusiast broods over the oppression of a people until he fancies himself commissioned by Heaven to liberate them. He ventures the attempt which ends in little else than his own execution."

But Lincoln was lacking in prevision, for he too, six years later, became one of the casualties of that conflict when he was felled by an assassin's bullet while watching the play, *Our American Cousin,* at the Ford Theater in Washington.

Brown's own words addressed to the court which was about to pronounce the death sentence upon him, are a touching vindication of his crusade against slavery. This is what he said:

"Had I so interfered in behalf of the rich, the powerful, the intelligent, the so-called great . . . it would have been all right. Every man in this court would have deemed it an act worthy of reward rather than punishment . . . I believe that to have interfered as I have done, in behalf of the despised Negro slaves, I did no wrong, but right.

"Now, if it deemed necessary that I should forfeit my life for the furtherance of the ends of justice, and mingle blood further with the blood of my children and with blood of millions in this slave country whose rights are disregarded by wicked, cruel and unjust enactments, I say, let it be done."

While John Brown's body lies a mouldering in the grave, his soul goes marching on. For he died to make men free.

J. Reuben Sheeler

Through the eyes of a professional historian, J. Reuben Sheeler (b. 1911) assesses Brown's influence during the hundred years following Harpers Ferry. Delivered at the annual meeting of the Association for the Study of Negro Life and History, held at Tallahassee, Florida, on October 16, 1959, the hundredth anniversary of the raid, Sheeler's address bore an appropriate title, "John Brown: A Century Later." To Sheeler, as to the other black commentators who had preceded him, Brown symbolized the spirit of social justice. Somewhat parenthetically it may be noted that in the course of his address Sheeler stated that in the hundred years after Harpers Ferry no professional historian had published a biography of Brown. Sheeler omitted the volume by James Malin, *John Brown and the Legend of Fifty-Six* (Philadelphia, 1942), doubtless on the ground of its limited scope, its focus centering largely on the Kansas scene. Sheeler's address was printed in *The Negro History Bulletin,* October 1960, pp. 7–10 (footnotes omitted; ellipses as in original); copyright by the Association for the Study of Negro Life and History, Inc., and Associated Publishers, Inc., used by permission.

Over one hundred years ago the John Brown Raid began at Harpers Ferry. "John Brown's body lies mouldering in the clay, but his soul goes marching on." The incident at Harpers Ferry reflects closer similarities to our present day problems and conflicts, domestic and foreign, than did most of the others of the past century. The incident ended all compromise on the continuation of slavery and brought the issues of a free America face to face with those of a slavery dominated America. Douglass says that "until this blow was struck, the prospect of freedom was dim, shadowy and uncertain." It was a clash between two systems of govern-

127

mental philosophy within America with each seeking to preserve
and extend its own way of life. The Northern free labor system accused the South's system of being wasteful and immoral. The
South argued that the Northern system was wage slavery which
failed to provide any security for the workers. The John Brown
raid at Harpers Ferry has been dramatized the world over as a
conflict between a system of free labor and that of slave labor.
Some months ago when this writer appeared to speak before a
labor school and organization in Sweden, the crowd, with direction, burst into one harmonious ring with "John Brown's body lies
mouldering in the clay, but his soul goes marching on." In Swedish
language the spirit or soul of John Brown had come to symbolize
free labor. While American Negroes attempting to integrate themselves into American society have been forced to give up the memories and celebration of their historical heroes and martyrs, the
spirit of John Brown goes marching on because one century later
not Negroes but all Americans find themselves in the plight of
struggling in a free labor system against the forces that would en-
slave them.

On the domestic scene in America, chattel slavery has been
abolished, but its aftermath has remained in segregation and so-
called legal as well as illegal schemes of discrimination. After one
century similar conflicting political systems for the utilization of
labor have taken on international significance.

For the present purpose we should like to discuss this spirit or
soul of John Brown through an analysis of the man, the Harpers
Ferry incident, and the influence it had upon American thought,
and upon social reform.

During these one hundred years since the John Brown raid at
Harpers Ferry no professional historian has published a biography
of his life. Myth and legend still hold much of the truth in secrecy.
Very little is known of the man before his advent in Kansas. He
was born in 1800 to a pioneer family and named for his grandfather who died in the American Revolution. Brought up in the

Ohio frontier country Brown had early developed a hatred for human bondage. His father had worked hard in Ohio for Negro emancipation as a part of his christian duty. Douglass told of an incident in Brown's childhood that may have been of great influence in the making of his character. While in Kentucky at the age of twelve delivering cattle to the army during the War of 1812, Brown had befriended a Negro boy whom he had seen cruelly beaten. This lay heavily upon his mind as the years passed on. The "beating of a Hebrew bondsman by an Egyptian created a Moses, and the infliction of a similar outrage on a helpless slave boy in our land may have caused, forty years afterwards, a John Brown and a Harpers Ferry Raid." He studied the Bible and refused to enlist in the army or carry arms until he was twenty-six years old. Poverty and failure had shadowed fifty-five years of his life. Father of twenty children, Brown had failed in more than twenty business ventures in six different states. All these years he had maintained the abolitionist beliefs.

The shocking murder of Elijah P. Lovejoy convinced Brown that slaveholders would not willingly abolish slavery without being forced to do so. Brown knew that any plan of force to abolish slavery would have to be kept secret. For several years he tried to effect a singleness of purpose with the abolitionists. He made friends with Negroes and tried to find out if they would support his leadership in a move to free the slaves. He found Frederick Douglass quite sympathetic with his views and he laid before him his plan for liberating the slaves.

In 1848 Brown obtained a plot of land from Gerrit Smith in the Adirondacks and moved his family to North Elba. Here he wrote a pamphlet, "Sambo's Mistakes" in which he issued advice for Negroes. A trip to Europe gave Brown much experience in the study of battlefields. After the passage of the Fugitive slave law and abolitionism grew stronger, Brown's spirit for action increased. His appearance in Kansas was an opening act of his private war against slavery.

Despite the fact that the period from 'bleeding Kansas' to Fort Sumter was filled with exciting incidents, the one at Harpers Ferry was most impressive to Virginia. It so happened that the place of the raid marks the northern point of the line that separated the Virginias. Harpers Ferry was the spot chosen by Brown to strike his blow against American slavery. For seventeen years he had acquainted himself with the surrounding territory. Brown had intended to take the arsenal on the night of October 24, 1859, and to take supplies and add them to his own in the nearby mountains. The freeing of the slaves being his motive, Brown had rented the Kennedy farm on Bolivar Heights about three miles from Harpers Ferry and moved his family to the place. It was observed by his neighbors before the raid that the female members of his family had gone and more men were joining his household.

On Saturday, October 15, 1859, a meeting of the liberators was held to discuss operations and on Sunday the council reconvened and adopted the program of Captain Brown. It was agreed that the attack would be made the next day, October 16, instead of the 24th. The liberators, twenty-two persons, seventeen white and five Negroes, extinguished the lights of the small village about ten o'clock that night, took the armory buildings and imprisoned three watchmen.

Brown had intended that Negroes should be armed and march northward to free territory. Some of the Negroes were given guns. Sixteen men took possession of the arsenal while six men went out the turnpike, toward Charles Town and captured Col. Lewis Washington, Col. Dangerfield and others with their slaves and confined them in the engine house.

Robert E. Lee, colonel, United States Army, on leave from a Texas command and at home in Arlington, was summoned by Secretary of War Floyd. Without a change from civilian clothes Lee joined the messenger, and with Lieutenant J. E. B. Stuart tagging along, proceeded to the War Department. There they were told of the happenings at Harpers Ferry. In the midst of rumors

Lee arrived by train with his horse marines from the Washington Navy Yard. Virginia militia men had come from many places. Early the following morning as thousands clamored to get closer to the engine house, the attack of Lee's forces was to last for not more than three minutes until the capture of Brown. With two of his sons killed in the struggle, Brown was badly cut about his head when Lieutenant Green dealt him a severe blow. Briefly sketched this was the incident. Historian Craven says it was "nothing more or less than the efforts of a band of irresponsible outlaws." But Henry David Thoreau, on the day of Brown's arrest, compared the death which Brown would face, to the crucifixion of Christ. Had Brown been killed at Harpers Ferry he would still have been a martyr in the eyes of those who knew him, but the fact that he lived and uttered his words of conviction, demonstrated an unbelievable faith in God, and showed unfaltering courage in meeting death, stamped his name as a martyr in the minds of all freedom seeking people, then and now.

The trial of John Brown at Charles Town, Virginia, is one of the most celebrated trials in United States History. Was it legal? John Brown was indicted and tried on the same day. This is quite unique in judiciary history. Denied counsel of his own choice for three days, Brown was finally granted the services of the interested, inexperienced twenty-one-year-old lawyer, George Hoyt, who was not given time to prepare a case for Brown. Of the seventeen charges against Brown, the state of Virginia was willing to drop all except the three capital offenses, treason against the state, murder in the first degree and inciting slaves to rebel. Treason is an act committed by a resident or citizen against a state. John Brown was neither a resident nor a citizen of Virginia. Captured in the arsenal Brown was on federal property. Article I, section 8 of the United States Constitution states that federal installations on state property with the state's permission are under jurisdiction of the United States. On the charge of murder, did John Brown kill any one? He could have been charged as an accessory before the fact. Did

John Brown incite slaves to rebel? He insisted throughout his trial that his only interest was freeing the slaves.

He was accused of disturbing the peaceable town of Harpers Ferry, but it must be remembered that there is no peace where slavery exists. There is no peace where discrimination and maltreatment exists for any segment of population, for uneasy lies that head each night that wears the crown of guilt. No slave community was at peace, for it was to John Brown nothing more than a den of robbers. He had declared that the slaveholders would never consent to give up their slaves until they felt "the big stick about their heads." Further substantiating this view Brown wrote these final prophetic words to the country, "I, John Brown am now quite certain that the crimes of this guilty land will never be purged away but with blood. I had, as I now think vainly, flattered myself that without much bloodshed it might be done." The state of Virginia spent more than a quarter of a million dollars to convict and execute Brown.

Twenty-five years before the Harpers Ferry incident such a case would have been tried in Federal Court, and after the Civil War the Federal Court would have exercised its jurisdiction with national support. But the situation a century ago was that the South was winning the battle for the court which had culminated in the Dred Scott decision and was lost in a Civil War and the Fourteenth Amendment.

It is estimated that more than sixty slaves were taken into the movement, although many others were opposed to joining. Of the first Negroes in Brown's company only one, Anderson, escaped and later wrote, *"Voices from Harpers Ferry,"* Dangerfield Newby and Lewis Leary of Oberlin, Ohio, were killed and another Negro named Gains, was taken prisoner. Shields (Emperor) Green and John Copeland were tried and sentenced to be hanged in a separate but equal hanging two weeks after Brown.

Of the bravery exhibited at Harpers Ferry, no doubt Shields Green was foremost. Anderson wrote that, "Newby was a brave fellow" and when he was shot through the head by the trooper who took advantage of a mutual withdrawal, "his death was promptly avenged by Shields Green," who raised his rifle in an instant and "brought down the cowardly murderer. Wiser and better men no doubt there were, but a braver man never lived than Shields Green. . . ." Frederick Douglass said, "If a monument should be erected to the memory of John Brown, as there ought to be, the form and name of Shields Green should have a conspicuous place on it."

On the day that John Brown's body was placed on a special train from Charles Town to Harpers Ferry where it was then to proceed to New York, Robert E. Lee looked on with a sense of satisfaction that this was the end. He had written to his wife on the previous evening. "Tomorrow will probably be the last of Captain Brown." This was the last of Captain Brown but the beginning of the spirit of John Brown that was to be reflected in American thought and social reform for another century. During the Civil War which was to break out after eighteen months, "John Brown's Body" was one of the most popular union war songs. Emerson declared that Brown would be a favorite in history while Henry David Thoreau wrote, "I foresee the time when the painter will paint the scene, the poet will sing it, the historian will record it." One scholar of John Brown in American literature has declared the task of collecting all about Brown in literature is almost impossible. His finding at almost one score years before the century's end was fourteen biographies, over two hundred fifty poems, eleven short stories and fifty-eight novels. Yet men fail to see him as he was. They either condemn him as a fiendish criminal or revere him as "God's angry man." This much is true: every battle for freedom has resulted in an expansion of human rights. The spirit of John Brown moves on in social reform.

In a speech at one of the meetings of the Southern Historical Society at Houston in 1957, Walter Prescott Webb of Texas, in pointing out why industry was moving into the South, said that the oppression of the Negro laborer in the South helps also oppress the poorer white laborer. In other words, demoralization of the one demoralizes the other, and thus both become "cheap and docile" laborers, who, along with favorable industrial legislation, are inviting to the South industry from the North, where labor is organized and well paid. Similarly, historians have raised the question: How extensive was there a spirit of revolution in the Northern states among whites based upon the attitude that Negro slavery oppressed and demoralized free laborers and free farmers of the North and East? These historians tell us that the Northern worker had come to fear competing as a free laborer with a slave laborer. They tell us that slavery was obstructing the idea of Manifest Destiny, and thus the spreading of "Northern democracy and non-slaveholding farmers" into the West. Howard K. Beale points out that during the 1850's there were "many places" where Jacksonian democracy continued to dominate, and that there was a "struggle of yeoman farmer and laborer against planter and merchant. . . ." William B. Hesseltine observes that by 1860 "wealth, industrial capitalists, great merchants, and bankers reigned supreme over a population of laborers, many of whom were crushed by poverty into squalid tenements, and small farmers whose total output, large as it was, seldom sufficed to give freedom from debt or opportunity for culture." Leland D. Baldwin believes that the working men of Northern cities "regarded themselves as very badly exploited" even "as late as 1850."

In the midst of the attempt of some laborers to move to the West to escape from the poor conditions experienced in the North and East, the panic of 1857 occurred, which meant increasing hardship for those at the bottom rung of the ladder. Seeds of rebellion were being planted in these conditions that would have sprouted into reform-agitation long before the Granger, Populist, and Progressive movements had it not been for the interference of the Civil War.

But for one man, a remedy for the conditions described above could not wait; such remedy could not be gradual. This man was

John Brown. Had John Brown not led his raid on Harpers Ferry, perhaps the historian would be denied a colorful description of the living condition of an Easterner, whose migration to Kansas was "probably . . . prompted by desire for land," and one that "felt that he had been cheated by proslave men." Let Frederick Douglass, who visited John Brown's home in New England in 1847, describe that living condition:

. . . I was a little disappointed at the appearance of this man's house. . . The house was a small wooden one, on a brick street in a *neighborhood of laboring men and mechanics* . . . Plain as was the outside, the inside was plainer. Its furniture might have pleased a Spartan.

It would take longer to tell what was not in it, than what was; no sofas, no cushions, no curtains, no carpets, no rocking chairs inviting to enervation or rest or repose. My first meal passed under the misnomer of tea. It was none of your tea and toast sort, but potatoes and cabbage, and beef soup. . . . Innocent of paint, veneering, varnish and tablecloth, the table announced itself unmistakably and honestly pine and the plainest workmanship.

No doubt there were many others living in similar conditions as those endured by John Brown and desiring to escape from these conditions by moving out to Kansas. And no doubt such wealthy and important men as Charles Francis Adams and Amos Lawrence, believing in the safety-valve theory, saw bred in such living conditions trouble for the "powers-that-be" in Massachusetts and New England, when they aided Eli Thayer in establishing the New England Emigrant Aid Society, which was organized to rid Massachusetts of its "John Browns" who comprised the so-called "surplus population."

Both the "John Browns" and the wealthy promotors of the Emigrant Aid Society, however, were to be disappointed. In Kansas, their New England Puritanism and free-soil ideals (and even Quakerism from Pennsylvania and Ohio) ran head-on against those that yet believed that Kansas offered a place where they could realize their dreams of becoming planters and slaveholders.

The clash of these two groups of people in Kansas did more to prove that Puritanism, Quakerism, and abolitionism could not be reconciled with slavery, and that the slavery issue was becoming quite rapidly a moral issue, which could not be compromised. "Bleeding Kansas" had become the first place where Easterner, Northerner, and Southerner met in close contact and thus could reveal why the Missouri Compromise, The Compromise of 1850, and popular sovereignty failed. "Bleeding Kansas" had become something like a place of last hope for those who had experienced the drab plight of the industrial workers in the East and North and for those who had suffered under the plantation system in the South. Perhaps there were those that said: "If I do not find economic satisfaction here in Kansas, then it is impossible for me to advance under the prevailing economic systems in the United States." If Senator Seward could say: "There is a higher law than the Constitution . . . The territory is a part . . . of the common heritage of mankind, bestowed upon them by the Creator of the Universe," then those that went to Kansas probably said it even more so. Deep vision was leading Seward to see developing out of the clash between a system of free labor and slavery "the irrepressible conflict." Although Charles A. Beard was referring to the Civil War, what he says in the passage below could also have been said about John Brown's war in Kansas:

Given an irrepressible conflict which could be symbolized in such unmistakable patterns by competent interpreters of opposing factions, a transfer of the issues from the forum to the field, from the conciliation of diplomacy to the decision of arms was bound to come. Each side obdurately bent upon its designs and convinced of its rectitude, by the fulfillment of its wishes precipitated events and effected distributions of power that culminated finally in the tragedy foretold by Seward.

When Frederick Douglass heard John Brown say "God and duty, God and duty," running "like a thread of gold through all his utterances," was Brown not saying, in other words, the same thing that Seward had said: that is, that the fight between free-soilers and slavery was a moral one?

One might say that John Brown was the champion of what Seward had seen in the struggle over slavery. Indeed, Seward had deep vision and a tremendous foresight, unexcelled by his colleagues. But Seward was a politician. John Brown, conversely, had learned through experience that the fight against slavery was a moral one—by suffering the plight of the poorer white Northerner. This experience forced him in carrying the white laborer's fight against slavery to Kansas, where many others of his economic station anticipated that last hope for success, or at least comfort. After striking an indirect blow in Kansas at what he believed the cause of his plight—slavery—he next chose Harpers Ferry, where he could strike a direct blow. . . .

Although the Civil War became a valve for the "surplus population" and potential John Browns of the North and East, its result did not improve the lot of the American worker. In fact, conditions in but a few years after the war were to worsen for the workers, because the Negro swelled the number of laborers. As early as 1865 it became noticeable that the ruling group had begun to fear again a possible cause of new unrest among workers and small farmers in the North. There had been talk during this year, 1865, of giving the freedmen "forty acres and a mule." Such talk was immediately squashed primarily because it might have suggested to the workers in the North that property should have been divided there too.

The strikes of the 1870's and 1890's should readily suggest that John Brown, the Spirit, was not "rottening" in its grave. Does not the spirit of the Grangers, of the Populists, of the Eugene V. Debs, of the Muckrakers, of the Robert La Follettes, of the Huey Longs, and of the Henry Wallaces suggest the ghost of John Brown, despite their different approaches?

John Brown, the spirit, truly taught the lesson that prejudice on the part of the whites against Negroes was hampering their understanding and improving of the bad living conditions, mutual to both Negroes and whites. He knew, no doubt, about the wretchedness of the living conditions of free Negroes in the North. Inviting Frederick Douglass to his home in 1847 was an indication that he was in great desire to have the cooperation of free Negroes, whose low wages afforded living conditions even worse than that of poor whites in the North. No wonder, then, Lovejoy was assassinated.

The strike in New Orleans in the 1890's symbolized the spirit of John Brown, in that for the first time Negroes were brought into labor unions. There was widespread fear that the Negro would "scab" unless he was given a part to play in the strike. Whites of New Orleans had come to realize that unless Negroes were brought into unions they would depreciate the value of white labor.

The Populists preached a similar doctrine. They desired to undercut Bourbon Democratic demagogy of race hatred with sound reasoning about making a living. Their approach was more constitutional but they aimed at the same thing as John Brown.

"John Brown's body lies mouldering in the clay but his soul goes marching on." It marches as the voice of reform. It is the voice of freedom of the common man that cries out in the wilderness for an equal opportunity at life, liberty and the pursuit of happiness for all men. It is the spirit that moved those venerable souls into the Niagara movement in 1905, and led back to Harpers Ferry in 1906 when that group declared that "We want full suffrage, and we have a right to know, to think and to aspire." It is the spirit that led the Martin Luther Kings, the Lonnie Smiths and caused them to seek to walk in dignity and live in peace. It provoked Emerson to write, "What is a man born for but to be a reformer, a remaker of what man has made, a renouncer of lies, and a restorer of truth and good. . . ."

Lerone Bennett, Jr.

Lerone Bennett, Jr. (b. 1928), senior editor of *Ebony* magazine, college and university lecturer, and author of the deservedly popular *Before the Mayflower: A History of the Negro in America, 1619–1962* (subsequently updated), combines a poet's imaginative thrust with the social insights of a seer. To both he brings the knowledge and the perspective of the historian. His evocative writing, the hallmark of his literary style, is richly evidenced in *The Negro Mood and Other Essays* (Chicago, 1964). Of the five thematically related essays in that volume, "Tea and Sympathy: Liberals and Other White Hopes" (pp. 100–104) is a lucid analysis of the reasons for the black American's distrust of white liberals. After bringing these ostensible friends to task in the essay, Bennett closes by turning to John Brown as a contrast figure, one whose broad humanity had carried him beyond the delimitations which bedevil most men, white liberals included. The essay is used by permission of Lerone Bennett, Jr., and the Johnson Publishing Company, Inc.

It is to John Brown that we must go, finally, if we want to understand the limitations and possibilities of our situation. He was of no color, John Brown, of no race or age. He was pure passion, pure transcendence. He was an elemental force like the wind, rain and fire. "A volcano beneath a mountain of snow," someone called him.

A great gaunt man with a noble head, the look of a hawk and the intensity of a saint, John Brown lived and breathed justice. As a New England businessman, he sacrificed business and profits, using his warehouse as a station on the Underground Railroad. In the fifties, he became a full-time friend of freedom, fighting small wars in Kansas and leading a group of Negro slaves out of Mis-

139

souri. Always, everywhere, John Brown was preaching the primacy of the act. "Slavery is evil," he said, "kill it."

"But we must study the problem . . ."

Slavery is evil—kill it!

"We will hold a conference . . ."

Slavery is evil—kill it!

"But our allies . . ."

Slavery is evil—kill it!

John Brown was contemptuous of conferences and study groups and graphs. "Talk, talk, talk," he said. Women were suffering, children were dying—and grown men were talking. Slavery was not a word; it was a fact, a chain, a whip, an event; and it seemed axiomatic to John Brown that facts could only be contraverted by facts, a life by a life.

There was in John Brown a complete identification with the oppressed. It was his child that a slaveowner was selling; his sister who was being whipped in the field; his wife who was being raped in the gin house. It was not happening to Negroes; it was happening to him. Thus it was said that he could not bear to hear the word slave spoken. At the sound of the word, his body vibrated like the strings of a sensitive violin. John Brown *was* a Negro, and it was in this aspect that he suffered.

More than Frederick Douglass, more than any other Negro leader, John Brown suffered with the slave. "His zeal in the cause of freedom," Frederick Douglass said, "was infinitely superior to mine. Mine was as the taper light; his was as the burning sun. Mine was bounded by time; his stretched away to the silent shores of eternity. I could speak for the slave; John Brown could fight for the slave. I could live for the slave; John Brown could die for the slave."

In the end, John Brown made of himself an act of transcendence. The act he chose—the tools, the means, the instruments—does not concern us here. His act, as it happened, was violent and apocalyptic; but it could have been as gentle as rain in the spring, a word perhaps, yes, or a name or a life committed to a piece of paper. Acts to the end grow out of the lineaments of men's lives and it is up to each man to create and invent not only his act but also the occasion of his act.

John Brown made his occasion, attacking the arsenal at Harpers Ferry in the hope of creating a situation in which slaves all over the South would flock to him. He begged his old friend, Frederick Douglass, to accompany him; but Douglass insisted that the plan was premature. The old white man and the young Negro argued from eight one night to three the next morning. While they argued, a tough cynical fugitive slave named Shields Green watched and weighed. After the argument, Douglass rose and asked Shields Green if he were ready to go. Green thought for a moment and then said: "I believe I go wid de old man." Shields Green was in the mountains and could have escaped when federal troops closed in on John Brown. A man suggested flight, but Shields Green said: "I believe I go down wid de old man." And he did—all the way to the gallows.

Why did Green deliberately sacrifice his life?

Not because he was irrevocably committed to John Brown's way but because he was irrevocably committed to John Brown, because, in a horribly bloody and horribly tangible way, a prayer had been answered; because he had at long last found a man, neither black nor white, who was willing to go all the way.

Who?

"I believe I go wid de old man."

Who?

"A man for all seasons," a pillar of fire by night and a cloud by day.

Who?

A John Brown or a Wendell Phillips or a Paine. It may be that America can no longer produce such men. If so, all is lost. Cursed is the nation, cursed is the people, who can no longer breed indigenous radicals when it needs them.

There was an America once that was big enough for a Wendell Phillips; there was even an America big enough for a Brown.

What happened to that America?

Who killed it?

We killed it, all of us, Negroes and whites, with our petty evasions and paternalistic doles, with our sycophantic simpering and our frantic flights from truth and risk and danger. We killed it, all of us, liberals and activists with the rest. Can the stone be rolled once again from the mouth of the cave? It is my faith—and all Negroes who do not have that faith are in or on their way to prisons, asylums or Paris—that buried somewhere deep beneath the detergents and lies is the dead body of the America that made Thomas Jefferson a lawbreaker and John Brown a martyr.

Can the stone be rolled away again?

Few American white men when sufficiently drunk can resist the temptations of toying with that mad idea. They come, martinis in hand, faces flushed, guilt waving, and they say: "There was this bright little old Negro boy in my class and I wonder what happened to him." Or, since speculations about the fate of bright black boys are dangerous, "There was this little old Negro girl." They say, oh, so many things and it dosen't matter for they are not saying what they are saying. What this man or that man is saying, really, is that, "I am ashamed of myself." He is saying, "There is something deep within me." He is saying, "I am better than I am."

He may be; but saying will not make it so.

"There was this little old Negro boy . . ."

Segregation is evil—kill it!

"We will hold a conference . . ."

Segregation is evil—kill it!

"But our allies . . ."

Segregation is evil—kill it!

For the Jew in Germany, the African in Salisbury, the Negro in New York:

Who?

A man beyond good and evil, beyond tea and sympathy, beyond black and white.

Who?

"A man for all seasons," a pillar of fire by night and a cloud by day.

Who?

"I believe I go down wid de old man."

Michael S. Harper

Holding degrees from California State College at Los Angeles and the University of Iowa, Michael S. Harper (b. 1938) is an associate professor of English at Brown University. A younger poet of exceptional promise, his published works include three books, *Dear John, Dear Coltrane* (University of Pittsburgh Press, 1970), *History Is Your Own Heartbeat* (University of Illinois Press, 1971), and *History as Apple Tree* (Scarab Press, 1972), in addition to poems appearing in a number of journals, including *New Letters, The Black Scholar, The Massachusetts Review*, and the *Quarterly Review of Literature*. The following stanzas (copyright, Michael S. Harper) were written expressly for this volume and will be included in a book-length poetic work-in-progress, *Sons and Ancestors: The Vision of W. E. B. Du Bois*.

HISTORY AS CAP'N BROWN

The price of repression is greater than the cost of liberty.

"*My name is John Brown; I have been well known as old John Brown of Kansas. Two of my sons were killed here today, and I'm dying too. I came here to liberate slaves, and was to receive no reward. I have acted from a sense of duty, and am content to await my fate; but I think the crowd have treated me badly. I am an old man. Yesterday I could have killed whom I chose; but I had no desire to kill any person, and would not have killed a man had they not tried to kill me and my men. I could have sacked and burned the town, but did not; I have treated the persons whom I took as hostages kindly, and I appeal to them for the truth of what I say. If I had succeeded in running off slaves this time, I*

144

*could have raised twenty times as many men as I have now, for
a similar expedition. But I have failed." ***

PLANS

Railroad routes;
Indian territory;
southwestern Missouri:

Douglass believed in Brown
but not in his plan:
a secret page of mountain
to strawbrick and turpentine.

These are accounts payable:
hidden arms in an Ohio haymow,
hung by the heavens in scarlet
on Blue Ridge Mountain,
even as the black phalanx fails;
though I am sick with ague,
truth fevers that new-made grave,
one thousand pikes as stones.

Earthwork inspections
from Roman provinces
to Spanish chieftains:
Schamyl, Circassian,
Moina, Toussaint, Hugh Forbes.

Hot bloody spots
at watered points—
Potomac/Shenandoah:
*I pledge my life to each slave,
with iron rather than in iron.*

* W. E. B. Du Bois, *John Brown* (New York: International Publishers,
1962), pp. 336–37.

REPORTS: KANSAS

"Osawatomie Brown
killed by pro-slavery
man named White—
Frederick Brown is dead—
Brown hit by spent grape
canister, rifle shot—
killed by scalping
so bruised he did not know
it 'til he reached the place:
with irons in hand I take
my scalp as Dred Scott
is taken in irons:

Come to the crusade:
blood is the issue,
not Negroes, *brothers."*

'EMPEROR': SHIELDS GREEN: FUGITIVES

Sunday Meeting: *I b'lieve I'll go wid de ole man.*
At Chambersburg Quarry:
I guess I'll go wid de ole man.
Black Monday: *I must go down to de ole man.*

GEN'L TUBMAN, AS WE CALL HER

$10,000: dead or alive won't catch her;
dreamer of dreams and sickness will:

"Serpent in rocks and bushes,
head of a white-bearded old man,
then two younger heads spoke:
Come!
I was sick,

dreaming wishful deeds:
the heads spoke in tongues."

While at writing table
two wrens flew in
from their porch nest
fluttering attention;
a snake on our post
set to eat our young in the nest;
father killed the snake,
the wrens' songs burst
a successful omen.

Heads as flowers
not birds,
and cut off
to blossom
on a table:
then I heard of Harpers Ferry.

FOUR WORTHIES: SOULS OF BLACK FOLK

To *Know,* in heart, in groin;
To *Move,* trestle, bog, boat, mask;
To *Love,* woman, child, land, tree;
To *Aspire,* where blood, sperm, bone join.

FUGITIVE PATHS

Submit, fight, run:
young woman
demented in childbirth,
a boy four dead:
Turner 'live and dead;
Crandall's burned school
checkers our stacked churches,

Lovejoy murdered,
Fayette's stories of woe:
I swear a blood-feud
with slavery,
my sword of Gideon
amidst this vast veil:
"it is right for slaves
to kill their masters and escape."
Plans form their towpaths
to arsenal gates,
Gabriel's glory, openended.

SAMBO'S MISTAKES: *An Essay*

Weaknesses:
small good reading,
thrown money on luxury—
no capital;
servility,
talkativeness,
disunity,
sectarian bias:
expects security with whites
by tamely submitting to
indignity, contempt, wrong.

Strengths:
guns.

"S.P.W.": JOURNEY OF CONSCIOUSNESS

These mountains are my plan:
natural forts conceal
armed squads of five

on a twenty-five mile line;
slaves run off
to keep them strong;
the infirm underground,
property insecure with blood:
"Subterranean Pass Way"

"LEAGUE OF GILEADITES": *Messages*

"Nothing so charms the American
people as personal bravery":
Cinques on *Amistad,*
Lovejoy and Torrey:
all traitors must die.
Count on division among whites:
teach them
not to throw fire
in a wooden house—
lasso slave-catchers:
hold on to your weapons:
man-stealing is *rescue work.*

SOJOURNER TRUTH: BLACK SYBIL IN SALEM

"Frederick, is God Dead?"
"No, and because God is not
dead, slavery can only end in blood."

JIM DANIELS: HAMILTON MASSACRE: *Parable*

From Fort Scott I met Jim Daniels
selling brooms as disguise,
handsome mulatto; less than a year
ago eleven citizens were gathered up

by armed force under Hamilton,
formed in a line without trial,
and shot: all left dead, all free-staters:

What action have the president,
governors of Missouri, Kansas taken?

Daniels came to Osage settlement
from Missouri, wife, children,
another black man to be sold next day,
asking for help: *rescue work* in Missouri.

Posse to "enforce the law":
man-stealing, no; killing free-staters,
yes: look up the barrel of this shotgun,
see if you can find your slaves.

PLANS: 2

I proposed a Negro school in Hudson: 1828;
in 1858 I fixed Harpers Ferry as spring
to the Great Black Way, central depots
spurred the Alleghenies, mountain arsenal:
pikes, scythes, muskets, shotguns,
Sharps rifles for skilled officers:
Forbes betrayed us in temper, money:
we delayed a year in fever.

At Chatham we met,
'League of Freedom':
swamped marooned,
Appalachian range,
Indian territory,
the route of Gabriel.

Rifle ball words
on rifle ball tongue:

most who gave arms
wanted use in Kansas only;
blacks hid me in Springfield,
rumors of scalping in Hartford,
cache of Harpers Ferry
in a guerrilla handbook:
I am through with Plymouth Rocks,
Bunker Hills, Charter Oaks,
Uncle Tom's Cabins:
those held accountable
are the mighty fallen.

I am without horses, holsters,
wagons, tents, saddles, bridles,
spurs, camp utensils, blankets,
intrenching tools, knapsacks,
spades, shovels, mattacks, crowbars,
no ammunition, no money
for freight or travel:
I have left my family poorly:
I will give my life for a slave
with a gun my secret passage.

BIBLIOGRAPHICAL NOTE

A FIGURE both historical and legendary, the enigmatic John Brown has been of enduring interest to his fellow Americans. The Brown literature has been enormous, including poetry, fiction, and drama as well as essays, history, and biography. Of the last named there are two that stand out for their original scholarship, those by Oswald Garrison Villard and Stephen B. Oates.

Villard's *John Brown, 1800–1859, A Biography Fifty Years After* (1910) was a landmark in its careful approach to the man. Although himself one of the founders of the National Association for the Advancement of Colored People, Villard did not let his liberal sympathies influence his analysis of Brown. His biography does not gloss over Brown's defects of character or errors of judgment. Villard was respectful of sound evidence, pointing out (in *The Nation,* February 12, 1914) that "undocumented recollections are a trap a wary historian must usually shun, particularly if recorded by one well on in years."

For a pioneer scholarly biography, Villard's work stood the test of time admirably. But in its five subsequent reprintings up to 1943 its text was never updated. This needed task went unaccomplished until 1970, when Oates's *To Purge This Land with Blood* made its appearance. Oates uses sources not available to Villard for all his spadework, such as the massive manuscript collection of Boyd B. Stutler of Charlestown, West Virginia, who died in 1970. Oates succeeds in his attempt to re-create Brown's life on the basis of contemporary sources, no mean feat since such sources were often shot with partisanship.

Hardly had the Oates book received its first favorable notices in the learned quarterlies than it was joined by another good biography—Jules Abels's *Man on Fire: John Brown and the Cause of Liberty* (1971). This realistic portrait, although somewhat less

scholarly than Oates and not as extensively buttressed in the manuscript sources, reveals a sound grasp of the man and his times. It
is evident that Abels had the lay reader more in mind—he eschews
footnotes, his pages are more laden with quoted dialogue and court
testimony than Oates's, his style is more informal (including such
terms as "soft-soap" and "soul brother"), and his tone is more
discursive. Abels's concluding chapter, "His Soul Went Marching
On," has an epilogue quality not found in Oates's final pages.

In their bibliographies both authors give brief appraisals of
Brown's previous biographers. Oates expands considerably on this
theme in an article, "John Brown and His Judges: A Critique of
the Historical Literature," in *Civil War History,* March 1971. An
additional sidelight on many of these authors, along with others,
may be found in Ernest Kaiser's "John Brown's Legacy," a review
essay on W. E. B. Du Bois's *John Brown* (the centennial edition),
appearing in *Freedomways, Summer* 1963. For those seeking a
general anthology of the man, *A John Brown Reader,* edited by
Louis Ruchames, is highly recommended.

Blacks who have voiced their sentiments on Brown range from
the well known to the relatively obscure. Two of them, Frederick
Douglass and W. E. B. Du Bois, are among the giants in black
history, both having left autobiographies and each in turn having
attracted a number of biographers. *William Wells Brown: Author
and Reformer,* by William E. Farrison (1969), is a scholarly
biography of an influential figure whose writings were widely read.
The prolific writings of Francis J. Grimké have received their due
meed in a four-volume work edited by no less a black historian
than Carter G. Woodson. Reverdy C. Ransom, a clergyman like
Grimké, has left an autobiography, *The Pilgrimage of Harriet
Ransom's Son* (1929).

As for the black poets herein represented, Countee Cullen and
Langston Hughes are the best known of their group in the twentieth
century, excluding the turn-of-the-century figure Paul Laurence
Dunbar. In their own volumes or in anthologies, Cullen and

Hughes are readily accessible to interested readers. The gifted Georgia Douglas Johnson is far less well known; a brief, earlier sketch of her may be found in *Who's Who in Colored America* (seventh edition, 1950). Another lesser-known twentieth-century commentator on Brown, J. Max Barber, is described, with a photograph, in *The Crisis* (New York) for November 1912.

For the black commentators who were contemporaries of Brown, the printed clues are, at present, somewhat meager. Osborn Perry Anderson published a slim volume in 1861, *A Voice from Harper's Ferry*, and an obituary notice of him appears in the *New National Era* (Washington, D.C.), December 19, 1872. A sketch of another Harpers Ferry participant, John Anthony Copeland, appears in *The Pine and Palm* (Boston and New York), July 20, 1861, its author the black abolitionist and writer William C. Nell. A number of references to Charles H. Langston are carried in brother John Mercer Langston's *From the Virginia Plantation to the National Capitol* (1894) and in Jacob R. Shipherd, *History of the Oberlin-Wellington Rescue* (1859). The Boston clergyman J. Sella Martin wrote a score of long letters to *The Liberator* (Boston) during the Civil War years, in many of them telling of his speaking engagements and other activities at home and in the British Isles.

INDEX